In a Contest ̣ ̣ ̣ ̣ ̣ ̣ ̣ ̣ ̣

Of Cythera, born in Cyprus, I will sing.
She gives kindly gifts to men; smiles are ever on her lovely face,
and lovely is the brightness that plays over it.

Hail, goddess, queen of well-built Salamis and seagirt Cyprus;
grant me a cheerful song.

- Homer, Homeric Hymn 10.1-6, c. 740 BCE, trans. Evelyn White

Love himself rises in due season, when the earth swells
And blows with the flowers of Spring;
Oh, then comes Love from Cyprus' beauteous isle
With joy for man throughout the world.

- Theognis, 6th century BCE

Since all things go by and men make narratives of all that comes to
pass, all have great desire to hear of the past and the old histories, for
they learn things that have passed and from them learn to look wisely
to the future. And in case anyone may find it hard to look and see how
he may come through safely, I will make by the grace of the all-holy
Spirit a brief record, in order that all men present may read it; and
they will find delight in histories of old times.

- from Leontios Makhairas' Recital Concerning the Sweet Land of Cyprus,
entitled Chronicle, 14th century, trans. R. M. Dawkins

In a Contested Realm

*An Illustrated Guide to the
Archaeology and Historical
Architecture of Northern Cyprus*

Allan Langdale

The Grimsay Press

The Grimsay Press
an imprint of
Zeticula Ltd
The Roan
Kilkerran
KA19 8LS
Scotland.

http://www.thegrimsaypress.co.uk
admin@thegrimsaypress.co.uk

Text and photographs © Allan Langdale, 2012

ISBN-13 978-1-84530-128-6

Note on Copyright

Since the northern part of Cyprus is not recognized the region is not obliged to follow international copyright laws. This gives rise to many copyright violations. Please do not buy any copies of this book that have been illegally copied.

Sources for frontispiece quotations: Homeric Hymn from *Sources for the History of Cyprus*, vol. 1, eds Paul W. Wallace and Andreas G. Orphanides. Institute of Cypriot Studies State University of New York, Albany and Cyprus College, 1990, p. 4; Selection adapted from Theognis, *Ibid.*, p. 5; Leontios Makhairas, *Recital Concerning the Sweet Land of Cyprus, entitled 'Chronicle,'* trans. R. M. Dawkins, Oxford: Clarendon Press, 1932, p. 3.

This book is dedicated to my mother, Nancy, and to my art history and archaeology students in Famagusta, who asked me to tell the world of the beautiful things to be found in their home.

Acknowledgements

I would like to thank my many friends in Cyprus who made my time in Famagusta so enjoyable and rewarding. Michael Walsh inspired me to make the most of what Cyprus had to offer and I happily joined him in his quest to tell the world about the medieval architecture of Famagusta.

My colleagues Sheelagh Frame, Uwe Müller, Anber Onar, Johan Pillai, Riza Tunçel, Özlem Çaykent, Matthew Harpster, Luca Zavagno, and Müge Şevketoğlu also provided daily encouragement.

Dan Frodsham and Sanem Şahin contributed much valued friendship and support. Benjamin Arbel pointed out many errors and inaccuracies I'd made in an earlier draft and any that persist do so despite his generosity and energies to extirpate them.

Thanks as well to Annemarie Weyl Carr, Patricia Fortini-Brown, Constance Penley, Edward Branigan, Margaret Mullett, Peter Edbury, Sharon Gerstel, and my colleagues at UC Santa Cruz for help in various ways.

My good friend Skip Norman, who has spent years photographing the social life of northern Cyprus, motivated me to keep working with the camera, while Suzanne Duca and Ross Quigley, Philip and Cassandra Grant, and Peter Sturman and Hui-shu Lee gave me shelter, sustenance and time to write back home.

Jim and Hawley Kusch also gave much appreciated friendship and support through the entire process of preparing this book.

I would also like to thank my mother, Nancy, for her patient support in my far-flung ventures, adventures, and — mostly — misadventures.

Contents

Illustrations

Maps

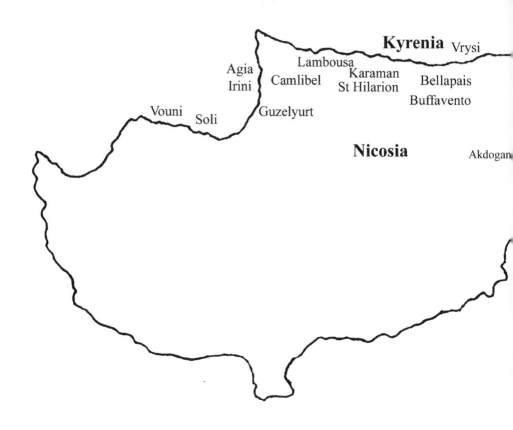

Karamanian Sea

Kyrenia Vrysi

Agia Irini
Lambousa
Camlibel
Karaman
St Hilarion
Bellapais
Buffavento
Vouni
Soli
Guzelyurt

Nicosia
Akdogan

Map 1: Principal Sites and Towns

Principal Sites & Towns in
the Northern Region of Cyprus

Sites & Towns in the Karpas Peninsula

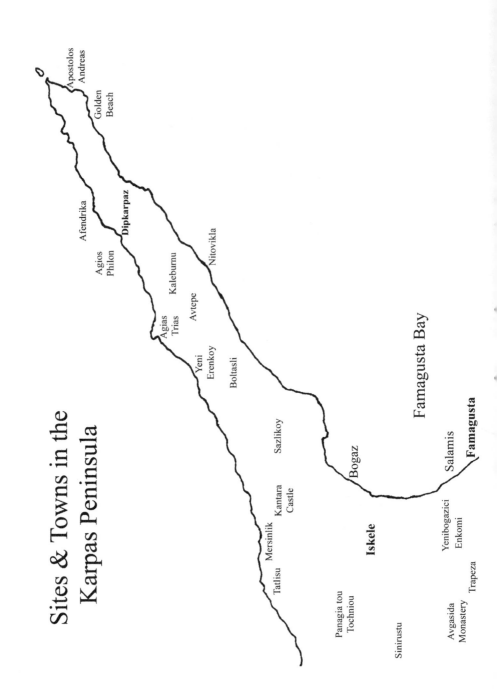

Apostolos Andreas

Golden Beach

Afendrika

Agios Philon

Dipkarpaz

Kaleburnu

Nitovikla

Avtepe

Agias Trias

Yeni Erenkoy

Boltasli

Sazlikoy

Bogaz

Famagusta Bay

Salamis

Famagusta

Kantara Castle

Mersinlik

Tatlisu

Iskele

Yenibogazici

Enkomi

Panagia tou Tochniou

Sinirustu

Avgasida Monastery

Trapeza

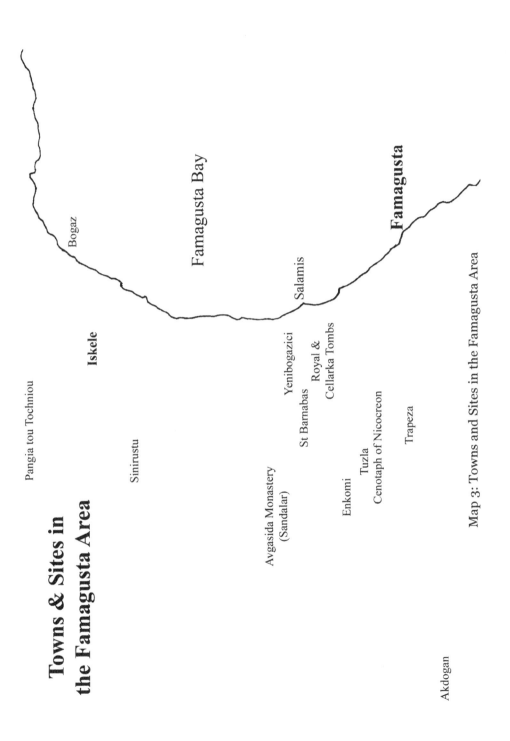

Towns & Sites in
the Famagusta Area

Pangia tou Tochniou

Bogaz

Famagusta Bay

Iskele

Sinirustu

Salamis

Famagusta

Avgasida Monastery
(Sandalar)

Yenibogazici

St Barnabas

Royal &
Cellarka Tombs

Enkomi

Tuzla

Cenotaph of Nicocreon

Trapeza

Akdogan

Map 3: Towns and Sites in the Famagusta Area

Introduction

In 2005 I began teaching art history at Eastern Mediterranean University in Famagusta in northern Cyprus. Before my arrival I had known virtually nothing about this unique island. Nevertheless, after a short time the place began to fascinate me, as it would anyone who loves history and the tangible remnants of past civilizations. The picturesque ruins of ancient cities, centuries-old churches, monasteries and castles all inhabit a relatively small area consisting roughly of the northern third of the island of Cyprus. I realized that the remarkable historical architecture of this region was decaying rapidly and was in desperate need of photographic documentation and the immediate intervention of specialists and conservators. By the end of the year I had amassed an archive of 17,000 digital images, which I hoped could be used by art historians, archaeologists, architectural historians, and others interested in the historical buildings that dotted the northern Cypriot landscape. This volume is my attempt to provide visitors with an up-to-date survey of these monuments of our world's common cultural heritage.

The main reason for the distressing circumstances of northern Cyprus's historical architecture lies, at least partly, in the island's recent history. The Republic of Cyprus, controlling the southern two-thirds of Cyprus, is a fully-recognized European Union country. In 1983 the area of northern Cyprus was designated the 'Turkish Republic of Northern Cyprus' almost a decade after the 1974 military action which effectively partitioned the island into Greek and Turkish sectors. The lack of recognition of the north as an independent political entity and the ensuing international economic and cultural embargo has limited the region's trading options and blocked, among other things, attempts at research and conservation work by international specialists. At the same time, Turkish Cypriots have been able or willing to dedicate only modest amounts of money to care for the many crumbling edifices, and they currently lack the expertise to undertake large architectural conservation projects on ancient, medieval, Byzantine, or even Ottoman buildings. The stunning monuments of the north's architectural and archaeological heritage have thus been caught for decades in the protracted stalemate of 'The Cyprus Problem.' Rainwater, seismic activity, invasive plants, erosion of foundations, vandalism, iconoclasm, and unchecked commercial and residential development are all factors contributing to the disintegration of these buildings and archaeological sites. Unless politics are set aside some of the remarkable structures of this contested realm will be known to the future only in photographs and important historical and archaeological information will be lost forever.

This book's geographical parameter does not reflect any political bias; it merely recognizes the current practicalities of travelling in the region and that visitors are likely to take the north and the south as distinct zones. The Green Line, with few crossings and numerous regulations limiting such things as rental cars, obliges visitors to investigate each area separately. The southern part of Cyprus is no less interesting than the north, and my decision to write a guide to the north was governed by the simple fact that I lived and worked there and thus became more familiar with that region. However, my decision was also influenced by the lack of information available for the north, and I felt that increasing peoples' awareness would help raise the profile of the sites and encourage international cooperation in trying to protect, restore and conserve these important monuments of cultural heritage.

Conflict on Cyprus is nothing new. Its history is scarred, as Lawrence Durrell observed in his famous novel *Bitter Lemons*, by the "ebb and flow of civilizations." The centrality of Cyprus on the eastern Mediterranean's maritime routes made it a vital nexus of trade and commerce for millennia. It was a stepping stone at the confluence of three continents — Europe, Asia, and Africa — and thus participated in the dramatic socio-political discords that often characterize the chronicles of such intercontinental crossroads. This contentious history can be read through the enticing remains of Cyprus's historical architecture. As Cyprus's wealth through many epochs engendered ambitious architecture, its many conquerors ensured a diversity of structures. Indeed, there are few regions of the world that are so restricted in size yet endowed with such a variety and density of architectural monuments. The sites documented herein include Neolithic habitations, Bronze Age tombs and towns, Greco-Roman cites, early Christian basilicas, Byzantine churches, Latin Gothic churches and monasteries, castles, and Venetian and Ottoman buildings from bastions to bath houses. They represent a historical scope of about three thousand five hundred years — much longer if one counts some of the older Neolithic sites — and over a hundred major architectural monuments, all found within an area of about 30 by 180 kilometres.

Despite the accelerated decay of recent years, these buildings have in fact been suffering for centuries. The first critical period of disregard for the medieval churches of Famagusta, for example, took place in the decades shortly after their construction in the late 14th and early 15th centuries when the town was controlled by the Genoese who, according to many contemporary witnesses, did little to maintain the city. The Venetians who followed focused mostly on the impressive fortifications, with ecclesiastical architecture receiving secondary care as the city's economy declined. When the Ottomans attacked Lefkoşa/Nicosia and Famagusta in 1570 the buildings took a beating. It is said that in the almost year-long siege of Famagusta the Ottomans fired 150,000 iron cannon balls into the city. While this may be the hyperbole of Venetian chroniclers, it is nonetheless true that homeowners still occasionally find these rusting ferrous spheres in their garden plots. The churches, rising visibly above the ramparts, presented enticing targets for the Ottoman gunners. Many hefty projectiles are still embedded in the ravaged facades.

Following the Ottoman conquest, those Latin (Catholic) churches that were not converted to mosques or donated to Orthodoxy began an inexorable decline, becoming convenient quarries for those seeking easy supplies of cut stone. This process accelerated after the British took control of Cyprus in 1878. Reports from 19th century visitors bemoan the fact that boats regularly stopped off at north coast ports and took on cargos of stone pillaged from ancient archaeological sites such as Soli and Aphrodisium. Desperate for materials to complete the Suez Canal and to expand Port Said in Egypt, the Cypriot churches were plundered by stone merchants eager for a quick profit. A sustained effort to curtail the disintegration came in the 1930s when the Cyprus Department of Antiquities began a campaign of architectural consolidation using untrained convict labour. The main weapon in the arsenal against dilapidation was a generous swabbing of reinforced concrete over the vaults and domes. But those cement coverings are now cracked and leaking, allowing roots and water to penetrate into arches, vaults, and domes. Collapse is imminent for many of them. One of Cyprus's frequent earthquakes — noteworthy culprits in the undermining of these buildings through the ages — could cause incalculable damage to the already compromised structures.

The degree of urgency for architectural conservation varies greatly from one instance to the next. The rustic 15th century Byzantine church of Panagia Kriniotissa, for example, has been so thoroughly neglected that numerous trees grow out of its fabric as the pine forests of the Kyrenia Mountains gradually reclaim it. Today it heroically holds itself together, defying the intrusions of the roots. Within five years it will be reduced to a pile of rubble even though it was restored as recently as the 1960s. Similarly, the rare 5th century floor mosaics of the basilica of Agia Trias in the Karpas peninsula, exposed to the elements, foot traffic, and invasive grasses, are rapidly disintegrating. There is no shortage of such distressing cases. The Gothic cathedrals of Lefkoşa/Nicosia and Famagusta were converted to mosques after the Ottoman conquest of 1571, a function they still have today, and have been repaired on numerous occasions over the centuries. Nevertheless, though cared for to some degree, these buildings are also fighting a losing battle with time.

This book includes several examples of architecture from the ancient world, including the Bronze Age site of Enkomi and the main structures of the extraordinary Greco-Roman city of Salamis. But the majority of the entries are on churches, and a brief account of Cyprus's history from the onset of the Christian period will help explain the impressive range of ecclesiastical structures.

Cyprus was Christianized early — beginning around 46 CE — and St Barnabas, the founder of the Christian community at ancient Salamis and the patron saint of Cyprus, was a companion of St Paul. Dating from the early centuries of Byzantine rule, the basilicas of Agia Trias, Soli, and the basilicas of Epiphanios and Campanopetra at Salamis are among the earliest Christian structures in all of Cyprus. Cyprus was under the control of the Byzantine Empire during most, though not all, of the period from the 4th until the late 12th century, with a severe falling off in church construction between about 700 to 1000 CE when the island suffered continually from Arab pirate raiding.

Byzantine rule on Cyprus ended in 1191 when the island fell briefly into the possession of King Richard I of England, who wrested it from the Byzantine despot Isaac Comnenos. Cyprus was then sold to the Lusignan kings in 1192 after a brief occupation by the Knights Templar. The Lusignans were French nobles whose predecessors had established a Christian kingdom in the Holy Land after the military successes of the First Crusade in 1099. A century after this, however, they were driven from Jerusalem and other Middle Eastern cities by the consolidated Muslim forces under Saladin. As other towns of the Holy Land subsequently fell to the advancing armies of Islam throughout the 13th century, Cyprus became richer and richer as it welcomed many prosperous Christian merchants and traders who were refugees of the conflict. Cyprus's wealth became renowned in medieval Europe. St Brigit of Sweden is said to have preached in the town square of Famagusta, decrying the sinfulness and vain riches of the city. Chronicles record that the brides of Famagusta were bedecked in jewels more valuable than those worn by the princesses of the kings of France. It was during this three-century Lusignan rule, between 1192 and 1489, that the numerous glorious 'French' Gothic structures were constructed.

Byzantine works of architecture did not cease to be constructed in the era dominated by the Roman Catholic rule of the Lusignans. Contemporary with the French Gothic structures, some of Cyprus's most beautiful churches, and certainly the most beautifully located ones, are Byzantine/Orthodox. Though much regulated by their Latin overlords,

Byzantine or Greek Orthodox Christians continued to build churches and monasteries during these times of Roman Catholic hegemony. Because the Latin monastic orders were linked closely with royal patronage and the urban contexts where the royal court and the nobility were located, much of Cyprus's Latin Gothic architecture is found in the larger cities and towns. Greek Orthodox churches, on the other hand, were often forced to the periphery or countryside, thus many of the medieval Byzantine churches are found in small villages and in remote mountain sites. There were exceptions. The churches St Nicholas ('Bedestan') in Lefkoşa/Nicosia — more properly called the Church of the Hodegetria — and St George of the Greeks in Famagusta are striking examples of urban Greek cathedrals or 'metropolitans' at the hearts of their respective cities.

A brief survey of the building types of Byzantine churches on Cyprus reveals much about the typological range and the unique features of Cypriot architecture. The variation in scale is remarkable, from tiny chapels just a few metres long to the monumental St George of the Greeks in Famagusta, which fuses Byzantine elements with soaring Latin Gothic architectural form and impressive proportions. The variety of models is also extensive, from a single, box-like barrel-vaulted nave ending in a semi-circular apse to the more complex cruciform plan, where two vaults intersect to form the squared base for a single, central dome. Two and three-nave churches are also common and one or more domes could be added to any of the designs. The picture is made more complex by the fact that some Greek Orthodox churches also had Latin chapels and altars inside them in the Middle Ages, thus serving the liturgical needs of both Greek and Latin worshippers in the same church. Moreover, many Byzantine churches went through many alterations, additions and demolitions over the centuries, adding to their fascinating complexity and hybridity.

The Latin Catholic churches of Cyprus, with their distinctive Gothic styles imported by the Lusignans from France but also filtered through their earlier Levantine crusader kingdoms, consisted of two main types. The first was the central nave with flanking side aisle configuration, as found in the cathedral of St Nicholas in Famagusta. The second type was the single-nave church with polygonal apse, a type exemplified by the Carmelite church in Famagusta where the church interior is one huge vaulted room, almost barn-like, without columns or arcades. Yet there are other exceptional variations such as in the Nestorian, Jacobite, and the Armenian churches of Famagusta, perhaps because these groups imported masons or architects from the Middle Eastern or Cilician shores from which they were refugees. The most impressive variation is found in the underground churches of Famagusta, which were carved out of solid rock.

Without doubt, the most striking churches of Cyprus are the cathedrals of Saint Nicholas in Famagusta and Santa Sophia in Lefkoşa/Nicosia, both of which were converted to mosques after 1571 and remain mosques today. Not only are these magnificent structures the equals of European churches, but, for the French scholar Camille Enlart — whose monumental 1899 study of the medieval and renaissance architecture of Cyprus is still an imposing authority — they were in one sense even superior to their European counterparts, as he found in them an unadulterated Gothic free from the excessive and flamboyant accretions of Baroque renovations and extensive 19th century reconstructions. The 20th century would make Enlart's proposition even more valid as so many Gothic churches of Europe were severely damaged in bombing during World War II, thus requiring extensive rebuilding.

However, churches were not the only types of buildings constructed in medieval Cyprus. During the Lusignan period great castles, begun by the Byzantines in the dizzying heights of the Kyrenia Mountain Range, were repaired and enlarged. Much remains of the castles of Kantara, Buffavento, and Saint Hilarion that is still impressive. In Famagusta and Lefkoşa/Nicosia vast city walls were begun in the Middle Ages, later to be augmented or completely rebuilt by the Venetians. The immense bulwark of the Kyrenia castle, on the north coast of Cyprus, another stunning example of military architecture, towers between the ancient Roman and the medieval harbours. The spectacular Premonstratensian abbey at Bellapais, perhaps Cyprus's most famous and beautiful medieval monument, was also a product of the Lusignan period.

The Venetians, who gained direct, overt control of Cyprus in 1489, also left a significant architectural legacy, most impressively in fortifications. At Famagusta a three kilometre long circuit of walls survives in its entirety, along with its imposing moat and counterscarp — a veritable compendium of medieval and renaissance military architecture. The Martinengo bastion, at the northwest corner of the city, impressively indicates the last military architectural forms devised to protect walled towns in the age of gunpowder, while at the Sea Gate, a marble Renaissance-style portal frames the lion of St Mark, angled towards the port where it proclaimed Venice's control over the furthest outpost of its maritime empire.

In 1571 the Turks subjugated the island and with Ottoman suzerainty new structures were built, though not as many as one might expect. For the most part the old churches and cathedrals were converted to mosques, thus making the construction of new mosques unnecessary. However, bathhouses were an integral part of Ottoman culture and some of the best examples of Ottoman architecture on Cyprus are the hamams of Lefkoşa/Nicosia and Famagusta. Here as well, however, the Ottomans re-used what they could. The Kertikli Hamam in Famagusta, for example, was originally a medieval bathhouse that was converted into an Ottoman-style bath with six distinctive perforated domes, and the Çafer Paşa bath, similarly, incorporated the chapter house of Famagusta's Franciscan church. Elsewhere, the Ottomans built aqueducts to bring water both to towns and farmers' fields, and in Famagusta an elegant *medrese* or traditional Islamic school, perhaps Cyprus's most beautiful work of Ottoman architecture, was constructed in the city's main square, integrating parts of a medieval loggia.

Thus many cultures and eras — Neolithic, Bronze Age, Greek, Roman, Early Christian, Byzantine, Latin, Venetian, and Ottoman — left indelible imprints on the island's heritage, making it one of the world's most fascinating places for lovers of architecture.

This book owes debts of gratitude to numerous scholars whose work has informed the text, not all of whom can be mentioned here. The work of Vassos Karageorghis still dominates the scholarship on ancient Cyprus whether pertaining to the Bronze Age or the Greco-Roman period, though the work of people such as E. J. Peltenburg on early Cypriot material has also been inspiring. Camille Enlart's monumental study of 1899, *Gothic Art and the Renaissance in Cyprus*, is still an essential volume, even though many have revised, challenged, or expanded his original findings and proposals. I have freely borrowed from his seminal volume herein. The two standard handbooks, also invaluable though long out of print, are George Jeffery's *A Description of the Historic Monuments of Cyprus* of 1918 (reissued in 1983) and Rupert Gunnis's *Historic Cyprus* of 1936. I have depended on Jeffery throughout, still finding his volume of great value. All of us who work on Cyprus are indebted to Claude Delaval Cobham's *Excerpta Cypria*, which I have used extensively for primary text sources. The work of A. H. S. (Peter) Megaw has also contributed much, as has the photo archive of Theodore Mogabgab who, like Megaw, worked for the Cyprus Department of Antiquities.

A host of contemporary scholars are revolutionizing our knowledge of Cyprus and its medieval history. Peter Edbury's publications have expanded our understanding of the domestic and international politics of Lusignan Cyprus, while Nicholas Coureas and Chris Schabel have revealed new dimensions of the economy, religion, and culture of Cyprus in the Middle Ages. The work of Annemarie Weyl Carr, focusing on Byzantine painting, has aided the understanding of Byzantine and Greek culture during the eras of Latin domination. Catherine Otten-Froux has also made contributions to the analysis of Cyprus's medieval architecture, while Jean Richard and Benjamin Arbel's work has similarly added much to our knowledge of Cyprus in the Middle Ages and the Venetian period. In another notable contribution Michael Walsh has produced a number of informative articles on the churches of Famagusta and spearheaded the campaign which resulted in Famagusta's inclusion to the World Monument Fund's Most Endangered Heritage Sites of 2007. A volume in French, edited by Jean-Bernard de Vaivre and Philippe Plagnieux, *L'Art Gothique en Chypre*, 2006, is generously illustrated and has essays by many leading scholars in the field. A number of other researchers are also making significant contributions, such as Panos Leventis with his beautifully illustrated and ambitious volume *Twelve Times in Nicosia* (2005), which I have borrowed from in my Nicosia entries, as well as Tassos Papacostas, Charles Anthony Stewart, and many others too numerous to mention. I thank them all for their dedication and scholarship without which this guide would have been impossible to compile. The sources listed for each of the entries, by no means exhaustive, provide references to the works of these and other authors. I hope that these scholars will understand that footnotes for each fact would have been cumbersome in a tourists' field book.

Although the contemporary political impasse on divided Cyprus is a central issue in the continued problems faced by the historical architecture of the north, the principal impediment to progress and conservation is a lack of international awareness. This book is an attempt to share with the world the beauty of what remains of these magnificent buildings and to bring attention to their predicament in this lovely but contested realm, providing both inspiration and a guide for explorers of the region. Architectural history, to invert the adage, does not repeat itself. Once gone, these wonders will be lost forever. I present this volume to the people of Cyprus, Greek and Turkish, with the wish that they may find peace, prosperity, and happiness.

Explanatory Notes

Citing Sources:

I have borrowed from three earlier books on the art and architecture of Cyprus and in the sources for each entry the citations have been shortened to Enlart, Jeffery, and Gunnis, followed by the page number. The full citations are:

Camille Enlart, *Gothic Art and the Renaissance in Cyprus*, trans. David Hunt, London, 1987 (org. 1899).

George Jeffery, *A Description of the Historic Monuments of Cyprus*, reprinted London, 1983 (org. 1918).

Rupert Gunnis, *Historic Cyprus. A Guide to its Towns and Villages Monasteries and Castles*, London: Methuen and Co., 1936.

I have also quoted freely from Cobham's 1908 volume *Excerpta Cypria*. Quotes from that text are followed by a shortened in-text form cited as: (*Excerpta Cypria*, followed by page number). Full citation is:

Excerpta Cypria: Materials for a History of Cyprus, translated and edited by Claude Delaval Cobham, Cambridge: University Press, 1908.

In several instances I've also quoted from R. M. Dawkins' translation of Makhairas' *Recital Concerning the Sweet Land of Cyprus*, cited as: [Makhairas, followed by page number]. Full citation is:

Leontios Makhairas, *Recital Concerning the Sweet Land of Cyprus, entitled 'Chronicle,'* R. M. Dawkins, trans. Oxford: Clarendon Press, 1932.

A few quotes are taken from D. G. Hogarth, cited as: [*Devia Cypria*, followed by page number]. Full citation is:

D. G. Hogarth, *Devia Cypria. Notes of an Archaeological Journey in Cyprus in 1888*. London: Henry Frouwde, 1889.

Some selections have been taken from the volumes in the *Sources for the History of Cyprus* series edited by Paul W. Wallace and Andrea G. Orphanides; namely, vol. I, *Greek and Latin Texts to the Third Century A.D.*, 1990; vol. III, *A Pilgrim's Account of Cyprus: Bars'kyj's Travels in Cyprus*, trans. Alexander D. Grishin, 1996; vol. V, *English Texts: Frankish and Turkish Periods*, ed. David W. Martin, 1998; vol. X, *Lusignan's Chorography and Brief General History of the Island of Cyprus (A.D. 1573)*, trans. Olimpia Pelosi, 2001. Shortened citations for the series are cited as: [*Sources History Cyprus* volume number, page number].

City Names:

In the entry headings the names of the buildings are followed by the names of the towns in which, or near which, they can be found, first in Turkish and then Greek, i.e. Akdoğan/Lysi. Travellers in the region will often find only the Turkish names posted on road signs, but will mostly find maps with Greek names. Many of Cyprus's towns have several versions of their names. For example, one might encounter Nicosia being called Lefkosia or Lefkoşa. Famagusta one might see as Mağusa, Gazimağusa, Ammochostos, Famagouste, or Famagouste in old foreign texts or maps. Kyrenia might appear as Girne or even Cerines in early texts. See bilingual place names lists on pp. 488-89

Dates:

Early dates are given as BCE ('Before Common Era', which replaces the old designation BC) and CE ('Common Era', which replaces AD). Later centuries are simply designated as 13th century for the 1200s and so on.

GPS Co-ordinates:

I have attempted to provide accurate GPS co-ordinates for all sites. Google Earth has made this possible and I thank Google for making this resource available. These co-ordinates can be pre-programmed into your cell phone or handheld GPS units before you travel. They also allow you to search Google Earth or Google Maps to do a little advance orientation before or during your trip to the region. The Y axis (north) is given first, followed by the X axis (east). I have included three maps herein (Maps 1-3, on pages xxii-xxv and 484-487), but these are not detailed and merely give relative locations of the major towns and sites. It is suggested that you have a good map of Cyprus to augment these less detailed maps. Variations in GPS between platforms has been reported. Thus Google Earth's coordinates may not be perfectly consistent with other satellite coordinates. Expect up to a 50 metre variable.

The Glossary:

At the end of this volume is a glossary to help with the various specialized terminologies used in the book. Some might find it useful to go through these terms before using the guide.

Exploring, Driving, Diving and Cycling:

If visiting Cyprus in the late spring or early fall you can count on hot weather; in July and August blistering heat. The month I suggest for exploring is April or early May unless you really like the heat and the beaches. In the mid-spring the island is green, wildflowers are thriving, and the temperatures are moderate, though a rainfall might be a possibility. One can search for wild orchids while investigating the ancient sites, and even see fields of wild cyclamen blooming. Indeed, the botanical splendours of Cyprus add a nice complement to your study of the archaeology and historical architecture, to say nothing of providing spectacular backdrops for your photographs. You might even see flocks of migrating storks or flamingos. October is very comfortable too, however, and one might well get mild weather into November.

A wide, full-brimmed hat is suggested, as is good sunscreen, even in the spring. If planning to hike or explore loose-fitting long pants are suggested since there are many thorned bushes in Cyprus and their spines are sharp and hard as steel, which is why sturdy but light footwear is also recommended. Sandals might not work if you want to go off the beaten path. Bring a couple of small flashlights, as these will come in handy in dark churches, caves, or tombs. They make small telescope-like monocles now that are relatively inexpensive. These are much lighter than binoculars and will help you see sculptural or architectureal details on buildings. It might also be good to have an insect repellent.

It is easy to rent a car in northern Cyprus, but you cannot drive it south into the Republic of Cyprus. The cars are often not in the greatest condition, so you must be in an adventurous mood. Be aware that Cypriots drive on the left side of the road, have cars with the steering wheel on the right, and aren't the best drivers. Traffic rules are routinely ignored and huge risks in overtaking another vehicle are often taken, so be prepared to be extra vigilant if driving. The authorities are doing a good job at improving the road system and have installed many speed cameras and it seems to be improving the overall safety of northern Cypriot roadways. You must have a valid driver's license and be over 25 years of age to rent a car. Because the distances are short, one can see a lot in a brief time in northern Cyprus.

Cyclists should be very aware of the dangers of cycling on Cyprus. Always stay as far away from cars and traffic as possible, opt for country roads over main roads or highways, wear bright clothing and a good helmet at all times, and do not cycle at dusk or when dark even if you have a light. You should have a good front and rear light. Bring lots of patches for your inner tubes and even a spare pair of tubes. You will get punctures, especially going off road with a mountain bike. There is a lot of broken glass and hard thorns on the roads. Be warned that northern Cyprus has among the highest *per capita* rates of traffic fatalities in the world. There are some options. If you are patient and adventuresome hitchhiking is remarkably good in northern Cyprus. That was my principal mode of getting around when I lived there, along with my mountain bike. There are also small buses that shuttle regularly between the main cities: for example, Famagusta to Lefkoşa, Famagusta to Girne, Lefkoşa to Morphou, back and forth. These buses usually leave every hour and are reasonably priced and fairly fast. The bus depots are conveniently placed in each city.

A snorkel and mask will allow you to see some underwater archaeological remains such as in the shallows at Salamis, but remember that it is illegal to take any artefact whatsoever from an archaeological site. Fins are probably not necessary unless you plan to do more serious diving. There are places to rent diving equipment or even take diving lessons in northern Cyprus.

One can easily mix sightseeing with beaches in northern Cyprus, and there are many small coves and sandy beaches. The beach beside ancient Salamis is quite good and there are a few small hotels on the beach within a kilometre or so of Salamis. There is a nice beach in Famagusta as well, by the Palm Beach Hotel, just a 15 minute walk from the old city. From here one gets the most impressive view of the coastal part of 'The Ghost City' of Famagusta, the old pre-1974 resort hotels now decaying in the military zone. The Karpas peninsula also has many beaches not very far from the archaeological sites and churches, the best being the spectacular Golden Beach along the south coast of the peninsula just off the road leading to Apostolos Andreas, about 2.7 km before one gets there [35° 38' 29.09" N / 34° 32' 54.70" E].

The Neolithic, Bronze Age, and Classical sites

Many of the archaeological sites listed early in this guidebook are extremely fragile and foot traffic can damage them. It goes without saying that one should not pick up or take artifacts from these areas, but one should also be careful where one walks. Avoid stepping on pavements or standing up on stones or walls. Stick to paths where they exist, otherwise use discretion when exploring. Some of the early Neolithic sites offer little for the casual tourist, as very little survives above ground. I have singled out some of the more important and impressive examples here, which more archaeologically inclined travellers may appreciate.

Neolithic, Ancient, and Early Christian/ Byzantine Cyprus

Fig. 1: *Archaeological reconstruction of a Neolithic Hut at Tatlısu/
Akanthou (Photo by Müge Şevketoğlu).*

The Neolithic Site of Tatlısu/Akanthou, c. 8000 BCE

[35° 24' 15.37" N / 33° 44' 52.29" E]

Tatlısu/Akanthou is one of Cyprus's oldest documented Neolithic sites with settlement layers suggesting dates as early as 10,000 BCE, but with more certain dates — based on radio carbon dating of some seeds — at around 8000 BCE. These dates place Tatlısu among the oldest identified sites of Cyprus, including Khirokitia, Akrotiri, and Shillourokambos. The site's archaeological material suggests a substantial settlement very active in the production of tools and decorative objects and having contact with mainland Anatolia, the source of the considerable numbers of obsidian blades (almost 5000) found at Tatlısu. Excavations also revealed the plans and some clues as to the elevations of the hut-like habitations of the occupants of the Neolithic village. The excavator of Tatlısu, Müge Şevketoğlu, found the outlines of round and quasi-rectilinear houses about 5-6 metres wide. Most had fire pits near the center, which were about 70 cm in diameter. Post holes indicated the use of timbers for support of the structures' roofs. One hole may have been a lime pit, suggesting that the inhabitants of Tatlısu were heating lime to manufacture plaster mortar. Some houses seem to have had their floors paved with such plaster materials. The houses — mud brick huts might be a more accurate description — were spaced very close together or abutted one another. There is evidence that one hut was built, then another room added on beside it, and so on, thereby enlarging the habitation as the family grew. The huts were only single storey, though Şevketoğlu noted one structure that had thickened lower walls, proposing that a second level may have existed in at least one of the buildings.

The obsidian blades are the most significant finds at Tatlısu, as their number far exceeds the number of such artifacts found anywhere else on Cyprus. Testing showed that most of the obsidian came from East Göllü Dağ in Anatolia (mainland Turkey) where a significant obsidian workshop at Kaletepe has been identified by archaeologists. Since no working cores (larger stones from which the blades were chipped) were found at Tatlısu, scholars have also concluded that the blades arrived ready-made and were not manufactured from raw material on site. The number of blades was so large that Şevketoğlu proposed that Tatlısu was a distribution point for obsidian tools not only on Cyprus but perhaps even further east in the Levant.

Cattle bones, too, were found in abundance. And since cattle were not indigenous to Cyprus, but were Anatolian, this is also evidence of Tatlısu's strong cultural and economic ties to the mainland, which even today is sometimes visible just 55 miles or so across the water to the north. Another type of animal bone that was found at Tatlısu was the moufflon, the mountain sheep indigenous to Cyprus. The bones of deep-water fish species indicate that the inhabitants of Tatlısu also fished in boats and not just from shore.

Professor Şevketoğlu and her team, having learned a great deal about the Neolithic huts that the settlers at Tatlısu lived in, undertook to reproduce one of them (Fig. 1). The site is useful to visit to see this small circular house, which gives an idea of the living conditions of the early inhabitants. Recent excavations in 2011 have continued to find a heavy concentration of small obsidian blades and small bones. The skulls of *caretta caretta* (sea turtles) have also been found, indicating an early food source. These endangered creatures are now a protected species and the beaches where they lay eggs in the Karpas are also protected sites.

Sources for Tatlısu: Müge Şevketoğlu, "Early Settlements and Precurement of Raw Materials. New Evidence Based on Research at Akanthou-Arkosykos (Tatlısu-Ciftlikdüzü), Northern Cyprus," TÜBA-AR [Türkiye Bilimler Akademisi Arkeoloji Dergisi] 11 (2008), 63-72; Müge Şevketoğlu, "Cypro-Anatolian Relations in the 9th Millenium BC: Akanthou / Tatlısu Rescue Excavation," Anadolu/Anatolia 30 (2006), 119-136.

Vrysi/Agios Epiktitos Neolithic Settlement, 4410-3750 BCE near Çatalköy /Agios Epiktitos [behind Acapulco hotel restaurant] 9 km east of Kyrenia

[35° 19' 56.49" N / 33° 25' 20.81" E]

It is difficult to write about this site in a book such as this, because it represents a tragedy in commercial overdevelopment in northern Cyprus, though one can certainly say that the Cypriots are not alone in this. The site is slowly being destroyed for lack of protection and the gargantuan Acapulco Hotel Resort has all but cut off the small peninsula from tourist access. This mega-complex includes a convention center, a large hotel and restaurant, and a casino. To visit Vrysi you must enter this complex through a large gate. They should let you park for free. Say you're going to the casino. Walk down towards the sea on the sidewalk and turn right and walk about 100m to the huge restaurant but don't go in the main door. Instead, continue past it and turn left around it at the wall about 50 m past the entrance. You will see the rear service area to the restaurant. Enter this and keep winding your way about until you find a tiny opening leading to the promontory overlooking the sea. What you will see is a sad sight indeed: one of the most important archaeological sites in Cyprus dissolving before your eyes and eroding into the sea. Exercise extreme caution while walking around this fragile and already damaged site. And be very careful if you go to the western edge to get a better view of the houses that remain as the cliff is steep and the soil unsound. Don't step on any unstable walls and do not pick anything up.

Vrysi, also known as Ayios Epiktitos after the Greek name of a nearby village, is a late Neolithic settlement dating from between 4410-3750 BCE. The site occupies a coastal headland, roughly rectangular in shape, about 100 by 80 metres in size. The site may have been chosen for the ease with which it could be defended, being surrounded on three sides by rocky inclines and water. Even more remarkable than its spectacular coastal setting, however, is the fact that the inhabitants excavated deep holes in the earth, living partially subterranean existences. The site was excavated by E. J. Peltenburg in a series of campaigns beginning in 1969 and ending in 1973, the 1974 season being cancelled because of that year's Turkish military action that divided Cyprus. During the excavations, 17 single-room houses (estimated to have been, on average, about 3 metres high, with walls about 60 cm thick) were identified. There seemed to be a clearly demarcated north and south sector, each sector consisting of a cluster of homes. It is difficult to determine the significance of this segmented aspect of Vrysi's 'town plan'. It may reflect two essential kinship groups, or maybe the gap between the two sectors merely indicates that the intervening ground was too hard to dig out. Though subtle differences in the layouts of the north and south sections exist, and there is some variance in pottery styles, there is too little information to come to any firm conclusion about Vrysi's north/ south segmentation. The two parts do seem to have been more or less contemporary with one another, as Carbon-14 tests show parallel dates. Still, there is some evidence that the north section was built first, and the south at a slightly later date. For example, the houses of the north section are much more uniform in size and the housing units are mostly more independent. Similarly, building techniques that evolved in the north sector were mirrored in the south, supporting the idea of sequential habitation and growth.

The plans and elevations of the individual houses varied, but, essentially, the groupings consisted of a row of adjoining houses with an average floor space of 14.4 metres square and narrow passages between each house. The plans were often oval-shaped, but some had irregular amoeba-like curved walls. A few were almost rectangular and some had benches for seating along the walls. A fire pit was typically situated a bit off center in the house. A recreation of one of the houses can be seen in the museum in Kyrenia Castle.

The stratigraphy of the interiors indicated 4-5 occupation levels and also gave some idea of the daily lives and economy of the citizens of this tiny settlement. Items found in the habitation layers included flints, pottery fragments, stone lamps, grinders, bone needles, and beads. All of the pottery found at Vrysi was handmade, not wheel-made, and the range of shapes indicates the varied domestic and light manufacturing character of the habitation: jugs, plates, many types of bowls, trays, and jars. Many were painted with simple geometric designs such as hatches, waves, circles, chevrons, dots, and parallel lines.

The bones of sheep, goats, pigs, dogs, and fallow deer were found, as well as traces of wheat, barley, lentils, olives, figs, and grapes. But fallow deer, sheep, and goat bones comprised 87% of the animal bones found at Vrysi, giving a good idea of the most common game eaten by the inhabitants. Indications are of a people who farmed some crops, hunted, made stone and bone tools, and built with stone, mud, and rough timbers. Several workshops for bead making, tool manufacturing, and stones for sharpening axes and other tools such as grinders, were also found.

The Vrysians did not import many objects and their production of axes and other tools seem to have been modest and only for local trade. Having said that, five pircolite objects attest to some intra-Cypriot trading from the Troodos Mountains, perhaps via some intermediary settlement. Only a single piece of obsidian was found at Vrysi, indicating quite limited interaction with extra-insular groups since obsidian came from Anatolia, though it is quite possible that the founders of Vrysi themselves came from the mainland of present day Turkey. Peltenburg concluded that the Vrysians had much in common with the inhabitants of the Neolithic settlement at Sotira — common pottery periods (age determined by thermoluminescence dating) and decoration, Carbon-14 dates of organic material, identical internal arrangement of dwellings — and thus classified Vrysi in the 'Sotira Group' of archaeological sites.

Timber posts, sometimes set on stone bases, helped support the roofs of the houses, which were mostly flat but sometimes slightly domed to facilitate water runoff during storms, something that must have plagued these houses during the rainy season on this poorly drained site. Peltenburg proposed that the houses suggested use by a single family unit as the size and organisation suggests a comfortable space for about four people. There were exceptions. House 7 (excavation level 2), for example, was so rich in artifacts that it may have been some kind of communal workshop for various culinary and manufacturing activities. Certainly, stone tools were made there as 1157 chipped stones were found, as were some bone hooks, 120 needles, 10 lamps, and 245 different pottery and stone vessels. Mollusk shells and flora and fauna remains were also numerous in House 7, indicating its multi-functionality. House 2B was also unique and an exception to the domesticity of most of the other houses. While many of the houses at Vrysi were independent units, standing close to one another but not with contiguous walls, House 2B shared a common wall with House 2A. Excavation levels 1-3 of House 2B yielded artifacts that pointed to that area's function as a stone-axe production area. One area of the settlement was left as a larger open space between houses, perhaps a Neolithic precursor to the town square or piazza.

A word should be said about subterranean settlement. The Vrysians were not alone in their impulse to construct underground or semi-underground habitations. Such sites are well known in other parts of Cyprus such as Philia and the slightly later Kalavasos-Ayious. In some cases these settlements included connecting tunnels, shafts, and porthole-doors and niches.

One of the features of such a settlement was that it could be effectively defended from attacks. Indeed, in the case of Vrysi, without telltale smoke from fires, boats could have sailed right by it without ever knowing it was there. Camouflage was a first line of defense. That the Vrysians may have had protection in mind in founding their unique home is also attested to by a wall and a ditch built in the south section, cutting off the neck of the small peninsula that they occupied. The significant energies expended in the construction of such a habitation are suggestive of a people who had very specific functions in mind. It may well indicate that the many small prehistoric settlements in Cyprus were not always at peace with one another and raiding, either by sea or land, may have been common. Farther west along Cyprus's north coast there is a striking Neolithic site called Petra tou Limniti. Now an island, it was once probably connected by a sandy spit to the mainland. Even more than Vrysi, it was naturally defended with steep cliffs all around. Similarly, there was a Neolithic settlement on the rocky hill right at the tip of the Karpas peninsula, this also indicating that Neolithic people felt the need to live in places that could be defended. There may have been other reasons for the underground chambers at Vrysi as Cypriot summers can be very hot and the subterranean rooms would have remained cool. Conversely, they may have been easier to keep warm in the winters.

After the 3000s BCE the settlement was abandoned but nobody knows why. No compelling evidence of environmental degradation, destruction, drought, or earthquake was found. However, there is evidence that squatters arrived at Vrysi in its later days, taking shelter in the tiny interstices or 'alleys' between the houses. Their tiny outdoor fire pits left telltale lenses of charcoal in the stratigraphy. These refugees may have been a sign that Cyprus was going through hard times. When the inhabitants of Vrysi left their unique settlement, never to return, they weren't alone, as many other Cypriots abandoned villages around 3700 BCE, indication of some island-wide upheaval.

Sources for Vrysi: E. J. Peltenburg, *Vrysi, A Subterranean Settlement in Cyprus: Excavations at Prehistoric Ayios Epiktitos Vrysi, 1969-1973,* Warminster, England: Aris and Phillips, 1982; E. J. Peltenburg, "Settlement Aspects of the Later Prehistory of Cyprus: Vrysi and Lemba," in *The Archaeology of Cyprus 1960-1985,* ed. Vassos Karageorghis (Nicosia: 1985), pp. 92-114; E. J. Peltenburg, *Recent Developments in the Later Prehistory of Cyprus* (Göteborg, Åströms, 1982).

Early/Middle Bronze Age Necropolis at Karaman/ Karmi (Edremit), 6 km SW of Kyrenia, near Lapta

[Palealona 35° 19' 21" N / 33° 15' 49" E]

The archaeological sites at Karaman/Karmi (Lapatsa) and Palealona, on the northern slopes of the Kyrenia Mountains below and just west of St Hilarion castle, were excavated by James Stewart of Melbourne University in 1961, but his untimely death the following year delayed the publication of a volume on the sites until 2009. The area in the immediate vicinity of Karaman/Karmi actually consists of four Early and Middle Bronze Age archaeological sites: the necropolis or cemetery of Karmi (Lapatsa), Palealona, Kapa Kaya, and Alakati. The following entry will deal only with the first of these, the tombs excavated at Karmi (Lapatsa). Each of the sites lies strategically west of the principal mountain pass that leads from the Mesaorian plain and Lefkoşa/Nicosia to Kyrenia, the Agridhia Pass. These locations were thus within walking distance of the shores of northern Cyprus on the cooler north slopes of the Kyrenia Mountains where fresh water was plentiful, and close to one of the island's principal transportation routes to the Mesaoria. The sites were also within a day's round trip walking distance from other more or less contemporaneous Bronze Age sites such as Lapithos to the northwest and Vounous (Bellapais, where there are also early tombs) to the east. To get to them one has to drive up towards Karaman, but as you pass through the village of Edremit on the switchbacks keep your eye open for the blue sign pointing right to Karaman. Don't pass it. Just go straight into the dirt road there and you should also see a yellow and black sign with 'Bronze Age Cemetery' on it. Take the paved road down to the left about 200 metres and park just past the big house. You'll see the path to the Karmi/Palealona tombs.

The tombs are in many ways typical rock-cut tombs of the Early to Middle Bronze Age, with tub-like *dromoi* off which bud one or more ovoid tomb chambers (Fig. 2), but there are some exceptional features to be found there. At Tomb 6, for example, carved into the entrance or *dromos* of the tomb, a rare relief carving of a human figure was found (this is the tomb in the concrete bunker built to protect it). The tomb entrance (*stomion*) also has simple carved decorations framing it; pilaster-like vertical elements with a zig-zag motif along the top. These 'architectural' elements suggest that the tombs might have been conceived of as 'houses of the dead'. Also at Tomb 6 a worn relief of a podium with a horn motif at the top is strongly reminiscent of the 'horns of consecration' found at the Pigadhes altar (see later entry) and the terra cotta shrine model in the Cyprus Archaeological Museum from Kotsiatis/Marki. Given the special treatment accorded Tomb 6 at Palealona (it also rests at the center of

Some Typical Configurations of Early Bronze Age Tombs

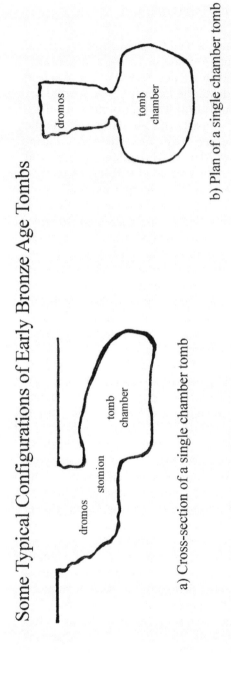

a) Cross-section of a single chamber tomb

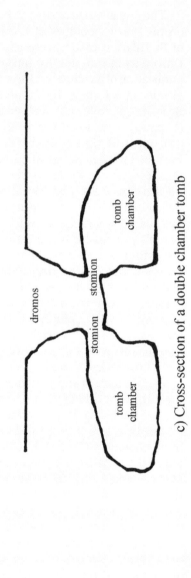

b) Plan of a single chamber tomb

c) Cross-section of a double chamber tomb

the grouping of all the tombs and it had some of the oldest and most impressive contents), archaeologists have theorized that Tomb 6 might have been a shrine. Thus its original function may not have been only as a tomb, though it eventually became one. Then, as a mortuary shrine, it continued in importance and others had their tombs assembled around the sacred site.

Tomb 11B at Karmi, imaginatively christened by Stewart 'The Tomb of the Seafarer', gives insight into the occupants of the typical tombs. The skeletal remains there indicated a male who had lived into his sixties. His teeth were worn smooth by the time he died and there was evidence of fractures and sprains, wearing of joints, and a defect of the lower spine that likely caused severe pain. It was in this tomb that Stewart found the beautiful and fully intact Minoan Kamares-ware cup that gave evidence of trade with the Aegean civilizations of the time, placing the small settlements of the northern coast of Cyprus among the many Middle Minoan, Bronze Age sites strung out along the Aegean and Eastern Mediterranean archipelago. For those interested in film, the 1970 film *The Beloved*, starring Raquel Welch, was filmed in Karmi. Alas, no traces of Raquel survive.

Sources for Karmi: Jennifer M. Webb, David Frankel, K. O. Eriksson, and J. B. Hennessy, The Bronze Age Cemeteries at Karmi, Palealona, and Lapatsa in Cyprus. Excavations by J.R.B. Stewart. Savedalen, Sweden, Åström Forlag, 2009; Paul Åström, The Swedish Cyprus Expedition Vol. IV part 1C, The Late Cypriot Bronze Age, Sweden; Wright, George R. H., Ancient building in Cyprus, 1992; Priscilla Keswani, Mortuary Ritual and Society in Bronze Age Cyprus, London: Equinox Publishing, 2004, esp. pp. 56-58.

Opposite: Fig. 2: a) Cross Section of a typical, single chamber Early/ Middle Bronze Age tomb with dromos, stomion, and tomb chamber; b) plan of typical single chamber Early/Middle Bronze Age tomb; c) cross section a double chamber tomb. Some tombs could have three or four chambers.

The Myrtou-Pigadhes Site and Altar, 1400-1300 BCE, near Çamlibel/Myrtou

[35° 17' 24.84" N / 33° 05' 16.38" E]

About three kilometres southeast of Çamlibel/Myrtou is a Bronze Age altar known as the Pigadhes altar, which was discovered in 1949 and later excavated by a British and Australian team, led by Joan du Plat Taylor, in 1950-51. Around 1300 BCE a large religious complex of some kind flourished at Pigadhes. Excavations revealed a site that had much in common with other ritual and religious shrines from Aegean civilizations such as the Minoan and Mycenaean cultures. Indeed, the shrine may have been founded by émigrés from Crete or other islands in the Aegean archipelago, though evidence suggests more significant influences from Anatolia and Syria. At the very least, pottery found there was imported to the site or brought there by travellers, and some of it came from the Aegean. There were various and telling pottery remains at Pigadhes, including Bronze and Iron Age ceramic techniques and decorative types such as Red Polished ware, Black and Red Slip wares, and Bucchero ware. The pottery shapes were also diverse: cups and bowls of many different sizes and designs, jugs, jars, cooking pots, craters (wine jugs with handles), kylixes (low drinking cups), pithoi (large storage jars), and plates. Among the most significant of the terra cottas were a few offering stands, which would have been used for rituals. They consisted of low bowls on stands that had handles for carrying in procession. Indeed, it is quite possible that much of the pottery at Pigadhes was used in ritual contexts as containers for votive offerings and the pouring of libations. The most impressive piece of pottery found at Pigadhes, and perhaps the most archaeologically important, was a Mycenaean rhyton (a cone-shaped drinking cup), almost complete, with palm tree and 'Mycenaean Flower' motifs, the style of decoration suggesting a date of c. 1300 BCE for its manufacture. A similar palm tree design was also found at Bronze Age Enkomi. Clay bull figurines from the site's earliest phases suggest the antiquity of the shrine, but snake and human figures were also found. In Room 15, bronze tripods were discovered, one with a lovely relief decoration showing animals being chased by hunting dogs, a motif also found in Mycenaean art. A small bronze bull was also unearthed. Animal remains were also plentiful at Pigadhes and included such animals as Persian Fallow Deer (*Dama mesopotamica*; or its Cypriot cousin), Cypriot Moufflon (*Ovis orientalis orientalis*), cattle, sheep, ox, and Screw Horned Goat (*Capra hircus*).

The most striking aspect of the site is the altar, which was reconstructed by archaeologists at its original location (Fig. 3). It is about three metres

Fig. 3: The reconstructed altar at Pigadhes Bronze Age ritual site.

high and has a pair of 'horns of consecration' on top of it, a religious motif with a long history in the Mediterranean. It should be noted, however, that the horns are a hypothetical reconstruction. Representing the horns of the bull and perhaps symbolizing fertility and/or strength, one also finds very similar designs at the Minoan palace of Knossos on Crete, but the altar also has similarities with other altar types found throughout the Eastern Mediterranean. Scholars disagree about whether the bull was actually worshipped as a cult animal or whether bulls were simply prominent sacrificial or votive animals for religious ceremonies for various deities.

The center of ritual sites such as Pigadhes was the cult house, consisting of one or two rooms, often entered from some kind of open court. The Pigadhes altar room or cult house was unroofed (Fig. 4). Such religious sites are called 'intramural' because they are enclosed in walls. Open air offering rooms were also found at other ancient sites on Cyprus, such as Agia Irini and Idalion. One wonders if observation of the heavenly bodies might also have played some role at such sites. An open 'court' leading to the cult house can be found at Pigadhes, although it was more like a roadway or long hall (along the northern flank of the site) with benches, presumably for people to sit while they waited for their turn at the rituals. As was fairly typical of such altars, their corners pointed to the cardinal points of the compass, even if this offset the altar from the orientation of the walls of the enclosure, thus indicating some awareness and importance of astrological orientation.

The reconstruction at Pigadhes recreates an altar with a high podium, as opposed to a more common low altar table. Such elevated altars were also known in the eastern Mediterranean, Middle East, and Mesopotamia. Indeed, 'tower altars' much higher than Pigadhes seem to have existed. Many of these high altars also had steps leading up to them, an element missing at Pigadhes (though the altar is stepped, these steps do not seem practical for someone ascending to the top of the altar). Scholars have proposed, therefore, that the altar table at Pigadhes, with the bull horns, was not used for sacrifices but rather for the display of a cult object or objects. The horns themselves may, in fact, have been the cult object. Such pedestal altars are known in Hittite art, sometimes with a bull statue atop. The Pigadhes altar resembles a variant called a 'ziggurat altar', with shallow stepping on all sides. The square within squares coffering is also similar to some paneling on other ziggurat altars from the Middle East and Mesopotamia. Generally, the Pigadhes altar suggests influences from Anatolia, Syria, and other regions east of Cyprus. Just to the east of the altar was a drainage channel, perhaps to facilitate the cleaning out of the sanctuary after blood and burnt offerings. The drain was covered over with heavy stones. These are still visible today, running more or less south to north through the site.

The remainder of the site has a cistern and rooms of various functions. There may have been rooms for pilgrims. Surrounding the main altar site are several small tumulus tombs made of roughly cut stone. The fact that some people chose to be entombed there attests to the popularity and veneration of the shrine.

Sources for Pigadhes: Joan du Plat Taylor, *Myrtou-Pigadhes: A Late Bronze Age Sanctuary in Cyprus*, London: Department of Antiquities, Ashmolean Museum, 1957; Erik Sjöqvist, review of Joan du Plat Taylor, "Myrtou-Pigadhes: A Late Bronze Age Sanctuary in Cyprus" *Gnomon* 30, n. 5 (1958): 328-330; Ora Negbi, "Urbanism on Late Bronze Age Cyprus: LC II in Retrospect" *Bulletin of the American Schools of Oriental Research* 337 (2005): 1-45; Jennifer M. Webb, *Ritual Architecture, Iconography and Practice in the Late Cypriot Bronze Age.* Jonsered, Sweden: Paul Åström, 1999.

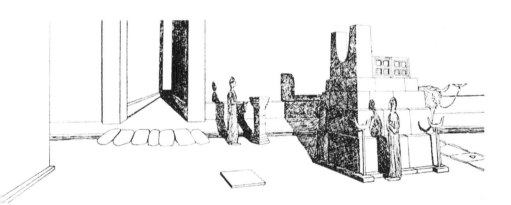

Fig. 4: Artist's reconstruction of Pigadhes cult room with altar [from G. R. H. Wright, Ancient Building in Cyprus, E. J. Brill, 1992].

Toumba tou Skourou, Bronze Age Potters' Quarter and Tombs near Güzelyurt/Morphou, c. 1600-700 BCE

[35° 13' 28.19" N / 33° 00' 05.36" E]

The remote archaeological site at Toumba tou Skourou is fascinating, enigmatic, and tragic. It may well have belonged to a much larger urban entity. Indeed, when the site was first considered, it was thought that it had the potential to be an 'Enkomi of western Cyprus'; another Bronze Age Cypriot metropolis. But in the early 1950s the whole area around Morphou and Toumba tou Skourou was heavily bulldozed to prepare the land for the planting of orange groves. Mounds and tumuli, even those of archaeological interest, were leveled by heavy machinery. Still, parts of the mound of Toumba tou Skourou ('Mound of the Slag Heap') were still intact when the devastating grading work was eventually halted. In the late 60s Vassos Karageorghis, the director of the Department of Antiquities, offered the site for excavation to Harvard University and the Museum of Fine Arts, Boston. These entities proceeded with excavations from 1971 to 1973 under the leadership of the late Emily D. T. Vermeule. Like other archaeological campaigns that began in the early 1970s, this excavation was cut short by Turkey's military action of 1974. Thus our understanding of the site is much hampered by both early demolitions by heavy machinery and by incomplete work done on what had survived.

The entire area seems to have been uncommonly rich archaeologically. A certain Mr. Tornaris, interviewed by archaeologists in the early 1970s, admitted to taking a hundred truckloads of cut stone from around the site of Toumba tou Skourou as well as eight hundred truckloads of walls and earth in the vicinity. Whatever Bronze Age city might have survived the millennia was hauled away in modern times to clear the way for the orchards of 20th century Cypriot citrus farmers. The aforementioned Mr. Tornaris and his sidekick Mr. Protopappas also greedily absconded with ancient 3500 year old *pithoi* (large earthenware storage jars) to store their own wine. In another blow to scholarship, the extensive pottery remains that had been excavated from the site and left in northern Cyprus were either broken or scattered during and just after 1974, although there have been recent efforts to safeguard this material at the Archaeological Museum at Güzelyurt/Morphou. Further, as was the case in so many places in Cyprus, tomb robbers had been active. One even forgot his newspaper in an underground tunnel, leaving an artefact from December 16th, 1968 for the excavators to find just three years later. Despite the vagaries of the site's history, in 1990 Emily Vermeule and Florence Wolsky published their findings, tentative though they might be, in a detailed monograph of the site.

The excavated portions of Toumba tou Skourou consist of an area of merely 66 by 36 metres, a small section of what was surely a much larger town, now completely lost. What Toumba tou Skourou may have been at its fullest extents we can now only dream of. What is visible, and what has been studied, is, as Vermeule put it: "an archaeologically perplexing industrial mound built of mud bricks, four adjacent 'houses,' and six tombs with twelve chambers". Though miles from the sea today, the town may have been a thriving river estuary port in former times. In fact, the Ovgos River was navigable up until the late 1940s, but silting and lowered sea levels have left Toumba high and dry and the Ovgos waterless for much of the year. The geographical aspects are also borne out in the evidence of the depth of the water table over time. An ancient well excavated at Toumbou showed that the fresh water table must have been between only twelve to thirty feet deep around 1500 BCE, since that's how deep excavated wells were. In the early 1970s, in contrast, fresh well water could be found only between three and four hundred feet, much deeper than in ancient times. Today, the almost nonexistent fresh water table is being ruined by sea water seeping in from miles away, threatening the very orange industry that helped create the problem in the first place through massive irrigation from wells and groundwater depletion.

The location's heyday was in the years between 1600 and 1200 BCE, but people still used the site for hundreds of years later, the archaeological record petering out around 700 BCE. Toumba tou Skourou's foundation, around 1600 BCE, occurred at a time when many towns and industries were established in western Cyprus, probably with commerce and industry generated by the copper mining and smelting operations that made Cyprus wealthy. This small remnant, Vermeule concluded, was a "specialized industrial quarter devoted to the manufacture of mud bricks, pithoi and fine pottery, with perhaps a little copper smelting".

Excavators identified five sections to the site, including an elevated rise christened the 'Mound', a rectilinear 'Basin' or catchment, an area of 'Fill', the 'Houses' (not habitations; probably workshops, though the workers may also have lived in them), and the Tombs. The Mound is a low rectangular prominence in the north part of the site, supported by a retaining wall about 30m long and creating a terrace. It shows signs of having been roofed at one time, but suffering a collapse around 1500 BCE. The burned timbers of the roof were discovered on the old pavements of the terrace. A new floor level was added atop this area, built up with a layer of fill made up of contemporary pottery debris — those valuable fragments, with their distinctive shapes and decorations, indicative of the date of the collapse and the time of rebuilding. The 'Basin' is an enigmatic structure, and may have functioned as a pool for the settling and refining of clays or for copper floatation, a process known to have been used in ancient times for the separating of copper from ores. It's roughly rectangular and about 14.0 by 5.5 metres in size. It had a waterproof lining and, at one point in its history, large pithoi sunk into the ground so that the mouths of the pithoi were at the floor level of the Basin. There was also a water channel cut into the wall to direct water into it. Two sacks of clay were found at the bottom of the Basin, supporting the idea that it was used for the refining of clay, but little other evidence helps define more clearly the Basin's function.

The four 'Houses', for lack of a better term, are rectangular buildings in the southern part of the site. One, House B, had five rooms in it, five wells, a baking oven or small kiln, and several fine, large pithoi, some with stone bases to stand on. Another room had twelve fully finished pots lined up against a wall ('Pot Row', the excavators called it). A stone gaming board, of a type found in other parts of Cyprus, was also discovered, indicating that the potters had some recreation. Other features included wells and water channels, indicative of the importance of water for the process of making pots. Evidence of kilns or furnaces were also unearthed, in some cases with parts of terra cotta bellows for increasing the temperature of the furnaces. So numerous were fragments of pithoi throughout the site and its immediate environs that it was thought that these large storage jars might have been Toumba's tou Skourou's principal manufactured product.

It is the tombs, found in the southeast corner of the excavated site, which are probably the most interesting aspect of Toumba tou Skourou. Each of the six tombs were of a fairly standard type found from Bronze Age Cyprus, with a tub-like pit (*dromos*) leading to a tomb entrance (*stomion* or 'mouth'), or, in most cases, a series of globular-shaped tombs budding off from the common *dromos* (Fig. 2). Tomb I had three such tomb chambers, for example, while Tomb II had four. Tomb III had one large chamber and one small niche off of the *dromos*, while Tomb VI had only one large chamber. Tomb I was by far the richest and the most interesting of the tombs at Toumba tou Skourou. When digging first began the archaeologists believed that they were just unearthing another well, since the tomb entrance didn't resemble the usual type of *dromos* associated with Bronze Age rock-cut tombs but it was, rather, more like a cylindrical shaft. However, it soon became evident that the shaft did indeed lead to large tomb chambers, and even more remarkably, that the shaft itself was not only pierced by the *stomions* of the large tombs, but was punctuated by fourteen small niches for infant burials. Although rare, this tomb configuration was not unknown in the region, for such a tomb with niches for child interment was also found at Agia Irini. Here, too, the niches for the infants were like miniature versions of the larger, adult burial chambers. Sometimes their tiny bodies were placed in jugs, with small cups or bottles for feeding close to their mouths, so their bottles would be there for them when they awoke in the afterlife. Sometimes the bones of two babies were packed into a single vessel, such as the newborn and the two-month old child in a Base Ring jug in Niche 2. Most of the infants found in the Tomb I niches were stillborn, newborn, or just a few months old, but in Niche 3 were found the jaw fragments of a three or four-year old child.

Tomb I's large Chamber I yielded an astonishingly rich hoard of pottery, by far the richest of Toumba tou Skourou's tomb chambers. Of the 516 vases from the 3 chambers of Tomb I, Chamber I contained 424 either complete pots or major fragments of others. These small jugs were essentially funerary gifts or votive offerings. There were also many human bones, but the skeletons were quite disarticulated and many bones were missing. Only one skeleton was more or less complete and coherent. It is thought that water ingress might have dissolved and shattered the tomb chamber's contents over the millennia. Thousands of bone slivers were scattered throughout its interior. Archaeologists determined that between twenty to twenty-four bodies might have been interred in this chamber. This is consistent with mortuary practices in other Cypriot Bronze Age sites. Tombs were used and reused over and over again, with bodies added and additional chambers cut over time. While Tomb I, Chamber I was the richest of the tomb chambers at Toumba tou Skourou, one of the more remarkable finds was in Tomb II, Chamber I: two painted ostrich eggs (although fragmentary unpainted eggs were found in Tomb I). Ostrich eggs, most likely from the Levantine Ostrich — *Struthio camelus syriacus* — were found throughout the Aegean world during this era. As funerary offerings, they may have had associations with being reborn in an afterlife, or were objects indicating the wealth of the deceased.

Chamber 4 of Tomb II also housed a revealing piece of remains: the skull of a woman about 25 years old. The top of her skull was flattened, probably from having been cradled in infancy with a headboard, a common malformation in the skulls of Bronze Age women in the Aegean, as many other remains of women of the time tell a similar story. So deformed was this young woman's skull, however, that it may well have been the cause of her premature death.

Sources for Toumba tou Skourou: Emily D. T. Vermeule and Florence Z. Wolsky, *Toumba tou Skourou: A Bronze Age Potters' Quarter on Morphou Bay in Cyprus*, Cambridge, Mass.: Harvard University Press, 1990; Priscilla Keswani, *Mortuary Ritual and Society in Bronze Age Cyprus*, London: Equinox Publishing, 2004, esp. pp. 2, 23-4, 28, 84-7, 90, 102-110.

The Kral Tepesi or 'King's Mountain',
Kaleburnu/Galinoporni, Late Bronze Age, c. 1200 BCE

[35° 31' 07.70" N / 34° 18' 36.21" E]

From the village of Kaleburnu's southeastern edge one can discern a high ridge about 100 metres high with dramatically sloping sides (Fig. 5). At the crest of this mountain, which is called the Kral Tepesi or King's Mountain, some university professors out for a hike in 2004 discovered a major Late Bronze Age archaeological site. The season's previous rains had washed away the soil and exposed the mouth of a huge ceramic pithoi filled with 26 bronze objects dating from about 1200 BCE. Archaeologists were contacted and for the past several years, in the summer months, salvage excavations have proceeded. Time is of the essence as local people are well known for their hobby of digging in search of archaeological treasures and, moreover, erosion is slowly destroying the vulnerable 3200 year old remains. Indeed, it is possible that much of the archaeological site lies strewn amongst the talus of the western slope. The bronze objects discovered in the pithoi included bowls, tools, a saw, a cauldron, offering stands, sickles, a jug with a lid, and other implements. Excavations have suggested that the mountain may have been the apex of a small town arranged on the terraces of the north and east slopes of the hill and even on the plains below. Today, these terraces, as well as the surrounding area, are used by farmers and annually ploughed, increasing the urgency for intervention. Just two kilometres away is a small cove that may have sheltered ancient ships that traded with the townspeople here. Certainly this coastline was a busy place in the Bronze Age, as it was so close to many contemporary ports on Anatolian and Middle Eastern shores. The distinctive hill of Kral Tepesi would have been a highly visible landmark for prehistoric seafarers.

The artifacts suggest some sort of light manufacturing at Kral Tepesi that involved small fires and liquids as many of the objects held liquid and excavations have revealed many places where small fires burned. Many flat round stones found at the site point to several large pithoi, as such stones were used as bases for these containers. Although inconclusive, perfumes may have been made here. Cyprus produced olive oil, and in the ancient world perfumes were oil-based, not alcohol-based. Cyprus is also rich with wildflowers in the spring, supplying some scents, and many herbs and plants that might supply fragrances were also common. It is even possible that opiates were processed here, as poppies were found in abundance on the island and drug production did exist in the ancient world.

The town around Kral Tepesi may have flourished around the same time as other significant late Bronze Age sites such as Toumba tou

Fig. 5: View of the Kral Tepesi ('King's Mountain') Bronze Age citadel near Kaleburnu/Galinoporni.

Skourou or Enkomi. Indeed, shovels and saws found here were also found in the 'Foundry Room' at Enkomi, suggesting connections with copper production. Bronze sickles were also found at Enkomi; but were they used to actually cut wheat or were they symbolic sickles used as votive donations to fertility gods? Sometimes it is difficult to separate ritual uses from practical ones. Unhappily, much of the archaeological context of the Kral Tepesi hoard was lost so it is difficult to know. Similarly, the hoard being packed away in a large terra cotta pithoi jar also presents interpretive problems. Why were all these bronze tools and vessels placed in there? Were they hidden and intentionally buried to save them from destruction? Or were the objects themselves a votive offering? Could the whole top part of the Kral Tepesi have been a ritual site since high places were so often dedicated to temples and gods, like an 'acropolis'? Or were they merely packaged for shipment? Further excavations will be needed to flesh out the context of the finds. The two offering stands/incense burners are in some ways the most compelling pieces in the Kral Tepesi hoard since they suggest the possibility that the area may also have been some kind of religious cult site where such offering stands would be used. Thus far, however, excavations have not yet with certainty uncovered such a cult house, though the rock-cut room with a vaguely apsidal end in the northernmost part of the hilltop is tantalizing in this respect.

The Kral Tepesi is extremely fragile. It is suggested that one admires the citadel from afar and does not disturb the archaeological site unless accompanied by a representative of the authorities. It is also dangerous at the top with no handrails or trails and a precipitous cliff on the west side.

Sources for Kral Tepesi: Martin Bartelheim, Bülent Kızılduman, Uwe Müller, Ernst Pernicka, and Hasan Tekel, "The Late Bronze Age Hoard of Kaleburnu/Galinoporni, on Cyprus," *Památky Archeologické* vol. 99 (2008), pp. 161-188.

Bronze Age tombs at Vounous (aka Kasafani), about two km east of Bellapais

[35° 18' 42.71" N / 33° 22' 08.23' E]

The collection of Bronze Age tombs at Vounous are about two kilometres east of the Abbey of Bellapais and were excavated in campaigns led by C.F.A. Schaffer in 1931-33, Eleanor and James Stewart in 1937-38, and Porphyrios Dikaios, who published findings on the site in 1940. There are two parts to the site, designated simply A and B, and there were well over a hundred tombs of the typical Bronze Age form with a *dromos* leading to either one, two, or three ovoid tomb chambers (Fig 4). As in the other Bronze Age tombs previously dealt with, the tomb chambers had an entrance called a *stomion*. Often, these were covered by stone slabs that closed the tomb. Several such slabs were found *in situ* during the excavations. Even by the 1930s many of the tombs had been robbed by the locals and the excavations were considered salvage digs. Water ingress over the centuries had severely disturbed the stratigraphy of the tombs and scattered pottery and skeletons around many of the chambers, thus destroying any sequence in the soil horizons. Still, the few undisturbed tombs yielded a huge amount of Bronze Age pottery and votive grave goods, including the famous 'Vounous Bowl' which was uncovered in Dikaios's excavation of tomb 22. Stewart's 1937-38 campaign retrieved a huge collection of fine pottery including vases, cups, bowls, and various ritual or cult vessels decorated with bull horns and dynamic zig-zag patterns etched into their sides. Sometimes other animal heads such as goats, sheep or rams adorned the rims and handles of the pots, possibly indicating the favorite animals for ceremonial sacrifice.

The aforementioned Vounous Bowl is an enigmatic sculptural group that seems to illustrate, in the form of a model, some ancient ritual. Some have seen it as a scene of sacrifice, as bulls are kept in a pen near an attendant figure. Some think it is simply a domestic scene. Perhaps the figures in the Vounous bowl represent a funerary ritual of some kind. The most compelling interpretation belongs to Edgar Peltenburg, who sees the Vounous Bowl as indicative of the emergence, on Cyprus, of a hierarchical, more socially stratified society. In some of the tombs at Vounous one finds clay knives or spear blades, sometimes with sheaths as well. In others one finds the same objects in bronze. Peltenburg thinks these grave goods represent rulers or warrior leaders of the Bronze Age communities. Earlier graves do not typically contain these items. In the Vounous Bowl one figure stands out as larger than the rest, and he (if it is indeed a he) is seated on a throne-like chair. For Peltenburg, it is not so important that the Vounous Bowl represents a ritual, but that that ritual event is an illustration of an emergent hierarchy where one figure dominated the proceedings, a king figure or soldier leader. Whatever the Vounous Bowl's meaning, it is a compelling and fascinating scene offering a glimpse, albeit enigmatic, into Cypriot life of the Bronze Age.

As this book was going to press, I received a notification that the site had been bulldozed to make a firebreak road and to construct a water storage tank. Several archaeological sites have been damaged in similar ways.

Sources for Vounous: A.E. Dunn-Vaturi, *Vounous: C.F.A. Schaeffer's Excavations in 1933. Tombs 49-79.* Studies in Mediterranean Archaeology 130, Jonsered: Paul Åstrom, 2003; P. Dikaios, *The Excavations at Vounous-Bellapais in Cyprus 1931-1932*, Oxford: Society of Antiquaries, London, 1940; Eleanor and James R. Stewart, *Vounous 1937-1938*, Lund, Sweden: Gleerup, 1950; E. J. Peltenburg, "Constructing Authority: the Vounous Enclosure Model," *Opuscula Atheniensa* 20, n. 10 (1994): 157-62; Diane Bolger, "Figurines, Fertility, and the Emergence of Complex Society in Prehistoric Cyprus," *Current Anthropology* 37, n. 2 (April, 1996): 365-373.

Agia Irini or Paleokastro, near Akdeniz/Agia Irini (Koruçam/Kormakiti), Pygmy Elephant and Hippopotamus Fossils and Iron Age Ritual Site, c. 700 BCE

[approx. 35° 20' 47.59" N / 32° 56' 23.66" E]

The remote archaeological site of Agia Irini is about 5.7 km north of the village of Akdeniz/Agia Irini in the far west of Cyprus, on the Kormakiti Peninsula, about 500 metres inland from the sea (it is also 6.4 kilometres west from the town of Koruçam/Kormakiti). No paved road leads to it, but a rough dirt road gets you to within about 200 metres of the site. While the cultural archaeological remains at Agia Irini are overgrown the still visible fossil remains are spectacular. Still, the cult site found here was a very important one and supplied much information about Iron Age ritual architecture and practices. In its time, it was probably the main town site in the immediate region. The first excavations were done in the late 1920s and early 1930s by the Swedish Archaeological Expedition, led by the seminal figure in early Cypriot archaeology Einar Gjerstad, who identified not just one but a series of buildings that he thought were sanctuaries of some kind. One of the most significant architectural finds was the semi-circular ritual structure at a spot named Paleokastro. In November 1929 a priest from Agia Irini, Papa Prokopios, walked into the offices of the Swedish Archaeological Expedition in Nicosia with a large terra cotta head that he had found while farming. This led to one of Cyprus's most magnificent archaeological discoveries: 2000 clay sculptures of human figures, many with distinctive conical hats or helmets. Some of these impressive statues are several feet high, life size, while others are merely a few inches tall. Presumably they were offerings to the gods or some kind of votive effigies. Some appeared to be dressed as warriors, others as priests in ceremonial garb. They were carefully arranged like an audience of worshippers around the semi-circular altar in the sacred enclosure. Most of these figures can be found today in the Archaeological Museum in Nicosia, though there are others in Sweden (in the Mediterranean Museum or *Medelhavsmuseet*, Stockholm,). They dated from around 700-500 BCE, the very end of the Bronze Age and beginning of the Iron Age. Not all the figures were depictions of human worshippers or gods. Some were minotaur-like men with heads of bulls. Some figures were of charioteers, complete with chariots, while others held instruments, indicating music might have been part of the rituals. Many male figures have beards and fanciful clothing. It is as if a large group of worshippers were magically turned to clay and buried in the midst of their ceremonies, only to be rediscovered 2500 years later. In another cache 33 scarab seals were found, some of Egyptian and some of Cypriot origin. Gjerstad reports that many local men in Agia Irini, who had for years augmented their incomes with clandestine digging for artifacts, were furious at Papa Prokopios for alerting the authorities about the site and letting foreigners excavate it.

Very little of the ritual altar and precinct are visible and one should be careful not to step on any walls or stones as the site is somewhat fragile. More visible are the nearby fossil remains, which should also be treated carefully. Take only photographs. The deposit of ancient bones at Agia Irini is at a site colourfully known as *Dragontovounari*, or 'Hill of the Dragons'. The villagers at Agia Irini believed these to be the bones of dragons that were all drowned in a cataclysmic flood eons ago. Less dramatically, but no less interesting, these fossil remains are actually of pygmy hippopotami and elephant. In many cases on islands such as Cyprus, Malta or Crete, some animals over time become dwarfed, getting smaller and smaller because of limited resources (conversely, some animals could become giant). Agia Irini is not the only place on Cyprus where there are impressive remains of the bones of ancient animals. They are often found in huge deposits because early humans hunted these defenseless animals to extinction, discarding their bones in heaps. These impressive remains gave rise to many myths about Cyprus and about the origin and magical properties of the bones themselves. Benedetto Bordone, from Padua in Italy, visited Cyprus in the 1520s and recounted some hearsay from the island:

> I say that in it [Cyprus] is a mountain a thousand paces in height, with a circuit of two miles, composed entirely of the bones of various beasts, and even of men. It is called Cirenes, and the dwellers there affirm as of perfect truth that whosoever is stricken by fever, and drinks a little of the powder scraped from these bones, has no sooner drunk than he is freed of his fever.
>
> *[Excerpta Cypria, 62]*

Of course, the tale grew bigger in the telling, and Bordone never saw such a mountain, but the story he tells of the Cypriots believing that grinding up the bones and dissolving them in a drink is true. He notes the mountain's name, Cirenes, but no such mountain exists. Rather this is an old name for the city of Kyrenia or Girne. Rupert Gunnis in 1936 noted that such religious rituals with the bones were, in fact, practiced well into the 20th century.

Near the sea is the tiny rock-cut chapel of St Phanourios. Beneath the chapel the rocks are full of fossil bones, called by the villagers the bones of St Phanourios, but in reality they are the remains of the pygmy hippopotamus. St Phanourios was a youth who lived in Asia Minor, he heard the call of Christ and came to Cyprus. He sailed across in a small boat with only his faithful horse as his companion, and, landing, tried to ride up the steep cliff, but his horse slipped and he and his steed were killed, in token of which the horse's footprints are shown to this day.

The chapel is much restored to by the villagers, who dig out from the rock the fossil bones and, powdering them, mix them with a drink of water. This draught is said to be a sovereign cure for nearly every known disease.

[Gunnis, 211-12]

These deposits and their association with St Phanourios suggested the scientific name of the Cypriot dwarf hippopotamus, which is *Phanourios minor* (though it is also known as *Hippopotamus minor*). Sometimes there are also in the intermingled bone deposits Cypriot pygmy elephants (*Elephas [Palaeoloxodon] cypriotes*), which are estimated to have weighed only 200 pounds — 2% of their full-grown relatives in Africa. The pioneering British paleontologist Dorothea Bate is credited with their discovery in 1902, but, in fact, earlier travellers had seen them. In 1683, Cornelius van Bruyn saw one of these bone sites, also noting how the locals venerated them.

We left the next day, taking with us some villagers chosen specially to show us a certain place in the mountain where are seen bones of men and animals incorporated in the rock, which hold there together in a state of petrifaction...I had brought with us hammers and scissors...

I extracted some of these bones from the rock. The chief was a bone which I took to be the radius of a man's arm. It was imbedded so firmly in the rock that it took us two hours to get it out, and despite all our efforts to preserve it whole, the rock itself broke and the bone with it. This after all was an advantage, for the fracture allowed us to see the marrow plainly defined. I carried it off carefully wrapped in cotton.

On the same spot I found plenty of fragments just hidden by the earth; some were human bones, others those of beasts, and some teeth of surprising size. All round the rock were candle-ends. I guessed the place was held in veneration, and found indeed that the Greeks came there occasionally to pray, believing perhaps that some of their saints may be buried there. I carried off my spoils, and noticed that the pieces which had been covered with soil were not so much petrified as the bone I had extracted from the rock.

[Excerpta Cypria, 237]

The "radius of a man's arm" that van Bruyn chips away David Reese claims was, instead, the humerus of a pygmy hippopotamus. In the 1860s Luigi Palma di Cesnola was also taken to a cave with an impressive deposit of elephant and hippopotamus bones:

It was a large cavern which my guide called 'Spilia Macaria', the entrance of which faces the sea. This cave contains a great quantity of bones, some of which competent authorities have recognized as human. It is about 60 feet above the level of the sea. I succeeded in penetrating into the cave, and found petrified bones on the floor and in the walls, forming a solid mass. How they ever came there will probably remain a mystery. My guide told me with religious awe they were the bones of 'forty saints', and that a few years ago it had been the custom of the peasants of neighbouring villages to make a pilgrimage to this cave, accompanied by their priests, on the anniversary of the 9th of March.

Thus these ancient bones, found at several sites on the island, but almost always near the coasts near settlements that go back to the Neolithic period, were fascinating artifacts for early voyagers, paleontologists and archaeologists alike. The oldest bones have been dated to 8100 BCE, giving an indication of the period of the earliest human arrivals. They were the first natural predators the poor elephants and hippopotami had to contend with. It is thought that these amazing creatures were hunted to extinction within a few centuries.

Sources for Agia Irini/Paleokastro: Jennifer Webb, *Ritual Architecture, Iconography and Practice in the Late Cypriot Bronze Age* (Jonsered: Paul Åström, 1999). For Agia Irini see esp. pp. 53-58, 163-166, 218-9, 243-48, 287-8, 296-7; David S. Reese, "Men, Saints, or Dragons?" *Folklore* 87, n. 1 (1976): 89-95; David S. Reese, *The Earliest Prehistory of Cyprus*, American Schools of Oriental Research Archaeological Reports Vol. 2, London, 2001; David Wilson, *Ayia Irini, periods I-III: the Neolithic and Early Bronze Age Settlements* (Mainz on Rhine: von Zabern), 1999; Alan H. Simmons, "The First Humans and Last Pygmy Hippopotami of Cyprus," in Stuart Swiny ed., *The earliest prehistory of Cyprus: from colonization to exploitation* (Boston: American Schools of Oriental Research, , 2001), 1-15; Dorothea M. A. Bate, "Further Note on the Remains of *Elephas Cypriotes* from a Cave Deposit in Cyprus", *Philosophical Transactions of the Royal Society of London*, vol. 197 (1905): 347-360; Stuart Swiny, "Prehistoric Cyprus, A Current Perspective," *Biblical Archaeologist* 52, n. 4 (Dec., 1989): 178-189; Einar Gjerstad, *Ages and Days in Cyprus* (Göteborg: Åströms, 1980), esp. pp. 106-118.

Fortress of Nitovikla, Bronze Age, c. 1500 BCE, South of Kuruova/Korovia

[35° 29' 17.61" N / 34° 17' 40.27" E]

The Bronze Age fortress site of Nitovikla can be found overlooking the sea 3 km SSE of the village of Kuruova/Korovia in the Karpas peninsula. Dating from around 1500 BCE, it seems to have been an outlook fortification built to monitor seagoing trade and guard the valley that extends inland towards the modern town of Kuruova/Korovia. It gives us a fairly good picture of a Bronze Age fortification, of which there was undoubtedly many more on Cyprus. It was destroyed sometime around 1600 BCE, but was rebuilt soon after the destruction, although on the same plan. It was essentially a square surrounded by four thick rubble walls with higher towers on at least three of the four corners, and square towers flanking the entrance gate, which was in the northeastern part. The western section has fallen down the slope of the hill. In general appearance, it seems to be consistent with such fortifications in that corner of the Mediterranean during this period, such as on Anatolian (Turkish) shores and the coastline of Palestine and Syria. There were storerooms, a kitchen, and an altar-like construction was found in the open courtyard. The fort itself was only the well-fortified stronghold of a somewhat larger trapezoidal walled citadel about 400 m long and varying from 100-200 m in width. This space is fairly legible when visiting the hilltop site, and the large stones flanking the entrance gate to the fort are also still discernable. It is thought that the larger enclosure offered refuge for the local population when the area was attacked by raiders. The large cistern helped supply fresh water for those who might have had to survive a siege of the fortress. The high position of the fort, in the southwest corner of the plateau, would have allowed sentries to espy the approach of unfriendly fleets and to sound an alarm to those who lived in the immediate area. It is estimated that the highest parts of the walls or towers were up to 6 metres in height. Squared masonry was used on the corners, but coarse rubble masonry made up the walls. Note that there is also a small natural harbour below. It is likely that this tiny anchorage sheltered Bronze Age boats long ago.

Sources for Nitovikla: Paul Åström, *The Swedish Cyprus Expedition*, vol. IV, Parts 1C and 1B, Late Cypriot Bronze Age (Lund: 1972), pp. 33-35; Einar Gjerstad, *Ages and Days in Cyprus* (Göteborg: Åström, 1980); esp. 49-59; Gunnel Hult, *Nitovikla Reconsidered* (Stockholm Sweden: Medelhavsmuseet), 1992.

Ruins of the Bronze Age City of Enkomi, near Famagusta (Tuzla/Enkomi), 1700-1200 BCE

[35° 10' 28.27" N / 33° 52' 19.54" E]

A few kilometres northwest of Famagusta, near the modern village of Tuzla ("place of salt") are the ruins of the Bronze Age city of Enkomi, which may be the place the Egyptians referred to as 'Alasia' (or 'Alashyia'), though some believe that this was actually the ancient name for Cyprus as a whole. As you first enter the archaeological site there initially seems to be little to get excited about, but as you walk just a few yards to the edge of the escarpment the land falls away, opening up to the vastness of the Mesaorian plain. On clear days you can see for miles and in spring this vista is clothed in a verdant carpet of newly sprouted wheat. Below this bluff lie Enkomi's magnificent remains. The early strata of Enkomi date from 1700 BCE, a time which corresponds to the Middle Bronze Age and the Middle Kingdom Period in Egypt. But this early city seems to have slowly passed away and been virtually abandoned for over a century (archaeologists found a fairly deep sterile layer). Around 1550 BCE, however, Enkomi began a spectacular comeback and prospered for several subsequent centuries. Enkomi was a port on the Pediaeos River, situated near the seacoast at the eastern end of the Mesaorian plain, the breadbasket of Cyprus. It had close cultural and trade contacts with one of the largest cities of the age, Ugarit, which lay a short voyage across the sea to the northeast. Artifacts tell us that Enkomi also had economic contacts with Egypt during the Bronze Age. Wheat, copper, olive oil, and wine were Enkomi's principal exports.

One of the most striking features of Enkomi, which is quite visible in the excavated area, is its regularized grid plan of narrow streets meeting at right angles. Two main arteries crossed in the center of the town and led to the four gates of the city walls. Such impressive urban orderliness anticipated the grid plan of later classical and Roman cities a millennium later. Yet Enkomi was not of a single construction, despite its organised appearance. Different parts were enlarged and added to earlier sections through different historical eras. Walls were extended or expanded, for example, as the city grew in population and wealth. Still, the attention given to the layout of the civic core of Enkomi is impressive for its time.

Many Bronze Age cities of the Eastern Mediterranean were severely damaged by an enormous and widespread earthquake sometime around 1365 BCE and Enkomi, too, seems to have been affected by the catastrophe. However, once again Enkomi emerged from devastation and the excavated grave contents from the post-quake recovery era reflect a very high, even luxurious standard of living. It is estimated that Enkomi's population eventually reached 15,000, making it a veritable Bronze Age metropolis, an indication of its continued prosperity. One of the things

Fig. 6: Tomb at Enkomi.

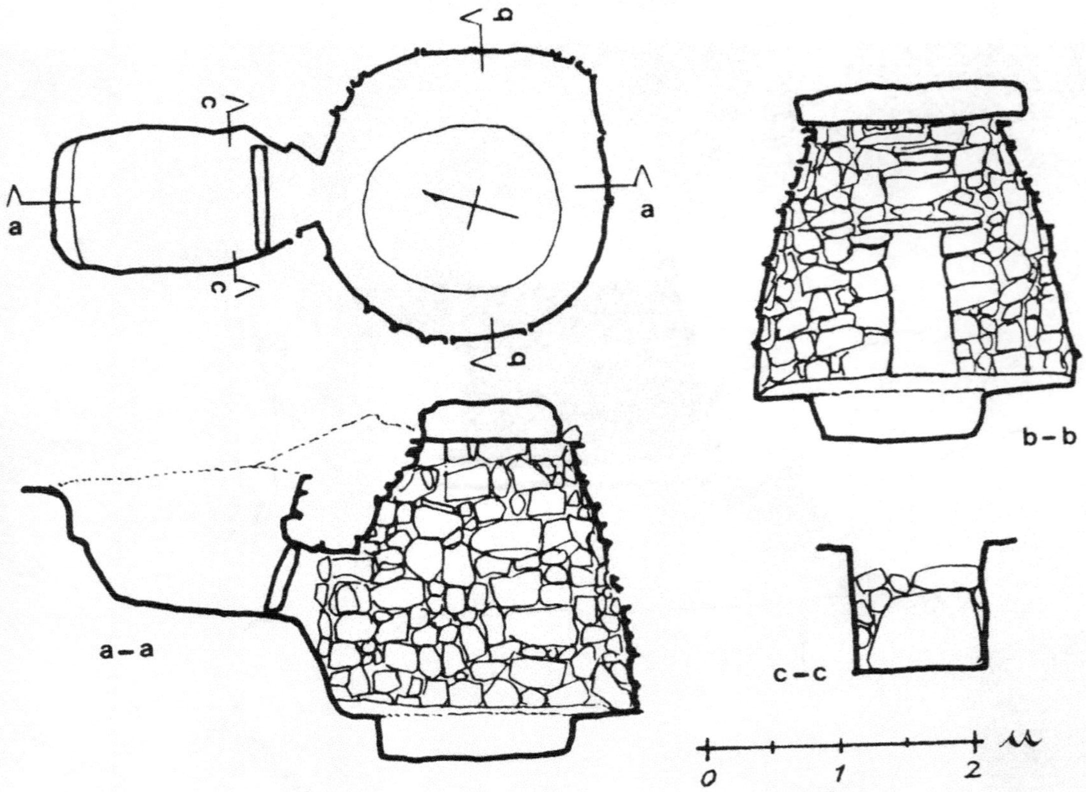

Fig. 7: Diagram of a tomb at Enkomi [from G. R. H. Wright, Ancient Building in Cyprus, E. J. Brill, 1992].

44

that made Enkomi so wealthy was bronze. The main ingredient of bronze — remember, this is the Bronze Age — is copper, and copper was Cyprus's main export. While we live in an age when oil is the commodity everyone wants, the Enkomians had the commodity everyone wanted in the Bronze Age. While the copper mines were in the Troodos Mountains, Enkomians seemed to have been active in processing the ore, as archaeologists found the slag heaps and other physical signs of copper production. The city also served as one of Cyprus's principal ports for shipping the distinctive ox-hide copper ingots produced at Enkomi. These ingots seem to have been so important to the Enkomians that they may have been given as votive offerings to gods or goddesses. Two small bronze statues were found at Enkomi, one of a warrior figure (christened 'the God of the Ingot', dating from about 1200 BCE) and another of a nude female; each stand atop bases that resemble the ox-hide copper ingots.

The excavated part of the city exposes an area of only a few hundred square metres, but one can learn many things while exploring the site. Almost every house had its own cistern which collected rain and ground water. The heads of these wells were inside the homes and were sometimes rimmed with nicely carved stone rings. Many of these remain where they were left over 3000 years ago. Some cisterns were stone lined, while others were crude pits. There were other more interesting cavities below the homes of the Enkomians, however, for they also buried their dead beneath their houses, and many of these tombs, too, can be seen today. Ancestors kept the living company in their labours and protected them from harm. This domestic burial custom also can be found in Ugarit, one of the many cultural parallels between the two cities. Some tombs were made of durable materials and given stone slabs as roofs (Fig. 6-7). These family tombs seem to have been planned from the initial designs of the houses and the dry climate of Cyprus ensured that the bodies dried out and mummified. Men were buried with fine bronzes and, later, iron implements and weapons. Women were often buried with elaborate jewelry and mortars and pestles used to make cosmetics, ensuring their beauty in the afterlife. One tomb was particularly significant as it was of a 'tholos' or beehive type design, similar to the famous Mycenaean tombs in Greece or even the impressive tumulus Tomb 3 at the King's Tombs just a couple of kilometres from Enkomi.

The milling stones of the ancient inhabitants can be found everywhere at the site, with some large earthenware pots still in the houses that they served thousands of years ago. These objects give a sense of the daily life of the inhabitants: the jugs of water, wine, and oil, and the diurnal grinding of wheat for bread.

In some of Enkomi's ceremonial buildings one can see extremely precise cut stone masonry with blocks so tightly fitted that barely a crack is visible. In one of these buildings a remarkable solid bronze statue of a god with a bull-horn helmet was found. It is over half a metre tall, seemingly part man and part bull, like the Minotaur of the Minoans. One wonders whether the people saw in him a savior or feared him as a punisher, though his archaic smile seems to preclude the latter and his right hand is outstretched in a gesture of blessing. Some think he is an early manifestation of the Greek god Apollo, into whom many fertility gods were later combined. Indeed, on Cyprus there was a particular manifestation of Apollo worshipped, 'Apollo Alasiotas', perhaps indicating his origin in 'Alasia', another name for Enkomi. As in so many places in the ancient world fecundity was the fundamental preoccupation of religion and the bull served as its masculine expression. This cult statue may have ensured the fruitfulness of cattle and crops as well as women, whom the Enkomians' depended on for their prosperity and survival. We might recall the Pigadhes monument, a four metre high Bronze Age shrine with huge, stylized bull horns [see earlier entry on Pigadhes]. The 'Ingot God' statuette was found in a large rectangular enclosure that was undoubtedly some kind of sanctuary or ritual site. In fact, the 'Horned God' just mentioned was also found in a sanctuary enclosure. Three of these enclosures were located in Enkomi's monumental core, each branching off of the main north/south street of the city (Fig. 8). Along the north wall of the Sanctuary of the Ingot God were many bull's skulls and some pottery remains of some fascinating figures the archaeologists christened 'centaurs'. Sometimes with four or three legs, they also had two human-like heads and faces. The hollowed out bodies of some of the 'centaurs' seem to have held liquid for ritual ablutions or offerings as there were circular openings on their chests for spouts.

Enkomi began to decline steadily from around 1100 BCE, just around the time that the coastal port of Salamis started to emerge, suggesting the possibility that the River Pediaeos had begun to silt up, obliging the Enkomians to make the short trip to the coast to develop the new seaport city. When leaving the site, it is interesting to visit the collection of stones strewn around the sheds near the entrance. There are some ancient architectural fragments, eroded statues, and some medieval and even Venetian carved and inscribed blocks.

Sources for Enkomi: See collection of essays in *Alasia, Mission Archaéologique d'Alasia*, ed. Claude F.-A. Schaeffer, 1971; Lindy Crewe, *Early Enkomi. Regionalism, Trade and Society at the Beginning of the Late Bronze Age in Cyprus. British Archaeological Reports*, Series 1700 (2007); C.F.A. Schaeffer, "Enkomi," *American Journal of Archaeology* 52, n. 1 (Jan.-March, 1948): 165-177; A. H. S. Megaw, "Archaeology in Cyprus, 1953" *The Journal of Hellenic Studies* 74 (1954): 172; A. H. S. Megaw, "Archaeology in Cyprus, 1955" *The Journal of Hellenic Studies* 74 (1954): 42. O. Davis, "The Copper Mines of Cyprus," *Annual of the British School at Athens* 30 (1928-29, 1929-30): 74-85. For readers of French see the series of articles in the journal *Syria* vols. 27 (1950), 30 (1955), 41 (1964), 45 (1968), 46 (1969), 47 (1970), 48 (1971), 50 (1973).

Fig. 8: View of monumental quarter of Bronze Age Enkomi.

47

The Royal Tombs and Cellarka Necropolis, near Famagusta, 11th to 7th century BCE

[35° 10' 33.50" N / 33° 53' 27.36" E]

About five kilometres north of Famagusta on Cyprus's east coast, and very close to the ruins of the ancient city of Salamis (and Enkomi and the church and monastery of St Barnabas as well), is a large field filled with tombs dating as early as the 11th century BCE. One set has been called 'The Royal Tombs' because of their monumental scale and opulent grave goods. Horses were buried with their masters to provide conveyance to the world beyond. Their skeletons and bridles were excavated in front of the tomb entrances, as if they lay in wait for their owners to mount them again and ride through the eternal fields of Elysium. One can still see these horse skeletons there today — turned to dust but still visible, protected by low greenhouse-like sheds. Work is currently underway to preserve these fragile remains. Marvelous collections of bronze artifacts were found in the ancient graves, including an elaborate bronze bridle, a throne, and a bed frame made of ivory. When Vassos Karageorghis excavated these burials in the 1960s a ripple went through the archaeological community because the findings provided evidence of funerary rituals as Homer had described them in the *Iliad*. Here were tangible, Bronze Age tombs which echoed the heroic Aegean past.

Most of the Royal Tombs have a similar configuration and excavations revealed certain consistencies in burial customs. In many ways their general configuration is very similar to earlier Bronze Ages tombs on Cyprus such as those found at Vounous, Karmi, and Toumba tou Skourou (see earlier entries). Typically, there is a sloping, ramp-like approach to the tomb chamber called a *dromos*. But unlike the *dromoi* of the tombs discussed earlier, in the Royal Tombs the dromos is decidedly monumental, as wide as a street in many cases (Fig. 9-10). The tomb chamber itself, constructed of huge stone slabs, had an entrance door (*stomion*), which was closed off by a large stone door. Many of the Royal Tombs contained the charred remains of the dead who were cremated in the *dromos* along with other sacrificial offerings. In many of the *dromoi* horses and chariots or funerary carts were found in place. In some cases, it is clear that the horses panicked and the attendants of the funeral had to stone the animals to kill them (Fig. 11). The unfortunate creatures were buried as they fell, their necks twisted and legs askew, with piles of the fatal stones lying around them. The horses were finely caparisoned with bronze blinders and bridles, and many still had the poles of the funerary carts attached to their yokes. The cremated remains of the dead were usually wrapped in cloth and placed in clay jars or bronze cauldrons. Several large amphorae, which contained honey or olive oil,

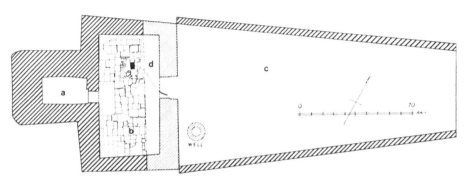

9: Cross-section and plan of Tomb 50 ('St Catherine's Tomb'), the Royal Tombs
r Salamis [from G. R. H. Wright, Ancient Building in Cyprus, E. J. Brill, 1992].

10: Tomb 50 of the Royal Tombs near Salamis ('St Catherine's Tomb') from the
of the dromos towards the modified tomb chamber. Note 'greenhouse' covering
horse burial.

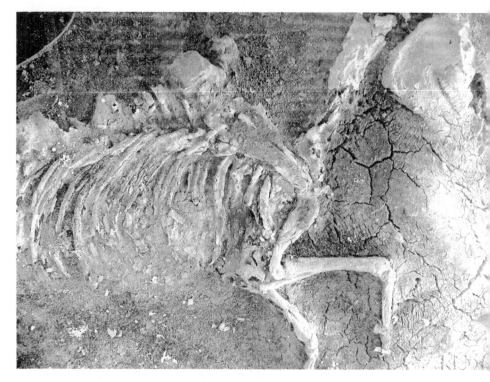

Fig. 11: The skeletons of the Bronze Age horse burials have turned to dust since the 1960s, but can still be seen through the glass roofs of the 'greenhouse' sheds. This is the one from Tomb 50 ('St Catherine's Tomb').

Fig. 12: The tumulus or mound of Tomb 3 of the Royal Tombs near Salamis.

were arranged as offerings against the walls of the *dromos*. In some cases, servants were also killed to follow their masters to the afterlife. They were often placed just outside the tomb, perhaps to guard it against desecration. These human sacrificial victims did not go willingly, it seems, as their hands were bound with leather straps.

The most impressive of the Royal Tombs is the great Tomb 3, a deep stone chamber with a large man-made hill or tumulus on top. The circular tumulus (*tholos*) itself is about 10 metres high (though it has been eroding for centuries) and about 50 metres in diameter (Fig. 12). Excavators had to remove tons of earth from the hillside to get to its entrance, even though it had been robbed in earlier times. It wasn't just a pile of dirt. Excavation revealed how carefully it was constructed, with radiating rubble stone walls surmounted by mud brick, which helped stabilize the hill. These features are visible in the cutaway portion under the modern roofing that protects the site. One can walk down into the tomb's *dromos*, even into the stone burial chamber itself, though it's not for the claustrophobic (Fig. 13). The chamber has stone walls and slabs that lean against each other to form a pitched roof as if creating an eternal home for the dead. Tomb 3 dates from around the year 600 BCE and, like some of the earlier tombs, had horse sacrifices in the *dromos*. Along with four horses and a war chariot, archaeologists also discovered weapons such as a sword, quiver, and an iron spear and arrow point. Clearly, the tomb was built for a great warrior or king of Salamis.

Another impressive tomb is also the most unique. The tomb chamber of this grave, excavated in 1965 and labeled Tomb 50, is preceded by a huge, barrel-vaulted structure and a wide *dromos* with a horse burial (Figs. 9-10). This was used, centuries after its original use as a tomb, as a church/shrine because, as the legend goes, this was the prison in which St Catherine of Alexandria was kept. Thus it is often referred to as 'St Catherine's Prison' in early guidebooks. For years this structure baffled archaeologists and travellers because they did not recognize that it was comprised of structures built in very different eras: an 8th century BCE tomb with a barrel vaulted chamber added much later in Roman times (though, to add to the confusion, this barrel vault used the huge stones of one of the earlier tombs). It became a shrine to St Catherine in Byzantine times and was used until the 20th century. During the Middle Ages and the Renaissance period, it was one of the most famous monuments to see when pilgrims and travellers visited Cyprus. It was also believed, as part of the myths about St Catherine that grew up around Salamis, that St Catherine had been born there as well. Nicholas Martoni visited Salamis in 1394 and wrote in his diary:

... I desired also to see the place of her [St Catherine's] nativity; wherefore on the fifth day of December of the third indication I went to that ancient city Constantia [Salamis] four miles distant from Famagosta, which was once a great city built by the Emperor Constantius, father of the blessed Catherine, but now is utterly destroyed, and went to the place where one can see [where] the castle of the city stood...and there directly is that room, now destroyed, where the blessed Catherine was born: near it now stands a seemly chapel, to which the people of Famagosta go with great devoutness and frequency.

[Excerpta Cypria, 24-5]

Clearly, the sites associated with the cult of St Catherine were actively being used around 1400. Many visitors from later centuries also make note of the sacred site.

The richest of all the Royal Tombs was Tomb 79, which was used (as were several of the tombs) for two successive burials which took place within a few years of each other. Four funerary carts were found, one of them a four-horse chariot with many bronze figural decorations. A spectacular bronze cauldron with heads of griffons and sphinxes surrounding the rim was also unearthed. Ivory furniture, such as a throne with Egyptian and Assyrian figures, are clear indications of the luxury goods which passed through ancient Cyprus.

Cellarka Tombs:

Not far from 'St Catherine's Prison', about 200 metres southeast towards the modern roadway, is an area of rock-cut tombs much simpler and more densely crowded than the Royal Tombs. These are the Cellarka Tombs, a warren of rock-cut graves of modest size all following the design of a stepped *dromos* leading to one or two rectangular tomb chambers. Excavated between 1964 and 1967, these graves date from a broad historical range between the 8th century BCE and the 4th century CE. Many of these were family crypts and were used over and over again. The artifacts found inside were modest: small clay animals, eggs, or little jars of seeds or fruit. The inclusion of fruits and seeds with the burials reflects the concept of *panspermia*, the notion of spreading life into afterlife through the dispersal of seeds. The concept survives in modern Greek Orthodox funerary rituals as well, where it is called *pankarpia*. An interesting phenomenon found at Cellarka was a preponderance of infant burials. Babies were placed in Rhodian amphorae and buried in shallow graves. Often, their bones were so soft that the skeletons did not survive.

Though smaller in scale than the larger Royal Tombs nearby, these tombs still sometimes had sculptural reliefs decorating their entrances, such as Tomb 84, which has a door of multiple frames with a crescent moon shape above. The gifts to the dead were also impressive and even beautiful, such as clay rosettes burned as part of an offering.

Sources for Royal and Cellarka Tombs: Claude Delaval Cobham and Max Öhnefalsch Richter, "A Pre-Historic Building at Salamis," *Journal of Hellenic Studies* 4 (1883): 111-116; Vassos Karageoghis, *Salamis: Recent Discoveries in Cyprus*, McGraw Hill, 1969; Vassos Karageorghis, "Tomb of St Catherine at Salamis," *Antiquity* 40 (March, 1966): 45-8; St Catherine and her mythology and Salamene cult sites are discussed in detail in Lorenzo Calvelli, *Cipro e la Memoria dell'Antico fra Medioevo e Rinascimento. La percezione de passato romano dell'isola nel mondo occidentale*, 2009.

Fig. 13: The dromos leading to the stomion ('mouth') of the tomb chamber of Tomb of the Royal Tombs near Salamis.

Ancient Greco-Roman City of Salamis, near Famagusta, 11th century BCE to 7th century CE

[Entrance Gate: 35° 11' 13.70" N / 33° 54' 12.27"E]

The remains of the ancient Greco-Roman city of Salamis are on Cyprus' east coast about six kilometres north of Famagusta. Dramatically poised on the sandy beaches of Famagusta Bay, the extensive ruins include an impressive bath complex, a gymnasium, public toilets, a theater, a forum, an immense water cistern, two Christian basilicas from the Early Christian/Byzantine period, two villas, and a Roman road currently under excavation. Recent excavations in the summer of 2011 revealed the *decumanus* and *cardo* (the main east-west and north-south streets respectively) of the city, a major find as now excavators can dig along these main streets to find the major architectural monuments, thus making their excavations more directed and efficient. Much of Salamis has yet to be uncovered, but its fame in the ancient world and a series of excavations beginning in the 19th century and continuing today, allow us to form a fairly detailed picture of the life and death of this legendary city.

Little is known of the foundations of the 11th century BCE city. Indeed, a single tomb is lone testament to any settlement from that bygone age. But it is probably not a coincidence that the city site of Enkomi was abandoned about the same time that Salamis, just a few kilometres away, arose. It is possible that Salamis was founded by citizens of Enkomi resettling closer to the coast. Salamis, which in some texts is referred to by an earlier name, Arsinoe (though this name, confusingly, is also sometimes associated with Famagusta), was likely founded as a port around the bay which still lies at the southern extremity of the city. There, too, was the mouth of the river Pediaeos, which supplied fresh water for mariners while at the same time offering transportation for goods from the Cypriot hinterland to the port and thence on to markets across the seas. The Pediaeos has long since dried up and mud flats, dried brittle in the summers, are all that remain of what was probably an exemplary sea bay and river port. It is possible that beneath the modern silts lies the preserved remains of ancient ships, which may have sunk in the harbour through the violence of battles, the mishaps of weather, or other perils of seafaring. It is also probable that the Pediaeos dried up even as Salamis grew, necessitating an eventual shifting of the port to the north and the construction of an aqueduct to bring fresh water from the Kyrenia mountains (of which one Byzantine period set of arches survives just to the north of the archaeological site's entrance and another small segment, also from the Byzantine/Medieval period, rests in a field about 2.5 kilometres west of Salamis).

If one walks along the beach, say, from near the main entrance to the site (where you buy tickets) south to just past the Basilica of Campanopetra, one can discern a narrow reef that runs parallel with the coastline about 100 metres out to sea. This is particularly visible at low tide. In an underwater survey done in 1974, N. C. Fleming published a report that told of two roads under the water, one running parallel to the shoreline and another running at a diagonal. Fleming was able to see many large ashlar blocks that were foundations of ancient buildings or port facilities, indicating that there were substantial structures here, and that the ancient shoreline is probably marked by the reef one sees today. Fleming estimated that ancient Salamis was 1.8 to 2.0 metres higher than it is today. A huge earthquake in 342 CE lowered Salamis's elevation, one historical document recording that Salamis was left partially submerged by the quake. Other earthquakes over the centuries could have magnified this effect. He also inferred that the port lay just south of the Basilica of Campanopetra, which overlooks the sea. The harbour, in Fleming's diagrams, is like a hooked finger pointing south and curving sharply inland to create a roughly circular haven for boats.

Assyrian inscriptions record the existence of a King of Salamis in 707 BCE and the historian Herodotus makes note of some kings of Salamis in the 6th and 5th centuries BCE when Greek/Aegean settlers were prevalent there. The earliest coins found on Cyprus date from the reign of Euelthon, which began in 560 BCE. Salamis's emergence as a significant port in the eastern Mediterranean region assured its character as a cosmopolitan city. It counted many Jews and other Levantine peoples among its population from early times. The city lay, after all, less than 100 kilometres from the shores of the Middle East. Phoenicians traders and settlers were among the peoples who inhabited Cyprus and Salamis as well.

The ancient Greeks on Cyprus composed a mythical story of the founding of Salamis. Like many cities in the Mediterranean region with Greek pasts, Salamis constructed a foundation myth linked to one of the heroes of the Trojan War. To have such a pedigree — having been established by one of the legendary champions of Homer's Heroic Age — lent prestige and honour to a city. The people of Salamis claimed that their city had been founded by the Trojan hero Teucer, son of Telemon and Hesione and step-brother to Ajax. Teucer's father, as the story goes, had expelled his son for not avenging Ajax's death, and Teucer's wanderings allegedly brought him to this shore of Cyprus where the ruins of Salamis now keep quiet vigil.

Whatever the facts of Salamis's very early history, we know that in 411 BCE a young man who claimed to be an ancestor of the aforementioned Tuecer, Evagoras, became the ruler of Salamis and later, the rest of Cyprus as well. His thirty-six year reign (411 to 374 BCE) was perhaps Salamis's most glorious era. Evagoras is a heroic figure for Greek Cypriots in particular because he established close ties with classical-era Athens (for which his historiographic star ascended in the years that Greek Cypriots were supportive of *enosis*, union with Greece, in the 1950s and 60s). Evagoras was a great statesman and warrior. His system of governance was regarded by some as being even more democratic than Athens', and the Greek orator Isokrates composed a famous eulogy praising him. Evagoras expanded his control beyond Cyprus to include cities along the south coast of what is today Turkey, securing previously Persian-controlled trade routes and ports of call. No doubt the Athenian praises sung of Evagoras were related to his courageous aggression towards the Persians, whose expansions west threatened Athenian dominions. Salamis prospered and as her merchant fleet plied the waters, moving goods back and forth across the Eastern Mediterranean, Salamis grew in size and prestige. Isocrates records a flattering impression of Evagoras' reign:

> After he had taken over the government of the city [Salamis], which had been reduced to a state of barbarism and, because it was ruled by Phoenicians, was neither hospitable to the Greeks nor possessed of a trading port or harbour, Evagoras remedied all these defects and, besides acquired much additional territory, surrounded it all with new walls and built triremes, and with other construction so increased the city that it was inferior to none of the cities of Greece. And he caused it to become so powerful that many who formerly despised it, now feared it.
>
> *[Sources History Cyprus I, 37]*

But Evagoras' successes and his inroads into Persian protectorates did not go unnoticed, and the Persians eventually besieged Salamis with an overwhelming force in 380 BCE. Evagoras was forced to negotiate highly disadvantageous terms of surrender, paying heavy tribute to the Persians, and just six years later he was assassinated after having lost Salamis and having tried to regain it by siege. By this time Salamis, weakened by war and competition from the ascendant Cypriot port of Paphos, began a decline, though it would have several significant resurrections. It would not be totally abandoned for another 1000 years.

Conquerors were not the only factors in the rise and decline of the city's fortunes. Many troughs in Salamis's history are marked by catastrophic earthquakes while several peaks are registered in the subsequent rebuilding campaigns. Other natural phenomenon had ramifications for Salamis. The southern harbour began to silt up and a new harbour was established in 306 BCE to the north end of the city. New public buildings thus began to appear at the north edge, and this is important for our consideration of the ruins because the gymnasium, baths, theater and amphitheater are all situated at this north end of the urban confines. If one walks along the beach of Salamis, one can see the aforementioned large blocks of stone that once were harbour roads or sections of wharfs. Snorkeling in the shallows reveals thousands of pieces of broken ancient pottery, and, even more dramatically, off the beach at the southern edge of the city one can snorkel amongst the remains of giant Roman sarcophagi — their pitched lids tilted and covered in seaweed — from Salamis's now inundated southern necropolis. When winter waves come, one sometimes can also see some large stone tombs partially exposed in the sands of the beach.

One of the first major earthquakes that leveled the city came during the reign of the Roman emperor Augustus (31 BCE to 14 CE). The city was rebuilt, only to suffer the same cruel fate again in 77 CE. The Romans rebuilt the city yet again during the reigns of Trajan (98 CE to 117 CE) and Hadrian (117-138 CE). Once more, in 332 and 342 CE, earthquakes severely damaged many structures. By this time Salamis had become a Christian city, even though paganism survived for several more years. The Byzantine Emperor Constantius provided the funds for a substantial rebuilding, though Salamis's golden age was by then long past. The city was renamed Constantia, after its new imperial benefactor, but was now much smaller and less prosperous than it had been in earlier centuries. Eventually depleted, Byzantine Salamis/Constantia would gain the nickname 'Ammochostos', that is, 'filled with sand' as the dunes gradually reclaimed its ruins, and its last citizens would abandon their ancient, dying town but take the nickname with them — a name that would eventually transform into 'Famagusta' — to a small natural harbour a few miles to the south. In the Middle Ages that city would also become, as both Enkomi and Salamis had been, famous and fabulously wealthy.

Salamis was the site of some terrible social upheavals. During the reign of the Roman Emperor Trajan, around 115-116 CE, there was an anti-Roman Jewish revolt, not only in Salamis but in all of Cyprus's major cities and, indeed, in other Middle Eastern lands such as Egypt, and Libya. This uprising has come to be called the 'Second Jewish-Roman War' or the 'Kitos War' (corrupted from the name 'Quietus', as Trajan's general Lucius Quietus was sent to subdue the Jews). There had been a significant Jewish population in Cyprus and in Salamis from early times. These Jews, fed up with Roman domination, rebelled against their overlords. Led on Cyprus by their leader Artemion, they are said to have killed tens of thousands of people. But the Roman reaction was even more violent. Some have estimated the number killed on Cyprus to be around 250,000. At the time, it is thought that the total population of Salamis alone could have been as high as 120,000. Salamis was utterly destroyed in the conflagration. After the Romans regained control, they prohibited Jews from living on Cyprus. There are stories of ships being driven by storms on to Cypriot beaches and the Jews on those ships being put to death for setting foot on the forbidden shores.

The Palaestra/Gymnasium and Bath Complex

[35° 11' 10.86" N / 33° 54' 10.85" E]

The bath complex that we see today represents the last of a series of three baths (Fig. 14). Not very much is known about the first, smaller bath structures, the earliest of which may have dated from the 3rd century BCE, except that they all occupied the same location as the ones we see there today. The earthquakes during Augustus's reign destroyed this first, already very old complex and a new, Augustan period gymnasium and bath complex was constructed over its ruins. This Augustan edifice also eventually fell into ruin but was heavily restored and renovated in the early Christian period around 350 CE on a smaller scale.

The architectural and functional components of the complex deserve comment because the gymnasium and palaestra were decidedly Greek architectural and cultural elements while the adjoining bath buildings reflected more the Roman infatuation with bathing. Still, the Greeks often appended baths to their gymnasia although Roman baths tended to be larger and more ostentatious. A palaestra was essentially a large, open exercise yard, more or less square in plan, which was used for athletic training, primarily wrestling. It was often demarcated by a columned portico running around its inner perimetre. Athletes would wrestle and engage in other physical and martial training regimens in the sand-covered yard. For the Greeks, the general procedure included a generous swabbing of olive oil on the body before exercise. Afterward, they would clean their bodies using a bronze implement called a strigil, which was a curving blade used to scrape away the accumulated sweat, oil, and dirt from the body. Only then might they visit the baths to sweat out the last of the dirt and oil from their pores.

The Romans also loved their baths, which often included a series of rooms of various functions and temperatures. The hot bath was called the *caldarium*, the sweating room the *sudatorium*, the warm bath the *tepidarium*, and the cold plunge bath the *frigidarium*. Often, in Roman culture, massages and sexual services — for varying proclivities — were also available at bath complexes. This is one reason why baths sometimes fell into disuse during the Christian period, as Christians saw the baths as places where sinful activities took place. For similar reasons, theaters and amphitheaters were often abandoned or dismantled when Christianity became dominant.

Plan of the Gymnasium and Bath Complex at Salamis

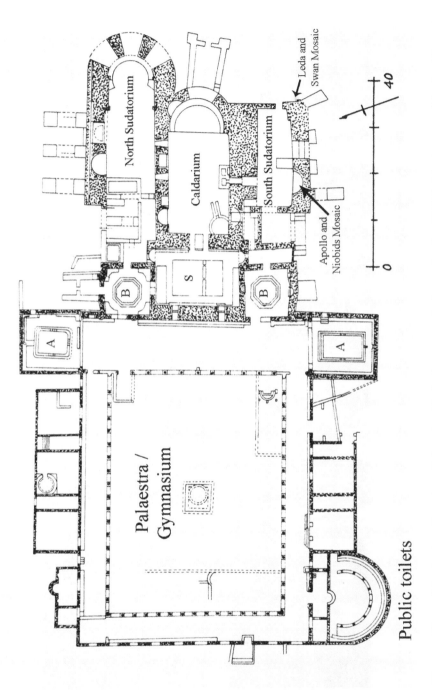

Public toilets

Fig. 14: Plan of the baths of ancient Salamis: A) piscina or cool plunge baths; B) frigidaria or tepidaria; S) west sudatorium [from G. R. H. Wright, Ancient Building in Cyprus, E. J. Brill, 1992; after Karageorghis].

Fig. 15: View from the southeast towards the palaestra/gymnasium of ancient Salamis.

The large open courtyard, porticos, and surrounding rooms found at Salamis at the west end of the bath buildings may have functioned both as a palaestra and a gymnasium. Both building types involved education and training in athletic events, although gymnasia often had many other rooms for overnight guests, kitchens, and, sometimes, a straight running track. A common feature of Greek palaestra are large stone basins for laundry and washing water, such as can still be found at Pergamum in Turkey. But if these ever existed at Salamis they have been lost.

The Romans adopted elements of the Greek palaestra complex and integrated them into some of their larger bathing compounds such as the imperial baths of Caracalla in Rome. The prominence of both palaestra and bath here at Salamis, too, represents a merging of the Greek athletic ideal of the exercise yard and the Roman emphasis on aquatic pleasures and luxurious, sensuous bathing experiences. It was a common combination, particularly in the eastern parts of the Roman Empire where the Greek heritage was powerful and enduring.

The palaestra/gymnasium, as it stands today, is composed of a series of columns which were re-erected during the 1952-55 excavations of the Cyprus Department of Antiquities (Fig. 15). The ones of the west portico are smaller than the ones of the east portico because these smaller columns were moved there from the scene building of the theater during the restorations after earthquakes in the 4th century CE. During that same era the Christians walled up the many rooms that surrounded the west, north, and south porticos. Benches were constructed against the new walls, offering places to sit and rest. Originally, the complete colonnade around the open yard carried a series of arches supporting a wooden roof which offered shelter from the rain and the heat of the sun. However, it is not known when the original colonnade around the palaestra was erected and it may in fact have been a very late, post-Augustan feature of the complex. Archaeological evidence of earlier sets of columns exists only for a limited, eastern colonnade during Augustus's time.

The roughly square open space of the palaestra/gymnasium — an impressive 53 by 40 metres in dimension — may not have been a sandy exercise yard during all the eras of its use. One inscription, found in the east portico, refers to additions in the bath's gardens, and it is hard to imagine any area other than the open area of the palaestra. But at some point the open court ceased to be used for the vigorous physical exercises for which it had originally been intended. In some even later era the space was paved over. The center of the open area still has remains of a small platform which was surrounded by a circular, shallow pool. A squat column was in the center of the podium and may have carried an imperial statue, perhaps of Augustus or, later, Trajan or Hadrian; all emperors who contributed significantly to rebuilding Salamis in the Roman period.

It is likely that in the earliest Hellenistic palaestra/gymnasium there were some latrines off the south portico. Certainly, by Roman times there was an impressive public toilet complex in the southwest corner, much of which survives today (Fig. 16). This large semi-circular room, with about 40 toilet seats arranged along the inside walls of the half-circle, had a series of monolithic columns holding up a roof. However, it is possible that only the 'seating' area was covered and the remaining part was open to the sky, allowing light in and air to circulate. It was a luxurious experience, if not very private. Water came splashing — the noise masking any embarrassing sounds — out of a spout set high into the wall at the apex of the semi-circle, most of it draining below to a continuous-flow flushing system which immediately carried anything away through its conduit. Sadly, none of the actual toilet seats survive, though a few of the supports for them do. Some of the water from the central spout was diverted to a small channel, still visible, which ran along at the feet of the toilets' patrons. This water was used for cleaning oneself after business was completed, like a sort of bidet. Quite civilized. And, if you felt like washing your hands again, another small cascading tap ran just outside the exit for a quick freshening up.

One of the most impressive parts of the palaestra/gymnasium is the east portico (wider and longer than the other porticos, approximately 50 x 10 metres), which fronted the bath complex itself at its western edge. Here the largest columns are arrayed. These columns do not belong where they now stand and represent another instance of the moving of columns from another part of the city during the 4th century, Christian-period restoration. It may be that these columns supported a higher roof which also makes it likely that there was a clerestory of windows allowing light into the upper portico. The capitals also do not match the proportions of the columns and so they also must have come from elsewhere in the city. By then, the Christian era, the classical temples and theater had become unwanted symbols of the perverse pagan past and the vain entertainments which may also have included, at times, the martyrdoms of Christians. It is likely that at this time the amphitheater (if, indeed, it had ever been completed in the first place) was quarried for stones used in repairs and new construction, which is why virtually nothing of it remains except for a few fragmentary vaults and a depression in the ground between the gymnasium and the theater.

The pavements of the east portico are also of some interest, for today they resemble a collage comprised of paving stones from myriad fragments. And this is indeed the case, for in those same Christian-period renovations flooring panels were torn up from the theater and reused here, while other various fragments, some with Greek or Latin inscriptions on them, were used to fill in the gaps in the pavement. This

Fig. 16: Remains of the toilet seats from the gymnasium latrines. Note channel for water along the lower section for cleaning up.

may be a very enigmatic feature for visitors to the site. But for Christians the reuse of these ancient inscription blocks in the paving of their renovations evoked the glory of the city's Greco-Roman past while at the same time indicating Christianity's triumph over paganism and the emperors who had persecuted them. They literally could now tread on the names of the ancient pagans who had persecuted them. They became as well symbols of vanity, and reminders to Christians of the virtue of humility, as even the greatness of Rome and its emperors had faded.

Archaeologists discovered an altar dedicated to Hermes in the middle of the east portico, dating from the 2nd century CE. Its dedication inscription was to a patron of the gymnasium, 'Diagoras, son of Teukros'. It is an eloquent testament to the system of civic patronage in the city, where wealthy citizens donated money for building in the names of the gods to both beautify their city and to gain public honour and divine favour for themselves. Many such monuments with similar dedicatory inscriptions are found both here and in the ruins of Roman cities throughout the Mediterranean.

It is in the great portico that one has, at least partly, entered the bath complex, because at the short ends — forming extensions of the portico north and south — are rectangular *frigidaria* or cool swimming pools. These were oval shaped pools in the Augustan period but were made rectangular in the Byzantine Christian restoration. The statues currently arrayed around this northern pool — all dating from around the 2nd century CE — decorated other parts of the bath complex originally, as a few statuary niches have been found. Some of these statues were uncovered close by in the east portico during excavations in 1890. It is even possible that some of them could represent Muses who, appropriately, decorated parts of the theater's scene building which was largely dismantled in the Christian period. One of these statues depicts Persephone and was made of a gray stone which is thought to convey her sad fate at the hands of the god of the underworld (unhappily, someone decided to emphasize this with a coating of modern gray paint). Her face is just a gouged out hole, it having been a white marble insert. Her hands, too, were made of the finer, lighter material. It is an effect that gave a dramatic life-like appearance to the statue: a lighter, warmer skin tone set against a darker drapery. The white marble face of Persephone was discovered in 1983 by a tourist, though its features were much eroded.

The southern pool may have been in use for a longer time, beyond the years when the north pool was abandoned. The south pool was lined with marble panels and there was a columned portico around it (parts of the columns were found inside the pool during excavation), which held a wooden roof that offered some shade on the pool's deck and benches.

Today, the tall west façade of the bath complex, which towers over the east portico, is dramatically eroded. In places one can discern column drums in the wall which were used as fillers in the repairs of the 4th century, Christian period. This façade was originally plastered over, so one would not have been able to see the inserts and irregular aspects of the masonry. There is even evidence that it was decorated with mosaics as tesserae were found in the dirt below the wall. It would have presented a much different face for the bathers of the second through the fourth centuries, pagan or Christian. Nonetheless, even today it is impressive. One can still appreciate the massive 3.66 metre thickness of its walls, which suggests at least the possibility of a barrel vault for the ceiling of the *sudatorium*, into which led the two now walled up entrances on the façade. There is even a possibility that there was a second, upper level in some parts of the complex.

It can be challenging trying to make sense of the baths today as one walks from one section to another, but we can begin to clarify the experience by indicating the general layout of the structure. The bath complex proper consists of six main rooms in all (Fig. 14). The three most easterly rooms are the larger while the three western ones are smaller. At the western end of the complex there are almost identical rooms with octagonal pools at the north and south that are connected to a large central hall which was one of the three *sudatoria* or sweating/steam rooms. This west side *sudatorium* is connected to an even larger middle hall — the largest interior part of the whole complex — about 35 metres long and 12 metres wide. This was the *caldarium* or hot bath. Both north and south of this large, central *caldarium* are other *sudatoria*.

The octagonal pools in their respective north and south rooms might have been *frigidaria* or cool plunge baths but it is also possible that the water entering them was warm, thus making these pools *tepidaria*. No heating elements were found under them but both were lined with marble and had fountains splashing in niches in their walls. However, they were also very close to the *praefurnia* or furnaces of the complex so the water flowing there may have been warm. Since the two rectangular pools in the wings of the east portico outside were certainly *frigidaria*, the octagonal pools seem the best candidates for *tepidaria* in the complex. Either way, one could cool off inside or out, as one wished.

Between the two octagonal pool rooms was the largest of the three *sudatoria* or sweating and steam rooms. It is in this room that one can read, in the broken walls and floors, the complex workings of the bath's heating system. Part of the floor has collapsed, revealing the stacked, brick pillars called the hypocausts (Fig. 17; these have been restored). Hot air was pumped into the open spaces beneath the floor from two furnaces (*praefurnia*; one to the northeast and the other to the southeast), thus heating the floor. The hot air was then channeled up through terracotta pipes embedded in the walls, keeping them hot as well. Some of these

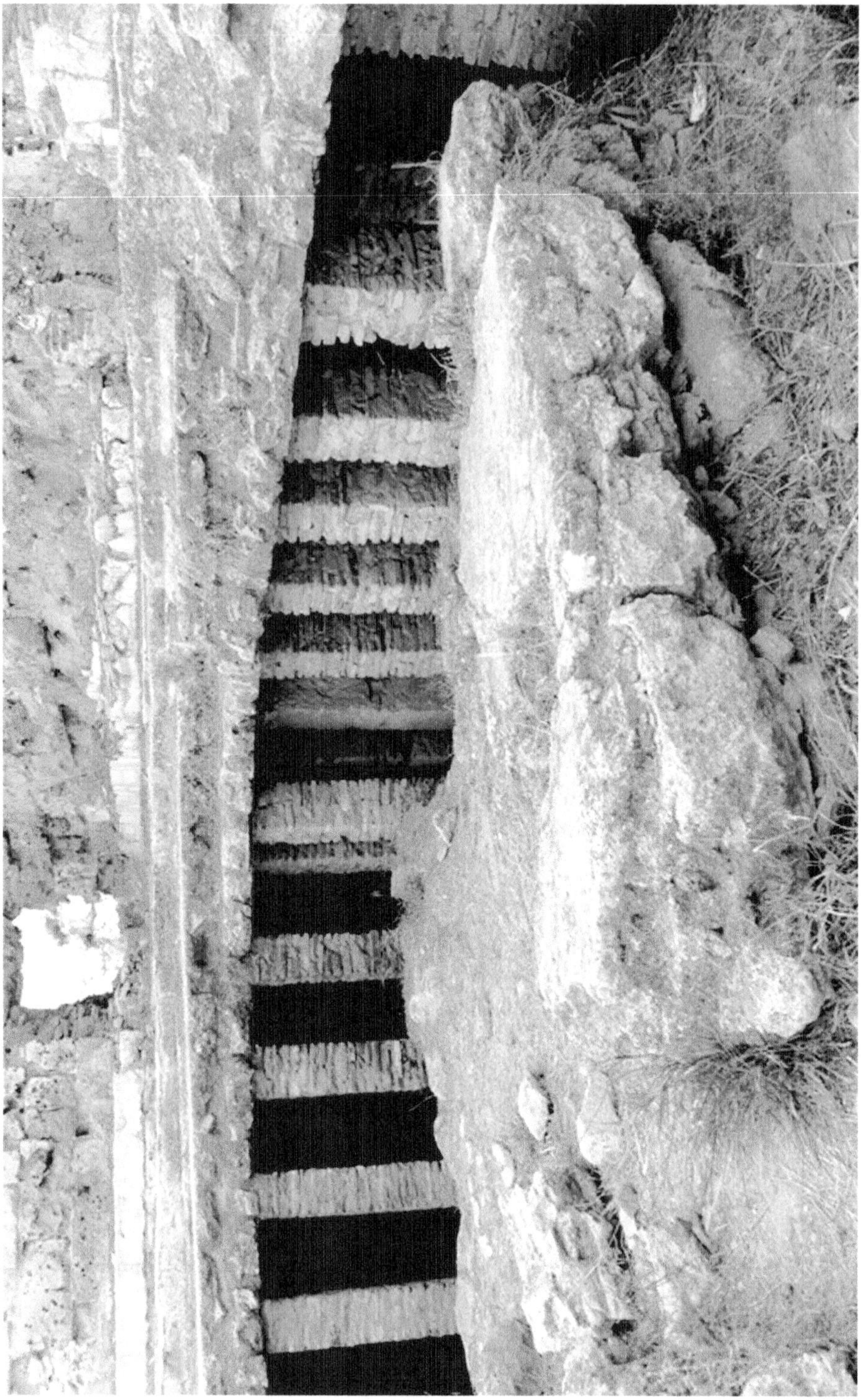

Fig. 17: Reconstructed hypocausts of the ancient baths at Salamis.

clay pipes can be seen in the lower parts of the wall, which was also faced with marble slabs. Many of these were probably torn off to use as flooring for the Christian basilicas of Epiphanios and Campanopetra (see following entries), but a few remnants can still be discerned on the bath's walls. There was a shallow pool of water in the center, also heated by hypocausts, to provide steam. As mentioned earlier, we might well imagine a large barrel vault over this room, finely finished with plaster and perhaps decorated with paintings or mosaics. At least one part of a fresco survives, although this appears to be a modern restoration. In a curving semi-dome over the south doorway, which leads indirectly to the south octagonal pool, is a fragment of a fresco depicting Hylas discovering a Nymph. Hylas, on the left carrying a spear, raises his hand in surprise as he espies a water nymph that has blue streams of water flowing from her hand. A story involving water, of course, is fitting for the setting. The style of the fresco, with its simple lines and draperies and large-eyed faces, places it in the late third or early fourth century CE. It is a pagan story depicted at the very moment of the Christianization of the Roman Empire. What they show us is that there was overlap between the Christian and pagan worlds. The Roman Empire did not become Christianized overnight, especially at its fringes.

The largest room, the *caldarium* or hot bath, had two doors connecting it to the east *sudatorium*. Its climate in parts may have been pretty much the same as the *sudatorium*. It is easy to imagine a steamy atmosphere and bathers relaxing on stone benches. At the east end of the hall, however, is a large, semi-circular pool with hypocausts beneath (one can get a peek at them through a small doorway; this part is also a restoration). This was certainly the hot plunge bath or *caldarium* of the complex. This large room had a barrel vault arching overhead, stuccoed smooth and painted with frescos. There were also some mosaics in arched niches in both the south and north walls. Some of this decoration survives in one of the niches on the north wall which, unlike those of the south wall, are still intact. These are only fragmentary, but other, better preserved mosaics can be found in similar arches in the south and north *sudatoria*. These arched niches, and their offending pagan decorations, were walled up in the Christian restoration of the baths, thus preserving mosaic fragments that otherwise would have been lost. In the north *sudatorium* there is a small hot plunge bath, so there was an option, at least at some point in the building's history, for a dip in a hot tub there. A bit of mosaic can be seen in an arched niche on the north wall: intertwining garlands of a vine and pomegranate fruit. At the crest of the arch is a circular frame which once held a representation of a female face; perhaps a figure associated with fruits and fertility, such as Flora, who represented springtime and flowers.

The best preserved mosaics of the entire structure — all of which date from the end of the 3rd century CE — are found in two places in the south *sudatorium*, which one gains access to from the east side. Both are fragmentary, but each nonetheless eloquently conveys the sophistication and style of the total compositions. In each, too, enough of the work has endured to allow us to determine the subject matter. The smallest is found high in a niche in the south *sudatorium* on the south wall in the eastern end. It partially survives, but it depicts a portion of the 'Leda and the Swan' myth. Only the bottom left corner of the total image is visible today, but we can clearly see the part of the reclining body of the old, bearded Evrotas (his name is written in white tesserae above his head), the river god who witnesses the erotic spectacle of Zeus who, disguised as a swan, makes love to the nymph, Leda. We see nothing of Leda, but one dramatic, outstretched wing of the swan reaches towards Evrotas. Fronds of reeds, depicted with green and turquoise tesserae, lend a sense of naturalism to the riverside scene. Such reeds also decorate the headdress of Evrotas. At the top one can discern an arm and another wing, this one likely belongs to Eros, who flies away, his amorous inspiration having had its intended effect. Below, rows of dark tesserae indicate water flowing from the large jar Evagoras would have been leaning on. He personifies the river's source and such river gods were typically represented this way in late Roman and even early Christian art. Indeed, in Christian representations of Christ's baptism the River Jordan is often personified as an old, bearded man leaning on a jug or amphora from which the river's waters stream.

The other south *sudatorium* mosaic is also on the south wall but in a larger niche in the west end. Here, only the lower two-thirds of the scene survive but there is enough to theorize about the subject matter. Archaeologists believe that the mosaic depicts part of the story of Apollo and Artemis slaying the Niobids. Of Apollo, who kneels at the middle top of the composition, only a part of his knee is visible, though his lyre and quiver of arrows — his attributes — lie on the ground before him. It is thought that Artemis is the much better preserved figure striding on the left hand side, though her legs are decidedly masculine. Perhaps the Niobids were depicted in the higher part of the semi-dome, which collapsed at some point (what you see today is a modern restoration of the semi-dome). Even if the true meaning of the figures may elude us, there is still much to appreciate in what remains of this mosaic, particularly in the lovely band of garlands that runs along the bottom with the well-preserved female face in a roundel in the middle (Fig. 18), Apollo's quiver and lyre, and the plants springing on the ground below Artemis, all giving a sense of the opulence of the original décor of the bath complex.

The easiest way to enter this south *sudatorium* is by walking around the whole complex to the south side and then entering at the sea side where the walls have fallen away. It's a bit out of the way, and thus many

Fig. 18: Detail of head from the mosaic of Apollo and the Niobids from the ancient bath complex at Salamis, south sudatorium.

visitors pass it by, but it's worth going around not only for the mosaics just discussed but for three other reasons as well. Firstly, one passes by the huge cistern on the south side which held the water supply for the bath complex. It is a long, rectangular structure still partly covered by its barrel vault. This stored water so that the baths wouldn't run out, possibly also supplying pressure. Secondly, if one looks closely around that southeast corner, one can see some of the water channels which distributed the water to the baths. These would, of course, have been invisible in the walls in ancient times, but have been revealed by the breaking down of the structure. It's a rare instance where one can examine the plumbing of an ancient monument. Finally, not far from the Apollo and the Niobids mosaic one can see parts of the underground furnace and hot air circulation system in the northwest corner. It is marked by a small and narrow brick arched opening about a metre tall.

The most fascinating book on Salamis is Vassos Karageorghis's *Excavating at Salamis in Cyprus 1952-1974*. It is filled with remarkable excavation photographs and the most striking of all shows a large house on top of the hill that completely filled and covered the bath complex. The excavators had to tear the house down to dig out the baths. Whenever I stand in the great central *sudatorium* of the Salamis baths I always imagine that house fifty feet above my head. We are reminded of the tons of earth that covered these sites and the work required to professionally excavate them. A poignant sign of that work remains just southeast of the bath towards the sea, where, in a small clearing, one can still see a short length of the little railway tracks that the excavation carts were rolled on. Some of those carts, now rusting, stand alongside as forgotten witnesses to the excavations headed by Karageorghis.

The Theater

[35° 11' 05.31" N / 33° 54' 08.69" E]

The theater at Salamis, discovered in 1959, was a typical Roman theater and was probably built during the reign of Augustus. It was semi-circular in plan with a semi-circular orchestra, a stage (*proscenium*), a tall backdrop wall behind the stage (*frons scenae*), now destroyed, with two entrance halls (*parodoi*) for the spectators at ground level flanking each side of the orchestra (Figs. 19-20). It was similar in design to the best preserved of all Roman theaters at Aspendos on the south coast of Turkey, which is not far from Cyprus over the Karamanian Sea. The orchestra is 27 metres in diameter and one can still see the circular footing for the altar where a sacrifice to the god of theater, Dionysus/Bacchus, would take place before each performance. At some later point

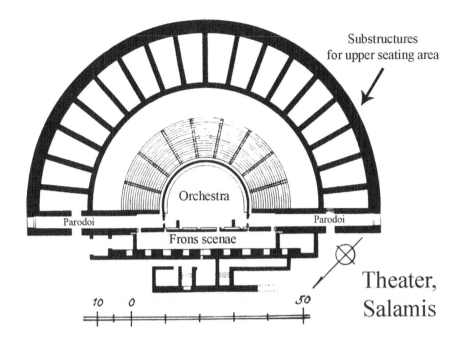

Substructures
for upper seating area

Orchestra

Parodoi

Parodoi

Frons scenae

10   0   50

Theater,
Salamis

Fig. 19: Plan of the ancient theater at Salamis [from G. R. H. Wright, Ancient
Building in Cyprus, E. J. Brill, 1992].

Fig. 20: View of the orchestra and seating area of the ancient theater at Salamis.

in the theater's history — likely the later Roman period — a metre-high solid stone fencing was erected around the orchestra (only the footings survive) perhaps so that it could be filled with water for aquatic entertainments and mock battles called *naumachia*, or to protect onlookers from dangerous combats, events that had usually been hosted by the larger amphitheaters. Much of the paving and fencing from this orchestra was torn up in the 4th century CE Christian era and taken to pave the east portico of the baths which were being restored at that time.

The sloping, radiating seating area is mostly modern restoration. Originally, the seats went considerably higher than what one sees today. There were initially over 50 rows of seats and it is estimated that the theater could have accommodated 15,000 spectators. The limestone facing endures only in sections of the first few rows. In the central part of the seating area, about 6 rows up, is a small platform and special honourary 'thrones' for important city officials. Ten sets of steps gave access to the levels, dividing the seating area into 9 separate and equal sectors. The substructure underneath the first few rows of the seats was solid rubble fill, but the outer part of the entire semi-circular plan was borne by a series of radiating walls with barrel vaults. So the seating area was partially supported by earth at its lower rows and by arches and walls underneath the uppermost rows. The foundations of the higher seats that are no longer extant can be seen by climbing to the top of the present-day seating area and looking down. One can then easily imagine the size of the original theater by projecting upwards.

The view from the seats is open today but in Roman times the massive stage wall (*frons scenae*) would have risen to the height of the seating area which has been estimated at 20 metres. It had several niches with statues of Apollo and the Muses, and of emperors as well. Inscription plaques were also found by excavators, one praising the Emperor Hadrian as a benefactor of Salamis. Just below the imposing scene building was the theater stage. It was a 40 metre long timber platform about 5 metres deep and about 2 metres above the level of the orchestra. In ancient times wooden planks would have provided a sturdy floor for the actors.

There was also an amphitheater at Salamis, located in the large depression of ground just beyond the stage of the theater towards the gymnasium, but it has never been excavated and its exact dimensions never revealed. If it was ever completed, most of its blocks were quarried long ago.

Opposite: Fig. 21: Plan and elevation diagrams of the Roman forum of ancient Salamis, with rectangular marketplace and Temple of Zeus, with monumental arched entryway at north end [from G. R. H. Wright, Ancient Building in Cyprus, E. J. Brill, 1992].

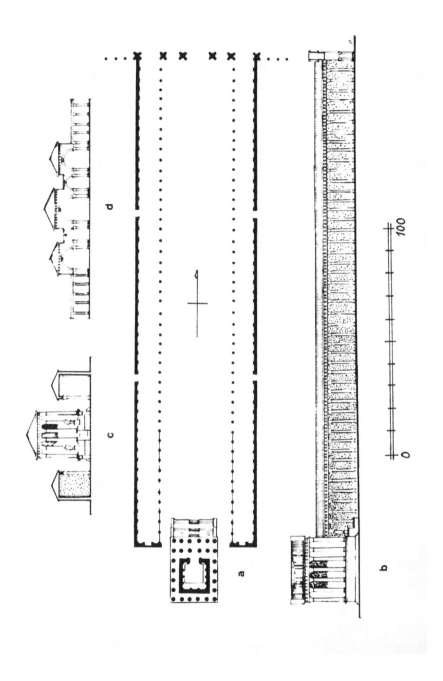

a

b

c

d

100

0

73

The Roman Villa ('*L'huilerie*')

[35° 10' 48.64" N / 33° 54' 15.15" E]

The extensive remains of what was a Roman period villa were unearthed at Salamis. One of its most distinctive features was an apsidal room that some think might have been a chapel. However, it should be remembered that apsidal rooms were very common in palatial residential Roman architecture, and a semi-circular element didn't necessarily mean that the room had some religious function. When you are in the main town square of Famagusta, look low along the south side and you'll see a marble bench with ancient reliefs of running animals in a vine motif. This huge slab almost certainly came from Salamis, and excavators of the villa also found a relief in stucco that looks remarkably like this one in Famagusta's main square.

Sometimes this complex is called '*L'huilerie*', a name given to it by French excavators, meaning 'Oil Factory'. What they found was that after the buildings no longer functioned as part of a villa they were used as an olive oil production facility.

The Forum, Temple of Zeus, and Cistern

[35° 10' 43.02" N / 33° 53' 56.79" E]

In the southern part of the city, about a ten-minute walk from the theater, is the forum of the Roman period. The forum was a rectangular open area about 250 metres long and 60 metres wide, resembling a broad boulevard. Flanking the long sides of the forum were monumental colonnades with 27 foot high columns which held up a timber roof to create a shaded portico along the fronts of the shops and market stalls (Fig. 21). Only one of the great columns survives; a reconstruction from fragments, with its Corinthian capital.

At the south end of the forum one can still find the foundations of the stepped platform upon which stood the massive Temple of Olympian Zeus which dates from the early years of the first century CE during the reign of Augustus. One of the inscriptions discovered there was a dedication to Zeus in honour of Livia, Augustus's wife. Virtually nothing survives, but if you proceed west for a few yards, you can find some of the Corinthian capitals and the drums of the columns lying peacefully under the boughs of the trees. They may belong to the temple or to the columns of the forum.

At the north end of the forum huge stone terraces lead up to the enormous cistern (sometimes referred to in guidebooks as the '*Vouta*' or '*Loutron*'), which dates from the Byzantine, Christian era (Fig. 22), though one theory dates it to as early as the reign of the Roman

Fig. 22: The great cistern near the Roman forum at ancient Salamis, with piers that once held up a vaulted roof. Sometimes referred to as the 'Loutron' or 'Vouta'.

Emperor Septimius Severus, since it may well have been during his time when the aqueduct from Kythrea in the Kyrenia mountains was built. This enormous cistern would have been an appropriate repository for the volumes of water brought in by the aqueduct. The terrace seems to have incorporated a large arched structure which may have been a monumental entrance gateway to the agora in the Roman era before the cistern was built (see Fig. 21). The cistern is a huge, rectangular pool which was covered over with vaults. At the eastern end, one can see some of the 39 square pillars that held up the vaulted roof. It must have contained tens of thousands of gallons of water. The size of the cistern may represent a greater concern about the supply of water in Cyprus. Nicholas Martoni, an Italian notary visiting Cyprus in 1394, was very impressed by the cistern and thought it to be the biggest in the world. He wrote:

> In the middle where the castle stood is a certain ancient cistern, no bigger one I think is found in the world, with a vault raised on 36 columns and with apertures above whence the water was drawn. Into this tank water flowed continuously from a certain mountain, along a conduit built with pillars and arches...
>
> *[Excerpta Cypria, 25]*

Evidently, what Martoni saw six centuries ago was in much better condition that we see today. In Martoni's time the cistern still seems to operate, and water from the aqueducts was still flowing into it. Moreover, its vaulted roof was still intact.

D. G. Hogarth also visited the still unexcavated area of the cistern and forum in 1888. He found a place inviting:

> There are, however, two places in this wilderness where I longed to set a few diggers to work; the one is near the southwestern corner of the site, just within the walls, where a fluted shaft of white marble, evidently deeply buried, is peeping out of the ground; the other is at the northwestern angle beyond the Loutron [cistern] where in a well-defined oblong depression [the forum], much choken with sand, lie half-buried a number of glistening granite shafts of very large diameter...
>
> *[Devia Cypria, 61]*

Such historical accounts give us eloquent literary images of the magnificent city, overgrown and filled with sand, which the early travellers saw.

Sources for Salamis: Vassos Karageoghis, *Sculptures from Salamis*, Nicosia: Department of Antiquities, 1964; Vassos Karageoghis, *Salamis: Recent Discoveries in Cyprus*, McGraw Hill, 1969; Joan du Plat Taylor, "A Water Cistern with Byzantine Paintings, Salamis, Cyprus," *The Antiquaries Journal* 13, n. 2 (1933): 97-108; J. Arthur R. Munro, H. A. Tubbs, Warwick Wroth, "Excavations in Cyprus, 1890: Third Season's Work, Salamis," *The Journal of Hellenic Studies*, 12 (1891): 59-198; N. C. Fleming, "Report of Preliminary Underwater Investigations at Salamis", *Cyprus, Report of the Department of Antiquities*, Nicosia, 1974.

Basilica of Epiphanios, Salamis (Constantia), late 4th to 7th century CE

[35° 10' 47.60" N / 33° 54' 02.22" E]

Salamis became Christianized in the 4th century, but there had been a Christian community there from a very early date, the city having been visited by St Paul around 45 CE. It was also the home of the patron saint of Cyprus, St Barnabas, who was Paul's contemporary and Salamis's first bishop. The city was renamed Constantia after the Byzantine emperor Constantius who funded extensive post-earthquake renovations in the late 4th century CE. Two basilicas date from Salamis's early Christian period and the impressive dimensions of these buildings and the materials used to construct them are indicative of the prosperity of this era. The first of these two churches, the Basilica of Epiphanios, was founded by one of Cyprus's most important early Christian saints, the Bishop Epiphanios, who was buried in his basilica in 403 CE. The church was thus begun during the famous bishop's lifetime, around 385 CE (he was born between 310 and 320 CE), though it was unfinished at the time of his death. During Epiphanios' time much of the population of Salamis was still mostly non-Christian (pagans and Jews) and his biography records that he was adamantly opposed to continued paganism in Salamis and, furthermore, fought Christian heresies there as well. Indeed, Epiphanios was a major early Christian theologian and an honoured Church Father. He spoke so many languages that St Jerome called him '*Pentaglossis*', or 'five-tongued'. His most famous work was the *Panarion*, which challenged the heresies or Origen and many others. It is a fascinating document of 4th century Christianity and the relatively new religion's impulse to codify its beliefs.

Because there was still religious competition in Salamis, Epiphanios was obliged to perform impressive miracles to raise money for the basilica. One story, by Polybius, tells of a rich pagan named Faustianos who was killed when one of the church's construction workers fell from the scaffolding on top of him. Epiphanios brought him back to life and converted him to Christianity. Alas, we do not hear the fate of the poor construction worker.

Fig. 23: View up the nave of the Basilica of Epiphanios in Salamis, with re-erected fragments of the columns, looking east from the narthex.

The basilica had seven aisles though the two outermost of them were merely halls with minimum communication with the main interior parts of the church (Fig. 23). One of these aisles could have been the *catechumena*, a place for those believers who were as yet unbaptised but who were awaiting their entry into the Christian fold. These converts would not be allowed in the body of the church during the Eucharistic ceremonies and had to sit on benches in this side chamber. The place of honour in the church was the *synthronon*, the set of stepped benches set into the curvature of the central semi-circular apse. Also in the apse, and in the area just before it, was the bema, a slightly raised platform that elevated the most important part of the church (this was demarked by a templon screen, a low fence that indicated the holy space and marked the threshold between the priesthood and laity). Here, Bishop Epiphanios himself would have presided, surrounded on either side by a group of clerics organised according to Church hierarchy. The entire structure, including its substantial narthex (a long hall running in front of the west end of the church, creating an antechamber), was about 60 metres long and 40 metres wide. Many of the columns of the nave still survive up to a few feet making it easier to envision the original layout. Some capitals, possibly pillaged from the city's classical period temples, lie on the ground amongst the ruins. A few fragments of colourful geometric *opus sectile* and mosaic work can still be found in places, providing an impression of how resplendent the floor decorations would have been, though some of these could well have been taken from the floors of the Salamis bath complex, which by now was a smaller operation than it had been in earlier centuries. Numerous mysterious substructures can be discovered near the eastern apse of the building, perhaps providing access to wells or spring water for drinking and religious rites such as baptism. The baptistery, in fact, survives east of the church. It has a cross-shaped pool that had a hypocaust underneath, which means that the baptismal waters were heated before the celebrants entered it. In the early Christian period baptisms were full emersion, so no doubt the warmth was appreciated by cold-weather converts. (For a more detailed discussion of baptismal fonts and the rites of baptism see the entry on Agia Trias.)

The triple-apse (*trichonos*) formation of the basilica of Epiphanios was inspired by churches in Palestine, and the apses were linked by passageways in the interior, something found in Syrian churches of the period. Such a configuration was to become common in Cyprus. Since Epiphanios had spent time in Syria and the Holy Land, it is likely that he brought ideas and perhaps even architects and masons from the nearby mainland. The liturgical function of these apse passageways is a mystery. Perhaps it allowed priests to inexplicably appear or disappear from the altar without the means of ingress or egress visible to the worshippers. At the very least, they provided separate short-cut entrances for the clergy, thus enhancing the stage-like function of the bema and *synthronon* and the hieratic separation of the clergy from the worshippers.

By the late 7th century the basilica was falling into ruin as Cyprus's economy declined in the wake of repeated Arab pirate raiding. The local Christians, much poorer than they had been centuries before, built a new but more modest church about 20 metres long off the southeast corner of Epiphanios' monumental original structure. Of this later structure, the great scholar of Cypriot architecture A. H. S. Megaw wrote:

> Such was the minuscule successor of Ephipanius' spacious church. Its meager congregation squatted in the ruins of the great city, which the sand dunes progressively engulfed. Already in the 7th century it was known as Ammochostos, "hidden in the sand", a name its inhabitants took with them when they moved to the site of the medieval city, the modern Famagusta.

The smaller church, sometimes referred to as the 'Annex Church', also had a more symmetrical form with a nave and a single set of flanking side aisles. Each ended in a semi-circular apse on the interior, but on the exterior the aisle apses were squared off. The architects and masons who modified the church in later centuries must have been reasonably skilled, as the nave was later roofed by a trio of domes. Nevertheless, the Annex Church also quickly fell into decline. When Salamis was completely abandoned, the body of St Epiphanios was brought to Famagusta, where it was said to have resided in the church of St Symeon. Eventually, the saint's relics were transported to the Byzantine capital of Constantinople.

Sources for Basilica of Epiphanios: George Jeffery, "Byzantine Churches on Cyprus," in *Proceedings of the Society of Antiquaries* vol. 28, 2nd series (March, 1916), pp. 111-134; George Jeffrey, "The Basilica of Constantia, Cyprus," *The Antiquaries Journal* 80 (1928): 344-49; Claudia Rapp, "Epiphanius of Salamis: The Church Father as Saint" in *The Sweet Land of Cyprus*, eds. A. A. M. Bryer and G. S. Georghallides, Nicosia, 1993, pp. 169-187; Charles Anthony Stewart, "The First Vaulted Churches in Cyprus," *Journal of the Society of Architectural Historians* 69, n. 2 (June, 2010): 162-189.

Basilica of Campanopetra, Salamis (Constantia), late 5th-7th century CE

[35° 10' 43.54" N / 33° 54' 24.41" E]

The larger and later of the two basilicas at Salamis was the Basilica of Campanopetra, which is spectacularly situated on a bluff just above the sea. The structure derives its name from an old name for the spot, which

Fig. 24: The synthronon in the central apse of the Basilica of Campanopetra at ancient Salamis.

literally means 'field of stones', and it was excavated by a French team from the University of Lyon. There may have been a Christian building here as early as the mid-4th century but most of what is visible today probably dates from the 6th to 7th centuries. Before the spring growth of fennel takes over, the general plan of the structure is still visible, with a clearly defined narthex, atrium, and a nave with two pairs of flanking side aisles. In the main apse is the well-preserved set of semi-circular steps of the *synthronon*, which served as a seating area for the bishop and high ranking ecclesiasts (Fig. 24). The complex actually had three large atria (pl. of atrium; a large rectangular open area courtyard surrounded by an arcade supporting a porch): two of them one after the other in the west and then a separate, third one to the east. This last, eastern one, however, may have been reserved for special ceremonies or functions or may have been associated with the Bishop's residence. The most distinctive feature of this east court was its monumental baldacchino, an arched portico with columns that may have been an architectural reliquary for a fragment of the True Cross, making the court an open air shrine for the veneration of the relic. As we shall see momentarily, the relic could also be worshipped from a quasi-subterranean chapel beneath the court.

The excavators of the Campanopetra basilica and its atria, baptistery, and other ancillary structures, everywhere found indications of the magnificent decorations of the church, including complex pavements in tiles, cut stone (*opus sectile*) and mosaic. There were numerous fragments of intricately carved marble capitals and mouldings, hinting at the decorative splendour of the furnishings. Columns of imported Proconnesian marble, their bases still discernable, held up arches which in turn supported a timber roof, and also indicate imperial patronage since this marble came from an island in the Sea of Marmara near Constantinople, the Byzantine Empire's capital. In several places, geometric pavements of yellowish limestone and marble are still visible, giving a sense of the opulence of the original interior (these are very similar to those found in the Salamis bath complex and may have been part of contemporaneous construction/renovation campaigns).

In the south aisle one can still find marble sarcophagi of ecclesiasts and former patrons of the church, their lids smashed long ago by treasure hunters (Fig. 25). When I first came here in 2005 the bottoms of these sarcophagi were intact, but by the time I left in 2007 the bottoms had been smashed out by grave robbers who hoped to find earlier, undiscovered burials underneath. The narthex of the church is substantial, just like the one at the basilica of Epiphanios. It is 32 metres long, almost 4 metres wide, and has small apses at the short ends, a feature also found in some churches of Constantinople. In one of these apses was discovered some detailed paving in *opus sectile* work. While many architectural

Fig. 25: The southern corridor (catechumena?) of the Basilica of Campanopetra at ancient Salamis, with sarcophagi and other burials.

elements of the basilica of Epiphanios are reminiscent of Syria, more of the features of the basilica of Campanopetra allude to contacts with Constantinople. The decorations and the sculpting of the capitals of the columns are suggestive of imperial workmanship, or, at least, work of very high quality and materials. The basilica of Campanopetra was larger and, most likely, even more sumptuous than the older, more venerable Epiphanios church. But this basilica, too, like all the buildings of Salamis, began to decline, certainly by the late 7th century CE, perhaps less than a century after its construction. Its splendour represents the last gasp of the greatness of Salamis/Constantia. There is also evidence of destruction and repair. For example, inset into a repaired wall of the narthex is a marble panel from an earlier *templon* or chancel screen.

As might be expected, the area around the altar was accorded special treatment. A bema, which is the elevated platform where the altar is, extended out into the body of the church, where it was further demarcated by a *templon* made up of low fence of solid stone panels about waist high. Many of these panels survived, some showing openwork patterns and others with reliefs of crosses and other conventional designs. The central apse was flanked by two large marble half columns. One of them, on the north side, survives to almost full height. Look closely at it, and you'll see some drill holes. They are pinnings for a couple of small bronze crosses that were probably votive offerings of some kind, possibly even a cross shaped *enkolpion*, which is an object that holds a small sacred relic inside.

In the north side aisle apse one finds a rectangular stone basin with two holes in it. It may seem like this was meant to be a lavabo or fountain, with the holes being spouts, but it was probably a reliquary for a saint's bones. The two holes in the bottom facilitated looking at or even touching the relics inside it, gaining their blessing. Originally there would have been a stone lid on the small sarcophagus-like reliquary.

Fragments of a marble roundel with an inscription were also found in the basilica, and while incomplete an important phrase appears: "...work of John...". A reference to a Consul named John in Cyprus appears in the 7th indiction of Justinian II (542-43 CE), and this may indicate a date for the basilica's construction. This is the same time that the great baths were being renovated on a smaller scale. It also suggests the possibility that some of the pavements in the basilica were taken from the portions of the ancient baths that were no longer being used. Indeed, some of the few pavements that survive in and around the *sudatorium* of the great baths at Salamis look very similar to some pavements in the basilica of Campanopetra. Many of the marble flooring panels at the basilica are also irregular in shape, comprised of a variety of rectangular shapes of different marbles. These, too, may have originally been the marble wall panels of the baths.

Another impressive and monumental part of the church complex was the *phiale* or font in the main atrium that was immediately to the west of the basilica entrance. It was an octagonal structure with monolithic marble columns holding up a series of arches. The pool, too, was octagonal, and at its center had a tall column with water spouting out the top, providing a flow of fresh water. Only the foundations of this *phiale* survive, but there is enough there to give an idea of its shape. One of the columns survives and has been re-erected.

One of the most important parts of the church uncovered by the excavators was the *ambo*, which survived only in fragments. These fragments were, however, more than enough to determine what the original structure looked like. The *ambo* was an elevated pulpit made of stone and was one of the most impressive pieces of ecclesiastical furniture in the basilica. The *ambo* of the basilica of Campanopetra was so opulent that it very closely resembled the *ambo* at Hagia Sophia in Constantinople (visitors to Istanbul can see that *ambo* reconstructed from its fragments near the entrance). Thus it is another indication of strong imperial associations. It was a sophisticated construction, with a steep set of steps up one side and down the other, with a circular podium at the top where the priest or bishop would stand while addressing the congregation. From this elevated position, the laity could better see and hear the speaker.

Baths and other buildings near the Basilica of Campanopetra

To the north of the main part of the basilica, attached to the church near the main altar, is the baptistery with a rectangular shape and a single apse in its east end. It had sumptuous pavements, as did most of the buildings of the basilica. Pilaster strips with elegant capitals along the walls with niches in between, perhaps for representations of saints, decorated the walls. There was no large or elaborate baptismal font here, which suggests that a tub-like font for infant baptisms may have existed, but adult baptisms by this time were no longer full emersion. Nearby were the toilets, which were less sophisticated than the toilets near the baths of Salamis, but still of similar construction and technology.

Just below the basilica, east of the east atrium and down the slope towards the sea, is a small bath complex with some pavements in striking circular patterns in *opus sectile* work. They are executed in marbles, limestone, fired brick, and a few pieces of valuable porphyry, a purple marble from Egypt which had imperial connotations. One can still clearly see the *caldarium* of the baths, with the remnants of the hypocausts still in place. Steps led from this complex to the beach just beyond. One can easily imagine an hour sweating in the hot baths followed by a dip in the sea to cool off.

Attached to the south of the baths are two other structures, both of which are quite visible today. One is just below the place where the baldacchino was in the east court above. One can clearly see that it originally had a broadly curved barrel vault. It was, in essence, a dark subterranean chapel where one could be near the sacred relic of the True Cross in the baldacchino above. It contained a small column that likely supported a small altar table for offerings. Fragments from the excavations indicated the room was beautifully decorated with painted plaster designs. Twenty-four coins were found there, ranging in date from 643-653 CE, giving a fairly accurate measure of at least one significant period of use. Since there was little light coming into the chapel it was lit by glass oil lamps, of which the archaeologists found ample if fragmentary evidence. These may have been part of a *polycandelion*, a metal chandelier that held several of these glass lamps. A *thymiaterion* (stand for burning incense) was also found, indicative of the devotions of the ancient worshippers. The structure may originally have been a cistern for water, but was only later converted into a chapel when the basilica was built or shortly thereafter. Just south of this is a large rectangular cistern about 5 x 10 metres in size, used for storing water for the bath complex. Perhaps this one replaced the one that had been made into the chapel.

Just a hundred metres or so from the Basilica of Campanopetra is a large cistern not accessible to the public (though one can look down the deep shaft), but I mention it nevertheless to give some sense of the more pragmatic architectural projects that also engaged 7th century builders in Salamis/Constantia. The impressive cistern is really two conjoined cylindrical cisterns about 16 feet deep and 8 feet in diametre, each cylinder connected to the surface by a rectangular shaft itself about 10 feet deep. This hydrological complex, capable of storing thousands of gallons of water, was excavated by Joan du Plat Taylor in 1932. One of the things that the cistern was clearly meant to address was water shortage, but du Plat Taylor's investigations also established that there were religious associations with the cistern's waters. Deep inside the cavernous interior, excavators discovered painted Christian crosses, an image of Christ Pantocrator, and several inscriptions. The inscriptions were from the Bible, and included passages having to do with water or the waters' blessing, such as this quotation from 2 Kings 2:21: "Thus saith the Lord, I healed these waters." Or, similarly, from Psalm 29:3, a fragmentary inscription: "The voice of the Lord [is] upon the waters...The Lord [is] upon many waters...." One also finds an inscription demonstrating local admiration for Salamis's most revered saints: "Barnabas the Apostle is our foundation. Epiphanios [is] our great governor." As du Plat Taylor notes, the quotation from Psalm 29 is also used in baptismal ceremonies, thus suggesting that these waters, or the cistern itself, may have been used as a baptismal font or at least supplied sanctified waters for baptism in the buildings above. Even a structure that might initially seem purely utilitarian could have had religious functions as well.

Sources for Basilica of Campanopetra: George Jeffery, "Byzantine Churches on Cyprus," in *Proceedings of the Society of Antiquaries* vol. 28, 2nd series (March, 1916), pp. 111-134; Georges Roux, *Salamine de Chypre 15: La Basilique de la Campanopetra* (Paris: Boccard, 1998); Susan Boyd, "A Little Known Technique of Architectural Sculpture: champlevé reliefs from Cyprus," Actes du XVI Congrès international byzantin, *Jährbuch der Österreichischen Byzantinistik*, 32, n. 5 (1982), pp. 313-325; Demitrios Michaelides, "*Opus Sectile* in Cyprus," in *The Sweet Land of Cyprus*, eds. A. A. M. Bryer and G. S. Georghallides, Nicosia, 1993, pp. 69-113; Joan du Plat Taylor, "A Water Cistern with Byzantine Paintings in Salamis, Cyprus," *The Antiquaries Journal* 13 no. 2 (April, 1933): 97-108.

The Cenotaph of Nicocreon, near Salamis (Tuzla/Enkomi), c. 310 BCE

[35° 09' 41.58" N / 33° 53' 06.25" E]

To the southwest of the tumulus of Tomb 3 of the Royal Tombs near St Barnabas — about 2.5 kilometres SW of Salamis — lays another tumulus that likely marked the southwestern edge of the necropolis which extended from ancient Salamis almost to the Bronze Age site of Enkomi. It was assumed by many — grave robbers and 20th century archeologists alike — that this tumulus was also a tomb. But scientific excavation disproved this assumption and in doing so revealed an even more compelling and unique monument (Fig. 26). There is no doubt that the tumulus was meant to allude to the tumulus tomb type of which the nearby and much earlier Tomb 3, a kilometre or so away, was an impressive model. When excavation began on the 10-metre high mound (likely much higher originally, almost two thousand years of erosion having worn it down) a very deliberate, layered system of construction revealed itself in the stratigraphic horizons of the soil. Some of the dirt fill used to make the mound evidently came from the digging up of tombs of an earlier period, since small artifacts were found chaotically intermingled in the upper layers. But as excavators penetrated to the heart and the base of the tumulus they began to uncover a more consistent assemblage of fascinating artifacts dating from the Hellenistic period, around the time of Alexander the Great. These included clay figures, life size and almost life size, which had been baked in place in a huge fire. They seem to have been draped in clothing as the bodies were rough cores and fragments of burnt cloth were found. Small bottles made of clay, called alabastra, which had been painted and gilded, littered the site. Burned wood, rosettes of gold foil from a diadem, charred terra cotta, and carbonized seeds — wheat, almonds, raisins, figs — all gave evidence of a fiery conflagration. Bits from clay human figures, including a foot and breast, as well as a horse's head, were also found. The clay heads, representing men and one woman, had naturalistic painting on their faces and bodies, such as red paint on their lips. It seems that these modeled sculptures were meant to create ephemeral representations for an elaborate funerary rite that imitated a funeral pyre. Underneath the tantalizing remnants of the ancient inferno was unearthed an extraordinary rectangular platform 17 by 11.5 metres in size. This podium was raised on four steps, elevating it about 1 metre, with a ramp leading up to it on the west side.

The archaeologists had a dramatic historical event with which to make sense of this otherwise perplexing array of elements. In the years after the death of Alexander the Great, Cyprus saw a great deal of warfare as powers tried to exert control over this rich and strategic island.

Similarly, the kings of the various Cypriot cities also sometimes rebelled against outside control to either gain or maintain independence. Such a situation existed in the years around 310 BCE, when the Egyptian king Ptolemy the First controlled Cyprus. Ptolemy had made Nicocreon, the king of Salamis, *strategos* or governor of the island as a puppet ruler. However, it seems that Nicocreon secretly agreed to an alliance with Antigonus, who wanted to resist Ptolemaic rule. Ptolemy sent his armies, led by two former friends of Nicocreon, Argaeus and Callicrates, against the renegade Cypriot cities and they besieged Nicocreon in Salamis. Nicocreon, facing defeat, took his own life. The historian Diodorus Siculus confuses Nicocreon with 'Nicocles' of Paphos, but his account of the suicides of the rest of Nicocreon's family is worth quoting:

> Axiothea, the wife of Nicocles [Nicocreon], on learning of her husband's death, slew her daughters, who were unwed, in order that no enemy might possess them; and she urged the wives of Nicocles' [Nicocreon's] brothers to choose death along with her.... When the palace had thus been filled full of death and unforeseen disaster, the brothers of Nicocles [Nicocreon], after fastening the doors, set fire to the building and slew themselves.
> *[Sources History Cyprus I, 93]*

Eventually the people of Salamis, proud of their king's courage and sacrifice, wanted some way to honour him. The noble bodies were long lost, so they concocted an elaborate funerary ceremony where clay effigies of the regal family were sculpted around wooden posts, surrounded with offerings and wood, and ignited in a funeral pyre which replicated a proper ritual for the souls who had not received suitable rites. This cenotaph commemorated the heroic Nicocreon and gave the royal family not only due honours but bestowed peace to their souls in the underworld. The ramp leading to the platform, perhaps used by the priests in a procession to anoint the clay figures and light the pyre, could later be understood as a symbolic ramp for the souls of Nicocreon and his family to descend westwards, in the direction of the setting sun, to their eternal home in the land of dead. The people of Salamis, having thus given tribute to their king, piled tons of earth atop the embers, marking the site and eternally commemorating their king and his family with a monument imitating the imposing royal tombs of the ancient kings nearby.

Soon the Athenians and other Greek allies would send a great armada to Salamis to liberate the fabled city, and the island of Cyprus, from Ptolemaic rule. The aforementioned Diodorus Siculus records in several pages of riveting description the siege of Salamis by the general Demetrius who, after a dramatic sea battle, emerged victorious. It was probably after this time that the citizens of Salamis honoured the sacrifices of Nicocreon and his family with the cenotaph.

Sources for Cenotaph of Nicocreon: Vassos Karageorghis, *Salamis: Recent Discoveries in Cyprus*, McGraw Hill, 1969; *Sources for the History of Cyprus, Greek and Latin Texts to the Third Century A.D.*, eds Paul W. Wallace and Andreas G. Orphanides. Institute of Cypriot Studies and Cyprus College, 1990, esp. pp. 92-99; George Hill, *History of Cyprus*, vol. 1; see pp. 159-161.

Fig. 26: The platform and western ramp of the Cenotaph of Nicocreon, Tuzla/Enkomi.

Rock-Cut Tomb east of Avtepe/Agios Symeon, Hellenistic Period, c. 330 BCE

[35° 29' 47.12" N / 34° 13' 44.27" E]

This is one of the most impressive tombs in the northern part of the island. As one drives east from Avtepe, continuing on the main road for about a kilometre, one makes a curving descent into a valley. At the bottom of this decline you'll see on the right a flat-topped mountain. The entrance to the cave is on the cliffs of the north side of this mountain, which is also the side that the main road runs along. Look immediately at the bottom of the hill for a turnoff to the right that will lead to the trailhead, which I've given as the GPS coordinates above. It's about a 400 metre walk along the new path to the base of the cliff below the tomb entrance. For many years this site was essentially inaccessible, but recently a path has been cleared to the cliff below the entrance to the tomb. One should be glad of this because when I first tried to get there in 2005 my experience was very similar to D. G. Hogarth's when he visited in 1887:

> It is while passing under one such hill, after abruptly descending from the central ridge ... that the traveller suddenly perceives high up in the cliff upon his right a dark patch, which a moment's scrutiny convinces him must be the mouth of an artificial cave. If he turns off his path... [he] bursts his way for five hundred feet of ascent through matted thorns and over rocks so hot as to blister his bare hands, until he reaches the foot of the scarp which forms the crest of the hill, he will have had no bad foretaste of purgatory.
>
> *[Devia Cypria, 72]*

In Hogarth's time there was still a bit of a ledge that one could climb to, and if one looks to the right of the cave mouth one can barely discern it and even perhaps the scant remains of a carved staircase along the cliff face. But the ledge that Hogarth used to get in has now eroded away. So the first time I visited I could see the entrance but had no way to get to it. The second time I went, however, a ladder had been set up. But it's quite a climb and it was by no means an easy ascent. Not for the faint of heart. But if there is access and one can make it up it is an amazing place. As Hogarth noted, "...the climber will not regret his labour, for the largest of the ancient Cyprian sepulchers lies before him". He also reproduced a diagram of its interior in his 1889 book *Devia Cypria* (Fig. 27). He estimated that the tomb was cut into the rock about 87 feet.

The central doorway was the main and probably original doorway, but flanking halls and windows were cut into the complex at a later date.

Some have suggested that the place served as a kind of fort or lookout at some point in Cyprus's history. Locals in the 19th century claimed that robbers used it as a hideout. Six large rectangular relieving piers have been left uncarved so that the excavated pseudo-cave would be more stable and wouldn't collapse. Everywhere one can see the grooves of the chisels that sculpted the interior out over two thousand years ago. As one enters, to the left there are 4 niches, presumably where sarcophagi, perhaps of terra cotta, once rested. Two more such niches are found on the right. But at the very end of the cave is a well dug deep into the earth. Was this excavated originally or was this done much later when the place was a habitation for the living instead of a home of the dead? Long robbed of the archaeological contents that may have solved the mysteries of this extraordinary 'structure', we can only guess at its function. But Hogarth suggested, probably correctly, that they were originally tomb complexes for powerful families of ancient Karpasian towns. Stripped by tomb robbers in later centuries they were modified and reused as habitations or refuges.

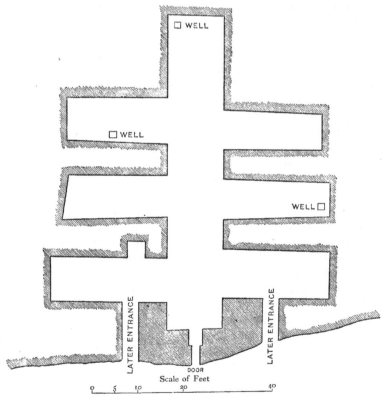

Fig. 27: Plan of the rock-cut Hellenistic Period tomb in the cliffs near Avtepe [from D. G. Hogarth, Devia Cypria, 1889].

Rock-Cut Tombs at Kaleburnu/Galinoporni, Hellenistic Period, c. 330 BCE

[35° 31' 21.42" N / 34° 18' 18.65" E]

The rock-cut tombs at Kaleburnu are more accessible than the cliff face tomb just discussed. Kaleburnu is also east of Avtepe, about 5 kilometres, just off the main road towards the north. Turn off the main road and park near the center of the village, at the top of the town, to walk to the tombs. The tombs are southeast, along a cliff face where there is a well-worn path to give access. Locals are happy to help out. When you are at the edge of town you'll get a wonderful view of the impressive little mountain to the southeast, the *Kral Tepesi* or 'King's Mountain' where in 2004 an important Bronze Age archaeological site was discovered (see earlier entry). The rock-cut tomb that is most accessible is only one of several at Kaleburnu. As Hogarth observed, while the Avtepe tomb stands more or less alone,

> ...at Galinoporni a hundred other rock-cut graves honeycomb the eastern slope on which the village is built: the houses are often built on to them, and they are used as inner rooms, as storechambers, as stables — indeed the natives are half troglodyte.
>
> *[Devia Cypria, 76]*

Some of the villagers still use these ancient tombs as part of their homes. Perhaps you'll get an invitation to tea and be able to see one. Here, too, as at the tomb near Avtepe, a well or even several wells were carved into the sepulchers, probably at later dates when people lived in them.

Ruined Ancient Village called 'Neta' (near Avtepe/Agios Sergios and Taşlıca/Neta), evidence of occupation from several eras from Bronze Age to Medieval

[35° 28' 16.51" N / 34° 14' 21.09" E]

While in the region east of Avtepe, exploring the rock-cut tombs discussed in the earlier two entries, you might consider driving south to a very interesting ancient village that, as far as I know, has never been excavated. During the rainy season the dirt roads may require a high-clearance and preferably four-wheel drive vehicle. The site is called ancient Neta, but there is also a modern village called Taşlıca/Neta, but this isn't where you go to see this particular site (though one can, it just isn't the easiest route). From Avtepe you take a dirt road that goes almost directly south from the west edge of the village. It will curve gently to a southeastern direction until you are actually heading east. At this point, about 2.3 kilometres from Avtepe, the road will fork. Keep to the right and that new road will take you directly south again. At about 800 metres from that fork in the road keep your eye open to the right and look for a tiny ruined church. This is the church of Agios Sergios, which is thought to date from the 14th century, during the Lusignan medieval period. Gunnis says it's a domed church, but if it ever had a dome it must have collapsed and the roof redone with a barrel vault. It might be the case, as there is some evidence of rebuilding in the vault above the center of the nave, and there are projections on the walls that might indicate the structural need for the greater support a dome would require. Mute shadows of frescoes remain on the crumbling plaster of the walls, but the church's frescoes were dilapidated even in the early 1930s when Gunnis visited. The apse and its semidome are completely collapsed. If you explore west of this church, and a bit south, you will feel like a real archaeologist exploring an ancient, unexcavated town site. Especially impressive are the large millstones that can be found in a milling factory just south of the church. It is tangible evidence of the processing of the wheat that grew in the fields nearby. Even today, the area produces a lot of grain. In one case, there's a huge millstone that was only half quarried out of the living rock before being abandoned centuries ago. Keep your eye open for the entry to a Hellenistic rock-cut tomb, also in the area. If you have the courage to go down into it you will be rewarded by the impressive sight of the tomb's three *arcosolia*, or carved, arched niches that once held sarcophagi. One of them is deeper than the others, suggesting that it held a several sarcophagi, perhaps of a family.

Rupert Gunnis claims to have seen some remarkable things in the vicinity just east of the modern village of Taşlıca/Neta [35° 28' 10.03" N / 34° 12' 52.03" E]:

East of the village [Neta] are the ruins of a large temple; remains of walls can still be seen, and two headless life-sized statues, one seated on a throne, lie on the hillside. About 200 yards south of this site is a small hillock covered with potsherds and fragments of terra-cotta figurines. Close to the school, also, is another site where terra-cotta statuettes can be picked up.

[Gunnis 253-4]

Such artifacts indicate some kind of cult or ritual site here from very early times. I found a headless limestone statue near the church of Agios Sergios in ancient Neta. Perhaps this is the one Gunnis is talking about. I didn't see the seated one. You might consider exploring around both modern and ancient Neta, then, and then cool yourself off by swimming in the sea nearby where there are some lovely beaches. Just 170 metres south of the church of Agios Sergios, turn left (east) on the dirt road, go about 750 metres, then turn right and in 250 metres you'll be able to see the sea. Park at the side of the road and walk west along the beach about 300 metres to a low promontory [35° 28' 09.72" N / 34° 14' 41.84" E]. At the top of that promontory you will find more ancient ruins to explore while you are enjoying the beach.

Sources for Ancient Neta: Gunnis, 253-4.

Hellenistic Rock-cut Tomb and Cult Sanctuary between Mersinlik/Phlamoudhi and Kapliça/Davlos

This is the only monument in this guide that I have not yet actually seen so I have no GPS coordinates. I am basing my approximation on D. G. Hogarth's description of the site's location from his 1889 volume *Devia Cypria* and the book's accompanying map. The site is west of and near the main road leading from Kapliça/Davlos, and northeast of the village of Mersinlik/Phlamoudhi about 200m from the sea coast. It is very difficult to find even though it's not far from the main north coast road. I searched for it for hours. Ahmet Genç at the Kapliça Hotel knows where it is. You might drop by and try to steal him for an hour or so. The beach there is worth visiting even if you don't find any tombs. Ismail Cemal also knows where it is, and you might think of hiring him as he's a guide for the region. Ismail and his wife Lois have for years been promoting eco-tourism in the region and have a small B&B in Büyükonuk/Komkebir. Visit their website at www.ecotourismcyprus.com and think about staying with them and promoting responsible tourism.

The site that Hogarth describes seems fascinating and very reminiscent of some of the rock-cut tombs that can be found in Paphos at the southwest corner of Cyprus. Hogarth thought it to be a royal tomb of a king of Aphrodisium, a lost city of the north coast. Hogarth included a diagram of the site and wrote the following:

> The tomb has a square court — 12 ft. 6 in. each way — sunk to a depth of 6 ft. 6 in. into the rock, and open to the sky. On the western and northern sides of this run covered colonnades, 5 ft. 6.5 in. in breadth, each supported by two fluted Doric columns, and a double column at the common corner, all cut out of the solid rock...the columns have supported a small architrave and frieze, with triglyphs and plain metopes...Crosses have been cut everywhere by pious Christian hands to conjure the evil spirits of the old sepulcher.
>
> *[Devia Cypria, 100]*

The site was first surveyed by the archaeologist Porphyrios Dikaios (who also excavated at Vounous) and by Hector Catling. Excavations and further archaeological surveys were done by Edith Porada, who ran a field school for archaeology at Phlamoundhi for Columbia University in the early 1970s. Porada, an expert on cylinder seals, found many artifacts in the area, many predating the Hellenistic period that the rock-cut tomb belongs to. Pottery from the Bronze Age was quite common, she found, leading one to think that the area was one of the many Bronze Age sites of the north coast of Cyprus. Much excavation remains to be done in this area as earlier archaeological surveys also revealed some kind of ancient, probably Bronze Age, cult site. This would be a good area for those who like to hike in open country to explore for ruins and remnants of past civilizations.

Sources for Phlamoudhi Rock-cut tomb: Hogarth, *Devia Cypria*, 100; S. Symeonoglou, "Archaeological Survey in the Area of Phlamoudhi, Cyprus,"*Report of the Department of Antiquities Cyprus* (1972): 187-198; Hadjisavvas, S., *KATAVOLES I. Archaiologiki Episkopisi 20 Katechomenon Simera Chorion tis Eparchias Ammochostou*. Nicosia. Ekdosi Kentrou Meleton Ieras Monis Kykkou kai Tmimatos Archaiotiton, 1991; Selma M. S. Al-Radi, *Phlamoudhi Vounari: A Sanctuary Site in Cyprus* (Studies in Mediterranean Archaeology LXV). Göteborg: Paul Åströms Förlag, 1983; Hector W. Catling, "Observations on the Archaeological Survey in the Area of Phlamoudhi, Cyprus," *Report of the Department of Antiquities, Cyprus* (1973): 107-115; Hector W. Catling, "The Phlamoudhi Survey Again," *Report of the Department of Antiquities, Cyprus* (1976): 29-34; also find several essays in J. S. Smith ed., *Views from Phlamoudhi, Cyprus. Annual of the American Schools of Oriental Research* 63, Boston: American Schools of Oriental Research, 2008.

The Palace at Vouni, 5th century BCE near Gemikonaği/Karavostasi

[35° 09' 30.99" N / 32° 46' 23.66" E]

The spectacularly situated Persian palace at Vouni is one of the great archaeological sites in northern Cyprus. The complex itself is relatively small and allows for a rewarding tour through the remnants of its numerous sectors comprised of over 130 rooms. As one walks around, studying the plan, a three-dimensional picture of the original palace and its luxurious surroundings begins to form in one's imagination (Fig. 28). The palace was built on a striking mountaintop location ('vouni' means 'mountain peak' in Greek) by Persians around 450 BCE, ostensibly as a headquarters for Persian representatives — and, one presumes, a contingent of soldiers — who wanted to keep the nearby city of Soli in line, as it had sided with the Persians' Greek enemies in an earlier revolt. The builder may have been Doxandros, a Persian puppet ruler of the city of Marion. The buildings were destroyed by fire after around a century of occupation, and so it represents a precisely defined historical moment in Cyprus's ancient past, even though there were four phases of construction (additional rooms added, or the configuration changed). It is also unique because no other Persian palace exists anywhere else in the Mediterranean, thus giving an exceptional sense of Persian court culture and elite residential architecture of the period.

Water management was always an issue on Cyprus even in very ancient times, and at Vouni water seems to have been plentiful, due partly to cavernous cisterns. Baths, well-appointed toilets, and even a sauna or steam bath seem to have been just some of the amenities provided by Vouni's abundant water supply. In one section one can still see the furnace area for the hot bath, though the room above that it heated has not survived. Ostentation continued in the royal apartments, a palatial residential quadrant with stunning views. A strange, double bass-shaped stone with an incomplete face — perhaps of a goddess — stands in a large courtyard and may have been a religious altar of some sort or simply part of a mechanism to bring up water from a cistern immediately below it (Fig. 29). Perhaps it performed both functions simultaneously. This cistern was filled by sluicing water from the roofs of the rooms surrounding the courtyard into the courtyard itself where it flowed into the mouth of the cistern, creating a courtyard 'well' that filled up when it rained.

Some early interpreters of the palace thought that it resembled the Minoan palaces of Crete, such as Knossos and Phaistos. However, though there are similarities, later architectural historians traced the origin of the layout to Mesopotamian palaces. In each prototype, however, there are residential quarters and quadrants of various functions gathered

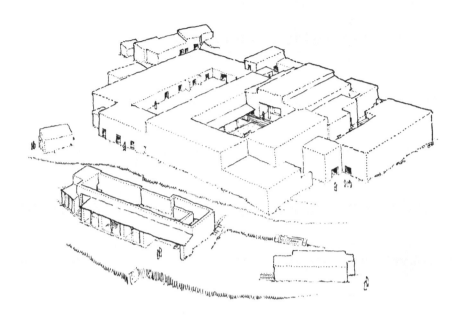

Fig. 28: Artist's reconstruction of the palace at Vouni [from G. R. H. Wright, Ancient Building in Cyprus, E. J. Brill, 1992].

Fig. 29: Sculptural relief above a cistern, in the great courtyard at the Palace of Vouni.

around large rectangular courtyards, just as at Vouni. Another feature of both Minoan and Mesopotamian palaces were the long corridor-like storage rooms. Excavators at Vouni discovered one such storage room filled with wine jugs still leaning up against the walls, highly reminiscent of the storage magazines at Knossos.

The site was excavated by a Swedish archaeological expedition in the 1920s. One of the artifacts they unearthed was a beautiful life size figure of a female figure called a 'kore', a youthful woman, similar to those found from the archaic period on the Acropolis of Athens. In another room were small but very fine bronze statues, one of a bull and another showing two lions attacking a bull. They found artifacts that were eloquent expressions of the splendour in which the ancient occupants lived: golden snake-bracelets, bronze statues, bronze and silver implements, as well as coins. One hoard had been hidden under a staircase. The keeper of that secret treasure must have been killed, perhaps in the conflagration that destroyed the palace in 380 BCE, and the hoard remained concealed under the collapsed stairs for 2500 years. This 'Vouni Treasure' consisted of 15 silver bracelets, 4 gold coins (very pure gold Persian coins called 'Darics' after the Persian king Darius who first minted them; they had the face of king Artaxerxes I on them) and 248 silver coins, including some of Greek and Phoenician mintages.

On the high point of the hill to the south are the remains of a temple that was dedicated to Athena. Only the foundations and substructures remain, but one can discern large rectangular holes which may have been sockets for statues. Look to the west along the coast if the weather is clear and you'll be able to see the tiny island of Petra tou Limniti, a Neolithic habitation site.

Sources for Vouni: Valentin Muller, "The Palace of Vouni in Cyprus," *American Journal of Archaeology*, 36, n. 4 (Oct.-Dec., 1932): 408-417; Einar Gjerstad, "Further Remarks on the Palace at Vouni," *American Journal of Archaeology* 37 n.4 (1933): 589-598; Einer Gjerstad and F. A. Schaefer, "Summary of Swedish Excavations in Cyprus," *Syria* 12, n.1 (1931): 58-66; Einer Gjerstad, *Ages and Days in Cyprus* (Göteborg: Åström, 1980), esp. pp. 86-105.

The Kyrenia Shipwreck, Girne/Kyrenia Hellenistic Period, c. 350 BCE in Kyrenia Castle Museum

In November 1967 a Cypriot sponge-diver named Andreas Cariolou took Michael Katzev and his team of archaeologists from the University of Pennsylvania to a site about a kilometre from Kyrenia's shore where a wreck of a wooden ship, wonderfully preserved, lay on the muddy seabed where it sank during the age of Alexander the Great, 2300 years ago (Fig. 30). Archaeologists concluded that the ship had been constructed just before Alexander's birth and went down soon after he died; that is, built around 350 and sank around 300 BCE. Coins date the wreck from circa 300-310 BCE, while carbon dating suggested the trees used to make the timber for the ship were felled around 380 BCE. It had been repaired many times before it sank. Indeed, it may have sunk because it was so old and leaky. Look closely at the ship's timbers and you might be able to see some of the repair patches on various parts. Another theory is that the ship may have been attacked by pirates who lingered offshore to pick off vulnerable vessels arriving or departing from Kyrenia. Yet why this would have led to its sinking is not easy to explain with the evidence at hand.

The find was not only important because such an old ship had been discovered, but the subsequent underwater excavation was a pioneering moment in scientific underwater archaeology, setting standards for later work. Eventually the project included scholars and scientists from Oxford and Oberlin College as well as those from University of Pennsylvania. Katzev wrote enthusiastically of the discovery: "The significance of the Kyrenia shipwreck cannot be overemphasized. It is, to date, the finest preserved ship from the Classical Period of Greek civilization ever found." Four hundred amphorae were found in the remnants of the ship's hold, the port side cargo barely disturbed from its original position. Cities in those times made amphorae of distinctive shapes, so archaeologists were able to trace at least parts of the ship's final voyages to ports of call such as Rhodes and Samos. In all, eight different amphora types were identified. The great majority of the amphorae were from Rhodes, indicating strong commercial ties, as might be expected, between the two large islands both located along the prosperous south coast of Asia Minor. Other amphorae were filled, and still sealed, with thousands of perfectly preserved almonds inside. You can see them today — no snacking allowed — in the Kyrenia castle museum. Smaller finds showed the personal items of the sailors who worked on the ship, including their drinking cups, plates, and bowls. Since these artifacts were found in groups of four, we assume that there were four crew members. Over twenty rectangular, stone grain mills ('hopper type') were also discovered, indicating the centrality of the grinding of grains in the region. Indeed, the artifacts from the ship were overwhelmingly agrarian in nature; either the products of agriculture (wine, almonds, etc.) or involved in processing (the mills).

The remains of the 47-foot long vessel, which J. Richard Steffy estimates was a 25 ton ship, are kept at a consistent temperature and humidity in a sealed room in Kyrenia castle, but one can get a great view of the ancient ship's hull from an elevated catwalk. Its staves, made of Aleppo pine, look like the ribs of a primeval whale. One of the most important elements of the wreck is the mast step, which you can clearly see in the restoration. Less visible is a part of the ship no less significant, the keel of the ship, which survived its full length though in 16 pieces. Also not visible when visiting today are the sections of lead sheathing that covered parts of the hull, which were glued to the timbers with a matting of agave leaves and pitch. Some pieces were also held together with copper nails. The preservation of the 6000 pieces of waterlogged timbers was the most complex scientific aspect of the expedition. After the wreck was photographed on the seabed and taken up, bit by fragile bit, to the excavation barge, the pieces were stored for months in tanks of fresh water, since to let them dry would have destroyed them. Contemporaneous work in Denmark, with 1000 year-old Viking ships, helped guide the Kyrenia conservation project. Eventually, the process used to preserve the wood was to soak the timbers in polyethylene glycol (PEG) for up to 6 months so that the solution penetrated into the collapsed organic cells of the wood and dried to a waxy solid. The process darkened the wood, which is why it is black in colour now.

Many remnants of Cyprus's colourful history can be found in the sea. Her shoals cradle ancient shipwrecks dating back millennia and scuba divers routinely come across old stone anchors or amphorae from antique ships long ago driven into the deep by raging storms. In 2006 a sixteenth-century galley that belonged to the armada of Lala Mustafa Paşa, the Ottoman conqueror of Cyprus, was rumoured to have been discovered. Its cannons and other artifacts await excavation by underwater archaeologists. Cyprus has been an archaeological wonderland for centuries, but even more lies in the seas around her shores. Indeed, one could argue that the future of archaeology in Cyprus is its underwater archaeology. Even World War II aircraft have been discovered in waters off the Karpas peninsula.

In 1986 a replica of the ship, the *Kyrenia II*, was built and sailed in New York harbour. If you visit Agia Napa on your trip to Cyprus, be sure to go to the Thalassa (Marine) Museum where you can see the reconstruction.

Sources for Kyrenia Shipwreck: See Michael Katzev's three articles in *National Geographic Society Reports*, 1974 (on the discovery, pp. 177-184), 1975 (on the conservation, pp. 331-340), 1976 (on the excavation, pp. 177-188). See also H. W. Swiny and M. L. Katsev, "The Kyrenia Shipwreck: a Fourth-century B.C. Greek Merchant Ship," in D. J. Blackman ed., *Marine Archaeology* (London: 1973): 339-359. For a detailed account of the ship's construction see J. Richard Steffy, "The Kyrenia Ship: An Interim Report on its Hull Construction," American Journal of Archaeology 38, n. 1 (Jan. 1985): 71-101. Thanks to Matthew Harpster for advice and material on this entry.

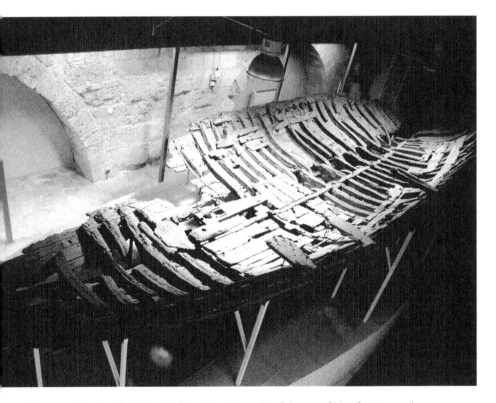

Fig. 30: The hull of the Hellenistic Kyrenia shipwreck in the Kyrenia castle museum.

Agia Trias Basilica, Sipahi/Agia Trias, 4th to 5th century CE

[35° 32' 40.71" N / 34° 13' 31.18" E]

About 5 kilometres northeast of the Karpasian town of Yeni Erenköy/Yialousa is a village called Sipahi/Agia Trias. At its eastern edge, tucked away in a picturesque olive grove just off a road that leads back to the main north coast road are the ruins of an early 5th century basilica known as Agia Trias, or "Holy Trinity" (Fig. 31-32). The remains of the three-aisled church reveal a plan about 21 metres long and 15 metres wide, including its nave, side aisles, and narthex. An atrium, measuring about 9 by 15 metres functioned as an open forecourt in front of the west entrance to the church.

Several ancillary structures surround the basilica, the most interesting of which are a catechumena attached to the southern flank of the church (also with a semi-circular apse, creating a veritable second southern side aisle) and the baptistery complex to the east. Agia Trias is best known for its geometric floor mosaics, which date from the building's early years if not its origin. These at one time covered the entire floor surface of the basilica and a substantial amount, about 70 percent, remains. The mosaics have been exposed to the elements for centuries and with a surge in tourism, increased foot traffic is also beginning to take its toll on these rare works of art.

Unlike the large urban basilicas (such as Soli, Campanopetra, and Epiphanios) Agia Trias was a smaller rural church that may have served a smaller local community or town and/or been a regional cult site. While the Karpas peninsula is only sparsely populated now, there is every indication that it supported a much larger population in ancient times. The ruins of the many Karpasian churches are just one indication of the Karpas's prosperity in former eras. Agia Trias' sumptuous mosaic decorations and substantial associated buildings suggest generous patronage. Medieval chroniclers often make mention of the many small and remote churches scattered in the Cypriot hinterlands and this church is one of the finest and earliest examples. The Karpas peninsula, in particular, was dotted with small timber-roofed basilicas in the 4th to 7th centuries such as those at Afendrika, Agios Philon, Sykha, and the Kanakaria church at Boltaşli/Lythrangomi. Some of them fell into ruin during the 7th to 9th centuries, but their remains were incorporated into newer vaulted basilicas some time in the 10th century. Agia Trias is somewhat unique, having never been reconstructed or built over, and thus offers an exceptional opportunity to study a reasonably well-preserved exemplar of its architectural type unmodified by later accretions.

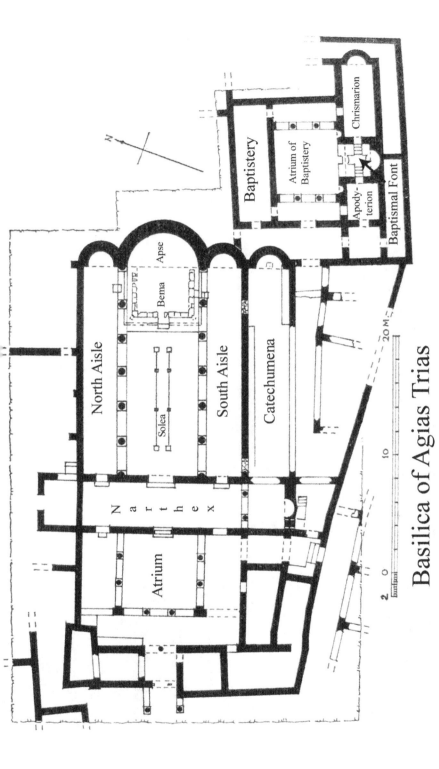

Fig. 31: Plan of the basilica and baptistery at Agias Trias, with atrium, narthex, solea, bema, nave, side aisles, and catachumena.

Fig. 32: View of the basilica of Agias Trias from the west, showing the columns of the atrium in the foreground and

Little of the church's elevation survives, though there is more than enough to clearly determine the building's plan and infer much about its superstructure. Some of the columns that held up the timber-framed roof were found during initial excavations and these fragments were re-erected on their bases and today give some sense of the building's vertical organisation. At the eastern terminus of the central apse is a bema which is elevated above the floor level of the rest of the church. At the bema's central edge, facing the nave, are three steps, possibly symbolic of the Trinity. The church's altar was situated on the bema, but nothing of it remains.

At one time a fence like stone screen (*templon*) probably helped demarcate the bema and altar area from the main body of the church where the laity stood during ceremonies. The bema almost completely fills the apse of the church, but not quite. As in other early basilicas, such as the larger and more famous basilica of Campanopetra in Salamis (Constantia), there is a narrow corridor between the bema and the wall of the apse. At the basilica of Campanopetra there is a *synthronon* in the apse, but no such remains were found at Agia Trias. Yet the presence of a substantial baptistery on the site suggests frequent visits by a local bishop and thus some arrangement of a *synthronon* in the central apse (where the bishop was seated during liturgies) is very likely. Perhaps it was a modest one such as at the Asomatos church at nearby Afendrika.

One of the most striking features of Agia Trias is the scant but significant remains of its *solea* (Fig. 33), which ran down the center of the nave from the bema steps almost to the church entrance. The *solea* consisted of a low fence, almost waist high, with stone posts which had grooves to support the openwork panels that slotted into them. Only fragments of these posts and panels survive, but there is enough to give an idea of the original configuration. One panel section, the best preserved, shows the bottom curve of a geometric circular motif with a flower in the corner. The *solea* was used by the officiating priests as a sacral passageway extending into the body of the church, functioning as a processional route during ceremonies. At times, a *solea* was coupled with an *ambo* or pulpit and it is possible that some kind of *ambo*, offering a slight elevation for the priest, could have been located at the center of this *solea*. At least one author claims that the remains of an *ambo* were found during excavations. The *solea's* construction closely resembles the stone barriers that divided the side aisles from the nave in many early Byzantine churches. These barriers, too, like the *solea*, segregated distinct spaces for clergy and laity, demarking strict hieratic thresholds.

The mosaic decorations neatly outline the *solea*, indicating that the liturgical furnishings and the pavement decoration were planned simultaneously. The nave mosaics are organised in three rectangular frames around the *solea* and include the mosaics of the *solea* itself,

which run in a consistent geometric design along its length. Two mosaic inscriptions can be found just beyond the *solea's* ends: one running in a strip along the front of the bema and another in a small rectangular panel immediately inside the entry way of the church. The first records the donation of Heraclius, the deacon who paid for the decorations in that part of the church, while the second, just inside the main entrance portal, tells of the brothers Aetis, Euthalis, and Eutychianos who made similar donations. The side aisles, narthex and catechumena are also filled with geometric mosaics, much in keeping with late antique and Early Christian designs. Though more rustic, they are reminiscent of the decorative borders and geometric floor mosaics found in Antioch, which is only 230 km away across the Latakia Basin to the east in what was Syria (now part of Turkey). This may be significant as the Cypriot Orthodox church was for centuries under the ecclesiastical jurisdiction of the Patriarchate of Antioch. The designs of the flooring display a splendid range of variations including wave patterns, chevrons, meanders, key designs, and myriad stellate, rectilinear, and curvilinear designs. Their exuberance and vitality are among their most compelling attributes. Although much faded by time, the tesserae were richly coloured stones of black, white, red, light and dark greens, and turquoise.

In the floor of the north aisle two exceptions to the non-representational decorative paradigm can be found, with two pairs of sandals and a depiction of pomegranates. One pair of sandals points to the interior of the church while the other points outwards. Perhaps they represented the sandals of pilgrims who visited the site, suggesting that Agia Trias might have been the site of a regional cult, or perhaps the simple footwear was meant to remind visitors of Christ's humility and poverty. The motif appeared most often in the pagan Roman context at the thresholds of baths where they functioned as reminders for people to take off their sandals. The sandals were often accompanied by the inscription "*Bene Lava*" or "Have a Good Bath". Pomegranates, also shown, were rich signs in both Judaic and Christian traditions, where they symbolized various concepts, from Christ's suffering with their blood-red juice, to the wealth of Christian salvation with their many seeds.

The narthex has a semi-circular niche at its south end and was set apart from the main body of the narthex by a pair of columns. This niche probably held a font for ritual ablutions. Since this specialized part of the narthex communicates only with the catechumena, it is probable that it functioned as a ritual component for the catechumens who were in the process of preparing to enter the Christian faith. Such additional, apsed corridors along the southern short ends of churches were common features in Cypriot basilicas of the Early Christian period. They are found in the Basilica of Campanopetra at Salamis, for example, and at the

Karpasian church of Agios Philon, which is very close to Agia Trias. In the atrium of Agia Trias one can still find a small monolithic stone font of a type fairly common in Cyprus, consisting of a flared and roughly fluted columnar base supporting a broad, shallow bowl or *phiale*.

Scattered among the ruins are mills for grinding wheat — made of volcanic stone — and deep bowls probably used for crushing grapes for wine or olives for oil. Given the liturgical centrality of bread and wine for the liturgy, and the sacral function of oil for anointing (chrism or extreme unction; an oil blessed by a bishop), these are eloquent signifiers of the diurnal religious activities which took place here centuries ago when a small monastic community may have been supported by local benefaction and the donations of pilgrims.

The existence of a substantial baptistery and baptismal font at Agia Trias points to the significance of the church in the region. In most cases, construction of a baptistery of such scale and elaboration would have indicated the presence of a bishop. According to Tertullian (140- c. 230 CE) in his work *On Baptism* there were instances when deacons or presbyters, if appointed to do so by a bishop, could administer baptismal rites. There is a similar baptistery at Agios Philon, not far from Agia Trias and also on the Karpas peninsula, but the two baptisteries may not have functioned contemporaneously. If the two baptisteries did function at the same time, this may indicate either a relaxed policy on baptism on Cyprus in the 5th to 6th centuries or, as was sometimes the case in North African early Christian communities, there were competing bishops or Christian sects who both baptized with similar ceremonies.

The baptistery at Agia Trias consists of an atrium with four monolithic columns in the north where witnesses to the baptism would observe the ceremony. Baptism in this period was a theatrical event with an audience for the rites. The spectators would have included the sponsors or guarantors of the initiate's character and sincerity, as well as those who had guided the candidate through their catechumenate and vouchsafed for his or her readiness to enter the faith. At the baptistery at Kourion, on the south coast of Cyprus, there is evidence of hook-like devices in front of the 'stage' recess in which the baptism would take place, so that the drawing back of curtains, revealing the sacred space for the drama of the ritual, would have heightened both the emotional impact and the solemnity of the event.

Since the baptistery of Agia Trias is one of Cyprus's best preserved we should take a moment to discuss the rites and how they relate to the surviving architectural elements. Baptism during this era was most often by full immersion. The baptismal pool or font is a cross-shaped 'processional type' (Fig. 34) where celebrants began the ceremony in a western room sometimes called an *apodyterion* ('changing room'; the

Fig. 34: The cross-shaped processional type baptismal pool at Agias Trias.

term is derived from Roman bath houses) where they would undress and prepare for the rites by renouncing the devil and evil. This room is very clearly visible at Agia Trias just west of the cross-shaped baptismal pool. The celebrant would then enter the central room with the baptismal font and descend down the 3 steps into the pool. They would then be fully immersed by the bishop three times (the number of steps and immersions both symbolic of the Trinity), and ascend the opposite steps and emerge into the eastern room, towards the rising sun. Remember, this would be witnessed by the audience gathered in the atrium for the ceremony. In this last, eastern room, called the *chrismarion*, they would be given white vestments and be anointed with *chrism* (sanctified oil) and perhaps receive the laying on of hands, which would complete the rituals of the entry into the Christian religion. This eastern room has an apse: this may be where the bishop stood for the anointing ceremony, since apse-shaped (semi-circular) architectural niches often indicate sacred spaces.

Other such cross-shaped processional baptismal pools can be found elsewhere on Cyprus, including the aforementioned basilica of Agios Philon and the basilica of Epiphanios at Salamis (Constantia). In some, such as those at Kourion and Epiphanios, the baptismal water was heated by an underground furnace to make celebrants and the presiding bishop more comfortable by warming the water. At both Kourion and Agios Philon there is evidence of later alterations of the cruciform font whereby arms of the cross were blocked off in order to facilitate infant baptism, which became increasingly the norm in later centuries as adult conversion became less common and children were born into already established Christian families. Precious water was also thereby saved with the smaller fonts.

The cross-shape of these baptismal fonts was highly symbolic. The four arms, filled with water, paralleled the promise of salvation in the Four Rivers of Paradise. In some North African cruciform 'processional' fonts mosaic decorations of flowing streams, fish, plants and birds make the Garden of Paradise symbolism even more explicit. They alluded directly to the heaven the baptized could hope to attain upon becoming Christian. In some instances, pipes and continuous drains permitted water to flow through the font, creating an impression of a natural stream and 'living waters' paralleling the River Jordan, in which Christ was baptized by John. The cruciform shape also alluded to Christ's death on the cross and, eventually, his resurrection. So the descent into the font was also a metaphorical descent into a watery tomb, and a symbolic death — of the former, sinful self — and one's re-emergence from the font indicated the promise of resurrection and a new, eternal life free of sin, which is also why the celebrants move from west to east, towards the rising sun. The time or baptism was also significant. Although in theory baptism could take place at any time of the year, there were favorite times for the rites, such as Easter, when the metaphor of Christian resurrection was especially powerful.

Sources for Agia Trias: Allan Langdale, "The Architecture and Mosaics of the Basilica of Agia Trias in the Karpas Peninsula, Cyprus," *Journal of Cyprus Studies* 15, n. 37 (2009): 1-18; Demetrios Michaelides, "Mosaic Pavements from Early Christian Cult Buildings in Cyprus", in *Mosaic Floors in Cyprus*, (Ravenna: Mario Lapucci, Edizione del Girasole, 1988), 81-151; A.H.S. Megaw, "Interior Decoration in Early Christian Cyprus", in *Rapports et Co-Rapports, XV Congrès International d'Études Byzantines*, Athens, 1976.

Basilica at Soli, Gemikonaği/Karavostasi early 5th century CE

[35° 08' 27.00" N / 32° 48' 47.03" E]

The basilica at Soli, found on the coast near Güzelyurt/Morphou Bay in western Cyprus, is one of the largest of Cyprus's early Christian structures. The city of Soli was a wealthy Greco-Roman port founded around the 6th century BCE, although habitation of the immediate region dates back to the Neolithic age, circa 1100 BCE. (If you drive just a few kilometres to the west, to Yeşilirmak, off the point you will see a dramatic little island called Petra tou Limniti, where there was a Neolithic settlement). Soli may have been named after the Athenian law-giver Solon. In one story Solon, exiled from Athens, visited a nearby town called Apeia and suggested to its ruler, Philocyprus, that he build a better situated city at a site not far away. This new city became Soli, and it became the central town of one of Cyprus's important kingdoms. In a related story, there was yet another city founded by Solon, also called Soli, on the Cilician coast of Asia Minor, where the citizens spoke a corrupted version of the Greek language, thus giving English the word 'solecism', which means to use a language in a non-standard or deviational way. The Greek geographer Strabo tells us that Soli had temples to Isis and Aphrodite in ancient times and that a friend of Alexander the Great, Stasanor, once ruled there. Probably one of its chief exports was copper, which was mined in the Troodos Mountains to the south. A few kilometres away at the site of Skouriotissa, archaeologists estimated that there were three million tons of slag from that area's copper mining and smelting activities.

Soli's affluence is reflected in the scale of the church and in the extraordinary mosaic floors with inscriptions, complex geometric designs, and figures of ducks, dolphins, a horse, a bear, and other animals. Long exposed to the damaging forces of nature, the entire site was roofed over in 1997 and pedestrian traffic has recently been restricted to a series of elevated walkways built in 2009-10, which help protect the mosaics and *opus sectile* pavements and give a good view of the architectural remains. Both Canadian and American visitors can be proud while visiting the site, as it was excavated by a team from Laval University in Quebec, Canada, from 1964-74, and the recent conservation work and walkway construction was funded by USAID through SAVE (Supporting Activities that Value the Environment), which supported many worthwhile conservation, environmental, and cultural heritage projects on Cyprus between 2005 and 2011.

The historical figure most important to Soli and its early Christian past is St Auxibius, who was the first bishop of Soli in 57 CE and was purportedly baptized by none other than the Evangelist St Mark. Although we cannot be certain, the ruins of the current basilica may well lie on top of the original church founded by Auxibius, or perhaps a martyrium for Auxibius became the focus of veneration for the people of Soli who constructed their basilica over the sacred spot. Certainly, earlier churches were, and are, there. The first large basilica, which was probably built in the 4th century (Basilica A), was demolished, and a new one constructed in the 5th or 6th century CE (Basilica B). Excavations have revealed some instances where one can discern both the earlier and later basilicas. For example, the large stone columns of the later basilica, almost a metre in diametre, which one can see today toppled like dominoes, rested on stone bases cut into the flooring of the earlier church (Fig. 35). The earlier basilica was supported not by stone columns but a series of wooden posts set on stone blocks. Similarly, the floor of one of the site's earliest structures (earlier than the first Basilica A, it is thought) is exposed in a cutaway in the east apse and reveals a mosaic with a partial inscription that reads: "Christ help him who made this mosaic".

The later Basilica B was to witness two of Soli's most tragic moments, a series of Arab raids around 653 CE and a terrible earthquake shortly thereafter. A lengthy inscription, found on a block discovered in the atrium, recorded the atrocities of the raids on Soli and the seismic aftermath:

...by reason of our sins [there was] an attack against the island and many were killed, others were carried off as prisoners, around 120,000, again the following year the island suffered another worse attack, during which were slaughtered more than the previous time and there were taken away thousands more ... and the basilica and all the bishop's household and the place of the holy bishops and other notables ... and the house became a holocaust of fire and in ... other places on the island there occurred the accursed earthquake, another ... [punishment] of God...

The newly established and rapidly expanding Muslim Umayyad Caliphate in Damascus found Cypriot coastal cities easy prey for plunder in these years. The heart-wrenching account is made even more powerful when it is known that the raiding did not cease, eventually leading to the abandonment of the city by the 9th century CE. Still, after the first large raid and the earthquake, the Solians had shown spirit in rebuilding their basilica.

Striking though the architectural remains are, Soli is best known for its beautiful mosaics. These survive from both basilica A and B. The most extensive to survival are found in the west half of the church, where many large rectangles of decorative flooring can be seen. Roundels with swans, pigeons, ducks and bears are found in the northwestern quadrant. Vine motifs and innumerable geometric designs characterize the borders of

Fig. 35: A fallen column from the basilica at ancient Soli.

Fig. 36: Mosaic of a swan from the basilica at ancient Soli (photo USAID, IRG, and the SAVE Project in Cyprus).

the roundels and the other mosaics in the northwestern section. A few very fine mosaics can be found in a long section down the center of the nave. This band marks the processional path that was the liturgical axis of the body of the church, and it likely led to the central door of the templon screen at the bema or raised platform in and in front of the central eastern apse. One might recall here the mosaics in Agia Trias where there is a similar path of mosaics down the center of the nave, although there this path was also marked by a *solea*. These processional-route mosaics at Soli are finer that the other mosaics in the church, being composed of smaller tesserae and thus done in more detail, indicative of the special and sacred corridor that the priests and bishops through Soli's history would have walked during religious ceremonies. The most complete figurative mosaic floor panel is found in the northwest quadrant and shows a beautiful swan in a roundel surrounded with a frame of lily-like blooms. Another frame has lens-shaped designs that look like paired leaves and a lovely border of vine motifs with partridges pecking at grapes (Fig. 36). The vines spring from elegant *kantharos* (a Greek vase shape) in the corners of the ensemble. The vine motifs are symbolic, as is the vase. A *kantharos* was a vessel in which wine was kept, and the grapevines that spring from it refer to the wine that symbolizes the blood of Christ. To the west of the church is the partly excavated atrium, which was originally, as at the basilicas at Salamis, a large open square surrounded on all sides with a covered arcade. Remnants of a *phiale*, or fountain pool, have been discovered there. Visitors to Soli can also ascend to the scenic Greco-Roman theater on the hill above the church. The view from the top is worth the climb.

As in many ancient coastal sites in Cyprus, especially those on the north side opposite the Turkish Cilician coast, Soli was robbed of its stones. Luigi Palma di Cesnola, who himself pillaged innumerable tombs during his tenure as American consul in Ottoman-period Cyprus, bemoaned the boats that regularly sailed to the area in the 19th century, bringing timber in their holds but leaving with cut stones pulled from the ancient structures of Soli including, no doubt, the basilica and the theater as well as other now lost monuments. The temples to Aphrodite and Isis seem to have been completely dismantled and taken away for other building projects through the centuries. When the Englishman Richard Pococke visited Soli in 1738 he noted substantial architectural remains that he characterized as "most remarkable". He saw giant stone piers with Corinthian capitals that had held up arches. By the time 19th century travellers like D. G. Hogarth and di Cesnola arrived, these magnificent remnants of Soli's glorious past had vanished.

Sources for Soli: Jeffery, 418-20; David S. Neal, *The Basilica at Soli, Cyprus: A Survey of the Buildings and Mosaics* (USAID and SAVE Project in Cyprus), 2010.

The Lambousa Fish Traps, near Alsançak/Karavas, 7th century

[35° 21' 29.58" N / 33° 11' 52.66" E]

On the north coast, just a few miles west of Kyrenia and about a mile north of Alsançak/Karavas, is the ancient site of Lambousa, a town founded by Phoenician traders about 2800 years ago and which continued to thrive through the Greco-Roman period to the Byzantine era. In 1902 nine remarkable 7th century silver plates were discovered there, an indication of Lambousa's flourishing economy. They show scenes from the life of the Biblical King David, with whom one of the kings of Lambousa identified. Lambousa also had vast mulberry groves and their leaves provided food for silkworms and a thriving silk industry.

At that time were carved, in the living rocks of the seashore, a complex series of fish traps and tanks, the weathered remnants of which are still visible today. (Note: They are not easy to find. One can drive to a parking lot at the church of St Evlalios and then hike east about 1 km along the seaside east until you find them. Don't worry about old rusted 'do not enter' Turkish military signs). There are three main tanks, two of them much eroded by the waves of the past 1400 years. One can plainly see the rock-cut channels leading to and from the main holding tanks and the subsidiary, smaller ponds. The largest of the traps is the most impressive, a rectangle of about 30 by 20 metres in size, with three of its four sides in an excellent state of preservation with only the seaward edge having succumbed to the scouring of the waves (Fig. 37). Maybe schools of fish were lured into the traps at high tide, and then the intricate arrangement of sluices was shut off when the tides receded. Perhaps small boats corralled schools and drove them into shore where they sought refuge in the narrow channels, only to find these shut behind them. However they worked, they evidently did work, and they are fascinating because they represent the ingenuity of the ancient peoples and a unique aspect of the daily life of these shore dwellers whose lives were so intimately connected with the sea.

Sources for Lambousa Fish Traps (and 'David' Plates): K. Nicolaou and A. Flinder, "Ancient Fish Tanks at Lapithos, Cyprus," *The International Journal of Nautical Archaeology and Underwater Exploration* 5, n. 2 (1976): 133-141. The silver plates found at Lambousa have generated substantial scholarship. For a recent and in-depth treatment, which includes the substantial bibliography, see Ruth E. Leader, "The David Plates Revisited: Transforming the Secular in Early Byzantium," *The Art Bulletin* 82, n. 3 (Sept. 2000): 407-427.

Fig. 37: The large rock-cut fish trap at Lambousa.

Early Christian Basilicas, Afendrika (aka Aphendrika, Asphronisy, Urania), 6th century CE, 10th century CE and later

[35° 38' 52.13" N / 34° 26' 27.48" E]

Afendrika was a large coastal city on the northern edge of the upper Karpas peninsula that flourished in Hellenistic and early Christian times. On the north coast, it was well-situated as a port for trade with the south coast of Asia Minor and the Middle East. Never excavated, though surveyed by the famous Swedish expedition of the late 1920s and early 1930s, the extensive ruins of the sizeable city still remain underground. Three major churches from later eras, however, still survive side by side: Agios Georgios, Agios Asomatos, and Panagia Chrysiotissa (Fig. 38). The dating of these latter two churches was for a long time indeterminate, mostly because the Asomatos and Chrysiotissa structures were perplexing conglomerations of the fabrics of earlier and later churches. Camille Enlart was so impressed at the similarities between these churches and Romanesque churches of France that he incorrectly dated them quite late—12th century—to correspond with that style of architecture in France. Thus the Chysiotissa and the Asomatos were wonderful puzzles for architectural historians. It was A.H.S. 'Peter' Megaw, one of the great scholars of Cypriot architecture, who first proposed that the Chrysiotissa was a really a set of three consecutive churches from the 6th, 10th, and 16th centuries, and the Asomatos two churches from the 6th and 10th centuries. Megaw was essentially correct, however, the 10th century date for the reconstructions/renovations from timber roofed basilicas to barrel vaulted ones was challenged by Andreas Dikigoropoulos in the 1950s. One of the assumptions that both historians and architectural historians such as Megaw had made was that, owing to repeated raiding by Arabs between the middle of the 7th century to the middle of the 9th century, it was unlikely that major church building would have taken place. But the historical record demonstrated that Cyprus continued to be quite prosperous during this era, and thus Dikigoropoulos suggested that the churches had indeed been ruined in the 7th to 8th century, but had been rebuilt with barrel vaulting right away, without a protracted period of abandonment and ensuing ruination.

The most interesting of the trio is Panagia Chrysiotissa, where the ruins of two successive early Byzantine churches were augmented with a much later and much smaller construction — probably from the later years of Venetian rule on Cyprus in the 16th century — added inside the earlier plans. Very little of the original 6th century church survives, but one can still see parts of its old semi-circular apse behind the newer

Fig. 38: View of the Byzantine churches of Afendrika.

Fig. 39: The church of Panagia Chrysiotissa, Afendrika, with parts from the 6th, 10th, and 16th centuries.

church. Exploration northeast of the apse reveals a sacred cavern which has curious shelves carved into its walls and channels for water. It gave access to a well from which worshippers could obtain the blessings of holy waters. The floor is littered with pottery fragments, supporting this idea. The many carved shelves may have been used for votive lamps or candles. At the far end of the cavern is a well so deep one cannot see the bottom of it. If you bring a flashlight (one should always have one or two if exploring on Cyprus) you can also see ladder notches in the well's walls, presumably carved there during the digging of the well itself. Look carefully at the wall to the left of the top of the well. There's a hole in the wall with a basin carved into it. Note that this basin leads to a channel cut into the wall that runs along the wall for several feet. Someone brought the water up from the well and poured it into the basin, from which the water would flow down the channel so devotees could collect vials of the healing water or even drink it.

The Chrysiotissa began as a 5th or 6th century timber-roofed basilica probably much like the basilica of Agia Trias. Some of the remnants of this earliest church include the stone columns incorporated into the arches on the south side of the Venetian-era structure (Fig. 39), although the inner part of the large apse is also from this earlier church. A later construction from around the 8th century was built incorporating some of the then long ruined stones of the earliest church. This 8th century version was also large, more or less the same size as its 6th century predecessor. But this later church was vaulted, and one can still see the slight curves at the tops of the walls along the south flank of the ruins (this would have been the south side aisle). Then, when the 8th century church was long since decayed, the smaller 16th century building was constructed on its ruins, abutting what was left of the earlier walls. It is this last church, built during the Venetian era, which one sees most clearly today.

Agios Asomatos, about 100 metres south of the Chrysiotissa, is also a complicated hybrid of earlier and later structures (Fig. 40). Its history is similar. The Asomatos church, too, began as a 5th to 6th century timber-roofed basilica. The large masonry blocks of the apse area belong to this early basilica. Look closely and see if you can discern the large, squared masonry blocks of the early church as compared to the smaller and more irregular masonry of the later church. If one looks low down along the interior north wall, one can see parts of the columns from the early church that were used as foundations for the barrel vaulted 8th century church, which is mostly what one sees remaining today. The vault of the south side aisle is mostly intact. One must envision a larger but similar vault over the nave and the north side aisle as well. Its sturdy piers and its triple apse (*trichonos*) formation make it a typical Cypriot formation. It would have been quite dark inside, with only a few small windows.

Fig. 40: The church of Agios Asomatos, Afendrika, with parts from the 6th and 10th centuries.

The fates of these churches are, in a way, typical for Cyprus and linked to the island's history. Megaw noted that many of Afendrika's earlier buildings probably fell into ruin during the hard times between 750 and 965 CE, when Cyprus was repeatedly invaded by Arab fleets and pirates, although Slobodan Ćurčić has argued that Cyprus's numerous earthquakes are also likely culprits in the destruction of Cypriot churches of the period. Perhaps both are right, recalling the account in the earlier entry on Soli regarding the destructiveness of both Arab raiding and earthquakes. While it is true that Cyprus gained greater stability under firmer Byzantine control after 965 CE, as mentioned above, Dikigoropoulos convincingly argued that the churches were likely rebuilt earlier. Despite numerous setbacks, then, there is evidence that the Cypriots continued to build, rebuild and renovate their cities and churches through the period of repeated upheaval.

Agios Georgios is the smallest of the three Afendrika churches. The supporting drum of its single dome is still visible and is not circular in shape (Megaw aptly describes it a "square with rounded corners") and is carried on transverse arches, a system later rejected by Cypriot builders, as was the imperfect dome shape. It is thought that this church represents an early experiment with the dome on Cyprus dating from around 975 CE, roughly contemporary with the Asomatos restoration. Just south of the churches one can find a dirt road that curves up the hill to the south. You may have to go through some goat or sheep pens. Watch out for those rams and billy goats and be careful with the gates as the kids will make a dash for it. On the crest of the hill you will be on the acropolis of Afendrika, from which there is a wonderful view of the churches, the expanse of the unexcavated city site, and the blue sea beyond.

Sources for Afendrika Churches: Enlart, 304-6; G. Jeffery, 257-8; A. H. S. Megaw, et. al., "Three Vaulted Basilicas in Cyprus," *The Journal of Hellenic Studies* 66 (1946): 48-56; Slobodan Ćurčić, "Byzantine Architecture on Cyprus: An Introduction to the Problem of the Genesis of a Regional Style," in *Medieval Cyprus: Studies in Art, Architecture, and History in Memory of Doula Mouriki.* Eds. Nancy Patterson Sevcenko and Christopher Moss (Princeton: Princeton University Press, 1999): 71-80 and figs. 1-22; Charles Anthony Stewart, "The First Vaulted Churches in Cyprus," *Journal of the Society of Architectural Historians* 69, n. 2 (June, 2010): 162-189.

The Sykha (Sykhada) Church (aka Panagia Afendrika) 6th century CE, 8-9th century CE about 4 km northeast of Kaleburnu/Galinoporni

[approx. 35° 32' 43.19" N / 34° 19' 54.31" E]

When Megaw wrote his article on the Chrysiotissa and Asomatos churches at Afendrika (previous entry), he included a discussion of the ruins of another remote Karpasian church called the Sykha church (Fig. 41; it is also sometimes referred to as Panagia Afendrika, which can be confusing because it's not at the site called Afendrika). It is in many ways a replica of the Asomatos church and has a similar scale, plan, and building history, having originated as a 5th or 6th century timber-roofed basilica and having been rebuilt in the late 8th century as a barrel vaulted structure. The Sykha church is very overgrown now but one can still make out the principal parts. The vaulting of the south side aisle is mostly intact, and parts of the north side aisle are also still standing. Like the Asomatos church, it had the typical Cypriot *trichonos* or three-apse formation. The Sykha church also has what seems to be a substantial narthex at the west end. Its walls are intact and it may belong to a period after the 8th century.

This church is not easy to find. Drive east on the main road from Kaleburnu for a couple of kilometres and keep your eye on the hills to the north (your left). Look for the pattern of three triangular, low, conical-shaped hills in a row all of about the same size. Park where you can and walk or drive on any dirt track (be careful of farmers' crops) towards these three hills. The church ruins are in what appears to be an area with low trees and bushes about 200 m from the hills' base. You have to get pretty close to be able to actually see the church. My GPS co-ordinates for this church may not be dependable, but they're close.

Sources for Sykha Church: Enlart, 307-8; A. H. S. Megaw, et. al., "Three Vaulted Basilicas in Cyprus," *The Journal of Hellenic Studies* 66 (1946): 48-56; Charles Anthony Stewart, "The First Vaulted Churches in Cyprus," *Journal of the Society of Architectural Historians* 69, n. 2 (June, 2010): 162-189.

Agios Philon, near Dipkarpaz/Risokarpaso, 12th century and ruins of the late 5th century CE

[35° 37' 48.82" N / 34° 22' 26.14" E]

The basilica of Agios Philon is on the north coast of the Karpas peninsula, just a few kilometres north of the town of Dipkarpaz/Risokarpaso (Fig. 42). It marks the site of an ancient town called Carpasia (or Karpasia), which was southwest along the coast from ancient Afendrika. Not much of the ancient town survives (recall from Soli that many stones were taken from the ruins of several of the north coast's ancient cities). When Richard Pococke visited in 1738 there was much more to be seen, including a long section of city wall extending from the port.

> We arrived at Carpass [Dipkarpaz/Rizokarpaso], and went about two miles northwards to the plain and to old Carpasy, called by the ancients Carpasia, the capital city of the kingdom of that name, which is now given to all the country. The island here is only three miles and three quarters broad. There are some ruins at old Carpass, especially the remains of a wall near half a mile in circumference, with a pier from it into the sea, at the end of which there are some signs of a tower. The whole seems to have been only a castle for the defence of the port. To the east there is a very good church in the Greek style...
>
> *[Excerpta Cypria, 257]*

This "very good church", now in ruins, occupies a picturesque location on a sea cliff. The church's three apses still survive, as do its south wall and parts of its façade and north wall. A section of one of the pendentives, which carried the most recent church's single dome, arcs gracefully in the structure's upper levels. Some of the heavy, rectangular piers still tower in the church's interior. Like Afendrika, the ruins seen here today are of a church built over the remains of earlier versions. The earliest church may have been the 'metropolis' (cathedral) of the See of the Karpas as Carpasia was the main city in the area in the 6th century. St Philon was said to have been made bishop of the Karpas by none other than St Epiphanios of Salamis himself. Constantius, the Archbishop of Sinai, visited Cyprus in 1766 and as part of his diary he recorded the story of St Philon.

> Then Carpasia, one of the most noble cities of the island, where Philo, the commentator on the Scriptures, was bishop. As a deacon he was at Rome, in the train of Pulcheria, the sister of [emperors] Arcadius and Honorius. There she fell sick, and learning that God

Fig. 42: The Byzantine church of Agios Philon, Carpasia.

Fig. 43: The apses of the Byzantine church of Agios Philon. Note the lower sections where one can see three successive apses from churches from three different periods: 6th, 10th, and 12th centuries.

healed the sick by the hand of Epiphanios, bishop of Constantia [Salamis], Philo was sent to bring the saint to Rome. He came to Cyprus, and, following a revelation from above, Epiphanios about A. D. 401 consecrated him bishop of Carpasia, and being himself about to sail for Rome, left Philo in charge of the church at Constantia.

[Excerpta Cypria, 316]

The earlier basilica, from the late 5th or 6th century CE, was about a third larger than the later one from the 12th century that we see today. Only parts of the outline of the earlier building are visible, mostly on the northern side. The history of the successive structures can be apprehended by looking at the three apses on the exterior (Fig. 43). There are three sets of apses, one built atop the other (not exactly matching, but pretty close on the central apse). The lowest one belongs to the early timber-roofed basilica of around the 5th to 6th century CE, the second belongs to a church that was likely from around the 10th century, while the last one, the current structure (much smaller than the previous two), probably dates from around the 12th century. One can thus discern the three principal stages of the structure's development.

South of the church are the remnants of several ruins dating from the same era as the 5th century basilica and later. In this area a large rock-cut cistern can be found below ground, presumably a water supply for the dry months. There is a processional type baptistery just south of the church, as at Agia Trias, and a large courtyard for spectators of the baptismal rites. This courtyard has a circular *opus sectile* pavement reminiscent of the one in the baths east of the basilica of Campanopetra in Salamis/Constantia. The organisation of these structures on the ground is not as clear as at Agia Trias, and there is some indication that the cross-shaped processional type of baptismal font at Agios Philon may have been blocked up or reduced to facilitate infant baptism.

While the church may seem inelegant in its sturdiness, therein also lies its beauty and geometric balance. Blind arch motifs provided articulation for the mural surfaces of the exterior, a motif reminiscent of the Romanesque architecture of Western Europe. But even closer prototypes exist just across the water in nearby Syria, notably in the church of Saint Symeon, not far from Aleppo.

Sources for Agios Philon: Jeffery, 254, Gunnis, 413.

Panagia Kanakaria, Boltaşli/Lythrangomi various phases 6th to 8-9th century and later additions

[35° 28' 41.92" N / 34° 09' 55.75" E]

Panagia Kanakaria is one of the most sacred of the Byzantine Cypriot churches and is located in a small village called Boltaşli/Lythrangomi in the lower Karpas (Fig. 44). Remnants of the apse date back to the 6th century but the structure underwent several repairs and enlargements over the years. One can also see part of a monastic complex and the ruins of several associated buildings dating from the 17th-18th century. Abandoned olive presses and giant millstones found in the yard give some idea of the agricultural activities of the monks who lived here over the centuries. One enormous millstone may have come from an ancient Hellenistic community that was situated on the rocky escarpment above the village. Some blocks of stone for the church's rebuilding campaigns may also have been taken from the ruins of that ancient town.

This church was the subject of an extensive study by two great scholars of Cypriot Byzantine architecture, A. H. S. Megaw and E. J. W. Hawkins, whose determinations on the building's history are still authoritative, even though some of his conclusions have been challenged. Unfortunately for the modern visitor the church is often locked. However, it is possible to obtain the key from the *muhktar* of the village of Boltaşli, who lives less than a kilometre away [Continue east on the main road for .5 km, turn left at the second road, go up about 200 metres, turn left, go 50 metres and his house is the first on the left]. Some planning and patience is therefore required if one wants to visit the interior. Barring this, the exterior of the structure is sufficiently fascinating in itself.

Of the first, early Christian church on the site virtually nothing remains, though whatever structure might have existed on this spot in the distant past may well have resembled in plan, size, and elevation the basilica of Agia Trias, which was timber roofed and is also on the Karpas peninsula (see earlier entry). The three capitals and one column base found lying on the ground in front of Panagia Kanakaria may have come from the nave colonnade of the early basilica, and the smaller column fragment that lies there may have been part of the portico of an early atrium peristyle. Some column bases, also possibly from the original structure's atrium, were reused in the monastery building's arcade just a few feet away.

Panagia Kanakaria is a striking work of architecture, conveying a sense of harmony despite its many drastic renovations and additions. Indeed, the signs of these many reconstructions are only apparent with careful observation. Aspects of the church's complex architectural history can be found, firstly, in the east end of the church and its three

Fig. 44: The church of the Panagia Kanakaria from the southwest, Boltaşlı/Lythrangomi.

Fig. 45: The church of the Panagia Kanakaria from the southeast, with apses, Boltaşlı/Lythrangomi.

135

apses (Fig. 45). The central apse is uncharacteristically large for the girth of the nave, spanning the entire width and thus dominating the central portion of the east end. This is partly because the masonry visible there today is a secondary sheathing covering and strengthening fragments of an earlier apse inside (yet, interestingly, this was revealed by taking away a more modern sheathing that was trapping water and hindering drainage). Close observation of the central apse's roofline also reveals that, while the south part of the apse is semi-circular, at the north end it becomes slightly polygonal. The three windows are unusually low to the ground and are also uncommonly wide for a Byzantine church, having been enlarged to allow more light into the apse interior in modern times. In addition, the apses of the side aisles are different from each other. The southern apse is higher and wider than the northern one, reflecting the differences in the heights and widths of the respective interior aisles. These two apses also had different functions inside the church. The southern apse functioned as the *diaconicon* while the north apse was the *prothesis* of the church. Structurally, these variant side aisles also provided buttressing for the church's vaults and, later, dome. C. A. Stewart has suggested that the Kanakaria was the first of the 'Afendrika class' churches (which includes the Kanakaria, the Asomatos, the Sykha, and the Chrysiotissa churches; see entries above) to be barrel vaulted.

One can discern variations in other parts of the church's masonry that give a sense of the instances of renovation, such as the seam in the southwest wall that demarks the addition (and/or later repair) of that part of the narthex. If one goes to the fields just north of the church and looks at the north wall, one can see how the building of the north aisle (or, more probably, the raising of the north aisle) cropped the bottoms of two windows. Invisible from the ground are a similar series of windows almost completely blocked by the higher south aisle. When you're inside the church look carefully at the piers of the nave that hold up the dome. Notice that they have been modified and added on to over the years, creating a kind of composite appearance. What this represents is the piers being called upon to do more and more 'work' over the centuries as the church's superstructure was changed and enlarged. When barrel vaults were added, they needed stronger piers, and when a dome was added, the piers needed to be strengthened yet again.

The church is best known today not so much for its architecture but for the infamous theft of its 6th century apse mosaic of the Virgin and Child in the mid-1970s. Thankfully, this magnificent work of art was recovered, along with other mosaics depicting several saints, and these can now be seen in the Makarios Cultural Center in Nicosia. Some mosaic fragments and frescoes still survive in place in the dark interior of the church, some of these dating from as early as the 13th century.

One of the additions to the building was a small domed porch over the south entrance. In the lunette above the doorway is a much damaged but still legible fresco from the 15th century depicting the Virgin Mary and the infant Christ on her lap. Two small donor figures kneel in supplication and worship at the bottom left. The donors wear Latin clothes and resemble other such kneeling donor figures in Cypriot art.

The narthex of the structure has a drum and a dome at the center (the drum, like the side aisles, having blocked an earlier window of what had been the earlier facade), and by the doorway an inscription giving a date of 1779 for some reconstruction done by Abbot Chrysanthos after some damage: "1779 Chrysanthos, monk and abbot, defrayed the cost of this building March 15." An English traveller, Alexander Drummond, who passed through in 1750, saw only the drum of the narthex dome intact; the curvature of the dome having fallen. It could be that Abbot Chrysanthos made repairs from damage from a severe earthquake in 1735 that ruined many buildings on Cyprus.

Probably the latest addition to the church's architecture was the small belfry or bell tower on the northwest corner of the church. As recently as the 1960s another bell tower survived just above the central doorway, partially blocking out the narthex dome. The monastic buildings to the south are probably not any more than a couple of centuries old, though the ruined ones to the north were likely older and perhaps even represented the location of the first monastic structures around the church. However, until scientific excavation of the entire area is undertaken, much of the earliest history of the Kanakaria and its satellite buildings will remain unknown.

There are a few theories about what 'Kanakaria' means. Probably the most convincing explanation is that the name referred to a now lost icon of the Virgin Mary holding the Christ Child. Specifically, 'Kanakaria' may be related to the Greek word *Kanaki*, which means 'caress'. Since one of the most common types of icon is one where the Virgin caresses the child (usually called the Virgin *Glykophilousa* or the Virgin *Elousa*), 'Kanakaria' might be a local appellation for an icon which depicted just such a tender moment between Mary and the infant Jesus. Kanakaria also means 'dearest' or 'darling', but, with either meaning the sentiment refers to the Virgin in an endearing or tender way.

One of my most powerful memories of the Kanakaria is of Easter day of 2007. That day the church door was already open and inside was a woman about forty years of age. She looked almost dazed. As she looked around, grasping a kerchief in her hands, I saw a tear fall down her cheek. "Hello" I said to her in Greek, being pretty sure she was Greek Cypriot. She looked at me and began crying. The last time she had been here was on Easter day of 1974, when she was à village girl of only seven. She could see in her imagination the flying banners, the brightly coloured decorations, the resplendent iconostasis, the crowds of happy celebrants, the smell of incense, and could hear again the resonant chanting of the priest. She could remember the still intact and radiant ancient 1400 year old image of the Virgin and Child still in the apse. She had herself, now, a daughter of seven and had returned alone to rediscover something of her recollections of the past. Perhaps she wanted to reconnect with something lost, so she could share her past with her daughter. I left the church to let her have it to herself for awhile. When she left, she grasped my hand for a moment and said, "thank you". From that point on I've always entered the Kanakaria with a feeling of reverence for that woman's memories.

Sources for Panagia Kanakaria: Jeffery, 261-3; A. H. S. Megaw and E. J. W. Hawkins, *The Church of the Panagia Kanakaria at Lythrankomi in Cyprus. Its Mosaics and Frescoes*, Dumbarton Oaks Studies No. 14, 1977; Andreas and Judith A. Stylianou, *The Painted Churches of Cyprus* (London: Trigraph and the Leventis Foundation, 1985), 43-48; Charles Anthony Stewart, "The First Vaulted Churches in Cyprus," *Journal of the Society of Architectural Historians* 69, n. 2 (June, 2010): 162-189.

Panagia tou Kyra, Sazliköy/Livadia, 7th and 12th century with later additions

[35° 24' 18.01" N / 34° 01' 48.01" E]

This small Byzantine church is one of the jewels of the lower Karpas region of Cyprus (Fig. 46). The word 'Kyra' may be related to the Latin 'Kyrie' used in the Latin mass, meaning 'lord', here feminized, or, similarly, a short form of 'Kyria', which one calls a woman one respects; here, obviously, the Virgin Mary, to whom the church was dedicated. Nestled at the foot of a rocky hill and hidden from the coastal raids of the Arab pirates who regularly assaulted the coasts of the island from the 7th to the 10th century, Panagia Kyra is typical of the tiny, chapel-like rural churches that must have been very numerous in Cyprus centuries ago. It was constructed in an area that seems to have been active with olive oil production and/or the grinding of wheat, perhaps as early as Hellenistic times, owing to the substantial remains of large millstones nearby. There are substantial wheat fields in the area even today. Indeed, the immediate region is very rich agriculturally, and in the Middle Ages, as we know from records of the Cartulary of the Cathedral of Santa Sophia in Nicosia, in 1197 Joscius, archbishop of Tyre, was awarded by King Amaury of Cyprus the *casale* (agricultural region) of Livadia and the right to import and export without charges. There is also evidence of an ancient underground tomb or cistern, now filled in. It is certainly possible that this place was a revered spot even in pagan times with a sacred spring located here. Excavations have never been done to reveal the earlier plan of the church or even monastic buildings that may have existed on this spot at an earlier date. In the interior of the church, inset horizontally high in the north wall, are two marble posts which came from the sanctuary screen (*templon*) of an earlier edifice.

The church has a cruciform, Greek cross plan with a single, conical dome that's not quite circular. The apse is likely the only part of the 6th-7th century church that survives, while the nave and dome probably date from the 10-12th century. In even later years a narthex was added and an enclosure on the south side, this last component upsetting the geometric equilibrium of the original structure.

Inside the church there is an opening in the floor which leads to a holy well (*ayasma*) which was once fed by a spring, supplying water for holy services. This cave extends far under the church towards the hillside but has filled in over the centuries. I had a student who told me that when he was seven years old his father and uncle made him go down the hole and explore the tunnel, presumably to see if he could find some treasure or artifacts. He went a few yards and then was too scared to proceed, but said that it seemed to go on for as far as he could see in the dim light. Please

Fig. 46: The church of the Panagia Kyra, near Sazlıköy/Livadia.

avoid the temptation to send your own offspring down there. There also seems to have been a low dam constructed behind the church to withhold water from the hills in a catchment area, perhaps holding back water for irrigation purposes. If you climb up into the hills nearby — which you should do because it's a lovely view — you can see how the church rests at the bottom of the hill's drainage area. The low land just beyond to the west was evidently amply fed by the waters coming from these hills as both the Turkish and Greek names for the village indicate a somewhat marshy area. In Greek, 'Livadia' means 'meadow' and 'Sazliköy' means 'village of reeds.' This ready supply of seasonal water, however, is also the cause of much of the building's current conservation problems, as the poor drainage around the church has allowed dampness to penetrate the walls. The frescoes, parts of which may well date from the 12-13th century, are almost completely destroyed because of it and even the sandstone blocks are disintegrating from the moisture. At one time an image of the Christ Pantocrator graced the dome of the Kyra church.

Tragically, the 6th-7th century mosaic of the orant Virgin Mary and infant Christ in the apse, parts of which had survived until modern times, was stolen or destroyed around 1979 and never seen again. Not much of the mosaic survived except for the right side of the Virgin's body with her right arm, part of her purple mantle (the *maphorion*) on her shoulder, and a tiny section of Mary's halo, all against a golden background. This mosaic, showing Mary with her arms outstretched in a form of worship called an 'orant' pose, was an important work because it survived the iconoclastic period in Byzantine art (8th century) when many frescoes and mosaics were destroyed throughout the empire. Only fragmentary glass tesserae in the plaster remain today. However, even before 1979 not much was left of the mosaic, partially because of a local superstition that if you pulled out a piece of the mosaic and carried it in your pocket, you would be cured of acne or diseases of the blood. The image's own miraculous efficacy thus doomed it to eventual destruction. Gunnis noted a fine 18th century iconostasis in the church in the 1930s, with icons dating from 1702 and 1708. What became of these we do not know.

Sources for Panagia Kyra: Jeffery, 250; Gunnis, 328; A.H.S. Megaw and E. J.W. Hawkins, "A Fragmentary Mosaic of the Orant Virgin in Cyprus," *Actes du XIV Congres International de Etudes Byzantines*, Bucharest, 6-12 Sept. 1971, vol. III, pp. 363-366; George Jeffery, "Byzantine Churches on Cyprus," *Proceedings of the Society of Antiquaries* 28 (1916): 111-184, esp. p.122-3; Andreas and Judith A. Stylianou, *The Painted Churches of Cyprus* (London: Trigraph and the Leventis Foundation, 1985), 52; J. L. La Monte, "A Register of the Cartulary of the Cathedral of Santa Sophia of Nicosia," *Byzantion* 5 (1929-30): 447; *The Cartulary of the Cathedral of Holy Wisdom of Nicosia*, eds. N. Coureas and C. Schabel (Cyprus Research Centre: Nicosia, 1997), no, 46.

Lusignan, Venetian, and Ottoman Cyprus

Byzantine/Orthodox Architecture of the Medieval Period

Antiphonitis, Bahçeli/Kalogrea, 12th to 15th century

[35° 19' 38.29" N / 33° 37' 08.08" E]

Tucked into a scenic cleft in the northern slopes of the Kyrenia mountain range about a half an hour east of Kyrenia is the Byzantine church of Antiphonitis (Fig. 47). The nearest village is Bahçeli/Kalogrea, but most people get there today via the town of Esentepe/Agios Ambrosios. The church gets its name from the *Antiphon*, which is a part of the Orthodox liturgy where a priest sings a line of chant and the laity responds by singing a response. This 'call and response' structure is integral to the Orthodox mass. The interior organisation of this church, with its open and roughly circular nave and dome, may well have provided a particularly good acoustic environment for the sonic aspects of the Orthodox ritual.

This church is rather unique in plan, with a Gothic arched narthex and a series of columnar piers inside creating an irregular, octagonal nave. In this respect it is reminiscent of the famous Byzantine church of San Vitale in Ravenna, Italy. In its general plan, Antiphonitis also echoes the designs of well-known Byzantine churches in Greece such as the famous monastery church at Hosios Loukas. From the exterior the church might appear to have a typical basilical plan, but in the interior the novel elements of the structure become more apparent. The shape of the nave is reflected in the dome, which is not quite circular (recall the 'squared circle' dome of Agios Georgios at Afendrika and Panagia Kyra). In this dome survives the best preserved fresco of Christ Pantocrator remaining in northern Cyprus, despite the vandalism of two shotgun blasts pocking the figure.

The interior still has numerous frescos dating from the 12th to the 15th centuries. Tragically, many parts of the impressive Tree of Jesse fresco, which had dominated the south wall, were stolen in 1975. The frescoes were retrieved by the authorities, but the images of the 'Ancestors of Christ' had been cut up into separate panels. Criminals also damaged the angel frescoes in the apse in an attempt to extract their faces. During the medieval period the church was patronized by the Lusignan royal family, who added an elegant loggia, once roofed with timbers and tiles, to the south side of the church. One can see the symbols of the Lusignans everywhere there: the rose, the cross with rose, and the singular drop-shaped elements of which there are so many variants in Lusignan architecture, a sort of 'cone and sphere' motif.

Sources for Antiphonitis: Enlart, 206-8; Gunnis, 194-5; Andreas and Judith A. Stylianou, *The Painted Churches of Cyprus* (London: Trigraph and the Leventis Foundation, 1985), 469-485.

Melandryna Monastery and Church of the Panagia, Near Esentepe/Agios Amvrosios, 15th – 17th century

[35° 20' 56.33" N / 33° 36' 34.98" E]

This church, dedicated to the 'Panagia' or most Holy Virgin Mary, is much ruined but majestic in its devastation. It is also not so easy to find but one can drive to within about 100 metres of it. Going east on the main north-coast road out of Kyrenia, keep your eyes open for the turnoff to Esentepe (Note: This is where you would turn off if you were going to Antiphonitis; see previous entry). Go past the Esentepe turnoff for about 3.4 kilometres. You will pass through an area with new housing developments on both sides of the road, go through these and look for a road to your right just after the housing development. It's hard to see, but there's actually a blue street sign for Klavuz Sokak. Turn right and go about 500 metres and park at a sharp turn left in the road. The Melandryna church is close, about 100 metres from the roadway to the south or southwest, depending on where you park your car. You can see it from the road on your right.

Though very dilapidated I like this place very much. It gives a good sense of a medieval Orthodox monastery of medium size, of a kind that was very numerous on Cyprus in ages past. One must use one's imagination to reconstruct the complex in one's mind. The church was originally a 15th century construction, probably very late in Lusignan times or perhaps even the early years of Venetian rule on Cyprus, which began in 1489. Enlart saw some fresco painting here in the 1880s, but these have long gone. He thought that they were in an Italian gothic style, which indicates a 15th century date. Like the church of Agios Sergios in Yeniboğaziçi/Agios Sergios just north of Famagusta, large and sturdy flying buttresses were added to the exterior flanks of the building, presumably because the interior barrel vaults were failing and needed additional support. Indeed, the interior vaults seem to have needed rebuilding at some time after initial construction. The earthquake of 1735 might have been the culprit, though Cyprus has had many serious seismic events over the centuries. Today it is really a shattered structure and it looks as if it will fall into rubble at any moment. Jeffery saw a 16th century iconostasis there in the early 20th century, and although he was not impressed with the icons it is a real tragedy that it has been lost. He thought that it resembled very closely the iconostasis at nearby Antiphonitis, also lost. The ruins of the cloister for the monks can also be seen at Melandryna as well as some later monastic buildings to the west on the flat area above the church.

Sources for Melandryna Monastery: Enlart, 208-9; Jeffery, 235-6; Gunnis, 195.

Church of Panagia Pergaminiotissa, near Tatlısu/Akanthou, 13th – 17th century

[35° 24' 17.72" N / 33° 46' 56.70" E]

This Byzantine church is just 400 metres off the north coast road NE of the town of Tatlısu/Akanthou. If you are driving east from Kyrenia you don't need to go through Tatlısu, but just go past the turn-off for the town and keep going for 3.7 more kilometres, then look for the dirt road on your right. You will be able to see it from the main road. The church's name derives from an ancient town that used to be here, or near here, called Pergamon. It is thought to have been associated with the Melandryna Monastery, which is about 18 km to the west (see previous entry). However, it could have been an independent church enjoying instead the benefaction some higher clergy such as the bishopric. Several other buildings seem to have been in the vicinity, but these were ruined long ago. The church's interior was also extensively frescoed, but these wall paintings were very dilapidated, though recent restoration work funded by USAID has improved their condition. This area, as well as a site nearby known as Aphrodisium (one of the claimants to being the birthplace of the goddess of Love, Aphrodite), await scientific excavation, though the sites have been plundered by locals for centuries. Gunnis reports a place close by where one can find the fossilized remains of pygmy hippopotami. He also notes a small acropolis on the hill and half of an ancient sarcophagus lid that he thought dated from around 400 BCE. Gunnis cites a mid-19th century German volume by Ludwig Ross (*Reisen Nach de Insel Cypern*, 1846), where the author records that he had seen extensive ancient ruins in this area. Exploring might be rewarding in the countryside around here. Bring your hat and camera.

Usually the church is locked, but you might be lucky enough to visit when it is open. The interior of the church is quite dark, but there are a few frescoes that may date from as early as the 12th century, making them very rare survivals even in their fragmentary condition. In the apse one can find a traditional depiction of Mary flanked by the archangels Michael and Gabriel. Some of the better preserved frescoes, however, are found just outside the conch or upper semidome of the apse. The art historian Annemarie Weyl Carr has identified and discussed the subjects of the main narrative portions of these frescoes, high on the north and south walls flanking the bema or the area just in front of the apse. They depict scenes from the *Protevangelium* that tell early stories from the life of the Virgin Mary, including her conception. One of the better preserved of the frescoes shows the Prayer of Anna (south wall, closest to the apse). One can see Anna kneeling in prayer for a child, her body covered in a red mantle. Beside this, one can make out Joachim holding open a book with Anna seated beside him, perhaps the open book representing the episode of the Consultation with the Twelve Tribes. The last image of the triptych shows the meeting of Joachim and Anna as they embrace and kiss, indicating that Anna has told Joachim of her miraculous pregnancy. Below the embracing couple of Joachim and Anna is a figure where the upper, squared half has clearly been cut out by robbers, likely because it was well preserved. At least the lower part of the figure with its impressive costume survives.

Sources for Panagia Pergaminiotissa: Gunnis, 150-1; Müge Şevketoğlu, Hüseyin Küçüksu, Ahmet Asher, *Church of the Panagia Perghamiotissa*. USAID/SAVE, 2009; Annemarie Weyl Carr, "The Program of the Panagia Pergaminiotissa: A Narrative in Perspective," in *Cyprus and the Balance of Empires*, ASOR Archeological Reports Series, ed. Charles A. Stewart. Oxford: Oxbow Books, forthcoming 2012.

Agios Ephimianos (aka Euphemianus/Themonianos), Akdoğan/Lysi, 13th century

[35° 05' 08.65" N / 33° 39' 52.97" E]

This striking, chapel-sized shrine lies in a lonely plain southwest of the town of Akdoğan/Lysi. It consists of a simple Greek cross plan with a single dome and apse (Fig. 48). Marked by a few eucalyptus trees, which were widely planted in Cyprus in the early 20th century to help drain marshy areas in the battle against malaria, the church is surrounded by grain fields quite close to the Green Line. In springtime it is surrounded in spectacular fashion by verdant stalks of wheat and a striking variety of wildflowers. The dome once had a well-preserved fresco of the Christ Pantocrator in its interior, but, as at Panagia Kanakaria and Antiphonitis, robbers cut out the frescoes, smuggled them out of the country, and tried to sell them on the world art market. In the dome one can clearly see the lines from the cuts the thieves made while extracting the sections of the frescoes. However, eventually these frescoes were retrieved. The fresco of the Virgin Mary with the infant Christ in the apse experienced a similar fate. These frescoes, restored by Laurence J. Morrocco, have been on impressive display at a consecrated chapel in the Menil Foundation in Houston, Texas, but were recently returned to Cyprus in March 2012. The frescoes and their fascinating story are the subject of a book by the great scholar of Cypriot Byzantine painting, Annemarie Weyl Carr.

Like Panagia Kyra, this church is one of my favorites. It stands isolated in the fields and served those poor workers who tended the crops in the Middle Ages. One can easily imagine, during the harvests over the centuries, these churches being used for the daily devotions of the peasant labourers.

Sources for Agios Themonianos: Andreas and Judith A. Stylianou, *The Painted Churches of Cyprus* (London: Trigraph and the Leventis Foundation, 1985), 492-5; Annemarie Weyl Carr and Laurence J. Morrocco, *A Byzantine Masterpiece Recovered: the 13th Century Murals of Lysi, Cyprus,* Austin: University of Texas Press and the Menil Foundation, 1991.

Fig. 48: The church of Agios Ephimianos (Themonianos), near Akdoğan/Lysi.

Agios Thrysos, 14-15th century (and nearby Phoenician Statues)

[35° 34' 11.86" N / 34° 15' 25.47" E]

When driving along the north coast road of the Karpas Peninsula it's worth stopping at the church of Agios Thrysos, which is just east of the Theresa Hotel. The more modern 19th century church is visible just off the main road and one can park nearby it and walk down to the beach to the modest medieval church on the seaside. It is a single rectangle with an apse and a small underground chamber or shrine. One still sees votive candles and icons left here by devotees who still venerate the site. It is in a lovely location and gives the impression of solid strength with its large stone blocks, but the salt and damp from the sea is taking its toll on the fabric of the building. While hitch hiking there I was once picked up by a chatty young fellow who said that his father had 'caught' a small golden statuette while fishing nearby. He abruptly forgot how to speak English when I asked him what his father had done with it. Searching for and illegally selling antiquities has long been a veritable second career for many Cypriots.

If you feel like a walk you might consider taking a hike up the dirt road that leads almost directly south from Agios Thrysos. A few hundred metres to the interior, in a small outcrop and copse of small trees one can find a truly remarkable thing: a couple of large Phoenician statues still in the quarry in which they were being roughed out by the sculptors. Unfinished and abandoned at the site, they are nonetheless spectacular finds. One feels like a real archaeologist coming upon them. The Phoenicians had colonies on Cyprus as early as the 9th century BCE, and these statues may date from between that time and the 7th century BCE.

Panagia Elousa, late 14th or early 15th century

[35° 35' 21.12" N / 34° 20' 14.17" E]

This small, two-aisled chapel-like church was part of a small monastery tucked away in the hills of the Karpas Peninsula. The epithet 'Elousa' means 'tender', and refers to any sacred icon of the Virgin Mary who tenderly caresses or rubs cheeks with the infant Christ on her lap. The eponymous icon has of course long since disappeared, and, like many interiors of orthodox churches in the north, the interior is sadly neglected. Ruins of the monastic buildings can be seen near the site. The structure still has its whitewash and makes a striking sight by the nearby groves. One can imagine the small monastic community here and the substantial veneration that this chapel-like church enjoyed in earlier times.

Panagia tou Tochniou Monastery/Buluşa Manastırı, Ağillar/Mandres, church 14th century, additional structures later

[35° 20' 56.04" N / 33° 49' 39.16" E]

Panagia tou Tochniou is a Greek Orthodox church and monastery, known in Turkish as the Buluşa Manastırı (Fig. 49). It's worth visiting simply for the scenic drive to get there, especially resplendent in the springtime. It commands striking mountainside views of the farmlands and olive orchards south towards Işkele/Trikomo. A new road from the village of Ağillar/Mandres gives easy access when as recently as 2004 one had to hike out for miles in fields to find it. A small Greek cross, single dome, single apse church marks this site, its façade facing an open, walled courtyard. Monastic structures surrounded this enclosure, the most modern of which occupy the southern part of the complex, taking advantage of the views to the plains below. Small columns and capitals, likely taken from much older churches, can be seen in some of the older monastic structures in the western and northern part of the complex. Many of the buildings have been heavily restored in recent years. A few fragments of fresco can still be found inside the church. Tochniou gives a good sense of the layout and isolation of the old, medium sized Cypriot mountain monasteries that might have had twenty monks or so (there was a similar modestly sized monastery a few miles east near Kantara).

One of the most interesting features of the monastery is the double gateway. This is often overlooked by visitors since today one enters from the direction of the parking lot. But this modern entry was not the original entrance to the monastery, which led down the hill and towards the agricultural land in the plains below. It's worth going out of the arched gateway off of the southwest corner of the open area in front of the church where one can clearly see the hinges for the old doorways that secured the walled compound at night. Leaving by this portal and walking down the path a bit, one can also get a view of the south façade of the monastery cells and the buttresses supporting that wall on the incline of the slope below. Then, coming back into the monastery, one passes through the entrance trodden by the monks and their donkeys when they returned from the fields and orchards ages ago. In the springtime, one might see wild asparagus hunters in this area. One time at Panagia Tochniou I met a whole family of men hunting asparagus, three generations of them: an old man, his son, and his grandson. They all looked very much alike, as if one was looking at the same man through his different stages of life. Each had verdant bouquets of slender asparagus stalks stuffed into their multiple vest pockets, making them look like fertility gods. The old man was beaming with pride that his son and grandson were great asparagus hunters like him.

Fig. 49: The monastery and church of Panagia tou Tochniou (Buluşa Manastırı), Ağıllar/Mandres.

156

St Barnabas Church and Monastery, various building periods 5th to 19th century, 4 km north of Famagusta

[35° 10' 29.41" N / 33° 52' 50.05" E]

St Barnabas is Cyprus's most important native saint and martyr and the patron saint of Cyprus. He knew several of the apostles, including Saints Peter and Paul, and was known to have traveled through Salamis, his home town, and parts of Asia Minor with Paul in 44-45 CE. He also likely knew the Evangelist St Mark and may even have been related to him. Barnabas was also the first bishop of Salamis. Salamis had a significant Jewish population in Barnabas's day and it was this community that he infuriated with his preaching of the new Christian religion, leading to his martyrdom in Salamis around 70-75 CE.

When he was executed his body was secretly disposed of in a remote marshy area so his burial place would not become a site of Christian veneration. For centuries the site of his grave was thus unknown, but this changed in 478 CE when the Archbishop of Cyprus, Anthemios, had a dream in which he envisioned the location of Barnabas' body. Anthemios excavated the grave and the identity of Barnabas was confirmed by the hand-written copy of St Matthew's gospel which, according to legend, Barnabas was holding at his death. With this 'discovery' of an early Christian martyr, a native of Cyprus, the Cypriot Church now had justification to petition the Patriarch and the Byzantine Emperor Zeno for independence from the suzerainty of the See of Antioch, which the Cypriot Church had been dominated by. The petition was granted and the Cypriot Church became autonomous or 'autocephalous'. The Emperor Zeno provided funds for the founding of the monastery in Barnabas's name, though nothing much remains of the structures from this early time.

The buildings seen today date from the 18th to the 20th century with only fragments from earlier foundations (Fig. 50). At the east end one can discern, in a reconstruction made after excavations in 1934, the curvature of the old apse further east than the current church's apse. There, one can find some marble remnants that may have belonged to the earliest structure, a 5th century basilica, including a small, broken marble *phiale* (its top is missing; compare the one in the atrium of Agia Trias) and some small columns and capitals. One can still see the curving steps of the synthronon for the bishop, indicating the church's status as a 'metropolitan' or cathedral of Salamis. Despite its relative modernity, the significance of the current church of St Barnabas to the Greek Cypriots is such that this building is still one of the most venerated on the island. It is one of the few Greek churches in northern Cyprus that still has its pre-1974 iconostasis with its icons intact. Note that the flanking wings of the iconostasis are later additions, with the central part being older.

Fig. 50: Facade of the church of St Barnabas, in the monastery of St Barnabas, near Famagusta.

At the very top of the iconostasis is a painted crucifix done in a 14th century Gothic style with trefoils at the terminals of the cross. The skull of Golgotha can be seen below Christ's feet. In the four trefoils are the symbols of the evangelists: the Ox at the bottom (St Luke), the winged man on the left (St Matthew), the Lion on the right (St Mark), and the Eagle at the top (St John). Rectangular panels flank the crucifix, with Mary on the left and St John on the right, mourning Christ's death. There are two registers lower down, with many of the older icons arranged across the width of the central part of the iconostasis. In the upper row are images of several saints and martyrs, done in different styles and belonging to different periods. In the register below are scenes both from the life of Mary and the life of Christ, also from varying times. The carving of the wooden superstructure is beautifully done with leaf motifs and decorative 'architectural' elements such as pilasters, capitals, and the elegant row of semi-dome 'arches' with pediments over them in the lower register of the upper section just mentioned. At the far left, in the new part of the iconostasis, are full-length icons of Cypriot saints, from right to left: St Spyridon, St Neophytus, and St Ephimianos.

As you walk around the inside of the church be sure to look up high to the tops of the heavy piers. There you'll see inserted into the corners splendid Corinthian capitals, which likely came from Salamis. They bear some resemblance to the capitals of the basilica of Epiphanios. Note also that the two domes are not circular, but the distinctive, more ovoid 'square with rounded corners' shape that we have seen at Antiphonitis and Panagia Kyra. In the squared apse in the south side there is a fairly modern fresco that shows scenes from the story of the monastery's founding. On the left wall Christ gives the vision to archbishop Anthemios about the location of St Barnabas's body. In the next scene, divided by an inserted classical column with spiral fluting (again, likely from Salamis), we see the scene of the discovery of St Barnabas's tomb and body. Then, on the back wall, Emperor Zeno receives the 'original' copy of the Gospel of Matthew that was found with Barnabas's body. Note the upper background behind the emperor, where the imperial city, Constantinople, is indicated by its high walls and the dome of Hagia Sophia. And this leads, on the right hand wall, to the Church of Cyprus receiving its independence from the See of Antioch. These frescoes, then, established St Barnabas and his church and monastery at the center of the most important single event in the history of the Cypriot church. Note how the inserted spiral-fluted column, clearly an ancient artifact, is used in the decoration to convey the ancient time for the story, thus emphasizing the antiquity of the foundation and of St Barnabas himself.

Just to the east of the church and monastery is a small shrine built in the 1950s to mark the purported grave site of St Barnabas. In fact, the rock-cut tomb beneath the shrine, which one may visit, could be much older than Barnabas's time, and might well belong to the larger series of ancient rock cut tombs found elsewhere in the immediate area (the Royal Tombs are just a few hundred metres away). In 2006 even more rock cut graves were found between the church and the shrine. Since it was common for ancient tombs to be used and reused in subsequent centuries, the tomb may have had many occupants.

The monastery was said to have been inhabited by a few monks, down to only three in the 1970s, and these stayed on briefly even after the Turkish invasion of 1974. Today, the buildings serve as the area's archaeological museum and the church itself has been converted to a museum of icons. Most of the artifacts in the archaeological museum are from the nearby Bronze Age site of Enkomi and include excellent examples of pottery from the Bronze Age through to the Classical and even Venetian Renaissance times.

Sources for St Barnabas: Jeffery, 237-9; Gunnis, 224-5; George Jeffery, "Byzantine Churches on Cyprus," *Proceedings of the Society of Antiquaries* 28 (1916): 111-184, esp. p. 123-4.

Church of the Panagia, Trapeza (aka Panagia Chrysopolitissa) near Famagusta, 13th and 16th century

[35° 07' 57.49" N / 33° 51' 27.90" E]

The extraordinary Trapeza church can be found in the middle of a flat plain at the eastern end of the Mesaoria about 7.5 kilometres northwest of Famagusta (Fig. 51). It is easily visible just south of the main highway to Lefkoşa/Nicosia. This lonely church is all that is left of the medieval village of Trapeza, which was destroyed in 1426 by the Mamluk Sultan of Egypt, whose ire had been raised by the Lusignan kings of Cyprus. After the attack, the only thing that seems to have been left of the earlier Byzantine church at Trapeza was a single dome standing precariously on fragmentary piers. That dome is today the smaller of the church's two domes, which probably date from the 12th or 13th century. In that smaller, older dome one can barely make out a shadowy image of Christ Pantocrator, much damaged by smoke from the fires of shepherds who still sometimes camp in the shell of the building. Beneath this soot may lie one of the most important medieval Byzantine frescoes on Cyprus, and yet no scholars seem to have noticed it before. It may be that the soot covering it has been there since the Mamluk invasion of 1426, thus obscuring for centuries the extraordinary work of art underneath.

After the destruction of Trapeza, the church, but apparently not the village, was rebuilt and the building's complicated history can be read in the structure's complex architectural elements. In the latter part of the 16th century a second dome and a nave and aisles were added around the dome of the older structure, incorporating it into the newer edifice. The seams of the many additions can be discerned with careful inspection. The aisles might have been added at different times. Certainly their styles are different. While the north aisle is a barrel vault with strainer arches, the south aisle is groin vaulted. It is also possible that the church's aisles were meant to serve both Latin and Orthodox rites, and their variances reflect accommodations for this dualistic function. The south aisle seems larger and more splendid, and may have given pride of place to the Latin rites. At the same time, it may instead reflect a variable treatment of the *prothesis* (north aisle apse) and *diaconicon* (south aisle apse) of the Orthodox church. For some unknown reason, the south aisle was made shorter than the nave and north aisle, thus creating a strange imbalance in the southwestern corner of the building. Did they simply run out of money and finish the corner with a wooden porch?

It is difficult to discern if, in fact, the secondary church additions that incorporated the earlier 13th-14th century dome date from the 15th century and not the 16th century, which was the main era of Venetian domination (1489-1570). Many Lusignan symbols can be found in the

Fig. 51: The Trapeza church near Famagusta.

parts of the church built after the destruction. Here, the drop-shaped motif is very sharp and dart-like. The additions thus have decorations that indicate a pre-1489 Lusignan date. However, it is thought that many masons still used Lusignan decorative motifs even in the Venetian era. Still, there are reasons to believe that most of the fabric of the contemporary edifice was constructed in the late 15th century. Gunnis cites a "date shown" of 1563, and thus credits the Venetians with a "half hearted attempt to restore it." If Gunnis is correct, then the work was done a mere seven years before the Ottomans conquered Cyprus. Perhaps the work on the church was halted by the invasion itself, leaving the building slightly incomplete.

The name of the ancient village, 'Trapeza', means 'refectory'. A monastic refectory of some kind may have been an important structure in the medieval village. Perhaps the church was rebuilt in an attempt to revitalize the ruined village of Trapeza (or the local monastery), but while the church was almost finished the village and monastery were never re-established. However, George Jeffery also notes that 'Trapeza' or 'Trapesa' means 'table' or flat 'table land', which accurately describes the immediate area, and this is a more likely explanation for the village's name.

On some maps (such as the UK Department of Defence, 1973), the church is called Panagia Chrysopolitissa (there is another church in Paphos with the same name), perhaps representing a later rededication of the church. There is actually a second church at Trapeza, just to the south, but virtually nothing of it remains above ground.

Sources for Trapeza: Enlart, 316-7; Jeffery, 200; Gunnis, 154-5.

Panagia Absinthiotissa near Taşkent/Vouno, 12th century and later. Renovated in the 14th century, reconstructed in 1963

[35° 17' 01.34" N / 33° 23' 20.79" E]

A dirt road winding above the village of Taşkent/Sykhari brings one to a lovely terrace in the southern slopes of the Kyrenia Range. There one can find the stunning church of the Panagia Absinthiotissa (Fig. 52). The name of the church means 'Our Lady of the Absinthe', referring to the herb *Artemisia absinthium*, also known as 'wormwood', which is what the infamous greenish liquor is made from. The church and monastery were already down on their luck in 1736 when the Russian monk Bars'kyj visited. He also explains the origin of the monastery's name:

> I...then went to another monastery, which was about an hour's walk away, and it is dedicated to the Most Holy Mother of God and is called Absinthiotissa, that is, wormwood. They say that it is so called because of a very old icon which was located here, before the foundation of the monastery, which was found in a small cave which was overgrown with these bushes. Concerning how, by whom, and when this monasterywas founded I could not determine as it is now largely deserted, and there lives a solitary hieromonk in poverty and answerable to the *hegumen* [abbot] of the monastery of Saint John Chrysostomos. It is situated on level ground near the top of the mountain, and in the past the monastery's buildings must have appeared as large and beautiful. In its structure the church is beautiful and spacious, and on top is covered on the outside with a dome, but now it is so old and neglected that it is ready to collapse. That year from the earthquake [1735] many stones from the building had been loosened and fallen, while the monks could not grow in number to take care of it, because of the crippling taxation of the Turks. There are two or three monastic cells in which live a hieromonk and a novice, and they feed themselves from the sweat of their brow. They have a small spring with healthy water, and the air there is also healthy.
>
> *[Sources History Cyprus III, 30-31]*

Very soon after Bars'kyj's visit, the monastery was abandoned, but it was virtually rebuilt in 1963 in an attempt to revive the monastery.

The church's location is striking and it is one of the most accessible of the Byzantine mountain churches since one can drive all the way there from the main highway in about 15 minutes. It is not far from the hard-to-miss Turkish Cypriot flag painted on the mountainside, which was put there

Fig. 52: Church and monastery of Panagia Absinthiotissa, near Taşkent/Vouno.

because in the 1974 offensive many Turkish soldiers lost their lives coming over the mountain above the church (which has led to the renaming of the nearby peak 'Commando Hill' or Komando Tepe by the Turks). Enlart also noted that the monastery of the Absinthiotissa was under the control of the monastery of St John Chrysostom, which lies at a similar position along the northern mountain slopes about 3 kilometres to the southeast and is, sadly, currently off-limits to visitors because it's on a military site. The church is dominated by its large central dome which rests on a high drum pierced by numerous windows. If the restorations have been true to the original structure, the use of brick voussoirs around the west entrance and the windows of the dome's drum, among other features, are reminiscent of church architecture in Constantinople. The dome is the last of many reconstructions, but Enlart thought that at least one reconstruction was done in the late 14th century and led by a French architect. The narthex of the church, which has apses on the short ends and sturdy Gothic rib vaulting, probably also dates from this period.

The monastic buildings are also reconstructions, including the large refectory (*trapeza*) of which very little of the original masonry remains. It was restored in the 60s. One can imagine the wooden tables of the monks filling the space, which is about twenty metres by five. The size of the refectory also lets us know that at some time, at least, there were probably more than thirty monks at this monastery. It is the only Byzantine monastic refectory left on Cyprus, and one might think of it when exploring the Latin, Gothic refectory at the monastery of Bellapais. At least some patronage came during the Venetian period, because a tomb slab with an effigy of a woman in Venetian dress was still there when Enlart visited in the late 19th century.

Sources for Panagia Absinthiotissa: Enlart, 205-6.

Church of St James, Işkele/Trikomo, 15th century

[35° 17' 01.85" N / 33° 53' 33.92" E]

This jewel of 15th century Byzantine Cypriot architecture occupies a location in a fork in the road in the middle of the town of Işkele/Trikomo about half an hour's drive north of Famagusta. Its simple design, based on the traditional plan of the Greek cross-in-square with a semi-circular apse and a central dome, lends the structure a compact purity. The drum of the dome is pierced by several small windows that allow light into the interior. Their lancet shapes, echoed in other parts of the building's articulation, are reminiscent of contemporaneous Cypriot Latin Gothic architecture and are indications of the Latin influences on the Byzantine architecture of the period. Entrances with hood moldings, lintels, tympana, and other Lusignan elements can be found in the south and west walls of the church, though there is evidence of a doorway once giving access from the north as well [Hint: If the south door seems locked with a chain, try unraveling the chain].

The interior of the church reveals even more clearly the simplicity of the building's geometry with its well-lit dome carried on four pendentives. The walls have inset plates and bowls, a decorative tradition seen elsewhere in Greek Cypriot churches, such as the narthex of the Panagia Kanakaria.

Although rather small in size it is one of Cyprus's most lovely works of architecture, beautifully integrating both Byzantine and Latin elements in a very harmonious expression. It is so well preserved that even the stone drain pipes still survive and function. Keep this structure in mind when visiting the nearby Panagia Theotokos (next entry), because the earliest version of the Theotokos church would have resembled St James before its nave was extended west and an additional nave and apse were later added on to the north end.

Panagia Theotokos, İşkele/Trikomo, 12th century

[35° 17' 00.61" N / 33° 53' 20.40" E]

This church, now an icon museum, also has some well-preserved and important 12th century frescoes, including an impressive image of Christ Pantocrator with a host of adoring angels in its dome. Other frescoes of saints can be found on a column and niche in the south wall (part of an even older church on the site) and another monumental image of Christ in a mandorla in the vault of the north aisle near the church's side entrance, which was part of a 15th century image of the Ascension of Christ. Oddly, a huge chandelier has been hung from the middle of this rare and significant fresco which is in need of cleaning as soot has severely darkened it. The fresco that gives the name to the church is found in the southern apse, hidden by the iconostasis (Fig. 53; you may have to ask permission to go back there to see it). It is an image of the *Theotokos*, Mary, the 'bearer of god'. The image of the *Theotokos* shows Mary standing with an image of the infant Christ in a circle superimposed on her womb. Mary's hands are outstretched in a worshipping attitude called the orant pose. She wears a blue gown which shows her role as queen of heaven, and the purple mantle called the *maphorion*, indicating her imperial stature. The infant Christ blesses with his right hand and holds a scroll, the word of god, in his left. The scroll is an interesting holdover from pagan times, in a way, for philosophers were often shown holding scrolls to signify their wisdom. Images of Christ as a philosopher or wise man/child picked up on this convention in early Christian art. Mary is flanked by the worshipping archangels Gabriel and Michael. There is also a broad arch in front of the apse, and here the Ascension is depicted, with groups of apostles on either side looking up at Christ rising to heaven. Another fresco shows Mary in a fairly rare depiction as she spins some wool into purple thread, a symbol of Mary's flesh giving corporeality to the Holy Spirit with Christ in her womb, alluding to the Annunciation.

The church's structure consists of two aisles divided by two broad arches resting on squat, circular piers. Each of the two aisles has its own apse, which suggests that one aisle was built earlier than the other. It is likely that the south section was an earlier single-aisled church. This two-aisled configuration is very typical on Cyprus and often denotes two or more building stages in different eras, but also probably indicated both Latin Catholic and Orthodox altars in the same church, not an uncommon configuration during Lusignan and Venetian rule on Cyprus. In some cases, as here, the Orthodox aisle is the one with the dome, while the undomed aisle is the Latin aisle, each terminating in an apse and altar where the rites of each denomination could be enacted.

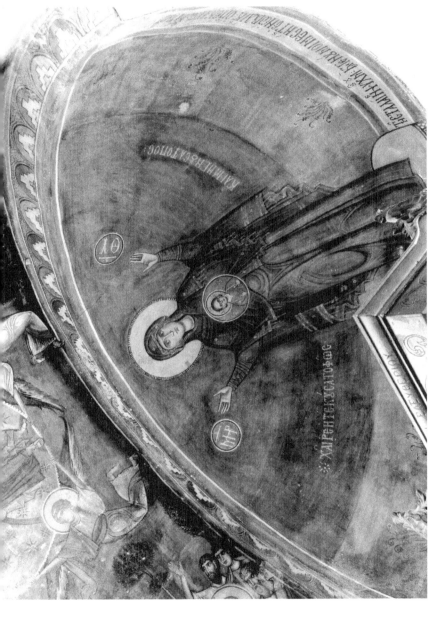

Fig. 53: Fresco of the Panagia Theotokos ('Bearer of God') in the older, south apse of the church of the Panagia Theotokos, İskele/Trikomo.

At some points in Cyprus's complex medieval history, the same priest administered the rites of each religion. The travelling monk Felix Faber, who visited Cyprus in 1483, was shocked to see this and thought it to be a great heresy. In later times, other Latin churchmen agreed and the practice was outlawed.

There is evidence that the earliest version of this church was a much smaller single domed cruciform church very much like the church of St James (previous entry). The oldest dome, in the south aisle, would have been the single, central dome in this earliest building, with its semi-circular apse to the east. This tiny structure could have dated from the 12th century. Be sure to walk around the outside of the church and look at the two apses and domes to compare them (Fig. 54). The oldest frescoes are also to be found in this older part of the church, and include the impressive image of Christ Pantocrator in the dome (Fig. 55). Here, Christ holding the Bible and raising his hand in a blessing gesture is surrounded in a lower ring by a procession of heavenly angels who approach the throne of heaven. Mary and St John the Baptist stand by the throne in orant worshipping poses, with a procession of saints lined up behind them. The act of giving reverence to this throne is called the *Hetoimasia* (*Etoimasia*; Ητοιμασία) or preparation of the throne of heaven for the second coming of Christ.

Sources for Panagia Theotokos: Andreas and Judith A. Stylianou, *The Painted Churches of Cyprus* (London: Trigraph and the Leventis Foundation, 1985), 486-491; see the interesting article by Maria Evangelatou, "The Purple Thread of the Flesh: the Theological Connotations of a Narrative Iconographic Element in Byzantine Images of the Annunciation," in *Icon and Word: the Power of Images in Byzantium, Studies presented to Robin Cormack*, eds. Antony Eastman and Liz James (Aldershot: Ashgate, 2003), pp. 269-285.

Fig. 54: Apses of the church of the Panagia Theotokos, İskele/Trikomo.

Fig. 55: Fresco of Christ Pantocrator and the Hetoimasia in the south dome of the church of the Panagia Theotokos, Işkele/Trikomo.

Panagia Kriniotissa (Krinia Sinaitiko Monastery), 15th century

One of the most striking and tragic images in northern Cyprus is the decaying remains of the Byzantine church of Panagia Kriniotissa. Nestled in a secluded forested cleft in the north slopes of the Kyrenia Range above the village of Karşiyaka/Vasilia, the site is accessed not from the town but from the St Hilarion ridge road a few kilometres west of St Hilarion. It's not far from a rather odd tourist attraction on that same road, a Turkish tank that was parachuted from a plane in 1974. However, the parachute didn't open properly and the tank is virtually embedded in the mountainside. Characteristically, the Turks made this dramatic mishap into a colourful victory shrine. You can't beat it for a photo-op. The Kriniotissa church, and the monastery that accompanied it, was built at the site of a sacred mountain spring (as the name implies), and the foundations of the monastic community may date to the late 11th century, though the church one sees here today was likely built in the 15th century. The monastery probably owned some agricultural terraces below on the mountainside near Lapithos or Vasilia to help sustain it.

Numerous trees have taken root in the building's crumbling fabric, gradually pulling the structure apart. The apse has already fallen and the narthex will follow soon without intervention. Amazingly, considering the dilapidation of some of the vaults that support it, the dome of the church still stands. The church was in even worse condition, however, before 1968 when it was partially reconstructed by the Cyprus Department of Antiquities. But one should not lose heart. When George Jeffery visited the church around 1918 he described it as "completely ruined". So things can be rebuilt. It is a beautiful setting surrounded by pine trees. One can see what an idyllic spot it would have made for a mountain monastery.

Source for Panagia Kriniotissa: Jeffery, 322.

Agios Evlalios church, 15th-16th century, Lambousa, on the coast 1.3 km north of Aslançak/Karavas

[35° 21' 15.09" N / 33° 11' 28.58" E]

This sizable medieval Byzantine church, almost certainly built on the remains of an earlier one, is just a stone's throw from the famous church and monastery of Akhiropietos ('Not Made By Human Hands', i.e. made by God, miraculously), which is currently occupied by a military garrison and closed to the public. One can see the remains of the earlier Evlalios church just outside the east end of the current structure. A walk of about a kilometre east of Agios Evlalios takes one to the impressive Lambousa fish traps, one of my favorite sites on the island, so the area is worth a stop. Agios Evlalios has a classic plan and elevation. There is a narthex in the west end, a nave with a dome on a high drum and a semi-circular apse in the east end, with entrances on the west, south, and north sides. The church interior has recently been closed to the public, but one can at least peer into the windows. The pendentives of the dome (the four triangular sections just below the drum that support it) are ribbed, which is a fairly novel characteristic; borrowed, one presumes, from the aesthetic of the ribbed Gothic arch. The side walls of the nave are articulated by blind arches that use ancient columns. Jeffery noted the church's lovely floor paving, but this is difficult to see now. Alas, the impressive iconostasis seen by Jeffery around 1918 is gone.

Sources for Agios Evlalios: Jeffery, 320-1.

Sina Monastery, above Karşiyaka/Vasilia (date uncertain)

[35° 20' 27.16" N / 33° 07' 32.01" E]

The Sina monastery occupies a wide shelf of land just above the town of Karşiyaka/Vasilia on the lower north slopes of the Kyrenia Mountains west of Girne (Fig. 56). One can walk to it from the village. Below the monastery are a series of terraces that were once farmed by the monks. These are fast disappearing as new homes for British retirees are being built above the town. Little is known of the history of the monastery and it may not be any older than the 18th century. At least the ruins of the buildings don't seem very old. Indeed, the whole complex might have been rebuilt in the 19th century but with an aim to keep the earlier styles of architecture. Still, some monastery could well have occupied the spot for a few centuries. Only archaeological excavations would reveal the plan of any earlier complex. One of the most fascinating aspects of Sina, along with its impressive vistas, is its irrigation system. Hiking above the monastery reveals the remains of an aqueduct that directed water from the mountains above. A more modern pipeline is still used today and it follows the same route as the older channel. The monks guided the water to the monastery via the small aqueduct, though some was also sluiced to a pressure tower from which other streams were redistributed (similar pressure towers can be found in nearby Lapta at the terminus of the Lapta aqueduct and at the village of Tatlısu/Akanthou). Much of this water system is still traceable today. The water went through the monastery itself, then out to a holding tank near the entrance, after which it could be directed to irrigate the fields on the terraces below. Exploring the crumbling structures today is somewhat dangerous as many walls threaten to collapse, but hiking in the surrounding area is rewarding. For stronger hikers, climbing to the rocks high above offers tremendous views of the ruins below.

Fig. 56: The ruins of the Sina Monastery above Karşıyaka/Vasilia.

Mill and Waterworks at Başpinar/Lapithos/Lapta. Originally medieval, but current construction 18th -19th century

The village of Başpinar/Lapithos has a short section of arcaded aqueduct that brought water into a tall pressure tower. This, in turn, supplied water to run the mills of the village. These mills may well have been operating in the medieval period and were certainly working during Ottoman, and even modern times. It would seem that the mills of Lapithos were working for centuries, powered by the water from the mountain springs from the slopes of the Kyrenia Mountains above. One can also see the ruins of a similar pressure tower above the ruins of the Sina Monastery above Karşıyaka, to the west. Water was always scarce on Cyprus, but the highlands of the Kyrenia Mountains (also known as the Beşparmak/Pentadactylos Mountains, after the 'Five Fingers' outcrop that are their most distinctive promontory) as well as the Troodos Mountains in the southwest, had a number of springs that supplied water for much of the year. These springs were the lifeblood of many Cypriots as the few rivers were seasonal, drying up completely in the summer months. A few arches of the aqueduct that brought the water to the pressure tower can be seen today. Restoration work is planned for the aqueduct and the mills of the town.

Avgasida Monastery, foundation date unknown, Originally 15th century, current ruins 18th century and later, near Famagusta (1 km northeast of Sandalar/Santalaris)

[35° 12' 53.64" N / 33° 48' 32.90" E]

There are some interesting ruins to see at the Avgasida monastery, which is found just north off of the road about 1.5 km west of Alitlar/Aloda and about 1 km east of Sandalar/Santalaris. A dirt track about 300m north of the road leads to the former monastery. The foundation of the Avgasida monastery is shrouded in mystery, but some of the remains suggest it was prosperous in the 17th or 18th century, and may have been a center of significant agricultural production. Its original foundation goes back at least to the late 15th century, since this date accords with what we know of the lost church's architecture. Today, the monastery complex has been divided up into sheep pens and the monk's cells in the southwest portion, with their elegant arched doors, are used for storing hay. The broad fields north of the monastery and the areas around the small villages are very fertile and seem to have been irrigated, at least in part, with water diverted from the ancient Roman underground aqueduct that in ancient times had brought water to Salamis. Ambitious hikers can explore this region north and northeast of the monastery and find the remnants of the 2000 year-old water system, which is all underground at this part of the aqueduct's route from Değirmenlik/Kythrea on the southern slopes of the Kyrenia Mountains about 30 kilometres to the west.

There was a Lusignan-era medieval church here at Avgasida until 1974 when the Turkish army destroyed it in retribution for the killing of Turkish Cypriot civilians in the nearby villages by a retreating EOKA-B contingent who were fleeing the advancing Turkish army (there is a mass grave and monument about a kilometre past Sandalar). There are photographs of the church, however, that give us a sense of its appearance, and Enlart made some drawings of it in the 1880s. It had a two-aisle plan with low arches separating the aisles, similar to the configuration of the Church of the Theotokos in Işkele/Trikomo, and had a single dome. It may be that this two-apse, two aisle church also had two altars in the medieval period, as we know that many Orthodox churches on Cyprus were required to also maintain a Latin, Catholic altar. Enlart noted that the north apse was not used when he visited in the 1880s, suggesting to him that this had been the former Latin apse, now derelict. Large flying buttresses had also been added, much like those that can be seen at the church of Agios Sergios in Yeniboğaziçi, north of Famagusta (next entry). These, too, are lost. A medieval tomb slab, noted by Enlart

178

and photographed by Theodor Mogabgab, showed a relief of a man in elegant, late medieval dress. This may have been the original patron of the church. Gunnis thought that he could discern the name 'George' in Greek on it, with the date 1482, a mere 7 years before Venetian rule officially began on Cyprus. Gunnis also saw, in the early 1930s, a fresco of Christ Pantocrator in the dome of the church. He noted that it was "fine and well preserved", so it is one of the many great losses of mural art on Cyprus. Gunnis also saw many icons on the iconostasis, some of which dated from the 18th century. What became of these no one knows.

There are a number of short pillars used to support arcades throughout the monastery. One should take a careful look at these because many of them are re-used bits of ancient columns or capitals and marble fragments from early Byzantine-era templon screens.

Sources for Avgasida Monastery: Enlart, 314-316; Jeffery, 240; Gunnis, 424.

Fig. 57: The large flying buttresses of the church of Agios Sergios in Yeniboğaziçi/Agios Sergios.

Church of Agios Sergios, Yeniboğaziçi/Agios Sergios, near Famagusta, 14th century with later additions

[35° 11' 50.92" N / 33° 52' 40.93" E]

The date of the earliest structure on this site is uncertain, but it could be as early as the 13th or 14th century. The church is dedicated to St Sergios, a bishop of nearby ancient Salamis (Constantia) in the 7th century. It is one of the many churches on Cyprus that began as a small single domed church but was enlarged in subsequent centuries. In some ways the evolution of this church is similar to the church of the Panagia Theotokos in Iskele/Trikomo, expanding to accommodate a Latin Catholic altar at some point during the Lusignan era. The ponderous but impressive flying buttresses added to the west end were added at a much later date, perhaps in the 17th or 18th century (Fig. 57). There was a catastrophic earthquake on Cyprus in 1735, and many buildings were severely damaged. These buttresses might have been constructed to give additional support to interior vaults that were compromised by the quake. Note that similar buttresses were built up against the north wall of the Roman baths at Salamis. This is interesting as it might indicate that part of the ancient bath complex was being used in subsequent centuries, long after the abandonment of Salamis, perhaps as a religious shrine or chapel.

The arcade on the south side was probably built in the 19th century, as many Greek churches had such arcades added to their south flanks during that time. It offered shelter from the sun on the side with the most exposure, and also helped keep the interior of the church cooler.

Sources for Agios Sergios: Gunnis, 203-4.

Chapel, Monastery and Church of Apostolos Andreas, Karpas Peninsula, 15th and later centuries

[35° 39' 33.42" N / 34° 34' 26.96" E]

The site at Apostolos Andreas is still an important pilgrimage site on Cyprus, located almost at the tip of the Karpas peninsula. The end of August was the time when the 'Cava Andrea' festival was typically held. Interestingly, Turkish Cypriots, who are Muslim, also frequently come and pay homage to the saint, indicating that the importance of his cult was trans-religious and was central to Cypriot identity over and above religious affiliation. This is one of the most fascinating elements to religious history in Cyprus, as its multiculturality often led to the blurring of religious lines. According to legend, this is where the apostle St Andrew first set foot in Cyprus (there is virtually no evidence that this ever actually happened), and that miraculous springs welled up at the spot. A small medieval chapel, about 7m square, was built in the 15th century to mark the site of the sacred springs. Unhappily, this old chapel, square in plan with a central pillar supporting the vaulting, is usually closed to the public. Even though the most important historical feature of the place is off limits, the trip here is still worthwhile as the Karpas peninsula is the most beautiful part of Cyprus, especially in the springtime when the fields are green. The larger church that was built above it is much later, probably dating from the 18th or 19th century. This is also true of the monastic structures appended to it, since the English traveller Richard Pococke visited it in 1738 and found the whole place uninhabited and ruined. So most of what we see today must have been built after Pococke was there. Enlart wondered whether the small chapel was meant to serve as a sacred crypt for a larger church either planned or destroyed on the same site of the 18th-19th century church currently there. He also believed that the stylistic elements of the chapel, and the indication that much of it remained unfinished in terms of decorative detail, pointed to the 15th century when French and Lusignan influences were giving way to Italian and Venetian ones. This was also a time, the late 15th century, of difficult economic times in Cyprus, which may explain the unfinished components, and may also be a reason why the larger church — if it was ever planned at all — was never constructed. The site is also connected with one of the most important historical events in the history of Cyprus, as it was to this place that the Byzantine despot Isaac Comnenus fled in 1191 and was finally captured by Richard the Lion Heart, who, in conquering Cyprus, led the island into centuries of western, Latin domination. However, regarding the flight of Comnenus the records vary, some have him fleeing instead to Buffavento or even Kantara castles, which makes more sense but is less dramatic than imagining Isaac cornered at the very tip of the Karpas.

Gunnis tells several anecdotes of the miracles of St Andrew (Andreas) as told by Greek Cypriots, such as the tale of the Turk who brought his blind son to be cured. As he approached, his son was suddenly able to see, but the Turk then turned back — not actually having arrived at the church to formally pay his respects and give his donation to the church — at which point the son's blindness returned and no amount of cajoling could make St Andrew cure the son again. Similarly, some thieves once broke into the church, only to find all the doors and windows had become solid walls. Returning their loot to the treasury, the doors reappeared. In a rather odd story, a worried mother prayed that her son would not pursue a perilous career as a sailor and would instead become a chauffeur like his brother. St Andrew, a patron saint of sailors in the region, granted her prayer — the son became a chauffeur — but he was killed in an automobile accident days later. Andrew, apparently, had little patience with those who didn't believe in his powers. According to Cypriot tradition, if you want to receive Agios Andreas' good favours you need not drive all the way to the end of the Karpas peninsula. One need only place some money in a bottle, seal it, and throw it into the sea from any shore on Cyprus. If Andreas accepts your offering the bottle will float to his church. If he doesn't think you're worthy and doesn't accept the offering, your bottle will float back to the shore. So you might stay and enjoy the beach for awhile after throwing your bottle in, just to see what the verdict is.

Sources for Apostolos Andreas: Enlart, 309-313; Jeffery, 256-7; Gunnis, 168-170.

Fig. 58: Church of St Mamas, Güzelyurt/Morphou.

St Mamas Güzelyurt/Morphou, 18th century

[35° 12' 01.56" N / 32° 59' 27.18" E]

The city of Güzelyurt/Morphou, in the western part of Cyprus, derives its Greek name from the word *omorphos*, which means 'beautifully shaped', and the Turkish name, Güzelyurt, meaning the same thing: 'beautiful place'. The area was once much more wooded and better watered in times past, though today its water table is being lowered at alarming rates (see earlier entry for Toumba tou Skourou). The church of St Mamas is one of the most important Orthodox shrines in Cyprus and St Mamas one of its most important saints (Fig. 58). There are sixty-six churches on Cyprus dedicated to St Mamas, but this one is the most revered as this is where the body of the saint lies. The church one sees today was likely built in the early 16th century, but was remodeled in the early 18th century after a catastrophic fire. More changes were done in the early 20th century, such as the addition of the bell tower in 1900 and the arcaded porches on the west and north sides in 1907. According to excavations done in 1958 by A.H.S. Megaw, a series of four churches, including the current one, seem to have existed on this site, the first being as early as the 5th or 6th century. A later church, Megaw estimated, was from the 7th century, while the third was from the 14th or early 15th century. The first literary reference we have of a cult of St Mamas is from the mid-14th century traveller Ludolf von Suchen, but he doesn't specifically mention Morphou. It is very likely, though, that this was an important pilgrimage site from early Byzantine times.

In the Middle Ages the fertile Morphou area — also called *le Morf* in Lusignan times — was an important feudal estate called 'Le Seigneurie de Morfu', which was under royal Lusignan supervision. The Venetians sold the Morphou estate to the Greek Cypriot Synclitico family around 1528, though they soon tried to purchase it back, perhaps an indication of its prosperity. This family is important for our consideration of the church because St Mamas was strongly supported by the Synclitico. In 1538, Eugene Sinclitico left substantial donations and grants to the church, even stating his wish to be buried there in front of the saint's icon. He also recorded his wish that 2800 besants a year to be given to the church so that the monks could pray for his soul in perpetuity.

The Russian monk Bars'kyj was impressed with the church when he saw it in 1727, even drawing a picture of it in his travel diary.

The church of the holy martyr Mamas is a very splendid construction, unlike any other church over which Christians now have possession, and surpasses in beauty any other church on Cyprus. It is of considerable height, length, and breadth, and on the inside is supported on ten large pillars. It is a church of three apses... the floor is handsomely paved with stone slabs... The church is indeed very attractive, and in it, on the right hand side wall, there is the icon to the holy martyr Mamas and a marble sarcophagus... from the sarcophagus a myrrh is emitted, with which the faithful rub themselves and are cured of illnesses.

[Sources History Cyprus III, 20]

Bars'kyj also tells the story of local Muslims who wanted to take the church over and make it into a mosque. The abbot (*hegumen*, in Greek) of the monastery agreed to build them a new mosque so that he could save the church for Orthodoxy.

When Alexander Drummond visited St Mamas in 1754 he saw a fairly new church, but thought it to be older than it probably was. Even so, he was very impressed with it. His description of the church, and his account of the story of the patron saint, is worth quoting at length.

Morfou is a very cheerful place, about a league and a half from the sea, and its church is the handsomest building of its kind on the island: the court is finely walled with hewn stone, about fourteen feet high, extending to two hundred and fifty-six feet on each side, with forty-five feet for cloysters, etc. It was almost finished, in a kind of Italian taste, when the Turks conquered the island...Saint Mamas, to whom this church is dedicated, performed abundance of miracles while he lived upon earth, and even now affords daily matter for astonishment. When alive he either could not or would not pay his *kharaj*, or poll-money [taxes], and the collectors were always restrained by the operations of some preternatural power upon their bodies and spirits, from using him in the savage manner in which they treated others who were deficient in their payments. The prince, being informed of this extraordinary circumstance, ordered him to be hunted out from the hollow rocks, caves, and gloomy woods in which he always lived, and brought into his presence; and Saint George and Saint Demetrius, hearing of his being taken, followed, overtook, and accompanied him in his captivity. During his journey to court, seeing a lion rush out of a thicket and seize a lamb, to the terror and astonishment of his guards, he ordered the beast to quit his prey, and his command was instantly obeyed by the lion, who fawned and wagged his tail, in token of submission. The good man, being tired with walking, took the lamb in his arms, and mounting his wild beast, rode forwards to court, to the amazement of all who saw him. He presented himself in this equipage to the king, who, being apprised of these circumstances, accepted the lamb, generously remitted the *kharaj* he owed, and gave orders that the Saint should live without paying any tax for the future: thus favoured he came hither and built a little church, in which at his death his body was deposited. This is one way of telling his story, which is varied by every papa whom you consult on the subject

[Excerpta Cypria, 297]

That such a tax-evading saint would arise on Cyprus, where the Greek indigenous population had been dominated by a series of foreign powers who taxed them heavily, is perhaps no surprise. In more modern times, St Mamas also became known for curing deafness, which is why one often sees wax votive representations of ears dangling around his tomb inside of the church; these given to the saint in the hope of a cure or in thanks for one. Many other types of cures are attributed to Mamas, including helping correct speech impediments.

Drummond's story also explains why St Mamas is shown riding a lion and holding a lamb in the many painted icons and relief sculptures that depict him. The Cypriot chronicler Leontios Makhairas, however, has a different story about St Mamas and the lion. He says that in life the saint used to catch lions and milk them, which really is pretty miraculous since the saint is usually shown with a male lion. Drummond visited Cyprus at a very low point in its economic history, and everywhere he saw buildings in advanced stages of decay, so this is why he may have been so impressed to see a well built ecclesiastical structure done in such finely finished stone. Drummond also notes that the church is completely surrounded by a high wall, and this feature is also recorded in a drawing done of the complex in 1727 by the aforementioned Russian pilgrim and monk Bars'kyj. This high wall seems to have been ruined and its stones taken away long ago.

Drummond also gives a good description of how the saint was worshipped, and this is still true, though few Greek Cypriots visit the spot today (on the saint's day, September 2 on the Orthodox calendar — perhaps a good time to visit).

I have related one of his performances while in life, I will now communicate one of the feats he has acted since he went to the other world. Just above the place where he lay interred, a marble sarcophagus was placed, and on the wall is a picture representing him riding on the lyon, with the lamb in one hand and shepherd's crook in the other: upon his right is Saint George, and on his left St Demetrius, both on horseback. The Turks, expecting to find a treasure in this sarcophagus, broke it up; and ever since, through two little holes, which were then made, water is continuously conveyed into a hollow, being supplied from the sweat that issues from the face of the above picture, which is never dry, though those of his brethren saints, who are close to him, shew no signs of moisture.

[Excerpta Cypria, 298]

St Mamas's sacred icon, then, in concert with the sacredness of his holy body, takes its place among some of the great icons of Byzantine and Orthodox history: those icons that bleed, weep, sweat, or even lactate, emanating sacred liquids that can thus be smeared, collected, even drunk by believers for whatever cure or blessing is needed. Visitors can access the tomb that Drummond described from either the church's interior or exterior, but the hollow that Drummond mentions is on the interior, where one can gather the 'moisture' of the sweating icon on the sarcophagus (Fig 59). The current situation, then, is not quite as Drummond describes it. The holy water doesn't emanate from the icon, but, rather, from the sarcophagus itself. Today, as in Enlart's time — the 1880s — one opens a hinged cover from the middle of the sarcophagus to access the 'sweat'. Enlart claims to have espied a priest emptying a pot of water into the hollow when he thought nobody was looking. The sarcophagus itself is an interesting artifact. It is actually an ancient Roman tomb and there is an inscription on its south side in Greek that records that it once cradled the bodies of two women belonging to the family of Artemidoros from around the 3rd century CE. Above the sarcophagus is a triptych of icons, with St Mamas in the center, and flanked by St Demetrios on the left and St George on the right. Above this, in the lunette of the arch, are a series of small icons showing scenes of martyrdom.

As Drummond implies, there are many versions of the St Mamas legend. One story is that he wasn't Cypriot in origin at all, but Syrian, and when the Muslims conquered that region his marble sarcophagus floated out to sea and landed on the beach at Morphou Bay. The people dragged the sarcophagus, which seemed light, until it became immovable and heavy, an indication that the saint therein had found his preferred final resting place.

Jeffery believed that the only element belonging to the earlier Gothic church on the site was some of the architectural framing around the tomb of St Mamas itself, which perhaps makes sense in that the saint's tomb would not be moved even if the building around it was completely redone. The archivolts of this frame seem as if they've been taken from an earlier Romanesque style French edifice, with a preponderance of leaf and vine designs and the face of the 'Green Man' at the apex. One theory suggests that there was another aisle to the earlier church where the north portico is now, and that this may represent a Latin altar existing in this north aisle, now destroyed and replaced by the north portico. Such an

Fig. 59: The sarcophagus and shrine of St Mamas in the church of St Mamas, Güzelyurt/Morphou.

189

arrangement would have fulfilled the stipulation, common in Lusignan times, that Orthodox churches also have Latin altars for Catholic masses to be held. In such a case, the double face of St Mamas' sarcophagus, being accessible from two sides of a wall, would make some sense. If one looks on the wall above the sarcophagus on the outside, there does seem to be some history of modification of that wall. Only further excavations underneath the north portico area (recall that it's an early 20th century addition) might lend more certainty to the hypothesis.

Drummond's sense of the church being older than it actually was might be attributed to the fact that Cypriot architects and masons continued to use building techniques, designs, and carving styles of earlier centuries, including those inspired by the French Gothic architecture of the island and even the Italian influences that came in the Venetian period. Still, there seems to be at least a few fragments that could have come from the earlier building, such as the aforementioned arch over Mamas' tomb, the marble colonnettes flanking the main door, a small wall shrine to the left of the main door, and the small marble columns of the 'royal' doors of the iconostasis. Enlart also notes that the bases of the large main columns in the church vary, so perhaps some of these came from the earlier building. Certainly it is true that the capitals of the columns were either from the earlier building or carved in the spirit of the Gothic period. In a couple of the capitals the 'Green Man' can be discerned, with leafy projections coming out of his beard or mouth.

Gunnis saw marble reliefs on the iconostasis that seem not to be there anymore, which is a shame since he thought them to have been made around 1500 (correlating with the current edifice's construction) and "... perhaps, the finest example of the Minor Arts of the Venetian era still remaining in the island." The panels, he wrote, were "decorated with figs, grapes, acorns, etc., carved in high relief, with Venetian heraldic shields at the corners." The elevated wooden *kathisma*, or abbot's throne is there in the church as well, with its detailed and ornate carvings. Especially powerful is the relief on the side showing Adam and Eve taking the fruit from the serpent in the Garden of Eden. The pulpit of the church also survives, clinging to one of the columns. Be sure to climb the stairs to the *gyneconitis*, the women's gallery, as it offers a good view of the nave from above.

Most other churches of the northern region of Cyprus have lost their wooden altar screens or iconostasis and the beautiful icons that decorated them. Many of these paintings were probably either destroyed or stolen and sold on the world art market, only to disappear into private collections. It is therefore rewarding to visit this important Orthodox church and see it intact both architecturally and in terms of its ecclesiastical furniture and decorations as it helps us envision what the interiors of the now vacant Orthodox churches in the north looked like before 1974. The 'royal doors' of the St Mamas iconostasis are beautifully carved and painted. One should stand immediately in front of these doors and note that when the doors are closed, the scene on the uppermost portion is the Annunciation, with Mary on the right door and the angel on the left. This event marks the moment of the incarnation of the Holy Spirit in the flesh of Mary. Just beyond the royal doors, at the very sight line of the Annunciation, is the altar table of the church, which represents the corollary of the incarnation: the place where the priest prepares the bread and wine of the liturgy, which will become the body and blood of Christ. The impressive crucifix towering over the top center of the iconostasis makes the sacrificial metaphors of the altar's rites and the Annunciation clear. This crucifix is similar in iconography to the one at St Barnabas, with Christ on the cross with the skull of Golgotha at his feet and the symbols of the four evangelists at the points of the cross: the eagle of St John at the top, the lion of St Mark on the right, the winged man (angel) of St Matthew on the left, and the ox of St Luke at the bottom.

If one is able to look into the altar area, one can also see one of the church's most magnificent artifacts, the early 16th century painted wooden ciborium that acts as a canopy over the altar table. This ciborium was recently restored so one hopes that the public will be given access to it. We are lucky enough to have a dedication inscription on the face of the ciborium that not only records the patron of the piece but one of the painters:

The present roof [of the ciborium] was painted with the support and expenses of the hieromonk, Lord Pavlos and Abbot of this monastery, and by my own hand, Sylvestros Axiotes [of Naxos].

The abbacy of Pavlos also helps us date the ciborium around 1501. This impressive 500-year-old ciborium is indeed a rarity and certainly one of the most important surviving examples of ecclesiastical furniture in Cyprus. In the north side of the ciborium is found a depiction of the Christ child on a paten (the small plate used to carry the bread for the mass), while on the south side one finds an image of the Christ child in a chalice, which is a symbol of Christ's blood. These two images paired are called the *melismos*, named after the moment in the rites when the priest breaks the bread. They make clear the symbolism of the mass and the bread and wine as Christ's sacrificed body. The inscriptions also help with the interpretation. In a band around the image of Christ in the chalice the inscription reads: "This is my blood of the New Covenant which is shed for you and for many for the forgiveness of sins." And around the image of Christ lying on the paten: "Here I am presented, the mystical lamb crucified. I am forever broken and feeding the worthy. Shudder in fear, O Man, and do not eat unworthily."

Numerous angels of various ranks — cherubim, seraphim, and thrones (these last indicated merely by whirling discs with wings) — decorate the ciborium, indicating the holiness of the rites that take place at the altar and the sacredness of the Eucharistic hosts. On the west face (the one you can see from the royal doors) are a row of cherubim and seraphim with a long inscription as commentary:

Holy, holy, holy, Lord Sabaoth, Heaven and Earth are filled with your glory. Hosanna in the highest. The incorporeal nature, the cherubim, glorify you with ceaseless hymns. The six-winged creatures, the seraphim, exalt you with endless voices.

The thrice repeated word "holy" at the beginning of the inscription is the *trisagion*, which is sung by the priest during the rituals. Thus the angels in heaven and the priest on earth sing the same praise of god. Be sure to look up inside to the ceiling of the ciborium, because there one finds the most impressive painting. It depicts Christ as both priest and emperor, wearing robes and a crown signifying each, with the sun and moon above and stars all around, indicating the heavenly canopy where Christ resides in eternity. The inscription in the red proclaims: "The King of Kings and Lord of Lords," while the inscription outside the frame, in the blue, reads "Jesus Christ, and Great High Priest." In the corners are roundels with the symbols of the four Evangelists.

Sources for St Mamas: Enlart, 166-170; Jeffery, 221-3; Gunnis, 348-51; Müge Şevketoğlu, Rita Severis, William Remson, Elizabeth Bolman *et. al.*, *The Canopy of Heaven. The Ciborium in the Church of St Mamas, Morphou*, Michael Jones and Angela Milward Jones eds., International Resources Group, 2010.

Fig. 60: The church of the Panagia (Virgin) at Hisarköy/Kampyli.

Church of the Virgin Panagia, Hisarköy/Kampyli, 12th century

[35° 18' 03.91" N / 33° 06' 30.43" E]

About 3.0 km southeast of Çamlibel/Myrtou, and 2.2 km northeast of the Pigadhes Altar archaeological site, is the village of Hisarköy/Kampyli and the Church of the Virgin Panagia (Fig. 60). It is a Byzantine church of the single-aisle type with a semi-circular apse which spans almost the entire width of the church. A small dome rests on a high drum. There is indication that some kind of ancillary chapel was appended to the structure on the south side, perhaps even a second aisle was there. Some masonry clinging to the upper levels of the south wall indicate the existence of such an additional component. The structure, if in fact ever completed (or, was it completed but then collapsed?), opened to the main body of the church through a wide archway, the outline of which is still visible on the south wall, though now walled up and pierced only by two slender windows. The breadth of the arch in relation to its height gives us an idea why the structure may have been unstable. The arch is quite wide in relation to its height, thus any building with its profile would have been unsound. What may have happened is that the south wall was opened up and an arch built, so as to open the south wall on to a new south aisle addition. However, this proved to be untenable and the project of enlargement abandoned. The south wall was thus walled up again, now incorporating the failing arch into its fabric. However, there is another possibility, and that is that the south aisle was built to provide a second apse and altar for Latin rites, which we know was often done in Lusignan times. Perhaps after the Lusignan and Venetian eras the locals intentionally destroyed the south aisle with its Latin altar as a way of returning the church to its original 'pure' Orthodox configuration. Excavations may reveal whether this is a valid hypothesis. The church is maintained today by the Maronite community of Cyprus and is usually closed to the public, though its exterior is sufficiently beautiful to warrant a visit. In the same village see the Gambili Hamam (Ottoman Bath; see entry at end of book).

The Armenian Monastery, or Sourp Magar (aka Agia Makarios, Agia Merkourios), Various historical periods, near Alevskaya area

[35° 17' 14.67" N / 33° 31' 19.72" E]

This monastery may have been founded in the early Middle Ages. Some scholars believe that it was first constructed by Coptic Christians from Egypt around the year 1000 CE, but virtually nothing from that time survives. The Armenians arrived in Cyprus in significant numbers from the 6th century onwards. Certainly they were there in the late 12th century as they are recorded as having assisted Isaac Comnenos in his resistance against Richard the Lion Heart. Willibrand of Oldenburg, who visited in 1211, noted how the Latin occupiers dominated the Greeks and Armenians: "Whence you can see that the Franks are the lords of this land, whom the Greeks and Armenians obey as serfs" [*Excerpta Cypria*, 13], so one assumes that the Armenians had established themselves with a noticeable presence. Their population was to be significantly augmented in 1322 when the Mamluk Sultan invaded Lesser Armenia (on the south coast of modern Turkey; also known as 'Cilician Armenia') and many were made refugees. King Henry II accepted these refugees into his Cypriot kingdom. Makhairas records that in 1412 the locust infestation destroyed much wheat and "the Armenian vines at Kalamoulli", which one assumes was a significant Armenian grape growing enterprise [Makhairas, 623]. The modern town of Armenochori, near Limassol, retains in its name the ancient heritage of the Armenian village there. There were Armenian churches in both Famagusta and Lefkoşa/Nicosia.

Located on the wooded slopes of the Kyrenia Mountains, the monastery is a lovely spot to visit, but visitors will find the place much ruined, though there are plans to clean thing up. It is reported that the Turkish military used it as an encampment for awhile after 1974 and did some damage. It is one of the most remote places in Cyprus. The monastery passed to Armenian control in the 16th century, and may have been a resting spot for Armenian pilgrims making the arduous trek to the Holy Land. Cyprus was a popular way-station for such travellers in the Middle Ages. The monastery was dedicated to the Virgin Mary but also seems to have been connected with some devotion to Saint Makarios, who is said to have occupied a cavern in the rocks above the monastery. Much of what one sees today dates from the 19th century, except for a fragment of the older 15th century church abutting the new church. The east wall of the complex also seems to have remnants perhaps dating from the 15th century. One can go outside to see the exterior of this wall as well as a portal with a couple of Gothic-style windows and hood mouldings. In the interior of the complex, despite the dilapidated condition, it is easy to reconstruct the place in one's imagination, especially with the squat but still beautiful series of arches that run along the east side. The several doors to monks' and pilgrims' cells can also be discerned. Nearby are the ruins of the Melanisiko church (Agios Georgios).

Sources for Armenian Monastery: Jeffery, 334-5.

The Three Mountain Fortresses of St Hilarion, Buffavento, Kantara, and the Castle of Kyrenia

The Castle of St Hilarion (Dieu d'Amour), 13th to 14th century
[35° 18' 40.72" N / 33° 16' 52.10" E]

The fortress of St Hilarion is named after the early 4th century hermit Hilarion who lived his last days on the precipitous, craggy mountain. In the Middle Ages and in some later periods the fortress was also called Dieu d'Amour ('God of Love'), likely a French corruption of the Greek name for the mountain *Didymus* (i.e. 'twin', because it has double summits). It is a magnificent sight, even in ruin, and in a spectacular location (Fig. 61). Enlart called it "the principal fortress of Cyprus, one of the most astonishing monuments of the astonishing architecture of the Middle Ages", and quoted Philip of Novara as writing that the castle "stands in a right noble position among right noble mountains." The recluse Hilarion was a significant and respected saint, his life written up by none other than St Jerome. His grotto is marked today by the Byzantine church found in the castle precinct. This 11th – 12th century Byzantine church may have belonged to a monastery that was here before the castle was constructed. It has a fairly rare type of layout, with engaged columnar piers supporting an octagonal superstructure which, in turn, supported a single large dome. In this respect it's similar to the church at Antiphonitis. Alexander Drummond visited the castle in 1745. He climbed up the north side to get there. Tired tourists will recognize the sentiments:

As we approached ... S. Hilarion, which is on the summit, we found the west side of the hill so steep that our beasts could not mount it. I therefore left my luggage at Carmi, and with eight mules took a turn to the eastward, in order to find an easier access. When I came to the rock on which it stands, I dismounted, and having refreshed myself, sat down to make a sketch of the extraordinary aspect, then taking my stick in my hand I ascended as well as I could, and walked through all the different parts of the castle. It has certainly been strong, both from its site and fortifications...I walked down the west side, and you will have some notion of the difficulty of the descent, when I tell you that I spent thirty-five minutes in reaching the foot of the rock upon which the castle stands.

[Excerpta Cypria, 299]

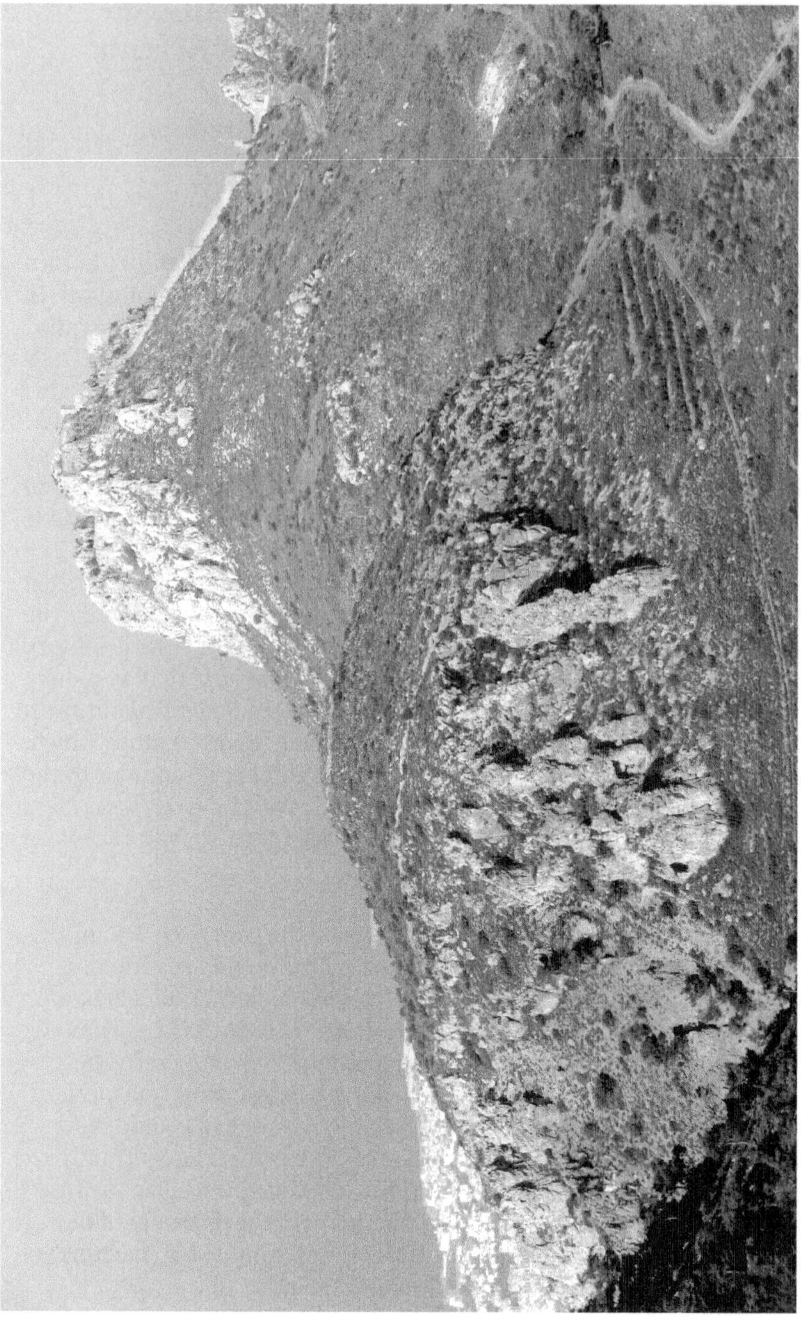

Fig. 61: The dramatic peak of the castle of St Hilarion, above Girne/Kyrenia.

Some sections of the fortifications on this naturally defensible site may date from the mid-twelfth century when there was a Byzantine fortress of some kind here, but the Lusignans enlarged it considerably in the 13th and 14th centuries. In fact, it must have been Cyprus's principal citadel in 1228 because it was to St Hilarion that the nobility of Nicosia went for security when the Emperor Frederick II invaded Cyprus. During the Lusignan period St Hilarion, which commands a position near the principal mountain pass between Lefkoşa/Nicosia and Kyrenia, became Cyprus's largest stronghold and the most important bulwark of a trio of citadels in the Kyrenia Mountains, which included Buffavento and Kantara castles (entries following). More than once Lusignan royalty took refuge within St Hilarion's extensive walls. Notice, however, how thin the lower set of walls are, and keep these medieval walls in mind when considering the much later walls of Famagusta, which are high but also very thick with several metres of earthen backing to withstand cannon balls. When you enter the barbican — the first gate you enter, where you buy tickets — look around and think about the design of the barbican and how difficult it would have been to attack the castle at this point. In some ways, the open space of the barbican was a well laid trap, since anyone entering it would have had defenders firing from above from many directions.

What remains today is but a tantalizing hint of what existed around 1375 when the castle was at its most developed stage. Jeffery notes that the complex is made up of three lines of defense: the outer walls that encompass the large, lower area of the bailey, the hillock upon which the most extensive building was done (just beyond the church), and, finally, the upper part of the castle in the west. Each section had walls and fortified gateways (Fig. 62).

There are nine semi-circular towers around the outer wall, including the two that are on the barbican or fortified gateway. The large bailey may have been essentially a village in medieval times, as everywhere there is evidence of human activity (Fig. 63). One can imagine walking through a smoky settlement here in the 14th century, through muddy tracks making one's way to the upper portions of the compound. Remnants of stables and other minor structures can still be seen. Past this trapezoidal open space, to the northeast, lies a second fortified area in which the most intensive building was done. Happily, many of these structures survive enough to give a sense of being in the narrow streets of a medieval town. This is where one finds the Byzantine church mentioned above with its distinctive brickwork. Other rooms with practical functions can be found in this part of the complex, many of them with their rib-vaulted ceilings still intact and offering stunning views. This is the core of the castle in many ways, and it is the part where the most survives. There

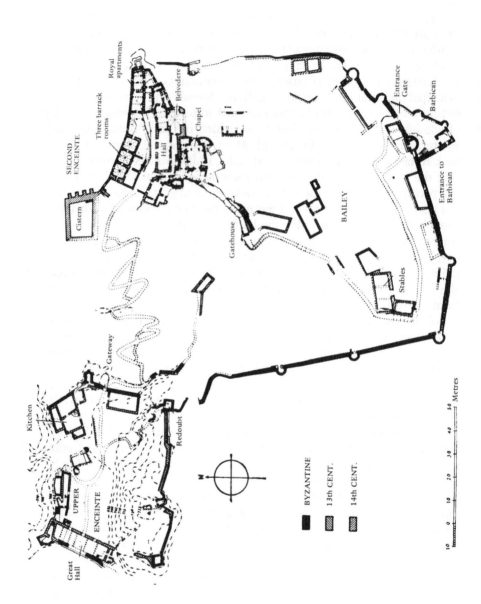

Royal apartments

Belvedere

Three barrack rooms

Hall

Chapel

SECOND ENCEINTE

Cistern

Gatehouse

Entrance Gate

Barbican

Entrance to Barbican

BAILEY

Stables

Kitchen

Gateway

Redoubt

UPPER

ENCEINTE

Great Hall

N

BYZANTINE

13th CENT.

14th CENT.

Metres

10   0   10   20   30   40   50

Fig. 63: View of the bailey and barbican of the castle of St Hilarion.

were several service structures, including a foundry for making weapons and a kitchen. A gate tower, elevated drawbridge and tunnel made the entryway to the second level the strongest of the three fortified gates of St Hilarion.

As one continues through the second level, emerging on the often sunless north side of the mountain, one finds the ruins of a set of apartments, from which there were spectacular views to the north and east. From here a steep track leads up to the upper part of the fortress. Along this north path, one passes some rectangular buildings that were soldiers' barracks. Beyond this one can see a large cistern, similar to a large swimming pool. It is one of the several cisterns that stored water for the castle.

Making use of an enclosed area between two steep outcrops north and south, a roughly rectangular open courtyard is created by walls and buildings in the east and west respectively. Enlart called this a "*cour d'honneur*" or "courtyard of honour" (look carefully at the ground, because you can still see some of the conduits that collected rainwater and sluiced it down to that large cistern you passed coming up). The west end of this open area is where the larger and more splendid royal apartments may be found. They offer magnificent views to the west from atop unscalable cliffs and from the upper levels on the east side the rooms no doubt looked down upon the court of honour. Only one place was more secure: the tower that occupies a lonely aerie on a pinnacle near the mountain's summit. It is from here, legend has it, that the Prince of Antioch, brother-in-law to the Lusignan Queen Eleanor of Aragon, had his bodyguards thrown to their deaths, victims of a false accusation from Eleanor, who wished him dead. Leontios Makhairas describes the betrayal:

And when the queen reached Lefkosia, she sent a letter to the prince [her brother-in-law]: 'My beloved brother, be on your guard against the Bulgarians [his bodyguards], for they are plotting together to kill you and take the castle of St Hilarion, and be careful for your own life. And because I love you, I tell you this.' The good lord believed this letter of his enemy, she who was more poisonous than poison, and so he fell into great sin, for he murderously took their lives without cause. For when the prince read the letter he brought them up to the castle and himself sat inside the keep [tower] and called them to him one by one. And at his orders they were thrown down from the window, and such was the height that they were killed.

[Makhairas, 547-49]

Thus depriving himself of his own bodyguard, and he thinking the queen true to him, Eleanor found it easy to have him killed when he returned to Lefkoşa/Nicosia.

The royal apartments consisted of two large rectangular halls, one on top of the other. It is likely that the lower part was more public and the upper providing more private domestic functions. Two Gothic windows in the upper portion still survive, giving some idea of the fine architectural elements that would have distinguished the structures centuries ago. The tracery in one of these windows hints at the possibility of a private chapel in this upper part of the royal apartments (Fig. 64).

Like all ruined castles, St Hilarion inspires the imagination. Though the central sections of the apartments have been destroyed, we might imagine walls painted in fresco with elegant tapestries and fine wooden furniture all lit at night with lamps and torches. One chronicler, Etienne de Lusignan, states that St Hilarion and the other mountain fortresses were reduced by the Venetians who feared they would fall into enemy hands, but this interpretation is not supported elsewhere in the historical records.

Sources for St Hilarion: Enlart, 428-437; Jeffery, 263-268; Kristian Molin, *Unknown Crusader Castles*, New York and London: Hambledon and London, 2001, see esp. chapters 7-10.

Fig. 64: Tracery window in the upper level of the western royal apartments of the castle of St Hilarion.

Castle of Buffavento (Castle of Kousouvendis, Castle of the Lion), 13th to 14th century

[35° 17' 13.78" N / 33° 24' 36.08" E]

The castle of Buffavento, also occasionally called the 'Castle of the Lion' (*Leone*) in some texts, or 'Kousouvendis' by Greeks, is the most remote of the three castles of the Kyrenia Range. 'Buffavento' was the name conferred by Italians on the castle, a corruption of 'Kousouvendis', simply meaning that it was buffeted by gusts (*'buffa'*) of wind (*'vento'*). The road to the base of the castle has recently been paved but a challenging climb still awaits visitors, though ramps and steps have been built to facilitate the ascent. Buffavento is the smallest of the mountain fortifications but it is also the loftiest, offering striking vistas north to the Karamanian Sea and south to the flat plain of the Mesaoria. Situated on a high point between St Hilarion and Kantara, signal fires could be set at the sighting of enemy ships, warning the other mountain castles and Kyrenia and Nicosia of any enemy fleet's advance. There were only a few buildings constructed here and some believe that it was more of a lookout than a castle proper. Two travellers of long ago left descriptions of their experiences there. The first was Cornelius van Bruyn, who made the ascent in 1683:

> At noon we reached the convent of St Chrysostom, and saw on a mountain near it the remains of a very large building. I started with three others to examine it. But we were not yet half way when the Greek whom I had taken from Larnica was too tired to go on — the hill is very steep — but the other two ...remained with me. But we were obliged to rest and take breath a dozen times.
>
> The ascent is as difficult and dangerous as I have ever made. The greater part of the time we had to climb with our hands as well as our feet, and whichever way we turned our gaze we saw only what made our hair stand on end. We took an hour and a half to reach the top. There one sees only the live rock, a number of ruined chambers, and large stone-built reservoirs. It must have been a huge building, with many rooms built at different levels. The sea is visible on all sides but one, and most of the island. The view of Nicosia, with many villages scattered over the plain, is very striking.
>
> *[Excerpta Cypria, 237]*

Another voyager, much later, was the Spaniard Ali Bey. This was not his real name. He adopted a colourful *nom de plume* to bolster his book sales and claimed to be from Aleppo, Syria, but actually lived in

Paris. He climbed up to Buffavento when he visited Cyprus in 1806. His colourful description reveals his desire to write a captivating adventure story for Europeans:

The peak itself is a rock nearly perpendicular on every side. There was no further trace of a path, so we climbed this natural wall, taking advantage of jutting rocks, projections, holes, anything to which our hands and feet would cling. Sometimes we had to help one another with a stick, at another the guide would stop to see where he could get the best foothold, so as to get over the parapet in front of him; and, to complete the picture, we had always beside us a horrible precipice...When one thinks of the labour and cost involved in the building of such a palace, on such a site: when one reflects on its antiquity, one is astonished indeed. It was decorated with all the luxury known at the epoch of its construction. The window openings are well proportioned: the marble was certainly brought from a great distance, as well as the lime and the bricks which could not have been made on the spot. The beauty, I might even say the magnificence, of the apartment probably used by the court, even the provision of water for a building so vast and situated on such a height, make one believe that the founder of the palace was a sovereign endowed at once with great talents, no ordinary spirit, and immense wealth.

[Excerpta Cypria, 399-400]

There must have been Byzantine-era late 11th or early 12th century fortifications here because in 1191, when Richard the Lion Heart conquered Cyprus, the despot Isaac's daughter surrendered to Richard according to the late 12th century chronicler Roger of Howden, who wrote: "On his [Richard's] approach towards the fortress the Emperor's daughter came to meet him, and falling at his feet, did him obeisance, putting herself and the castle at his mercy. Then was delivered to him the exceeding strong castle called Buffavent[o]...[*Excerpta Cypria*, 8; quote misattributed to 'Benedict of Peterborough']. It is this story that may be the origin of the tale that a mysterious legendary Queen founded this castle and why some Cypriots in former times referred to it as the 'Queen's Castle'. Other chroniclers tell us that Buffavento was often used as a prison during the Lusignan period. King Henry II, for example, imprisoned two of his fellow nobles there in 1311, the Constable Chamerin and Balian de Ibelin, who had supported a coup against him. In 1368 King Peter I locked the unfortunate John Visconte in Buffavento's cells. An innocent victim of palace intrigue, Visconte had the misfortune of bearing the unsavory news of the queen's infidelities upon Peter's return from an extended sojourn abroad. In 1385 Buffavento hosted more

Fig. 65: View west along the Kyrenia Mountains from the castle at Buffavento.

Fig. 66: View of residential structures in the castle of Buffavento.

aristocratic guests: two challengers to James I's reign were incarcerated and later executed there.

There are two main levels to the Buffavento complex, though these are arrayed on a few other sublevels as the construction jumped about the mountainside settling on whatever bits of level terrain could be found. The lowest level begins with a sturdy entry gate with a pointed archway which leads to a small open area off of which modest guardrooms and/or stables were built. A short stairway leads up to an assemblage of buildings on the second level, which must have been the residential portions of the castle. Some of these rooms retain their vaults and one even has a stone fireplace still in place. Shepherds who camp here with their flocks in winter still use the rooms for shelter. A water cistern is under the floor. Architectural elements point to some pre-Lusignan construction with Byzantine-style alternating stone and brick voussoirs in the doorways. Walking to the west one can find wonderful views of the Kyrenia Mountains (Fig. 65).

It is just below this level where one can look down to the most impressive part of the castle, which arcs out over a deep ravine running up from the northern slopes of the mountains in a dramatic and precarious positioning (Fig. 66). This two-storey structure was the most sophisticated of any in the compound. If there were any royal apartments at the site, these rooms were probably intended for that purpose. Bastion-like in appearance, it has impressive mural elements that curve around the profiles of the rocky outcrops. One of the reasons that the castle was situated here may have been to guard the narrow but still traversable pass that lies below this part of the fortifications. The upper rooms of the second level could have been barracks and might have been used to incarcerate the many nobles who were imprisoned there at one time or another. At the very western tip of this series of rooms one has a good view of the ravine below.

The highest level of Buffavento is today accessible by a modern metal staircase. The stone staircases, once carved into the cliffs by the Lusignans, have long ago eroded away. Three buildings occupy the site on the pinnacle of the mountain, although there are signs of one or two more that have been destroyed. Each of the structures had several rooms, but it is difficult to determine their specific function. One could have been a chapel of some sort because an indentation in one of the walls is reminiscent of a niche used to store liturgical instruments.

There are several cisterns visible throughout the site, some of them even showing signs of having been used in modern times (perhaps by the Turkish military, which had lookouts here for a time after the 1974 military action). This is a feature of all three of the Kyrenia Range fortifications because a short rainy season meant that water had to be stored to last through the long Cypriot summers.

In attempting to envision the original appearances of these places one must also try to imagine significant wooden construction in the form of shelters, stairways, catwalks, and small bridges or even drawbridges at certain points. All of these elements are, of course, lost, though signs of postholes and other indicators of timber structures are evident in each of the castles.

Sources for Buffavento: Enlart, 437-443; Jeffery, 274-5; Gunnis, 296-302; Kristian Molin, *Unknown Crusader Castles*, New York and London: Hambledon and London, 2001, see esp. chapters 7-10.

Kantara Castle (*La Candaire*), late 13th century

[35° 24' 22.22" N / 33° 55' 25.97" E; location of parking lot for site]

Kantara castle occupies a spectacular location at the eastern end of the Kyrenia Mountains just as they begin to descend into the lower hills that form the tapering spine of the Karpas Peninsula. Just a few kilometres east of the village of Kantara, it provides one of the most impressive vistas on the whole island of Cyprus. Of the three alpine strongholds Kantara is the best preserved and gives an excellent impression of the organisation of a medieval mountain fortification (Figs. 67-68). The eastern towers with their galleries of arrow loops are the complex's most impressive feature as they give a real sense of the defensive logic of the architecture. Almost all the buildings are gathered along the southern side of the peak. Kantara, or *La Candaire* as it was referred to in French texts, was taken for a short time in 1228 when imperial troops loyal to the Holy Roman Emperor Frederick II (who had designs on Cyprus in those years) were besieged there by Lusignans trying to drive the ambitious invaders from the island. Historians report that the Lusignans had to use a very destructive catapult (called a *trebuchet*) to destroy the walls of their own citadel to regain it from the hands of the occupiers. In the years after 1373, when the Genoese took over the city of Famagusta from the Lusignans, Kantara, with its excellent view of the northern top of Famagusta Bay and the land routes to the Karpas, became a good position to check Genoese raids.

The entrance to the castle is flanked by formidable double bastions, the north one with a dramatic slope (called a 'battering') at its base. These bulwarks envelop the area in front of the entrance, making any approach from that quarter dangerous for any attacker. One can go into them and look down through a gallery of arrow loops and get a defender's eye view of the area below. Please resist the temptation to shoot other tourists. A horseshoe-shaped tower dominates the southwest corner of the fortress contiguous with other western structures, including a large cistern in the northwest that fills with rainwater even today. At the apex of the site the ruins of a small chapel, with a single Gothic window, gives an idea of the religious devotion of the inhabitants of this isolated fortification.

Sources for Kantara: Enlart, 468-473; Kristian Molin, *Unknown Crusader Castles*, New York and London: Hambledon and London, 2001, see esp. chapters 7-10.

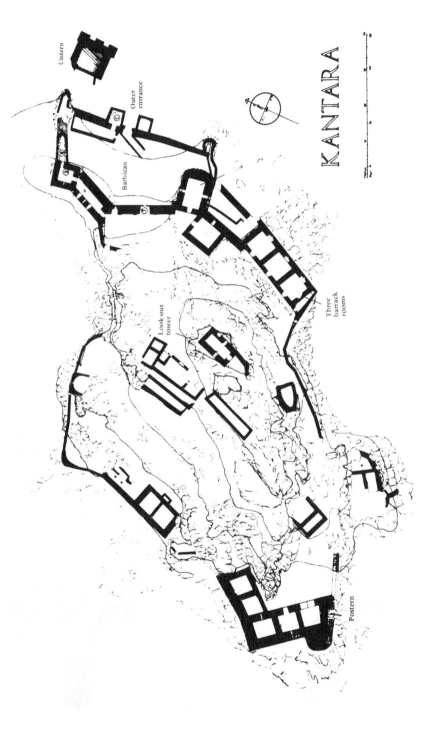

Fig. 67: Plan of the castle at Kantara [from Camille Enlart, Gothic Art and the Renaissance in Cyprus].

Cistern

Outer entrance

Barbican

Look-out tower

Three barrack rooms

Postern

KANTARA

211

Fig. 68: View of the walls and bastions of Kantara castle from the east.

The Castle at Girne/Kyrenia, 10th to 16th centuries

[35° 20' 29.64" N / 33° 19' 20.37" E]

One of the most important ports on Cyprus was Kyrenia (in Turkish, Girne), which was called 'Cerines' in Byzantine and medieval times, but referred to as 'Schernae' by Oldenburg who visited in 1211. Pero Tafur, around 1438, uses the name 'Aherines', and Stochove uses 'Gerines' in 1631, in which one can discern how the name 'Cerines' became the modern Turkish 'Girne'. The early name 'Aherines', so the story goes, was adapted from 'Achilles', the hero of the Trojan War who was said to have founded the city. It was the major north coast port and was connected to Nicosia through the Agridhia Pass through the Kyrenia Mountains (also called the Pentadactylos or Beşparmak, i.e. 'Five Fingers' Mountains, after an impressive, fist-like outcrop that marks another more easterly pass). The site was not only favourable because of its port and its strategic location near the pass to Cyprus's center, but because the north slopes of the Kyrenia mountains also had many springs that supplied abundant fresh water to the towns and villages along those shores. Moreover, Kyrenia lay on the coast opposite the many harbours on the southern seaboard of Asia Minor (Turkey) and was thus a convenient port of call for those ships ferrying goods across or along the Karamanian Sea. These characteristics made this coastline, as we have seen, one of the prime areas of settlement right back to Neolithic and Bronze Age times.

There had been a classical Roman harbour there, the outline of which is still visible just east of the castle. Indeed, one gets a wonderful view of its semi-circular shape from the ramparts. In medieval times the port was relocated to the west of the castle stronghold, where it was lightly fortified and protected with a chain across its mouth. The chain tower still exists in the contemporary harbour, around which today there is gathered a quaint, curving esplanade of restaurants and small hotels, making a very picturesque scene indeed. In Wilbrand von Oldenburg's aforementioned visit of 1211, he noted the following: "We first touched land at Schernae (Kyrenia) a small good town but fortified, which has a castle with walls and towers. Its chief boast is its good harbour" [*Excerpta Cypria*, 13]. The description supports the architectural and other historical evidence, that there was a substantial set of fortifications here in Byzantine times, ones that may have already been improved upon by the Lusignans by the time Oldenburg arrived. By the time of Stochove's visit in 1631, the town seemed down on its luck: "We stayed a day at Gerines which was once one of the finest and most important towns in the island, it is now chiefly ruinous. The larger part of the inhabitants are Greeks. A square castle commands the port, to which the Turks retire at night. The harbour is small, and suitable for boats and small craft only" [*Excerpta Cypria*,

216]. His observations were echoed forty years later by Noel Dominique Hurtrel in 1670:

> Then, having (by God's grace) got safe out of this dangerous gulf, we arrived at the town of Cerines in Cyprus, and there anchored. We saluted the castle, a square structure which guards the harbour, and to which the Turks retire for the night. The town is almost all destroyed; there are but a few poor dwellings which the Greeks have built up after their own fashion on the ruins; and here they live, for they form the greater part of the population, the Turkish families being few. The ruins which you see bear witness that it was once one of the chief towns of the island. The harbour is of no manner of use to large vessels, but is well enough for small craft.
>
> *[Excerpta Cypria, 232]*

When Richard the I of England advanced on Isaac Comnenus in 1191, Isaac sent his wife and one of his daughters to what he thought was a safe stronghold, the castle at Kyrenia. Assisted by Guy de Lusignan, who would become the founder of the Lusignan Cypriot dynasty (though Aimery de Lusignan would be the first Lusignan king of Cyprus), Kyrenia's castle was forced into surrender and Isaac's empress and daughter became Richard's prisoners while Isaac retreated to Kantara. This Byzantine period castle lies mostly invisible inside the later medieval and Venetian expansions of the walls and bastions we see today (Figs. 69-70). However, one impressive component of the era survives, a Byzantine church that once served the earlier castle now lies dramatically ensconced within the later additions (Fig. 71). Enlart thinks that this chapel-like structure must have been the *St George de la Donjon* in the French, or *Santo Giorgio del Castello* in the Italian records. But the church one sees today is probably a rebuilding of the earlier church, likely from the 16th century during the Venetian modifications, which were extensive in this quadrant of the castle.

Kyrenia castle was the site of two important early sieges in 1228 and 1232, when supporters of the Holy Roman Emperor Frederick II were testing Lusignan rule on Cyprus. In both instances the Lusignans managed to gain surrenders from the imperial forces and their faction. Challengers to Lusignan rule were also imprisoned in the castle's famously dark and horrible dungeons. Enlart notes that one prisoner, John le Miege, was able to write out a copy of the *Gestes des Chiprois* while incarcerated there in 1343. King Hugh IV (r. 1324-1359) briefly imprisoned his impetuous sons — Peter, who would become King Peter I, and his brother John — in the Kyrenia castle in 1339 for their disobedience. These youths had left the island without their father's permission and managed to get to Rome, either to drum up crusader zeal or simply assuage their desire

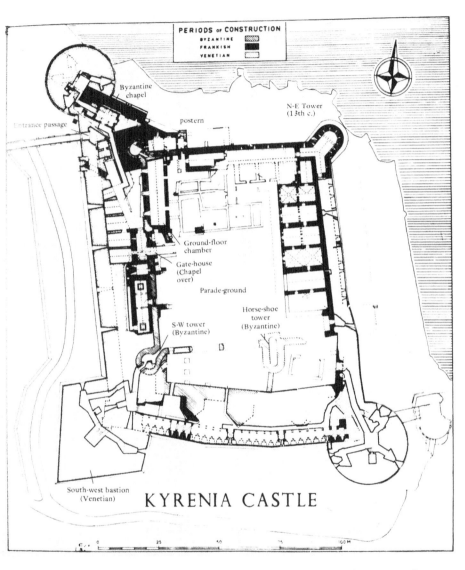

PERIODS OF CONSTRUCTION
BYZANTINE
FRANKISH
VENETIAN

Byzantine
chapel

Entrance passage

postern

N-E Tower
(13th c.)

Ground-floor
chamber

Gate-house
(Chapel
over)

Parade-ground

S-W tower
(Byzantine)

Horse-shoe
tower
(Byzantine)

South-west bastion
(Venetian)

KYRENIA CASTLE

0   25   50   75   100 M

Fig. 69: Plan of Kyrenia castle [from Camille Enlart, Gothic Art and the Renaissance in Cyprus].

215

Fig. 70: View of the eastern walls of Kyrenia castle.

to see the world. The pope sent them home, chastised, to their enraged father. Their time spent imprisoned in the castle varies from three days to two months in the annals of various chroniclers, but Hugh meted out slightly more severe punishment for a friend who had aided the boys, their compatriot John Lombard, who was hanged after having a hand and foot cut off. Nevertheless, Peter was reconciled with his father before his accession to the throne just before Hugh's death in 1359. Kyrenia castle would play a tragic role in Peter's own reign just a few years later. As king, in 1368, Peter allowed himself the journey to Europe to rally for crusade that his father had earlier curtailed. Leaving at home a wife and two mistresses, the energetic and amorous young king also left a void that rumour and jealousy was soon to fill. One of these mistresses was married, but the other, Jeanne d'Aleman, Lady of Choulou, was unmarried and, moreover, eight months pregnant with Peter's child. The queen, Eleanor, finding out about Jeanne, had her brought to the palace and tortured. The child, soon born, was immediately killed and Jeanne thrown into the darkest and most miserable dungeon of Kyrenia castle. The tragic story inspired one of Cyprus's greatest medieval folk songs, the *Arodaphnoussa*, in which a beautiful young woman suffers the vengeance of a jealous Lusignan queen, a thinly disguised revision of the story of Eleanor and Jeanne. Peter returned to Cyprus, freed Jeanne, and put his own queen on trial for she had had her own affairs. The queen was absolved by the court, but the unfortunate John Visconte, who had informed Peter of his queen's infidelities, was charged with calumny. So he, too, ended up in prison in Kyrenia castle, in an infamous cell, circular in shape like a cistern, in which John could not stand up in. Eventually transferred to a cell in Buffavento, John was starved to death merely for telling the king the truth about his queen's infidelities. Peter's response to all this, which was to seduce the wives of as many nobles as possible to even the scorecard with his philandering queen, earned him a brutal assassination in 1369 after only one tempestuous, adulterous decade in power. Peter's death left a much weakened monarchy and his unpopular, Machiavellian widow Eleanor on the throne. Cyprus descended into virtual anarchy. The Genoese saw this weakness and attacked, hoping to wrest Cyprus from the Lusignans. They sacked both Famagusta and Nicosia in 1373 and besieged the Kyrenia castle, where the Lusignans, under Constable James, put up an inspired defense. The chronicler Leontios Makhairas gives a vivid description of the siege apparatuses that the Genoese used to attack the walls, giving us a good sense of the designs of the engines of war in the late 14th century:

And at once they began the attack. And by land they brought up a machine called *Truie*, that is the *Sow*, and it had three storeys. And there were other machines; and they made a very violent attack. The first machine was a wooden tower with three storeys and three fighting platforms one above the other: in the middle of it was a ram and its gear, by which to make a hole in the wall of the castle: on the next platform was a great company of men with crossbows, who shot their bolts on the one side to engage the enemy, (so that the men might be able to make a hole in the wall), the height was so great that it was level with the battlements of the outer castle, and so high was this wooden tower, that those on the top platform were able to see what the people in the castle were doing. And this tower they called the *Cat*, and the next was the *Falcon*: this was a wooden tower filled with men and with ladders for climbing up upon the walls of the city. And the third was a cage set at the end of a beam, and it was filled with men with crossbows.

The defenders were able to burn and shatter these impressive constructions, and also used the *trebuchet* (a catapult) to good effect. For a time the Genoese were thus repelled from Kyrenia. Many more bloody sieges and miserable prisoners did this noble castle endure in the ensuing century. It is such a beautiful and picturesque place now, it is hard to imagine the horrors of war, torture, and incarceration witnessed here over the centuries. These towering walls silently observed many miserable sights during the three centuries of Lusignan rule. It was also under the shadow of Kyrenia castle that the Catalan ship bearing the aforementioned Queen Eleanor would sail away, she having been deported back to Aragon by her own son, King Peter II, against whom she had been plotting.

When the Venetians gained official control of Cyprus in 1489 — though in fact their hegemony was established in 1474 — all of Cyprus's defenses were evaluated and found wanting. Kyrenia castle was no exception. Extensive renovations were undertaken by 1544, but when the Ottomans came in 1570 the small castle surrendered without much resistance. Indeed, Venetian engineers had warned of the castle's defects and limitations. In fact, the Proveditore Ascanio Savorgnano had suggested demolition of the castle and the building of a new castle at the top of the Agridhia Pass, but such a project would have been prohibitively expensive, so extensive renovation was chosen as the most expeditious strategy.

The castle is essentially a large rectangle, with bastions at its four corners, enclosing a large open space or parade ground in the center. The Venetians thickened the walls, improved the moat, and completely sheathed the northwest corner, which had a small medieval square bastion, with a new circular bastion. This was a crucial corner as the entrance and drawbridge to the castle was here, so the larger bastion gave defenders a better position from which to defend the gate and enfilade the moat and harbour. One enters the fortifications by this original gateway today, and, as one enters, one can also see the upward sloping and switchback ramps that led into the castle, giving defenders advantages in position should any besiegers manage toget in.

The older medieval bastion in the southeast was also enlarged, and the design of the southwest bastion changed to an angled-bastion type to help provide more enfilading fire to the more exposed landward moats in the south and west flanks of the castle (the other sides, north and east, were protected by the sea). The thirteenth-century medieval bastion in the northeast corner is actually the most impressive, and the Venetians seemed to have kept it for the most part in its original form with few modifications. That horseshoe-shaped extension (compare the bastion in the northeast corner of Kantara castle) looks very dramatic from the end of the modern breakwater in the morning sun. As at Famagusta's walls, the long and narrow arrow loops were mostly filled up and the smaller musket loops built up along the crenellations of the upper levels. Stables for horses can still be found in the buildings of the east side of the castle. Horses were needed for the quick transport of munitions — cannon balls and gunpowder — to the walls and bastions. As one walks through the tunnels of the castle it is easy to envision these horse-drawn carts racing noisily through the cavernous and impressive barrel-vaulted passageways.

It is likely that the upper levels of the western interior of the castle were the residential part of the fortification (there is also a small chapel there), though the Venetian alterations make it difficult to come to any firm conclusions. But the remnants still there are strongly suggestive of royal apartments with the remains of what seems to be more elegant vaulting and refined construction as compared with the other parts of the castle. The tragic Queen Charlotte took refuge here between 1460 and 1463, while late Lusignan-era Cyprus dissolved into the chaos of war as Charlotte's illegitimate brother James challenged her throne. It is likely that the prisons of the castle were in the lower rooms of the north side of the complex.

It should be remembered that the town of Kyrenia itself was a walled city and the castle was a final line of defense, and there are scant but impressive remnants of two medieval bastions still visible. One is a fairly well preserved round tower with several stone projections of the machicolations lying about 150 metres southwest of Kyrenia's little harbour on one of the main streets that leads west out of town [at 35° 20' 25.45" N / 33° 19' 09.46" E]. It originally formed the southwest corner of Kyrenia's land walls. The other surviving bastion is more fragmentary but one can still make out its general shape.

Fig. 71: The old Byzantine church embedded in the Venetian additions of the bastions of Kyrenia castle.

Other Lusignan-Era Medieval Architecture

Fig. 72: The monastery of Bellapais from the west.

Bellapais Abbey, Bellapais, late 12th to late 14th century

[35° 18' 25.41" N / 33° 21' 18.33" E]

The cloister and refectory of Bellapais Abbey are two of the four jewels of Cypriot medieval architecture, along with the stunning façade of St Nicholas cathedral in Famagusta and the elegant porch of Santa Sophia in Lefkoşa/Nicosia. Bellapais derives its name from the French 'Abbey de la Paix' or 'Abbey of Peace', but it was also known as the 'White Abbey' (*Abbadia Bianca* or *de' Bianchi*) after the white robes worn by the monks who lived there. The French form *'de la Paix'* became corrupted in Italian to *'Bella Paese'* ('beautiful countryside') and, finally, 'Bellapais'. Early in its history it was also referred to as *Episcopia* or *Piscopia*. One of the monastery's 13th century abbots, Hugh de Fagiano, who had come to Cyprus in 1248 and who eventually became archbishop of Nicosia in 1251, returned later in life to Italy and founded a monastery in Tuscany, which he called *Episcopia* in memory of his tenure at Bellapais. Founded in the early 13th century the abbey is nestled in the picturesque slopes of the mountains that rise above Kyrenia on the north coast of Cyprus (Fig. 72-73). On the clearest days, one can make out the tops of the mountains on the south coast of Turkey sixty miles away across the water. The village, which grew up around the monastery in the 13th century, is best known as the place where Lawrence Durrell wrote his 1957 book *Bitter Lemons*.

Bellapais abbey was lightly fortified with a wall and an entrance gate that still survives (Fig. 74). One can see the arched gateway for carts with flanking, squared entrances for pedestrians. The imposts of the doors have sculptures of an ox and eagle, perhaps symbolizing the Evangelists Luke and John (Mark and Matthew are alluded to in the imposts of the main portal of the refectory). Evidently the monks thought that both Evangelists and fortifications alike would provide protection from whatever might arrive at their doorstep. One can also see, flanking the main fortified doorway above, the slots for the chains that would have raised and lowered the drawbridge over the small moat that filled in long ago. Above are the machicolations of the gate's tower. One can climb the stairs and enjoy a pleasant view from the top.

If you walk from the current entrance to the site towards the cloister you'll pass through an arched gateway that probably acted as part of a second lower wall around the western buildings. Note that the lintel of the doorway has a modern repair job in the middle, and notice that the coats of arms on either side are slightly worn on their inside edges. George Jeffery led the repair efforts here in 1913 and he tells us that the coats of arms were worn by the humps of camels rubbing up against them. The middle part of the original lintel had been carved away by stone robbers (presumably destroying the central coat of arms in the process) to allow

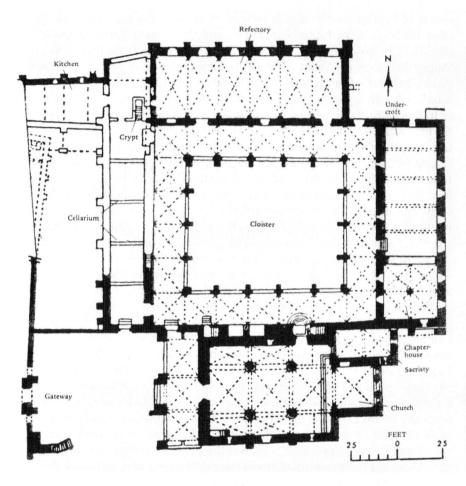

Fig. 73: Plan of the monastery of Bellapais [from Camille Enlart, Gothic Art and the Renaissance in Cyprus].

Fig. 74: The fortified gate and the façade of the church at the monastery of Bellapais.

the tall camels to pass through the gate. These camels were used to carry blocks away from the abbey as the thieves took away the shattered remnants of the buildings that once existed in the western section. When Jeffery was entrusted to conserve the abbey he estimated that villagers had been sporadically quarrying stone from the structures for three centuries, but that other more 'professional' robbers had recently started to take stones away more systematically. He also noted that the locals used the cloister for small garden plots and were growing orange trees in various spots, bringing in topsoil and digging irrigation channels. This brought water into the site rather than draining it away, thus threatening the buildings' stability by eroding and undermining their foundations.

Jeffery was particularly concerned about the solidity of the west end of the refectory, finding it already leaning six inches from the perpendicular. He built buttresses to restore the now lost supporting function of the kitchen buildings that once existed at the west exterior end of the refectory (these were subsequently taken down in more modern times). Today, one can see outlined in the west exterior wall the profiles of the arches of those lost kitchen structures. Repairs made by Jeffery that are still visible include the tall, square piers he constructed between the Gothic arches of the west side of the cloister. The stone robbers had taken away all of the support for these elegant arches and they were standing alone, ready to collapse at the smallest tremor.

The chapter house was almost completely filled with dirt in 1913 and, on the roof of the refectory, Jeffery found trees growing. He cleared these, as well as many other plants, took away the accumulated soil, and reinforced the roof of the vaults with cement. He estimates that hundreds of cartloads of earth were removed from the site to clear it of debris. The elegant Gothic tracery of the cloisters had been ruthlessly knocked out by the stone merchants' workers, so Jeffery carefully gathered what remained and tried to put the pieces of the complex puzzle together. Even though only the edges of the tracery survived, he could still determine the overall design, and it was thus possible to note stylistic differences in the traceries of the different arcades. The western arcade suggests that it was one of the first to be built, its tracery being more geometric. The other arcades are later — and perhaps the south the latest of all — with a more flowing and elegant 'flamboyant' style of tracery, which indicates a mid- to late-14th century construction. Surviving 'flamboyant' tracery is rare in Cyprus, though one can see a wonderful example reconstructed in the court of the Lapidary Museum in Lefkoşa.

The Dutch traveller Cornelius van Bruyn visited Cyprus in 1683 and his description of Bellapais is the most extensive account of the abbey before the 19th century, yet it is as if he were visiting the site today. You might see if you can recognize the things he writes about.

The next morning we journeyed towards the convent called De la Paix, said to have been built by the Templars. The road is carried with great difficulty across the mountain: at last one sees close to one the convent pleasantly situated in a wood; orange trees, olives, palms and other fruit trees surround it, and above them all towers a very tall cypress.... The entrance gate is remarkably high, quite the height of eight men, and nine palms thick. It is a kind of fortress in itself, and is pretty well entire. Passing this gate you turn to the left, and about twenty paces further on pass a second gate. On its cornices are carved in marble three different coats of arms. To the right of this gate you mount twenty-seven steps, nearly all ruinous. Descending again, you go to the left, and see the remains of rooms. Next you cross a large open space where are a few trees, and twenty-eight paces further on come to a building composed of four great arcades, to the left of which is a fine square apartment, now unroofed; again you pass through another room and enter the cloister, a quadrangle of great beauty and dignity, and as fair and whole as if it were but just finished. Between the two first columns at the entrance of the garden there is a fine marble cistern. It is in the form of a tomb and carved around it is a wreath which a little child on either side holds up with both hands, one of the children is somewhat injured, and the other is headless, and in other parts the tomb is mutilated. Round it are six lions' heads, two on each of the longer sides, and one on the narrower. At each of the corners is the head of a young ox, all in low relief, and of fair execution. The passage in which the stone stands is 112 feet long, and 48 wide.... The ornaments of the arcades are all broken, but you can see their style....Then one can mount thirty-six steps to a great passage full of wild plants, and seventeen more to reach the roof of the great hall, and again twenty to the top of the convent walls. One sees other rooms, mostly ruined: the view both towards the sea and landwards is very fine. I came down to the vestibule of the convent, and then descending on the left a flight of twenty-one steps came to a room 32 feet broad and 66 long, with a well built vault upheld in the middle by two pillars, three times the height of a man. One might fancy it all built five or six years ago.... The church, excluding the choir, is about 60 feet long and 46 broad. In the middle are four pillars of ordinary stone and of fair height. The walls are adorned with six or seven ancient paintings. Beyond the choir is another room. It is indeed a pity that this convent is not inhabited, for it is rich in conveniences, and the site is as pleasant a one as could be found.

[Excerpta Cypria, 238-9]

Van Bruyn was not easily impressed, but he clearly is captivated by the site, as most are today. There is much that he sees that we can lament the loss of, such as the mosaics around the church door or one of the coats of arms on the lintel destroyed by the stone robbers to let their camels through, but much of what he describes can still be seen. When Camille Enlart visited the abbey in the 1890s the monastery complex was grandly situated alone along the slopes of the mountains where it stood out sharply against a backdrop of "differing greens of great olive-trees, bushy-topped orange trees and carobs". Such a view we cannot enjoy today, no "cloisters framed in greenery" as Enlart saw, since the modern town has grown up around the abbey, but it is still a stunningly beautiful place.

Another visitor was the Russian monk Bars'kyj, who passed through Bellapais in 1736. He seems to think that the ruination that he sees, still magnificent, could never be restored to its former glory.

I stayed there for a whole day and explored and examined that wonderful building, and was amazed at the skillful artistry of the masons. I had intended to produce a faithful rendering of the scene, but I was overwhelmed as I saw in many places collapsed and destroyed ruins which were totally deserted and overgrown with trees and foliage. And there is no hope or power which can restore them or take care of them, and they will forever remain forsaken, deserted, and abandoned. This place is called Bellapais, from the Italian *bella pais*, that is a beautiful place, which is because it has such a wonderful location. It is surrounded by high mountains with dense forests and decorated with trees, and flowing springs and planted groves of cypresses, while on the east and north sides it commands views of the sea.

[Sources History Cyprus III, 31-2]

The exact date of the foundation of the abbey is unknown, but it must predate 1206 because records indicate that in 1206 the Bellapais monks, who had had Augustinian canons, entered the Premonstratensian Order, founded by St Norbert in 1120. We might recall that after the success of the First Crusade many monastic orders streamed eastward and innumerable new monasteries were constructed along the route from Europe to the Holy Land. Bellapais was one of these 11th century crusade-inspired foundations. The abbey eventually became very wealthy, receiving substantial royal patronage. In 1246 they obtained a relic of the True Cross and a legacy from a knight named Roger the Norman, making them even more prosperous. The Abbey's golden years were in the 13th and 14th centuries when the most impressive architectural elements were constructed, possibly by French architects and masons from Champagne or Burgundy. The church may be the earliest building that we can see on the site today, dating from the reign of King Hugh III (r. 1267-1284) who was an early benefactor of the abbey. It was he who conferred upon the abbots of Bellapais the royal honour of being allowed to wear the mitre and bear a sword and spurs when riding. Much of the later architecture was probably built during the reign of the Lusignan King Hugh IV (r. 1324-1339) who was another of the abbey's major patrons. Parts of the cloisters, however, with their more decorative and flamboyant tracery, probably date from the late 1400s or even early 1500s. Both Enlart and Jeffery saw the influences of 15th century Spanish Gothic in the cloisters of Bellapais, Jeffery noting that there was "more than one princess of the house of Aragon on the Lusignan throne".

In the early 14th century the monastery seemed to have been held in very high regard. In 1305 an Armenian named Hayton, Seigneur of Gorhigos and connected with the Armenian royal family, was so impressed that he gave up all material possessions and joined the monastic community at Bellapais. In the 15th and 16th centuries, however, the buildings and the quality of their inhabitants declined. In 1565 the Venetians controlled Cyprus and one of their nobles, Bernardo Sagredo, passionately addressed his colleagues in the Venetian Senate about conditions at Bellapais. He told them that the French monks were openly living with women and taking wives (some more than one!) and only their illicit progeny were being admitted as novices. The graceful buildings of Bellapais, once jewels, were decaying without proper upkeep and care. His exhortation to the Venetian Senate is worth quoting in full:

The 'White Abbey', of French religion, is all in ruins; the services are not maintained; all of the brethren have wives, and the revenues are assigned to their children so that the brethren live in great penury. If the Signory (which has the patronage of the abbey) will not take steps to put an end to this misappropriation, which has neither its own authority nor that of the Pope, everything will go to perdition. It is a great sin to see so great an abbey, such a miracle of architecture, falling into ruin. It will be pious and godly work to cause it to be served by religious of pure life, and not leave it, a shocking example and a scandal, in the hands of persons who serve it according to neither Greek nor Latin rite, but, one may say, according to the Arian or the Turkish; for one of them has affirmed to me that some of them have as many as three wives.

But the Venetians had more pressing problems on Cyprus than a few backsliding monks. Within five years they would lose their precious bastion in the eastern Mediterranean to the Ottomans. When the Turks took over the island in 1571 the Bellapais church was given to the Greeks and converted to Orthodoxy. This is why when one enters the church at Bellapais today one sees an iconostasis and other ecclesiastical furniture associated with Orthodoxy. One would have had a much clearer view of the apse in Latin times, without the tall iconostasis blocking one's view. The apse in the Bellapais church is squared off, a rarity in Cyprus, and one can see this clearly on the exterior. When Enlart visited the church in the last decade of the 19th century, he saw traces of paintings in the apse interior, the pathetic remnants of the "six or seven ancient paintings" van Bruyn saw in 1683.

The area around Bellapais may have been occupied in ancient Roman times and in the cloister's north arcade is an extraordinary Roman sarcophagus with garlands and lion heads, which may have come from the necropolis at Salamis or some other ancient Roman city (Fig. 75; note how similar it is to the 'Tomb of Venus' in Famagusta's main square). One can read on it the graffiti of countless travellers, one as early as 1735. Look underneath and you'll even see a Star of David inscribed in the supports on the garden side. The holes at the bottom of the tank — presumably once fitted with metal spouts — allowed this to drain into yet another, plain sarcophagus from which the water could be drawn. Both were probably filled by sluicing some water from a mountain spring behind the monastery or perhaps by gathering rainwater through a system of roof gutters. This fountain, or *lavabo*, stands just outside the refectory door so that the monks could wash their hands before and after meals.

This refectory door, in the southwest corner, is near where the kitchens were, though these have long since vanished, having been among the structures to the west of the surviving buildings. Indeed, it is thought that up to one half of the monastery has been lost, including not only the kitchens but the stables for animals and other utilitarian structures, perhaps even a hospice. Jeffery thought that there might be a residence for the abbot in that western quadrant. In former times, the abbot entered the refectory from a special door in the east end, which was closer to the chapter house, while the other monks probably used the door through which one enters today. This southwest refectory portal, just beside the impressive sarcophagus-lavabo, is beautifully decorated with a marble lintel with three perfectly preserved coats of arms. They are so crisp I suspect that they might be reproductions from the British period. On the right one sees the arms of the Lusignans with the lion rampant, the arms of the crusader kingdom of Jerusalem in the center with the cross surrounded by 'Maltese' (equal arm) crosses, and, finally, the arms of Cyprus/Jerusalem at the left. These last two indicated the Lusignan's continuing claim to the throne of Jerusalem, the crusader

Fig. 75: The lavabo made from an ancient Roman sarcophagus outside the refectory at Bellapais.

kingdom that they had lost long before. Note that the shield on the left is actually made up of the heraldic devices of the other two. In the impost on the right, one can see a crudely sculpted lion holding an open book, Venice's symbol of the Lion of St Mark. The other side has an angel as a symbol of St Matthew.

The lofty and imposing refectory is a huge, six-bay rib-vaulted room 33 metres long and 10 metres wide with vaults 11.30 metres high (Fig. 76). It is one of most impressive medieval refectories anywhere in the world. A stone pulpit built high on the north wall was used for the reading of the scriptures during mealtimes, filling the cavernous space with the sound from its elevated perch. Usually, one can go up the staircase to reach it. The shorter end sections of the refectory are peppered with small holes as these walls were once backdrops for an indoor rifle range during the British Administration of Cyprus, though at first they used it as a hospital in 1878 as so many new arrivals came down with fevers. Like so many historical buildings in Cyprus the refectory has had many uses, including stints as the village school and even as a prison (some of the occupants left graffiti on the walls), while today the venue is used for musical recitals and concerts. Yet it is in peril. The refectory's north wall is beginning to lean very slightly and one hopes that the international community may be given permission to consolidate the structure or the whole thing may tumble down in the next big earthquake and a rare and magnificent example of medieval architecture will be lost forever. Much has already vanished in recent centuries. One large section of wall that survived until 1911 was the tall eastern wall of the dorter (dormitories) and chapter house. During van Bruyn's visit, even the barrel vault survived, it seems, as he notes "a room 32 feet broad and 66 long, with a well built vault upheld in the middle by two pillars". That vault was gone by Enlart's time in the late 1890s, and the high east wall fell just over a decade later. More than one 19th century photograph shows the east wall surviving to its full and impressive height. Jeffery tells us that the collapse of the great height of the eastern wall happened because the stone robbers, the same ones who had taken all of the blocks from the western sector, had intentionally chipped away at the foundations and buttressing of that high wall, hoping that its collapse would supply them with more free building materials to take away and sell.

Jeffery gives us a good account of the refectory that helps us imagine how it was used. One must imagine the long wooden tables for the monks, arranged in their preordained positions. Citing the well known plan of the great monastery of St Gall, Jeffery invites us to envision the abbot's table at the short east end, slightly elevated. The regular monks' tables would have been arranged along the long walls, leaving the center open for the tables of honored guests of the monastery. Jeffery also notes that

Fig. 76: The Gothic rib vaulting of the refectory at Bellapais.

233

there are drain holes beneath each north window to facilitate the washing of the floor. Apparently the monks of the Middle Ages were messy eaters.

Beneath the refectory are the remarkable basement rooms of the cellars (*cellarium* or undercroft) with their utilitarian but elegant rib vaults that spring from central pillars [Note: some diagrams, and the signs at the site, call the lower room beneath the dormitories in the east side the 'undercroft', there is thus some variation in the use of this term with two different parts of the monastery]. There are two sections to the cellars, the easternmost with a door that led to a path down the hill in ancient times. Perhaps this is where peasants and farmers delivered goods to the monastery in a long gone era. One can easily imagine large clay jars of oil, wine, grain, and other staples stored here in the cool and dark where they would be preserved and close to the kitchens in the west end of the complex. Perhaps, too, in times of famine or other shortages, the monks might have distributed food to the poor who came to the east door for charity. A.H.S. Megaw also believed that there was another cellarium along the western section of the abbey, probably contiguous with the kitchens. He claims that in the area between the refectory and the kitchens were the latrines of the monastery, with remains of the water channel used to flush sewage running under the kitchen, a convenient but perhaps not altogether hygienic arrangement.

The cloisters and their arcades are among the loveliest anywhere and in several places their tracery remains, giving an idea of the grandeur of the abbey's past (Figs. 77-78). While many have seen the cool gray stones of western European abbeys, the stones here are a warm tan colour that radiates against the rich, blue Mediterranean sky. It is a shame that the full vaults of the western cloister are gone, but a few fragments of the arches survive and we are lucky enough to have the other three sides of the cloister in good preservation. And they are spectacular. The seven bays of the north and the south wings and the six bays of the east are among the most impressive works of architecture on Cyprus. Much figural sculpture remains in the corbels of the cloister but the best works are found in the chapter house, which must have had an extraordinary interior, with an elegant spray of Gothic ribs radiating out from a central pillar, each of these ribs springing from a decorated corbel on the walls or corners (Figs. 79-80). When Jeffery excavated this room in 1913 he discovered the column and capital (very likely taken from ancient Greco-Roman or Byzantine ruins) that you can now see re-erected in the center, along with the block that belonged on top of the capital that shows how the ribs of the radial vault sprung (it's lying upside-down on the ground nearby). On one of the corbels one finds Ulysses flanked by the Sirens, an ancient pagan story redeployed as a Christian metaphor for resisting temptation, while another portrays the ladders of St Augustine (one

Fig. 77: View of the arches of the cloister and the refectory at Bellapais.

235

Fig. 78: The vaulting of the north cloister at Bellapais.

Fig. 79: The chapter house at Bellapais, with its single column at the center of the room's vaulting.

Fig. 80: The chapter house (foreground) and 'undercroft' at Bellapais.

which leads to heaven, the other to hell) fancifully arrayed on either side of Augustine's head, indicating, one supposes, the cerebral origin of the famous Church Father's theological concepts (Fig. 81). His appearance is related to the fact that the monastery was originally Augustinian, from which the Premonstratensians were derived. Indeed, the latter Order was sometimes called 'Reformed Augustinian' or the 'White Canons' of St Augustine. Yet another corbel, even more whimsical, has a monkey eating the fruit of a fig tree, a grotesque figure holding a basket, and a lion-like monster, side by side. Nobody has been able to interpret this parable if, indeed, it alludes to one at all. In two corners monks cower, their faces vandalized by musket or rifle bullets. One can imagine the monastery's abbot and canons seated on the stone benches that still surround the edges of the chapter house, with the strange sculptures gazing down at them. Such grotesque and imaginative carvings were common in the monastic architecture of the Romanesque and Gothic periods. These depictions at Bellapais remind us of the complaint of St Bernard of Clairvaux (1090-1153; possibly alive when the first structures were being built here at Bellapais), a famous reformer of the Cistercian monastic order, who wrote around the year 1140:

What are these fantastic monsters doing in the cloisters under the very eyes of the brothers as they read? What is the meaning of these unclean monkeys, strange savage lions and monsters? To what purpose are here placed these creatures, half beast, half man?... Surely if we do not blush for such absurdities we should at least regret what we have spent on them!

Such caprices can also be found in the corbels of the cloister, with the triple-heads of dog-like creatures, a man whose arms are being bitten by weird monsters, and the ancient fertility symbol of the Green Man, who has a beard and moustache of leaves.

The dorter or dormitories of Bellapais, and the formerly vaulted room below (Jeffery called it a 'Common Room' while Enlart called it the 'warming room' and thought that it may have been some kind of workplace; it is labeled 'Undercroft' at the site), which extended on the upper level north from the chapter house, is now very much ruined, but the blocks lying below offer a good opportunity to search for mason's marks. There are dozens on the walls and on the blocks on the ground (Fig. 80). There are also good examples of ship graffiti here, some that may date to the 18th century judging by the tall-masted sailing ships depicted. As we have already noted, the eastern wall survived to its full height until the early 20th century, and the barrel vault of the longitudinal structure had survived at least until van Bruyn's visit in 1683. The storey

Fig. 81: The sculpted corbel showing St Augustine from the chapter house at Bellapais.

above included dormitories for the monks. In that upper storey one can see a series of windows with niches right beside them. These correspond to the monk's cells, each of which had a single window and wall niche for their meager belongings. A central hallway would have run down the center, giving access to the flanking monks' cells in the east and west. One suspects that the more privileged monks were given the cells on the now fallen east side, which had spectacular views and faced the rising sun. Other monks' cells may have been constructed above the refectory in the north but very little remains of any superstructure that may have existed there.

There is a small, chapel-like room on the upper level. It is the only complete structure that survives in the higher section of the monastery. It is thought to have been the treasury of the church, isolated above, perhaps, for the safety and security of its contents. It is a lovely little Gothic room with rib vaults springing from wall corbels in the Lusignan fashion. The corbels have a drop motif below them (note the similar designs in the church), one of the many variations of that motif in Lusignan-era architecture. Niches in the walls likely held valuable liturgical implements. Note the recessed edges where the wood of the doors was fitted. One can also see broken bits of masonry where the hinges of doors would have been, thus securing the valuables. The broken part of the stone may well indicate someone breaking the hinges open to rob the contents. It is very possible that the abbey was looted around 1373 when the Genoese rampaged through Cyprus, stealing all they could.

The church is a lovely building. It has a high belfry with four spaces for bells running across the top of the façade and there is a graceful vaulted porch in front offering shelter for visitors. One of the arched niches at the north end of the porch may have been the tomb constructed for King Hugh III, who had wanted to be buried at Bellapais (though he never was, being interred in Santa Sophia in Nicosia instead). Vague remnants of fresco decoration survive on the stones of the arch on the left, showing a figure of an Evangelist or Prophet in a quatrefoil frame. Another one of the niches at the south end, A.H.S. Megaw suggested, may have been the tomb of Guy d'Ibelin, who was buried at Bellapais in 1309. Mute traces of Venetian period coats of arms survive high on the wall in the south section of the porch. A remnant of a fresco, showing the Virgin Mary enthroned with the infant Christ on her lap and flanked by angels, can still be seen in the lunette over the main doorway, though it is not very old.

The church interior is a bit dark, as the windows are small and the apse windows' light is blocked by the iconostasis, but the space is still striking. Rather hefty, low columns hold up the broad arches, quite reminiscent of some Cypriot Byzantine churches. The apse or chancel is not accessible today, which is too bad since there are fresco remains on the walls (one can see its distinctive squared end from the exterior in the east). One might also make note of a closed door to the left of the chancel — at the end of the north aisle — which led to the sacristy with its elegant two-bays of rib vaulting (it, too, visible from the exterior in the east). Along the north wall of the church interior there are two doorways. The easternmost one led to a night stair, by which the monks would descend into the church from their dormitory for midnight masses or Matins. The one further west (closer to the entrance) led to a spiral staircase that took one to the roof and to the treasury. In the west end of the interior, one can see the wooden structure of the *gyneconitis* or women's gallery, a construction of more modern times that, like the iconostasis, reflects the later Orthodox organisation of the church's interior. The iconostasis, happily, survives, with many of its old icons still in place, as does much of the other Orthodox ecclesiastical furniture such as the wooden seats for the monks (called *stasidia* or *kathismata*), the special seat for the abbot (*kathisma*), the pulpit up high on the left, and the holders for large candles. On the upper row of icons on the iconostasis is Christ in the center, flanked by enthroned saints on either side. In the second row are scenes from the life of Christ. Beautiful chandeliers light the interior.

Sources for Bellapais: Enlart, 174-200; Jeffery, 323-335; George Jeffery, "The Cloister of Bella Paise Abbey, Cyprus, 1913," *Journal of the Royal Institute of British Architects* 21 (1914): 482-488; George Jeffery, "The Refectory of Bella Paise Abbey, Cyprus," *Journal of the Royal Institute of British Architects* 22 (1915): 181-85; A.H.S. Megaw, *A Brief History and Description of Bellapais Abbey*. Nicosia, Department of Antiquities, 1964.

A Late Lusignan or Venetian Period Chapel, Sınırüstü/Syngkrasi, 14th-15th century

[35° 16' 19.83" N / 33° 51' 06.07" E]

This small Lusignan-era chapel lies in an abandoned yard beside a school in the village of Sınırüstü (Fig. 82). It is not known whether it was the private chapel of a larger residential complex, such as a Lusignan period villa, or stood on its hillside in solitude as a pilgrimage chapel. Gunnis reports that it was called the church of St Nicholas, but doesn't give his source. He confidently states that it is a 16th century building, though it could certainly be late 15th century. Little remains of the chapel itself and there is evidence that it may have been an Orthodox rather than a Latin Catholic building, since its plan most resembles the two-aisle, two-apse structures like the church of the Panagia Theotokos in nearby İşkele/Trikomo. Like that church, the small chapel has an arcade dividing the body of the church into two aisles. It may have had two aisles and two apses, in fact, to accommodate both Latin and Orthodox rites. The monk Felix Faber, passing through Cyprus in 1480, was scandalized to find a monk giving Latin rites to Catholics and then, in alternation, walking to an Orthodox chapel and administering the Greek rites. Faber felt that this meant neither of the rites was valid and that it was a heretical act. A few tantalizing artifacts lie scattered in the yard beside the chapel, including a Greco-Roman period funerary marker (cippus) with Greek inscriptions on it, as well a few architectural fragments belonging either to the chapel itself or whatever building it may have been coextensive with. The columnar funerary marker could well have supported the altar of the chapel, as it was not unknown for such classical fragments to be used in this way.

Sources: Gunnis, 434-5.

Fig. 82 · The Late Lusignan or Venetian Period Chapel at Saranda/Saranta/Saranteion (Somakaosi

The History and Architecture of Lefkoşa/Nicosia

The city of Lefkoşa/Nicosia lies more or less at the center of Cyprus and has been the island's principal city and capital for centuries. There seems to have been a Roman castrum settlement there but nothing of that remains. The city's name in ancient times was 'Ledroi' or 'Ledra', reflected nowadays in the name of the central north/south thoroughfare of the old city, Ledras Street. Some say that the Latins corrupted the name Lefkosia (also 'Levkosia' or 'Lefkosia'), which the Greeks used for the city, to 'Nicosia' in the Lusignan and Venetian eras. Roads radiate out from the city north through the Agridhia pass to the north coast at Girne/Kyrenia, south to Limissol and Larnaca, east to Famagusta, and west to Güzelyurt/Morphou. Its central location in the Mesorian Plain, with ready access to the mineral deposits of the Troodos Mountains, made it an ideal location for a major city. In ancient times Cyprus's coastal cities were preeminent, and it was only in the late Byzantine period that Nicosia emerged as an important center. Today, the city's inland location might not seem logical, but being inland ensured that pirate raids — common in the 7th to 10th centuries — or enemy fleets could not take it by surprise, something that often happened with the seaside towns. And while the area around Nicosia seems very dry today, the Pediaios River once flowed through the city, although even in the Middle Ages, as today, this was a seasonal watercourse that often went dry in the summer months. Still, Nicosia had a high and plentiful water table as water from Mount Olympus, where the headwaters of the Pediaios began, flowed towards it. Medieval visitors noted Nicosia's plentiful wells.

Felix Faber, an Augustinian monk who visited in 1483, wrote his impressions:

> In the whole realm of Cyprus are four bishoprics or dioceses. The first is in Nicosia, which is the capital, now a great city, not on the sea but five German miles away in the heart of the island; surrounded by fertile and pleasant hills. A large torrent runs through its midst, which at certain seasons rushes down in a mighty stream. When I was there it had not a drop of water.
>
> *[Excerpta Cypria, 41]*

The account of an even earlier traveller, the German priest Ludolf von Suchen, who was there around 1338, shows his admiration for Nicosia:

> There is another great city in Cyprus called Nycosia. It is the capital of the island, and lies under the mountains in a fine open plain with an excellent climate. In this city, by reason of its well-tempered air and healthfulness, the king of Cyprus and all the bishops and prelates of his realm, the princes and nobles and barons and knights, chiefly live, and daily engage in spear-play and tourneys, and especially hunting.
>
> *[Excerpta Cypria, 18]*

Von Suchen is not the only visitor to Nicosia who commented on the popularity of hunting among the Lusignan nobles of Nicosia. He tells of hunting the Moufflon, the mountain sheep famous in Cyprus, with trained leopards, and of the hunting excursions of the Nicosians:

> There are in Cyprus wild rams which are not found in other parts of the world. But they are caught by leopards, in no other way can they be taken....they spend all on the chase. I knew a certain Count of Japhe... who had more than five hundred hounds, and every two dogs have their own servant to guard and bathe and anoint them, for so must dogs be tended there. A certain nobleman has ten or eleven falconers with special pay and allowances...when they go to the chase they live sometimes for a whole month in their tents among the forests and mountains, straying from place to place, hunting with their dogs and hawks, and sleeping in their tents in the fields and woods, carrying all their food and necessaries on camels and beasts of burden.
>
> *[Excerpta Cypria, 20]*

Nicosia began to grow rapidly as the capital of the Lusignan kings, but it had already begun its ascent to being the premier city of Cyprus in the late Byzantine era in the 11th century. Certainly, by the 12th century, Nicosia was the main city of the island. When the self-appointed emperor of Cyprus, Isaac Comnenus, was chased down by Richard the Lion Heart in 1191, Isaac first fled to Nicosia, which one presumes was a significant stronghold, though Richard was able to conquer it and eventually take all of Cyprus. When the crusading Lusignans assumed control over Cyprus in the late 12th century, just a couple of years after Richard's conquest, the royal Lusignan court and palace was located in Nicosia, as was the island's principal cathedral, Santa Sophia. Most members of the noble class lived there, even while their agricultural holdings or fiefs were in various places throughout the island.

The Venetian Walls and Bastions of Nicosia

The Lusignans built a substantial circuit of walls around the city, but these were destroyed by the Venetians in the 1560s in their attempt to redesign the city's fortifications. Scholars have tried to discover the extents of these earlier walls and there are some conflicting ideas about the arrangement of their circuit. Indeed, much of the city's historical architecture has been lost. Many convents, monasteries and churches were long ago destroyed and not very much is known about them except that virtually all the major orders were represented and some monasteries were quite large. Destruction by invasions and sackings were augmented by natural disasters, such as the catastrophic earthquake of 1222.

There was likely a castle in Nicosia in the 13th century. Enlart notes that the counter-seal of the lead bull of King Hugh I (1205-1218) shows the castle of Nicosia with the inscription CASTELLUM NICOSSIE (Enlart, 387 and Jeffery, 21). However, in the late 14th century King Peter II seems to have undertaken the construction of a more extensive set of urban fortifications to guard against Genoese incursions, which did indeed come in the early 1370s. By that time the Genoese had already taken Famagusta and would hold that city for about 90 years. While the outline of the Lusignan-era city walls is unknown, it is certain that they followed a different circuit than the walls the Venetians made starting in the late 16th century. These earlier walls are thought to have nonetheless been quite extensive and perhaps up to four miles in perimetre, virtually as large as the later Venetian walls that replaced them, though square in plan rather than circular. Some sections of the medieval fortifications seem to have survived until 1738 when Richard Pococke noted: "The walls of the ancient city, which were built with semi-circular towers, may be traced all around, and they seem not to have been much less than four miles in compass" [*Excerpta Cypria*, 260]. This corresponds with what scholars believe about the roughly square circuit of walls built during the Lusignan era. They were probably begun around 1300 during the reign of King Henry II, though it is unlikely that they were finished in his lifetime, as some sources mention ongoing construction into the reign of King Hugh IV in the 1340s. Panos Leventis traces major renovations of the walls in 1360 and, later, in 1373 after the Genoese invasion. Indeed, at that time the Genoese took control of part of the city, probably the southeast section, and made improvements to the fortifications in that quarter.

In one version of the hypothetical layout of the medieval fortifications the walls are essentially square in plan, with corners to the cardinal points, with a castle or citadel in the western corner and the course of the Pediaios River circling the great western bastion before entering the walled city. Today, the so-called 'Green Line' segregating the city into Turkish and Greek halves roughly follows the course of the Pediaios. There were four corner bastions, all circular in plan at the north, south, east, and west corners, and on the long walls between these great corner bastions were two smaller, semi-circular bastions on each of the four sides. The castle shared the great western bastion, but had three other bastions of its own and, of course, its own set of walls. F. S. Maratheftis, in his 1977 book on the city, believed that the circular set of later Venetian walls would have fit into this large square that measured about a mile per side, with the Pediaios River bisecting the city from west to east. By the 1450s the medieval walls were seen to be so inadequate, and the strategic island of Cyprus in such jeopardy from Ottoman expansion, that Pope Nicholas V

...enjoined the whole of Christendom to send troops or money to Cyprus; King John was exhorted to complete the fortifications of Nicosia (indulgences were granted for contributions to the cost of this work)...A bull of 12 April 1455 granted plenary indulgence to those who before 1 May 1455 should give assistance to Cyprus by personal service or subsidy.

[Hill, 523-4]

One thing is certain; when the Venetians assumed control of Cyprus in 1489 the fortifications of Nicosia, like those at Famagusta, were found to be anachronisms. When John Locke visited in 1553 he observed of Nicosia: "This is the ancientest citie of the Island and is walled about, but it is not strong neither of walles nor situation" [*Excerpta Cypria*, 70]. In 1565 the Venetian military engineer, Giulio Savorgnano, reported to the Venetian Senate that Nicosia's walls were old-fashioned and useless from a military point of view. The crumbling bastions had become so dilapidated, the townspeople had taken to planting garden plots in them. The Venetian campaign of refortification, which seems to have commenced in 1567 under the supervision of the Venetian Proveditore Francesco Barbaro after Savorgnano's designs, was indeed ambitious and obliterated many churches and monasteries that lay in the path of the new defences. The work must have proceeded at a terrific pace, since three years later, in 1570, the military engineer and theorist Bonaiuto Lorini could observe that:

The fortress of Nicosia was seen by me two months before the Turks invested it, and everything about it seemed well considered. I observed that although of earth, it was the finest work of the kind that could be made. I was still more astonished at hearing of its construction by the illustrious Signor Giulio Savorgnano, with the greatest ease, within the short space of eight months.

[Jeffery, 27]

When Lorini writes "although of earth" one assumes that he means that the earthwork ramparts were not yet faced with stone. Yet it may well be that they were never intended to be completely covered with stone. Savorgnano's designs called for only the lower half of the walls to be finished in masonry, while the upper part remained an earthen slope where the energy of incoming iron cannon balls would be easily absorbed. When the Ottomans attacked, however, the walls were still not totally finished. In fact, some of the stone faced walls that one sees today were completed by the Ottomans after they conquered the city. Savorgnano had been recalled to Venice early, and there are reports that, without his leadership, progress slowed in the last months before the Ottoman attack, thus leaving the work incomplete.

Citing Gilles Grivaud, Leventis writes of the Venetian building campaign that began in earnest in 1567:

The refortification project required five to six thousand workers. The river was diverted in order to flow in the new moat surrounding the city. The old walls with all structures lying outside the new enceinte (1800 houses, 80 churches and chapels, two large monasteries and numerous gardens), were demolished, and the smaller, circular fortress with eleven bastions was constructed.

[Leventis, 319]

The wealthy nobles whose money paid for the bastions, and whose names were therefore given to them, also had to oversee their respective construction projects. Again borrowing from Grivaud's research, Leventis gives a vivid account of the undertaking:

Shelter for the roughly 10,000 people that were displaced who, in their overwhelming majority, were poor masses, was never provided. Most of the displaced became workers in the project, and constructed make-shift wooden rooms in order to live in. Roughly 500 to 800 workers, men and women, worked on each bastion, from 6 am to 1 pm, and again from 7 pm until midnight or 1 am, with the groups shifting every two weeks, and with music, dance, and entertainment apparently provided each night on the construction site for the workers.

[Leventis, 319]

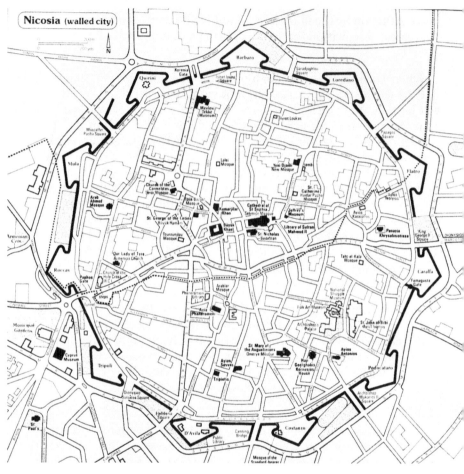

Fig. 83: Plan of Lefkoşa/Nicosia [from Camille Enlart, Gothic Art and the Renaissance in Cyprus].

250

One can easily imaging the chaos and urgency in Nicosia in the three short years between 1567 and 1570. All for nothing, for it was followed by a thorough sacking by the Ottomans. The citizens, those that remained alive, must have been completely destitute and dispirited.

The plan of the Venetian walls was of a type often designed on paper by Renaissance military architects but rarely executed in reality: a circular layout with angled bastions at regular intervals along the curves of the curtain walls (Fig. 83). Such a layout was often described as an 'ideal city', such as the circular design of the imaginary city of 'Sforzinda' by Filarete in the 15th century. One such city, Palmanova, was in fact built in 1593 by the Venetians in their territory in Friuli. However, while Palmanova was entirely planned, in Nicosia the city retained its medieval urban plan, though now ringed by a highly organised circular set of walls. Humanist inspired Renaissance military architects liked the circle. It was, after all, a perfect geometrical form. But this perfect form was also justified from a military point of view, though later it would be superseded by even more efficient star formations as the range of siege cannons increased. The angled bastions arrayed around the walls' circumference were deployed so as to protect each segment of wall with enfilading (literally 'infilling') fire, as well as to provide platforms for defensive barrages. Their large cannons, tucked away in the protecting curvatures of the two 'ears' (*orrecchiae*) of the bastions, covered the whole extent of the defenses. The low walls were thick and could withstand cannon, while the broad moat kept the enemy sufficiently distant. The eleven bastions were spaced so that there was no section of the city that was not equally defended. However, while the circular form with a ring of angled bastions was the ideal form of the time — witness Lorini's admiring description quoted earlier — there were those, even at the time, who expressed reservations about the fortifications. One problem lay not in the fortifications themselves, but in the fact that a number of low hills around the city were not included within the walls, thus giving both shelter and high ground to the enemy at several strategic points. Indeed, these hills would be exploited by the Ottomans in their siege. However, Nicosia was undermanned as it was, and a longer stretch of city walls would have been more expensive, would have taken longer to build, and would have had required many more men to defend its lengthier perimetre. The noble Venetian walls of Nicosia, then, impressive in their modernity and in the rapidity of their construction, were a classic case of too little too late.

Panos Leventis claims that the 11 bastions are symbolic of the 11 *contrade* or administrative districts of Cyprus. Thus the principal city's fortifications represent the defense of all of Cyprus, the bastions named after the magistrates of the Republic, Venetian and Cypriot, who energetically constructed them in the months, weeks, and even days before the Ottomans arrived in 1570: Barbaro, Loredano, Flatro, Caraffa, Podocataro, Costanzo, D'Avila, Tripoli, Roccas, Mula, and Quirini.

Sources for Nicosia and its Fortifications: Enlart, 387-390; Jeffery, 18-30; Leventis, 307-321; Gianni Perbellini, *The Fortress of Nicosia, Prototype of European Renaissance Military Architecture* (Nicosia: Leventis, 1994); Nicola Coldstream, *Nicosia: Gothic City to Venetian Fortress* (Nicosia, Leventis, 1993); Gilles Grivaud, "Aux Confins de l'Empire Colonial Vénetien: Nicosie et ses Fortifications (1567-1568)," *EKEE* 13-16/1 (1984-87): 269-79; Gilles Grivaud, "Nicosie Remodellée (1567): Contribution à la Topographie de la Ville Mediévale," *EKEE* 19 (1992): 281-306.

The Kyrenia Gate, Lefkoşa/Nicosia, 16th century (with later modifications)

[35° 10' 53.79" N / 33° 21' 42.40" E]

The Kyrenia gate, as we see it today, is not as it looked when this spot was the north gate of the Venetian city walls (Fig. 84). It is called Kyrenia Gate because it led to the road north (as it still does today) to the town of Girne/Kyrenia on Cyprus's north coast. Its original name, however, was the Porta del Proveditore, named after the Venetian Proveditore (regional governor) Francesco Barbaro, who also gave his name to the bastion just to the east of the gate. This part of the walls was altered in 1931 as part of a reconfiguration of this entry to the city, allowing for the wide, modern roads for cars. Today, it is a tourist information office. Luckily, there are late 19th century photographs that show it more or less in its original configuration, though the gate had also undergone renovations in 1821, just before the age of photography, so we cannot be completely sure of the original design. Jeffery claims that in 1821 the chamber above the gate was added, but he was not alive then so we must trust his source. The reliefs and inscriptions that can be found on the gate today are in some ways representative of five centuries of foreign occupation of the island of Cyprus. There is a Venetian inscription with the date 1462, the Ottoman sultan Selim II's *tughra* or ceremonial signature and a block with a *surah* (verse) from the Koran in Arabic, and the monogram of King George V (GVRI: 'George the Fifth Rex et Imperator', reigned 1910-1936). The date 1931 marks the year of the British-era renovation. That date is of some importance for Cyprus, as it marked the first revolt of Greek Cypriots against British rule. Most people point to the late 1950s as the time that Greek Cypriots rebelled, but the October 1931 rebellion was not insignificant. One principal demand then was the same as the one that came later in the 1950s, *enosis* or 'union' with Greece.

The Kyrenia Gate was probably the smallest of the city gates of the Venetian fortifications. The Porta San Domenico in the west was likely a bit larger than the Kyrenia Gate, though changes to both over time complicate any conclusions. Much larger and more impressive is the Famagusta gate ('Porta Giuliana'), for which one must cross over to the Greek side of Nicosia. It, like the Sea Gate in Famagusta, has an impressive domed interior. Even if greatly modified, one can easily imagine today how the flanking walls of the city, now cut back several metres from the Kyrenia gate, would have continued on to make a solid defense while the gate offered a simple but serviceable small arch through which carts and pedestrians could pass in and out of the city. During Venetian times, the square or piazza just inside the Kyrenia gate was called the 'Piazza dei Pisani', perhaps because traders from Pisa lived in that neighbourhood.

Fig. 84: The Kyrenia Gate, Lefkoşa/Nicosia.

Just outside the gate we must use our imagination and picture a broad moat with a drawbridge that would have been brought up at night and the doors shut tight, securing the city. Walking west along the sidewalk outside the walls, there are at least some parts where one can more easily imagine the outline of the moat. Until more recently, when the Ledra street crossing from Turkish to Greek Nicosia was opened, this was the route one took to cross the Green Line, walking outside the western flank of the city walls (past the Quirini, Mula, and Roccas bastions), to the Ledra Palace crossing, then down to re-enter the walled city at the Paphos Gate ('San Domenico Gate'; after the nearby monastery of the same name).

Just inside the Kyrenia gate is a dervish mosque and lodge of the Mevlevi Dervishes, also known in the west as 'whirling dervishes' after their distinctive 'dance' ceremonies. Their sect was founded by the 13th century poet known in the west as Rumi (1207-1273), who lived later in his life in Konya, Turkey, which is still the center of the sect's devotion around Rumi's stunning Selçuk-style tomb. The lodge dates from the 17th century and has the tombs of several sheikhs who led the *tekke* or dervish lodge.

Sources for Kyrenia Gate: Jeffery, 29.

The Venetian Column, Lefkoşa/Nicosia, 16th century

[35° 10' 41.16" N / 33° 21' 39.24" E]

Virtually everywhere the Venetians went they erected columns, often decorated with a sculpture of the lion of St Mark on top. Sometimes, they came in pairs, as at Famagusta, where they echoed the twin monumental columns at the Bacino waterfront in Venice beside the Ducal Palace. These columns were part of the ubiquitous iconography that helped the Venetians reproduce their authority in the many towns they controlled along the sea routes from Venice to the Middle East and the Black Sea. The columns often marked the place of public punishment, as they did in both Famagusta and Venice, though they often also played roles in articulating the urban space when used in civic ceremonies. Here in Nicosia, the column also marked an important part of the city, as it still does today, with the meeting of several crossroads, although it was moved just a few metres to its present location in 1915. Jeffery notes that the original configuration of column and base had a small water fountain but that this was not reproduced in the new location. Nearby was the 'Palazzo del Governo' of the Venetians, the central administrative building, which is completely lost. It was demolished in 1904 but had been dilapidated for decades. The current government buildings were built by the British on the site just west of the column. The column itself, which was the case in many of the columns throughout Venice's colonial cities, was 'spolia' (literally, 'spoils'), or a fragment of architecture that came from some earlier ancient Greek, Roman, or Byzantine building. This column may have come from Salamis, Paphos, or Kourion, all major Greco-Roman cities on Cyprus. Like the columns from Salamis in Famagusta, it is a monolith of grey granite over 20 feet high, though the high hexagonal base makes the whole monument seem even loftier. On the faces of the hexagonal base are Venetian coats of arms. In one, surmounted by the ducal *corno* or doge's cap, indicating the family of a doge, is the Donata (Donà) family arms with three roses and two bars. Francesco Donato was Doge of Venice from 1545-1553. Jeffery believed that the column may have been erected as a memorial at the death of the doge in 1553, while Arbel thinks it is simply the arms of the *luogotenente* Giovanni Battista Dona (1556-58). Other legible arms include those of the Contarini, Pesaro, Michaeli, and Querini families. There is an inscription in the base as well, which reads:

FIDES INCORRUPTA NON PULCHRITUDO NON
HUJUS UBERTAS SPECETUR INCOLAR

It's difficult to translate, but it means something like: 'Let neither the beauty nor the fertility of this place be seen, but rather the incorruptible fidelity of its inhabitants.' It is likely that a sculpture of the lion of St Mark surmounted the column originally, but the Ottomans would have been sure to destroy that. Today, a ball sits rather uninterestingly atop the monument.

Sources for Venetian Column: Jeffery, 59-60. Thanks to Frank Bezner for the translation.

Saint Sophia Cathedral, 13th to 14th century, Lefkoşa/Nicosia

[35° 10' 35.25" N / 33° 21' 50.66" E]

The great cathedral of Santa Sophia, certainly begun by 1209 (though some scholars trace its inception to as early as 1193) with subsequent building campaigns running well into the 14th century, was medieval Cyprus's principal Latin Catholic church and was the site of the coronation ceremonies of the kings and queens of Lusignan Cyprus. The first significant patron of the cathedral was the Archbishop Eustorge de Montaigu (1217-1251), and it is on his seal that the first representation of the cathedral is found. So dedicated was Eustorge to his building that a papal legate, Eudes de Chateauroux, complained to Eustorge that he was spending too much on the construction campaign and not enough on the divine liturgy. Camille Enlart, who visited Cyprus in the late 1890s, noted in his subsequent classic work *Gothic Art and the Renaissance in Cyprus*:

Nicosia is still a city of low houses widely spread out, with numerous gardens in between, and in consequence the great Gothic cathedral of St Sophia, though deprived of the crowning glory of its towers, dominates the broad townscape in a remarkably imposing way. Such a noble building rising among a swarm of dilapidated hovels gives a very good idea of what a medieval city looked like.

[Enlart, 82]

One can imagine what Enlart saw and, indeed, some early photographs exist that confirm his observations (Fig 85). Famagusta's cathedral of St Nicholas also gave such an impression. The name of the church, Santa Sophia, would suggest that the church was Byzantine, the appellation 'Hagia Sophia' being common in Byzantine churches (and the name, moreover, of the most famous of them all, in Constantinople/Istanbul). Scholars are of two minds about this unique name. Some believe that the name derived from a Greek, Byzantine church that might have existed at this very spot, and that the name indicated the Latin/Lusignan conquering of the site for Catholicism. However, more scholars today believe that the 'Byzantine' dedication of the church may instead indicate the Lusignan's desire to co-opt the name so as to placate and attract Orthodox Christians to Catholicism, thus proclaiming Lusignan rule over both Latin and Greek subjects on Cyprus. These scholars believe that Santa Sophia did not replace any earlier church, and that the Greek cathedral currently just south of Santa Sophia, the church of the Hodegetria (see entry below), was the site of the Orthodox cathedral or 'metropolitan' all along.

Fig. 85: Photograph of Santa Sophia cathedral in the late 19th century, Lefkoşa/Nicosia.

Just as the cathedral of St Nicholas in Famagusta was converted to a mosque in 1571, so too was Santa Sophia, which was renamed the Ayia Sofya mosque, simply a Turkish version of the same name. However, it was later renamed the Selimye mosque after the Ottoman Sultan Selim, the conqueror of Cyprus. While St Nicholas was adorned with a minaret only on its northwest corner, Santa Sophia received two towering minarets at the corners of its façade. Even today, these are visible from miles away.

Santa Sophia had a long and complex building history with campaigns grinding to a halt during times of invasion or economic slowdowns caused by natural disasters such as earthquakes or the great flood of 1330 in which it was estimated that 3000 people died. Many who had lost their homes that year found themselves refugees huddled in the cathedral for shelter. Scholars agree, however, that the construction began at the east end with the choir and crossing, and that this was more or less completed by 1228, enabling the church to be used for services. The visit of King Louis, the King of France, in 1248 is seen by some to have been a significant moment in the history of Santa Sophia as the king brought in his entourage artists, masons, and sculptors who may have worked on the cathedral. Since Louis also spent money liberally while he lingered in Nicosia, he helped the economies of the local religious institutions, including the cathedral. Some artisans of his court may have remained in Nicosia when Louis's planned military campaign to the Holy Land came to naught.

The cathedral was witness to other significant historical events. In 1360 the papal legate Peter Thomas invited the Greek bishops into the cathedral, locked the doors, and began trying to forcibly convert them to Catholicism. The Greek citizenry got wind of this, revolted, and tried to break down the doors of the cathedral. Some Latin nobles finally intervened and defused the volatile situation. This event reminds us that Greek and Latin relations in Cyprus were not very cordial through the periods of Latin domination. Indeed, there were numerous uprisings during the three centuries of Lusignan rule, such as the Kanakis rebellion of the first years of King Amalric's reign (1194-1205). Such struggles of the Greek majority against foreign hegemony mark many centuries of Cyprus's history. The year 1373 was a sad one for the city as the Genoese sacked it repeatedly, and the financial hardship of those events also must have strained Santa Sophia's coffers. Yet the cathedral often received generous benefices from the Latin citizens of Nicosia, and its impressive size and magnificent decoration is an indication of substantial royal and noble contributions made over the centuries.

Many visitors to Nicosia recorded their positive impressions of the great church. In 1394 Nicholas Martoni, after a harrowing trip from Famagusta in an ox cart with an argumentative companion and a night spent in a bed with ravenous fleas, nonetheless had good things to say of Nicosia. Of the cathedral he wrote:

The said city of Nicosia has an Archbishop, and his church is dedicated to St Sophia, it is a fair and great church, vaulted, and the whole of the vault from the choir arch to the high altar is painted with fine blue and golden stars.

[Excerpta Cypria, 26]

Reading Martoni's description of the richly painted vaulting of Santa Sophia, glittering with golden stars, reminds us that much of the church's splendour is lost to us today. Historical documents tell us of numerous altars besides the main altar, which also had a magnificent screen that divided the choir from the nave. The unobstructed view that we get today of the choir and its ambulatory would not have been available in the Middle Ages. The apse was also filled with choir stalls of wood, adding to the richness of the interior decorations. Many nobles were buried in Santa Sophia in floor tombs covered with slabs that often had effigies of the deceased carved on them, and some of these can be seen on display in one of the cathedral's south side chapels (an extra 'donation' to the caretaker might help get you access if the doors are closed). In the Middle Ages these would have been visible to all on the cathedral's floor.

The church also had a large octagonal marble baptismal font, constructed between 1319 and 1330, of which nothing remains, though Enlart mused whether parts of it might have been used to build the fountain for Muslim ablutions (shadirvan) that currently sits in the small garden of the church. That small forecourt, so confining today, reminds us that there once was a much more spacious parvis or cathedral square in front of Santa Sophia in medieval times and that the view of the western façade would have been much augmented by the more generous perspective. Today, one gets a better impression from the area north and northeast of the cathedral where more breathing room for the building has been retained. During the archbishopric of John de Polo (aka, Giovanni del Conte, John de Conte; 1312-1332) it is said that many furnishings were commissioned for the church, such as altars, paintings, silver angels, tapestries, and an embroidery of the Transfiguration of Christ. As the traveller Jacques le Saige noted when he visited the cathedral in 1518, there were also venerable relics in Santa Sophia: "...we were shown the right arm of St Lawrence enshrined in silver but I only saw a finger joint. And we were shown a double cross in which I saw a piece quite four inches long of the holy and true Cross of our Savior, and also many other relics" [Excerpta Cypria, 59]. Greffin Affagart, visiting in 1534, claims to have seen "one of the hydriai in which our Lord turned the water into wine" [Excerpta Cypria, 67] in Santa Sophia, but he may have been confused with the church in Famagusta called Santa Maria della Cava, which was famous for having such a relic. Felix Faber, in 1483, observed:

> It [St Sophia] is pretty large and well decorated, and maintains an archbishop, canons, and clergy. On the right of the church is a chapel dedicated to S. Thomas Aquinas, in which the legends of the holy doctor are exquisitely painted, while a gilt plaque on the altar sets forth his deeds.
>
> *[Excerpta Cypria, 42]*

Faber was most impressed, however, with a strange monument other travellers also made note of: a giant sarcophagus made of green jasper (a type of chalcedony). "For I cannot suppose that any king would have had a tomb of so great value," Faber wrote, "for jasper is more precious than gold, in which the dying Alexander ordered his remains to be placed" *[Excerpta Cypria*, 42-3]. These eyewitness accounts give us a much greater sense of the opulence of the church and impressive objects that were found in the cathedral in former times.

Perhaps the most impressive architectural element of the cathedral is its stunning Gothic porch at its west entrance (Fig. 86). Three graceful quadripartite Gothic rib vaults create a covered area just in front of the cathedral doors. George Jeffery notes that such a narthex-like porch was sometimes called a 'Galilee' in medieval times. The rhythm of the ribbing and the striations of the compound piers that support them compose one of the three great Gothic monuments of Cyprus, along with the Abbey of Bellapais near Kyrenia and the cathedral of St Nicholas in Famagusta. Justine Andrews has written on the function of the porch and the iconography of the figures in the archivolts of the 'royal portal', the main entryway of the church. This portal was likely constructed during the reign of King Hugh IV (1324-59) and during the tenure of the aforementioned Archbishop John del Conte, while the first coronation ceremony that took place there was probably King Peter I's in 1359. While Andrews sees similarities between the ornate foliage reliefs surrounding the portals with crusader decoration in the Holy Land, she also sees similarities in style to the rich border carvings that can be found in Reims cathedral in France. Reims was the cathedral in which the French kings were crowned, and Andrews sees an intentional reference here to the subject of coronation, since Santa Sophia, too, was a coronation church. Andrews also makes a connection between Reims and Santa Sophia in the sculpted figures of the archivolts of the main portals. In each, Old Testament kings and queens, saints, angels, bishops, and prophets are depicted (Fig. 87). The kings and queens are in the innermost register of the archivolts, thus in the place of honour in the portal's iconographic

Fig. 86: The Gothic vaulted western portico of Santa Sophia cathedral Lefkoşa/Nicosia.

Fig. 87: Figures in the archivolts of the main portal of Santa Sophia
cathedral Lefkoşa/Nicosia.

264

program. Andrews notes a correlation between the sculpted procession of kings and queens in the archivolts with the Lusignan coronation procession that would have passed under the portal itself. Unhappily, the relief sculptures of the tympana have been destroyed, probably as part of the 'purification' of the church in its conversion to a mosque in 1571. All that remains are two angels swinging censers (incense burners) in the lower corners of the central tympanum.

One of the more intriguing and unique elements of the portal and its organisation are the flat-paneled jambs. The jambs are the splayed elements that flank the doorways. In many Gothic churches these are composed of niches with full-figure statues of saints or other holy figures. At Santa Sophia, however, there are simply a series of tall panel-like frames, each surmounted by a relief carving of a crown being lowered from heaven by the hands of God. They were chipped away by the Ottomans as they depicted part of God's body, a heresy in Islam. Here, too, is an allusion to the sacred nature of kingship and how coronation supports the notion of the divine right of kings to rule. We might recall that Thomas Aquinas's treatise *On Kingship* (*De Regno*) was dedicated to the Lusignan King Hugh II for the latter's support of the Dominican Order, though the youthful king may well have died before ever having read it. In some of these jamb panels small metal hooks were discovered at the top. It is assumed that icon paintings of saints were hung from these hooks. This must have given an entirely different look to the portals and to the porch in general. Their presence would have obviously multiplied the imagery of the ensemble and also added much vibrant colour to the space. One wonders, given Andrews' convincing argument, if painted icons of Old Testament kings and queens might have echoed their counterparts in the archivolts and similarly augmented the theme of coronation that the portal seems to embody. However, saints also are said to receive the crowns of sainthood or martyrdom, so they, too, could have been appropriate subject matter. The panels are surrounded by reliefs of the wild rose, which was one of the symbols of the Lusignans, a motif found in many Lusignan buildings in Cyprus. This unique configuration of painted panels rather than sculptures also points to the possibility that it may have been very difficult for the Lusignans to obtain sculptors who were proficient enough to do full size figures in the round, whereas icon painters were fairly common on Cyprus. Today, one can see traces of medieval and Renaissance period graffiti on the walls surrounding the southernmost of the porch doors. Enlart was in the late 19th century still able to clearly see a Maltese cross with the date 1410 etched into the stone.

Both Enlart and Jeffery thought that there was intended to be a second level added above the vaulted porch of the western façade. Jeffery thought that it might be an open, vaulted porch mirroring the architecture below, but creating a large balcony from which royal or religious benediction could be given to audiences gathered in the cathedral square, or, similarly, icons or relics could have been displayed. The upper level could have played other various roles in church or royal ceremony. It might be noted that the cathedral of St Nicholas at Famagusta has a narrow but still significant porch running along the middle level of its western façade.

There were five chapels appended to the cathedral, most of which endure in some form today. One was reused by the Ottomans as a recess in the south wall of the mosque for the *mihrab*, or niche that indicates the direction to Mecca. Of this chapel little survives in the original form. However, the other four retain their medieval configurations. Each of these remaining chapels is similar in design: a rectangular body with a semi-circular apse with half-dome in the east end. Two of these opened up on to the nave and essentially served as the transept or crossing of the church. The one to the northeast was likely a sacristy or cathedral treasury. It also has a second storey on top of it. Enlart believed that this upper part, generously lit by lovely Gothic windows, might have been the Chapel of St Thomas of Canterbury, but he also proposes that its raised position, with a bench near a window looking out into the choir, might have been a safe place for the king or the archbishop to witness church ceremonies. The aforementioned surviving tomb slabs are kept in the southwest chapel. My favorite shows the 14th century effigy of Charles Doudiac, with his two children kneeling and praying for their father's soul at his feet (Fig. 88).

Comparison between the plan of St Nicholas at Famagusta (Fig. 128) and Santa Sophia (Fig. 89) reveals significant differences in the plans of the two churches. While St Nicholas's nave and side aisles each end in semi-circular apses — the side aisle apses being smaller than the central nave's — Santa Sophia's nave and side aisles all lead to the wide central apse, which has a series of four columns arranged in a semicircle, thereby creating what is called an ambulatory. Notre Dame in Paris has a similar configuration. The four columns in the hemicycle are not all the same, as one might think at first glance. One of them rests on a base that is actually a capital from some earlier structure. Two of the capitals are Gothic and beautifully carved, while the others are plain. Today, one sees a series of tie-beams between the vaults. These were probably added by the Venetians after a serious earthquake of 1491, soon after they had gained control of the island. One finds similar tie-beams in the vaulted churches of Venice to help stabilize the arches and vaults, such as in the Frari or San Giovanni e Paolo.

While the central, western portal is the most impressive of the church's entryways there are also two other attractive doorways, one on

Fig. 88:
Effigy on
the tomb
of Charles
Doudiac
with his two
children,
Santa Sophia
cathedral,
Lefkoşa/
Nicosia.

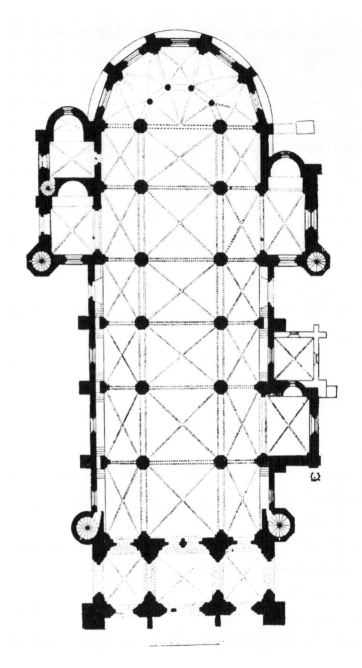

Fig. 89: Plan of Santa Sophia cathedral Lefkoşa/Nicosia [from Camille Enlart, Gothic Art and the Renaissance in Cyprus].

the north side and another that was taken away from the south side in the conversion of the building from cathedral to mosque. Jacques le Saige made note of the cathedral's portals in 1518:

> Then I breakfasted well and went to rest in the great church called S. Sophia, which is a very beautiful little church. There is the finest possible beginning of a bell tower of well cut sandstone, and already there are five porches [portals], three of which open a way under the said tower before one enters the church, and at the two ends of the transept there are two beautiful little doorways of fine stone, and the church is vaulted throughout.
>
> *[Excerpta Cypria, 58]*

The great south doorway may have been in an inappropriate place for the liturgical focus of the mosque, which was the south wall, although the portal was at the crossing and not exactly where the *mihrab* is located. The doorway was, for whatever reason, entirely disassembled and rebuilt along the southeast corner of the apse (Fig. 90). Made of marble, it has crockets along the top of the arch over the door, and in the tympanum some blind Gothic tracery that now holds an Ottoman inscription giving the date of 1584. Jeffery says the date is 1577, noting, in addition, that when De Mas Latrie visited in 1846 the south door seems to have been still in its original position. Enlart thought very highly of this Gothic portal and believed that it was designed by a French mason of the 13th century, perhaps even one that came in King Louis' entourage in 1248, maybe the architect Eudes of Montreuil who is said to have accompanied Louis on an earlier journey. The capitals of the colonettes run together to form a frieze of lovely leaf designs, and one can just make out some human faces above the imposts. The north doorway, while not as impressive as the others, has marble imposts with beautiful ivy and leaf reliefs on them.

As one walks around the exterior of Santa Sophia one can observe many interesting elements besides the portals. Up high, there are several gargoyles visible. On the south side, on one of the piers of a buttress, one can make out a sun dial. Also on the south side are several coats of arms of the de Pins, with their pine cone family symbol. Walking around the apse, there is a fragment of a figure of a camel driver raising a whip to goad his camel along.

Sources for Santa Sophia: Enlart, 82-130; Jeffery, 64-82; Leventis, 25-31 and 299-303; Justine M. Andrews, "Santa Sophia in Nicosia: The Sculpture of the Western Portals and its Reception, *Comitatus* 30 (1999): 63-80.

Fig. 90: South portal moved and reconstructed by the Ottomans, Santa Sophia cathedral Lefkoşa/Nicosia.

The 'Chapter House' of Santa Sophia, Lefkoşa/Nicosia, 14th century

[35° 10' 34.87" N / 33° 21' 55.62" E]

The beautiful Gothic structure at the southeast corner of the apse of the cathedral has been called the chapter house of the church. However, it is by no means certain that this actually was the building's function. Without question, though, it was one of the city's most splendid Gothic-era houses. It may have been designed so that the ground level was to accommodate shops for generating retail or workshop space that would help support the household, while the inhabitants of the house would live on the floors above.

The Church of the Hodegetria (also called St Nicholas, or the 'Bedestan'), Lefkoşa/Nicosia, various structures 6th to 16th century

[35° 10' 34.02" N / 33° 21' 50.12" E]

The Byzantine church that most guidebooks and signs refer to as St Nicholas or the 'Bedestan' should more properly be called the Church of the Hodegetria, referring to its earlier name that was likely derived from an icon of the Hodegetria type that was venerated in the church (Fig. 91). The name 'Bedestan' comes from the church's use as a market in the Ottoman period, 'bedestan' meaning a type of marketplace. The name St Nicholas seems to have been a spurious attribution of the 19th century that was simply repeated by later historians. The term 'Hodegetria' is an epithet of the Virgin Mary that means 'The One Who Shows the Way', and this is the name of a type of icon in which the Virgin Mary holds the infant Christ and points towards him. With her gesture, she 'shows the way' to salvation. The original Hodegetria image was a famous icon in Constantinople and many imitations were made of it. One of these, apparently, was housed here in the early church on the site. The church that one sees today is simply the last of many built at this location, fragments of earlier constructions are only mutely present. Much of what is visible now is from the Lusignan or Venetian period, and this is evident in the splendid portals on the north flank of the structure with their ornate sculptures, the pointed arches of some of the interior arcading, and in the well-preserved gargoyles along the roofline of the north side, all of which in their style and decoration indicate late Lusignan and Venetian eras (Fig. 92). A row of Venetian coats of arms can also be found on one of these portals, indicating that during the Venetians' brief tenure on Cyprus there was at least some patronage of the church, if not major building campaigns. Indeed, in other parts of the south section there is evidence of considerable renovation. This south section also contained an arcade which, at least by the 19th century, had begun to lean dangerously. However, it did not collapse and in 2009 a major restoration project began, thus ensuring its survival into the 21st century. The arches still lean, but have been stabilized. The dome and its pendentives were also in poor condition even around 1900, based on contemporaneous descriptions.

The Hodegetria church was the most important Byzantine church in Nicosia, being the 'metropolis' or cathedral for the Orthodox Christians. Some scholars wonder whether the Gothic cathedral of Santa Sophia was built atop an earlier Byzantine church, but many now believe that the Lusignans built their cathedral beside the Orthodox cathedral as a

Fig. 91: Arches of the church of the Hodegetria ('the Bedestan' or 'St Nicholas'), Lefkoşa/Nicosia.

274

way of embodying the now dual religious heritage of the island. Like St George of the Greeks in Famagusta, the metropolitan church of that city, the Church of the Hodegetria is a synthesis of Latin Gothic and Greek Byzantine architectural forms. George Jeffery was put off by this syncretism, demonstrating that in matters of aesthetics he disliked a fusion of styles and preferred 'pure' archetypes. Many historians studying Cypriot architecture today, however, have very different scholarly values and find the complexity and hybrid nature of Cypriot architecture one of its most compelling features.

There are numerous sculptures adorning the church, mostly dating from the late Lusignan period or from the Venetian era in the later 16th century. There are many vibrant ornamental reliefs around the portals on the north side facing Santa Sophia cathedral. Some show fantastic faces or coats of arms or are decorative bands or capitals of colonettes. In the lintel of one of the north portals (the westernmost) is a marble relief of the Dormition of the Virgin (or, in Greek, the *Koimesis*). It was a popular theme in both Latin and Byzantine art. The Virgin Mary lies on her deathbed, surrounded by mourning apostles. Christ stands behind her with her soul, represented as an infant, in his arms, ready to bear it to heaven, though this is difficult to see because it has been chipped off (Fig. 93). While for centuries during the Ottoman period the church was used as a marketplace, in the late 19th century it was used as a grain and lumber storage yard. Today, the building has been restored and part of it is used as a concert hall.

Sources for Church of the Hodegetria: Enlart, 136-146; Jeffery, 84-89; Leventis, 23-25 and 285-299; Michael Willis, "Byzantine Beginnings of the Bedestan," *Kypriakai Spoudai* 50 (Nicosia, 1987), pp. 185-192.

Fig. 93: Sculptural relief of the Koimesis or 'Death of the Virgin' above the north portal of the church of the Hodegetria ('the Bedestan' or 'St Nicholas'), Lefkoşa/Nicosia.

276

Church of St Catherine (Haydar Paşa Camii), Lefkoşa/Nicosia, 14th century

[35° 10' 38.60" N / 33° 21' 57.59" E]

Located just a short walk northeast of St Sophia is the church of St Catherine, one of the best preserved and beautiful churches on the island (Fig. 94). It dates from the late 14th century, when the stylistic phase of Gothic was highly decorative. It is useful to recall this church when one visits Famagusta and sees the church of St George of the Latins because St Catherine's gives a good sense of what St George looked like when it still had its vaults and south wall. The church was converted into a mosque after 1571 — renamed the Haydar Paşa Camii — as is evident by the minaret in the southwest corner. One sometimes also sees the building called the 'Bishop's church' because it was so close to the Archbishop's palace in medieval times.

Like many Lusignan-era churches on Cyprus St Catherine's consists of an open, single space with no side aisles or columns. It has only two ribbed vaults forming its nave and a beautiful vaulted apse of three sides at the eastern end. Appended to the northeast corner of the church is the pentagonal sacristy with graceful rib vaulting, which is entered through a doorway with a trefoil design atop it. Another room built on top of it might have been the treasury. This upper room, according to Jeffery's observations made in 1918, was itself divided by a timber floor into two chambers, the lower may have offered a communication with the convent buildings that may have been situated immediately to the north and perhaps abutted the apse itself (one can still see traces where walls attached on the exterior). From the upper room one could get a good view of the church's interior through a lancet window with tracery. Also on the interior of the apse, at the southeast facet, one finds a *piscina* niche, with tracery and a gable, where holy water was stored in medieval times.

There are a couple of beautiful doorways on the church exterior, one on the south side and one on the west façade. The south door is framed with a border of Lusignan wild roses, while its lintel has three shields with the coats of arms obliterated. Pairs of marble and sandstone colonnettes flank the doorway and lead up to gracefully carved archivolts with leaf decoration. The whole ensemble is crowned by a Gothic finial at the apex. In the tympanum is some blind Gothic tracery with trefoil and quatrefoil patterns. Note at the base of the colonnettes the Lusignan drop motif, a design found somewhere on most works of medieval architecture in Cyprus, though the specific forms vary, sometimes tapering upwards and sometimes downwards. The west portal is similar in design to the south doorway, though it has relief sculptures on the lintel showing flowers and winged dragons. It is worthwhile to walk right around the church to

Fig. 94: The church of St Catherine's, Lefkoşa/Nicosia.

the north side, as the antiquities department seems to use that space as a 'bone yard' for sundry architectural fragments and even classical and Byzantine objects. Once I saw a classical Greek relief in white marble with egg and dart (ovolo) molding and a fragmentary relief of a fighting Amazon, an amazing work of art that should have been in a museum.

The most recent scholarship has proposed that St Catherine's was associated with a hospice for the poor. Leventis cites two papal indulgences of April 1st and March 31st, 1362, which mention such a hospice and chapel of St Catherine. Leventis also notes that St Catherine's proximity — perhaps even virtually attachment — to the Archbishop's Palace would have made a hospice for the poor an appropriate extension of the charity of the archbishopric. While St Catherine's may seem too large to be a chapel one could certainly note that other chapels in Europe were this size or larger, so the church's size does not exclude it from this designation. It is unfortunate that the medieval structures just north of the church, whether convent or hospice, or both, have been destroyed. Perhaps future excavations may reveal the foundations of some of these lost structures.

Sources for St Catherine's: Enlart, 152-157; Jeffery, 90-94; Leventis, 227-229.

The Yeni Cami ('New Mosque'); ruins of a medieval church of uncertain dedication, Lefkoşa/Nicosia, 14th century

[35° 10' 43.95" N / 33° 21' 57.86" E]

Just a short walk north from St Catherine's are the ruins of a church that at one time might have looked a lot like St Catherine's. It is likely, however, that the church had suffered substantial damage even before the Ottomans took over in 1571. At any rate, the building was rebuilt as a mosque, incorporating what little remained of the earlier Gothic church. But this mosque, too, fell into ruin, and thus it is the ruins of both church and mosque that we see today on this site. Some mute details of the Gothic articulation give us a vague sense of the beauty of the original structure. There is a legend that the mosque was destroyed not by a natural disaster or poor construction, but by a greedy pasha who believed there was a treasure ensconced somewhere in the fabric of the mosque, and who tore the building apart searching for it.

Nearby is the small, newer mosque that gives the ruins their name, *Yeni Cami* or 'New Mosque'. Here there are three Ottoman tombs, one of which is the grave of the well-known poet Hassan Hilmi Effendi, who served as the *mufti* of Cyprus around 1800. Another tomb belongs to Mentish Ismail Aga, who apparently took his own life in 1735 rather than face criminal punishment. His son is also entombed at Yeni Cami, across the lane. He died not long after his poor father, in 1749.

Sources for Ruins at Yeni Cami: Enlart, 150-2; Jeffery, 99.

Saint George of the Latins (Büyük Hamam), Lefkoşa/Nicosia, late 13th or early 14th century

[35° 10' 36.84" N / 33° 21' 41.99" E]

This interesting early church was turned into a bath house or Ottoman hamam in the 1570s when the Ottomans conquered Cyprus, a function it still has today. It was called the Büyük Hamam or 'Great Bath', though in some earlier texts it is called the 'Women's Baths', as in George Jeffery's book of 1918. Like the Çafer Paşa Hamam in Famagusta, the 'church' part was used only as a part of the bath complex, and domed structures in Ottoman style were added on to it. Being a modern business restricts visitors' access to the interior of the structure, which is its most impressive component, though one can always pay for a bath and get the full tour. Perhaps that's not a bad option after a day of heavy sightseeing.

Jeffery cautions that there is no definitive information about this structure being St George of the Latins and notes that its north-south orientation suggests that it may not have been a church at all. Perhaps it was some other Gothic, vaulted building that had a secular function, even, as Jeffery suggests, a medieval bath house simply reconfigured to an Ottoman one. If true, a similar instance of renovation and reuse is the Kertikli Hamam in Famagusta, which was a medieval bath house much reconstructed and added on to by the Ottomans. Leventis has agreed with Jeffery on this point.

Although it may seem a bit out of the center of town now, St George of the Latins — whether this building or not — was beside Nicosia's medieval market and the Lusignan royal palace was also nearby. Today one can see that the church occupies a low level as the modern streets have been raised around the front portal. In 1330, when there was a great flood in Nicosia, this church was half submerged in the waters. At one time there was a nail in a wall that marked the impressive height of the water. Because of its proximity to the market and the palace it was a natural civic rallying point and many historical events occurred at the church, including the oaths sworn by noble Nicosians to Amalric, Prince of Tyre, after he successfully challenged the throne of his brother Henry II in 1306. Similarly, King Hugh IV received the oaths of the citizens in this church in 1324. Hugh's son may have been buried here, as a fragment of his tomb was found in the church. It was also the place where, according to the Greek Cypriot chronicler Leontios Makhairas, the assassins of Peter I gathered to discuss their plans on the fateful Wednesday, January 17th of 1368. R. M. Dawkins, in his translation of the Makhairas, calls the church 'St George of the Halfcastes', translating Makhairas' Greek *ton Ornithion*. These are equivalent to a name the Latins used for the church, Sant George des Poulains, who were, as Dawkins writes, "... the children of Frankish fathers and Syrian mothers." It may have been a vernacular name with some derogatory implications. Makhairas also says that cotton thread was sold near the church and just outside it was an enormous marble trough.

The apse of the church no longer exists, if it ever did. Perhaps it was demolished in 1571. The current building consists only of three vaulted bays. The most impressive element of the structure is a beautifully sculpted portal, with archivolts of cable, dog-tooth, dentil, floral, leaf, and grapevine designs. The portal may or may not have belonged to the original structure, as it appears to have been dismantled and reconstructed here. (Note the wedges inserted just above the imposts, as if parts of the first voussoir blocks were missing.) Nevertheless, it is still quite impressive. The colonnettes are all but obscured by the raised street level, but one can get a glimpse of them by walking down the stairs. Flanking and above the doorway are two nicely carved corbels with acanthus leaf designs. Perhaps they helped support a timber-framed roof that once sheltered the doorway similar to the modern one just above. These corbels, too, were likely brought from some other building.

Sources for St George of the Latins: Enlart, 157-160; Jeffery, 61; Leventis, 203-05.

Notre Dame de Tyre (Notre Dame de Tortosa) and later the Armenian Church (Sourp Asdvadzadzin), Lefkoşa/Nicosia, early 14th century

[35° 10' 30.08" N / 33° 21' 28.77" E]

George Jeffery noted that we cannot be sure that this church is the Benedictine church of Our Lady of Tyre, a designation which Enlart seemed to be quite certain of. Certainly a church of this name existed in medieval Nicosia. Many today accept the alternative contention that the church is more properly Notre Dame of Tortosa, an opinion shared by Jean Richard, Brunehilde Imhaus and Panos Leventis. This church's name also appears in the pages of several chroniclers. Whatever the correct designation, that this was a major nunnery in Nicosia is not debated, as the numerous tomb slabs and effigies found in the church bear witness to the many nuns and nobility who had themselves interred there. These tombs are eloquent evidence of the high regard that this nunnery had in medieval Nicosia. If the church is Notre Dame de Tyre, the convent and church was in a sense imported from Jerusalem. Baldwin I had founded a convent in Jerusalem, but when that city was lost to Saladin in 1187 a new institution was founded in the city of Tyre on the Middle Eastern coast. After that city was also lost to Islam in 1291 the institution was shifted to Nicosia. The same is true with the name Notre Dame de Tortosa, as Tortosa was a city on the coast of Syria, modern Tartus, where, incidentally, the 12th century cathedral church of Notre Dame de Tortosa still exists. This institution was also, then, an import from the Middle East to Cyprus.

From the beginning the church had structural problems, and today it is undergoing a thorough renovation. The nave is about 20 m long and 10 m wide, making it a bit smaller than St Catherine's, but here the vaulting is lower than at St Catherine's, giving a much different feeling inside. The increased breadth of the vault in relation to its height may have added to the instability of the architecture. Jeffery thought that the tall, broad, bare lower walls were meant for paintings, and one can only imagine what lovely frescoes might have existed there. One odd feature of the church's architecture is that the nave is made up of two types of vault, each comprising a fairly equal segment of the nave, though the westernmost vault is slightly larger. This westernmost vault is a barrel vault, while the easternmost vault is a ribbed cross-vault. Indeed, it is instructive to see the difference between the two vaulting techniques and how the ribbed vault — a defining feature of Gothic architecture — allowed for the large windows while the barrel vault necessitated the buttressing counterweight of a more continuous solid wall. The apse is pleasingly ribbed in the Gothic style and hence well lit by tracery windows, though these in recent years have been filled in. Hopefully, in the process of restoration, the windows can be reopened and re-glazed, and the apse returned to its original Gothic glory.

Jeffery gives an account of some of the tomb slabs of nobles that were found there, such as Mary de Bessan's (d. 1322), a woman from the crusading family of the Bethsan, or the one belonging to Balian Lambert (d. 1330), where the effigy shows the deceased in chain mail with a helmet; possibly he was related to Bishop Lambert of Famagusta from around that same time. In one case three women chose to be buried together, Alice de Tabarie (d. 1357), Isabelle de Nevilles (d. 1393), and Mary de Milmars, (d. 1393). Perhaps the more long-lived Isabelle and Mary wished to be reunited with their friend Alice who had died young. The effigy is of a single woman only, however, in elegant courtly dress of the period. The names of many nuns are recorded on the broken pieces of their tombs: Sister Anne de Montolif (d. 1348), Sister Eufemia Scaface [Escaface?] (d. 1348), Sister Anne de De (d. 1348), and Sister Sebille d'Agulier (d. 1348).

Armenians were said to have been supportive of the Ottoman campaign to take Cyprus from the Venetians, supplying sappers for the sieges of Nicosia and Famagusta. One story even recounts that in the Ottoman siege of Nicosia they opened the Paphos gate for the attackers. As a reward they were granted this church for their use either in 1571 or some time shortly thereafter. Some sources, such as George Hill, note that the Armenians may have had control of the church before 1571 when the Ottomans took it over and briefly used it as a salt storage facility before it was returned to the Armenians. Of course, it is entirely possible, even probable, that there was another Armenian church in Nicosia that has been lost, and that some historical documents may refer to this lost church. The present church has remained under the ownership of the Armenian Church until modern times.

Sources for Notre Dame de Tyre/Tortosa or Armenian Church: Enlart, 131-136; Jeffery, 50-55; Gunnis, 40-42; Leventis, 109-115; Jean Richard, "Un but de Pelinerage: Notre-Dame de Nicosie," in *Mosaic. Festschrift for AHS Megaw*, eds. J. Herrin, M. Mullet, C. Otten-Froux (Athens, 2001), 135-8.

Ottoman Architecture in Lefkoşa/Nicosia

Fig. 95: Inner courtyard and elevated mosque (pavilion mosque or kösk mescit) of the Büyük Han, Lefkoşa/Nicosia.

Büyük Han, Ottoman, Lefkoşa/Nicosia, late 16th century

[35° 10' 34.50" N / 33° 21' 45.10" E]

The Büyük Han ('Big Han') was originally a caravanserai or hostel for traveling merchants, offering safe accommodation for traders visiting the city (Fig. 95). Resembling such structures in Anatolia, it was one of the first buildings constructed by the Ottomans when they conquered Cyprus in 1571. The building is essentially an open square. It looks like a fortification from the outside, with its high walls pierced by tiny windows. Indeed, this was the idea, and the two gates of the han — wide so as to admit carts — were locked at night so that the visitors could rest easy with their merchandise and pack animals safely stored away. The lower levels were used to lay up the traders' goods and stable their animals, which in Cyprus included not only horses and donkeys but, even up to the early twentieth century, camels. The upper levels had several small vaulted rooms, each with its own sturdy door and windows. These were the 'hotel rooms' where the traders slept. Some rooms were also equipped with a brazier for cooking and heating and today one of the distinctive features of the structure is the series of peaked chimneys along part of the roofline. There are 78 rooms in all. During the British period the han was used as a prison, while in later years it provided housing for the poor.

A remarkable feature of the han's large open courtyard is the octagonal mosque elevated on a series of columns with Ottoman style capitals with stalactite designs. These columns support a series of ogival arches underneath which is a fountain for ritual ablutions. A small stone staircase curves up one of the sides of the mosque, giving access to the door and the interior. Windows can be found on all the remaining faces of the octagonal plan except for the section with the *mihrab*, the niche in the interior wall indicating the direction to Mecca.

Sources for Büyük Han: Jeffery, 98-99.

Kumarçilar Han ('Gambler's Inn'), Ottoman, Lefkoşa/Nicosia, 17th century renovation incorporating parts of medieval structures

[35° 10' 36.90" N / 33° 21' 45.10" E]

The smaller but very elegant han built near the Büyük Han was constructed some time in the later 17th century and parts of the entryway seem to have used a section of a Lusignan period medieval structure. In fact, it could be that the han was essentially a renovation of a medieval monastery. Recently restored, this han's smaller scale and less geometric design makes it somewhat more inviting than the monumental Büyük Han which looms beside it. A lovely arched gateway gives access to the intimate courtyard of the building. Sandstone pointed arches surround the courtyard at the lower level, while a porch supported by columns runs around at the second level above. The porch gave access to the rooms where the guests stayed. As in the Büyük Han, the lower levels were used to stable animals and store goods. It gained the name 'Gambler's Inn' because in the 19th century men would often play gambling games there to pass the time.

The History and Architecture of Famagusta

Famagusta is also called Ammochostos in Greek, which means 'filled with sand', a name transferred from a vernacular appellation for Salamis/Constantia, which in the medieval period became covered with sand dunes. Turkish Cypriots call the city 'Gazimağusa' or just 'Mağusa', in which the Turkish word for a war veteran or hero, *gazi*, is, essentially, attached to 'magus(t)a'. The name 'Famagusta' is the result of a long history of corruptions and Italianization of Ammochostos, along the lines of: 'Ammochoste', 'Famagouste', and 'Famagusta'. However, an alternative theory is that it derives from the Latin *Fama Augustae*, meaning 'Fame of Augustus'. Though it sounds good, no convincing argument has been forwarded to explain why such a Latin phrase should be related to the city. An earlier name seems to have been, in some sources at least, Arsinoe, which may date from some early foundation by the Egyptian pharaoh of the same name. The city was likely founded by citizens from Constantia (Salamis) who were seeking higher ground and a better location for a port. They found what they needed about 8 km south of the location of their ancient city. While driving from the ruins of Salamis to the walled city of Famagusta it may seem as if the ground is completely level, but Famagusta is founded on a low promontory of stone that slopes gently up from the seaside (Fig. 96). This extensive stone bed, sandstone cemented by an admixture of lime (or a sandy limestone, one could say), supplied a ready building material for the new city. The original quarries not only provided stone for building but would eventually help create the moat around the walled city, largely carved out of the rock especially on the north side. Some of these quarries became the numerous cavities under the city which in later centuries were used as cisterns for storing water and for underground cellars and even churches. Today there is still substantial evidence of subterranean Famagusta, though with unchecked development these cisterns and ancient cellars are being filled with concrete or covered over with new houses and apartments.

The port's secure anchorage was protected by a reef along the east and south sides a few hundred metres offshore, leaving only the northern end of the harbour as an entry way. The mouth of the port was protected in the late Middle Ages and Renaissance period with a huge chain

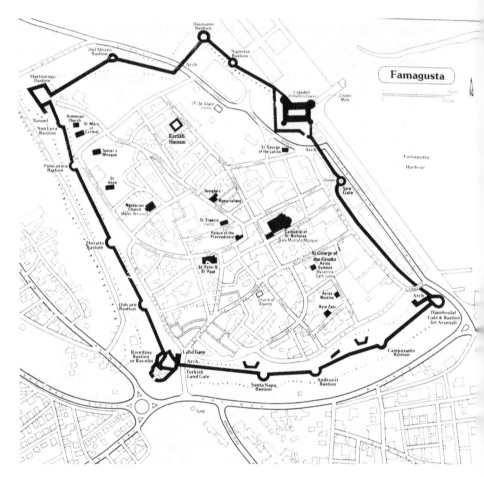

Fig. 96: Plan of Famagusta and its walls [from Camille Enlart, Gothic Art and the Renaissance in Cyprus].

that was drawn across it, thus impeding the entry of any enemy ships. For this city's first few centuries it seems not to have been very large or important, merely a fishing village. When Richard the Lion Heart pursued the Byzantine despot Isaac Comnenus in 1191 he is said to have sailed around to Famagusta, so it was likely a port of some significance by the late 12th century.

So for centuries, from around 600 CE to 1000 CE, Famagusta was a very minor port, a mere shade of the great cities of Enkomi and Salamis that preceded it centuries and even millennia before. However, a change of fortune was imminent when the First Crusade was launched to take the Holy Land from the Muslims. Famagusta lay just 172 kilometres from the coast of Syria (the port of Latakia) and while crusader kingdoms were set up on the profitable shores of the Middle East, Famagusta's proximity and strategic importance helped make it prosperous. For almost a century the Levantine Christian Crusaders grew rich controlling the Middle Eastern terminus of important trade routes, but at the close of the 12th century the Muslims were united by a new ruler, Saladin, who began to repossess these Middle Eastern lands for Islam. The crusaders retreated in defeat, town by town, gradually giving up their mainland possessions. Over the next century, more and more cities would be reclaimed by Saladin's armies.

The Lusignans, French crusaders who had lost the kingdom of Jerusalem in the Holy Land, eventually purchased Cyprus from Richard of England, who had only recently acquired Cyprus by wresting control of the island from the aforementioned ruler Isaac Comnenus. Guy de Lusignan had aided Richard in his defeat of Isaac, thus perhaps gaining the regent's favour. After a brief Templar rule, the Lusignans took over Cyprus and ruled for three hundred years. Thus Cyprus became the new emporium of the east, Christianity's easternmost port at the very threshold of Muslim expansion. With the fall of the major Middle Eastern port of Acre in 1291, Famagusta became Cyprus's most active and profitable trading center, so that by the mid-14th century it was thought to be one of the world's richest cities. Certainly, chroniclers record that the merchants of Famagusta were very wealthy. The German priest Ludolf von Suchen noted in his visit to Famagusta around 1338:

It [Famagusta] is the richest of all cities, and her citizens are the richest of men. A citizen once betrothed his daughter, and the jewels of her head-dress were valued by the French knights who came with us as more precious that all the ornaments of the Queen of France...But I dare not speak of their precious stones and golden tissues and other riches, for it were a thing unheard of and incredible. In this city dwell very many wealthy courtesans, of whom some possess more than one hundred thousand florins. I dare not speak of their riches.

[Excerpta Cypria, 19-20]

Leontios Makhairas also condemns Famagusta because he claims sodomy is often practised there, and that men keep male slaves as homosexual partners. St Brigit of Sweden visited Famagusta and decried the vanities of the wealth and sinfulness of its citizens while preaching in the cathedral square.

Traders from dozens of Mediterranean ports, all the major European and Levantine players, were there. One could hear Arabic, Italian, French, Greek, and Syriac spoken in the streets. Von Suchen also observed: "And daily from the rising of the sun to its going down are heard rumours and news. And the tongues of every nation under heaven are heard and read and talked; and are taught in special schools" [Excerpta Cypria, 20]. As one might expect, translators were as busy as businessmen. Even though the Middle East was controlled by the Muslims, trade did not cease, but now many of the goods passed through Famagusta, making it a bustling, cosmopolitan marketplace of the Levant. But trade was not Famagusta's only source of riches. The valuable article of clothing or type of wool — the same word might have been used to refer to both — called 'camlet' was also produced in Famagusta. It was so prized that the Sultan of Egypt (the Spanish traveler Pero Tafur tells us) asked that the Kings of Cyprus pay their annual tribute to him with 2000 coloured camlets. So crucial and precious was this industry that the women who wove the camlet wool were forbidden to leave the city. Nicholas Martoni visited Famagusta in 1394 and observed:

...there is made a great quantity of camlet. There is one custom in force in this city...that no woman can go out of the city of Famagosta without the leave of the Commandant...and this is rarely granted to any woman. The reason alleged is that men cannot live in that city but for the women who spin and prepare wool for the camlet, for they have hardly any other means of living.

[Excerpta Cypria, 22]

Obviously camlet was a hugely important commodity for the city, and must have contributed substantially to its wealth, though camlet was also made in Nicosia. David Jacoby has done a detailed study of camlets, tracing their origin, trade, and types. We don't know exactly what camlets were or what they were made of, but it may have been a fine goat hair or even the hair of camels. So regulated was the camlet production and trade that an Italian named Pegolotti mentions in his manual on trading from the 1330s that each shipment should have a seal on it vouchsafing the contents' size and quality. We also learn that Venice is a port to which many Cypriot camlets are shipped, and he records the tariffs charged on their shipments. They were made in a wide range of colours, as many documents attest, and found their way into the wardrobes of popes, kings, and the nobility of Europe.

It is during the almost three-century rule of the Lusignans that most of Famagusta's significant architecture was produced, though the city was under the control of the Genoese for ninety years. The Genoese occupation was not looked upon very favourably by chroniclers of the time. When the Genoese took over Famagusta in 1373 Philippe de Mézières, a contemporary witness, concluded that "The tyrannical oppression and the inhuman avarice of the Genoese" had impoverished not just Famagusta itself but the whole kingdom of Cyprus. Similarly, the Cypriot chronicler Leontios Makhairas, writing about the Genoese, lamented that "a malignant devil has become jealous of Famagusta," as he watched the city begin its terminal decline. Indeed, it is difficult to imagine today, as Famagusta's old city seems such a sleepy place, but the city's history is marked by violence. Not just the large and dramatic wars, but writers also tell us of riots, murders, raids, and brutality of all kinds. Medieval Famagusta was a rough place.

A compelling snapshot of Famagusta in 1563 is given by Elias of Pesaro, whose observations give us insights into the minutiae of everyday life. We learn, for example, that renting a house costs about the same as in Italy, but the bread in Famagusta is expensive, though it's the best he ever tasted. The olive oil is bad, so people often use sesame oil for cooking instead. He praises the Famagustans for assiduously enforcing the quarantine of 40 days for ships in the harbour if they come from a region where the plague is known to be infecting the population. He observes that opthamalia (eye infection) is common in Famagusta. Indeed, many travellers to Cyprus make note of Famagusta's bad air and the fevers and diseases it breeds. The apples aren't so good but the pomegranates large and "as good to look at as to eat". The green markets of Famagusta are full of a variety of fruits and vegetables, and the salt is "wonderfully fine". But the most historically significant aspect of Elias of Pesaro's letter is how his observations about the lively money lending business demonstrate that the Venetians had returned Famagusta to prosperity after its decimation during the Genoese occupation. Elias makes note of Famagusta's "large and pretty square," and observes that, "at all the street corners are fountains of running water." Historians argue about whether Venetian rule on Cyprus was good or bad, but Elias' letter suggests that, at least in Famagusta, Venetian hegemony led to a fairly good and even prosperous life. In fact, Elias says that "...every mechanic, every labourer, has in his house vessels of silver or jewels, for they are all rich."

The Venetians had been an active presence on Cyprus and in Famagusta through the early Middle Ages. Their influence and power increased steadily until they were poised for a takeover when they arranged the marriage of Caterina Cornaro, from one of Venice's most noble families, to King James II. The Cornaro family had many profitable holdings in Cyprus and the family had established itself on the island from the 14th century. King James did not live long after his union with Caterina, and his infant son and heir also died, leaving Caterina, adopted daughter of Venice, as the sole heir to the Lusignan throne. Caterina was essentially a puppet of the Venetian Senate, and after a few years they obliged her to abdicate and donate Cyprus to Venice. The chronicler George Boustronios gave a compelling description of the Queen's last days:

And on the fifteenth of February 1489 the queen went from Lefkosia on her way to Famagusta to cross over the sea. She went on horseback and all the knights' ladies and the knights were in her company; six knights were at the bridle walking by her horse. She had put on a dress of black stuff. From the time she came out of Lefkosia all the way the tears never ceased to flow from her eyes; and at her going the people also wept loudly. Order had been given that all the soldiers should come to Lefkosia and as soon as the queen came out of the court they shouted: "Saint Mark! Saint Mark!" And on the first of March 1489 after Christ she went aboard the galley and sailed for Venice.

Thus the Venetians gained this prosperous island realm without doing battle. But Cyprus, and Famagusta, were past their glory days. The Venetians put substantial efforts into trying to revitalize Famagusta and prepare it for a much feared Ottoman attack. It is thus in military architecture — the walls and bastions — where we see the most visible traces of Venetian activity. These fortifications, along with the Gothic churches of the Lusignan era, are today the most spectacular remains of this once fabled city.

Readers wanting a visual tour of Famagusta should watch the award-winning documentary film on the city and its history and architecture, *The Stones of Famagusta: the Story of a Forgotten City* (2005; 70 min.). More information can be found at the website: http://www. stonesoffamagusta.com.

The Syrian Quarter of Famagusta

The Syrian Quarter is the northwest corner of the city and there one can find the Armenian Church, the Church of St Mary of Carmel (Carmelite Church), the Jacobite Church ('Tanner's Mosque'), the Maronite Church (Church of St Anne), two underground churches, the Nestorian church, and the Martinengo Bastion.

The Armenian Church (Church of the Gantchvor Sourp Asdvadzadzin Monastery, 'Monastery of the Caller', Sainte-Marie-de-Vert), Famagusta, 14th century

[35° 07' 38.43" N / 33° 56' 10.94" E]

The Armenian Church lies in the northwest corner of the old city and is one of a sextet of interesting churches in the immediate vicinity, all within easy walking distance of one another (Fig. 97). Although we associate Armenia with the region now called Armenia and the regions in eastern Turkey around Lake Van which were once Armenian territories, the nation was once comprised of an area along the south coast of Turkey called 'Cilician Armenia' or 'Lesser Armenia'. The Armenians were continually under pressure from Muslim forces that began entering Asia Minor beginning in the 10th century, and through the Middle Ages they often turned to the Latin Lusignan kingdom of Cyprus for support. In fact, after 1375 the Lusignan kings not only held the titles of kings of Cyprus and Jerusalem but of Armenia as well. But Armenians could have been in Cyprus in significant numbers as early as the 6th century as refugees of a war during the reign of the Byzantine emperor Justinian II. They are recorded as having assisted the Byzantine despot Isaac Comnenus in his skirmishes with Richard the Lion Heart in the late 12th century. It is likely that there were Armenians settled in Famagusta from early in the Middle Ages. Other members of the Armenian community arrived at Famagusta in a large influx in the early 14th century as refugees fleeing a Mamluk invasion of Cilicia. Jacopus of Verona happened to have been in the city at this time and he wrote a heart-wrenching eyewitness account of what he saw in June of 1335 as he arrived in the port of Famagusta:

> ...and that very hour that I entered the harbour several large vessels and galleys and *gripparia* from Armenia, from the city of Logaze, crowded with old men, children, women, orphans and wards more than fifteen hundred in number, who were flying from Armenia because the Soldan (Sultan) had sent hosts, many and mighty, to destroy it, and they burnt all that plain and carried off captive more than twelve thousand persons, over and above those they had slain by the sword, and they began to destroy it, as I was told by the Venetian merchants who were there, on Ascension Day, which fell on May 25th.
>
> O Lord God, sad indeed it was to see that multitude in the square of Famagusta, children crying and moaning at their mothers' breasts, old men and starving dogs howling.
>
> *[Excerpta Cypria, 17]*

Fig. 97: The Armenian church, Famagusta.

Famagusta was no stranger to receiving émigrés (such as those that flooded in after the fall of Acre, Sidon, Beirut, Tortosa, and others around 1291) and the city seems to have been able to absorb this significant influx. Apparently this refugee community was able to get on its feet quickly in the rarified commercial environment of 14th century Famagusta, perhaps owing to an already established Armenian presence in the city. By the second half of the 14th century, certainly, there was a substantial and prosperous Armenian community, with an Armenian Bishop and a number of important civic offices held by members of the community. Still, the Armenian Church was dominated by the Latin, Roman Catholic Lusignans, as were the Greek Orthodox people. Wilibrand von Oldenburg, who visited Cyprus in 1211, noted the subjection of the Armenians and Greeks:

> But the Greeks, over whom throughout this land the Latins have dominion, have thirteen bishops, of whom one is an archbishop. They all obey the Franks [Catholics], and pay tribute like slaves. Whence you can see that the Franks are the lords of this land, whom the Greeks and Armenians obey as serfs.
>
> *[Excerpta Cypria, 13]*

This modest church is the lone survivor of three Armenian churches in Famagusta and is located in the northwestern corner of the old city, right beside the church of St Mary of Carmel and the cannon ramps for the cavaliere of the Martinengo Bastion. Numerous other buildings surrounded it, perhaps even a monastery, though these were likely destroyed during the Venetian period when the Martinengo Bastion was constructed. When the church was visited by George Jeffery in 1917 he saw the remnants of a small sacristy attached to the apse. Late 19th century photographs still show this sacristy, though much in ruin, as well as the excavated remains of several ancillary buildings. Although now vanished, one can just make out where the sacristy abutted the northern part of the apse.

It has been argued that a construction date of 1311–1317 should be attributed to the surviving Armenian church of Famagusta, making it very early in the chronology of Famagusta's medieval churches. However, I think it could well date from mid-century. Indeed, it is tempting to see it as a votive church built by those refugees observed by Jacopus of Verona who found a new home in Famagusta in 1335. The church is a simple, single cross-vault with a semi-circular apse at the east end. There are three entrances that lead to the interior. Some frescoes survive but they are currently difficult to see. At the time of writing, plans for cleaning were in the works and so one might find the church closed through 2012.

One of the more legible frescoes is on the north wall, in the west end, where there is a scene of the Flagellation of Christ (look up high; can you see Christ's crossed legs and his hands tied to the pillar?). Also on the north wall there is an angel, who holds Christ's clothing in a mostly invisible and much damaged scene of the Baptism of Christ. On the south wall is a weathered image of the *Koimesis*, or Death of the Virgin Mary as well as a 'Pantocrator', a large face of Christ, Ruler of the Universe. A fresco of St George on his horse is to the left of the main east entrance. There is an elegant *piscina* in the north wall near the apse, where liturgical instruments were stored. A bit of its Gothic tracery remains. On the outside walls of the church one can see Latin and 'Maltese' crosses inscribed into the stones around the west and south portals. These may have been a kind of graffiti carved by pilgrims passing through the city. Michele Bacci identifies these crosses as *khachkars*, which means 'cross-stones' in Armenian, and these are sometimes found on other Armenian churches. On the south wall, just to the right of the doorway, one can make out the remains of a sun dial.

Sources for Armenian Church: Enlart, 286-8; Jeffery, 143-4; Gunnis, 101-2; Allan Langdale and Michael J. K. Walsh, "The Architecture, Conservation History, and Future of the Armenian Church in Famagusta" *Chronos* 19 (2009), 7-29; Philipe Plagnieux and Thierry Soulard, "Famagouste. L'Église des Armeniens (Sainte Marie des Verts)," in *L'Art Gothique du Chypre*, de Vaivre and Palgnieux eds, Paris, 2006, pp. 257-60; Michele Bacci, "The Armenian Church in Famagusta and its Mural Decoration: Some Iconographical Remarks," in *Culture of Cilician Armenia*, proceedings of the international symposium, 14-18 January 2008, Antelyas: Catholicosate of Cilicia, 2009, pp. 489-508.

The Carmelite Church (St Mary of Carmel), Famagusta, 14th century

[35° 07' 37.58" N / 33° 56' 11.56" E]

The Carmelite church rests alongside the Armenian Church in the northwest corner or Syrian quarter of the old city (Fig. 98). St Mary of Carmel was the home church of the Carmelite monks in Famagusta and their monastic buildings, long ago destroyed, were likely in the vicinity of the apse. The southeast sections show many signs of large timber roofed structures appended to the church as there are many post holes, though it is uncertain whether these dated from the time of the church's construction or were later accretions. The fact that the post holes seem as if they were part of the initial masonry, that is to say evenly and neatly squared as opposed to being roughly gouged out, may indicate that they are part of the original complex. It is possible that these traces represent a residence for an abbot or a chapter house that was part of the original plan. Michalis Olympios notes that when Nicholas Martoni visited the church and its ancillary buildings in 1394, he "commented on the beauty of the church, with its chapels and wall-paintings, and on the cloister, the dormitory and other rooms of the monastery, as well as the relics he saw in the church." It is possible that the plans of these structures still lie east, though this area has been aggressively leveled with heavy machinery in the recent past and was in a restricted military zone up to just a few short years ago.

The Carmelite church was one of the larger churches of Famagusta. Only St Nicholas cathedral, St George of the Greeks, and Saints Peter and Paul were bigger. Its walls also survive to full height in most places, and some of the unribbed vaulting of the apse remains as well. Unlike the other large churches, however, the structure of the Carmelite church consists of a single nave with no side aisles, ending in a single, three-sided apse, making the interior of the building essentially a large vaulted hall, similar to St George of the Latins, just a five-minute walk away, or even St Anne's, which is even closer and has all of its vaulting intact.

The church had tombs in it, indicated by the shallow funerary niches in the interior walls. Such features are common in Famagusta, the clerics and monks raising money by selling burial spaces. It is also believed by some that these renovations to accommodate tombs may have weakened the supporting capacities of the walls, thus contributing to the eventual failure of the roof vaults. The church's most famous sepulcher, St Peter Thomas', for which the church was widely known, is lost, if it ever was indeed in this specific church. It was a floor tomb, however, unlike the wall tombs in niches, and the self-effacing Peter wished to be interred there, as Olympios notes, "so that all men will be able and obliged to

Fig. 98: The Carmelite church, Famagusta.

tread upon my corpse, and, if possible, even goats and dogs." Such was the saint's humility. Yet from this modest tomb St Peter Thomas performed many spectacular posthumous miracles. One of his most impressive feats while still alive had been witnessed by many in the neighbourhood, including some Armenians: while St Peter prayed in the church fire came down from the heavens, so ardent were his entreaties to God. In the north part of the apse one can see a today shallow rectangular inset where there used to be a marble plaque — Enlart discovered it in fragments in his excavations of 1901 — that recorded the establishing of a daily Mass at dawn in commemoration of that miracle. While Enlart believed Peter's tomb to be situated in the Carmelite church, it is nonetheless true that no physical evidence for it has been found. However, the tomb slab of Guy Babin was still in place in Enlart's time. The honourary position of Babin's slab indicates that he may have been the founder of the present church, even though the coats of arms painted in the apse, as well as in relief on the façade of the church, indicate substantial royal contributions, very likely from King Hugh IV, whose predilection for patronizing monasteries is also reflected in his generosity to the Abbey of Bellapais. A boss in the crossing of the vault above the tomb also carried Guy's coat of arms. George Jeffery notes that the collapse of that vault and its boss stone may have shattered the Babin tomb slab directly below it, an eloquent metaphor for Vanity. You can see this still lying on the ground. Guy Babin was a knight of Nicosia who had been a devoted vassal of King Hugh IV. Doge Francesco Dandolo had conferred the honour of Venetian citizenship upon him in 1332, and he was a royal emissary to Pope Benedict XII in 1336. He was married to Maria of Morphou as a diplomatic gesture to help mollify a powerful enmity between Guy and John of Montolif, Maria's cousin, which threatened the realm's stability.

The two large arches in the north and south walls may also indicate ambitious funerary chapels of some kind. These were likely added later in the building's history. In the apse are aumbries and a piscina: shelves and niches for liturgical implements, reliquaries, and holy water.

Numerous ghost-like frescoes, much faded, are discernable in optimal light conditions. Their disappearance is one of the great losses of medieval mural art in Famagusta. George Jeffery could see many things in 1918 than we cannot see today, and Enlart in 1888 could see even more inscriptions and paintings. Had those scholars not recorded these our knowledge of them would have been forever lost. One of the most impressive of these frescoes, even if visible only as a shadow, is the scene of St George and the Dragon on the north wall near the apse. In the right light the long, curved teeth of the dragon are visible. Someone has destroyed the heads of both the maiden and St George, but one can make out the radiating halo of St George, as well as his horse and the delicate hands of the maiden he rescues. One can see the elegant, curving swath of the maiden's dress as she leans away from the dramatic event, and you can even see her hand on her chest as she registers her surprise. Yet over a century ago Enlart could see even more details. It's worth quoting him to get a sense of the particulars that have been lost to time: "In the background a red brick Italian castle makes a contrast with Cypriot architecture which is always in stone or mud-dried bricks. In the foreground to one side the maiden with curling blonde hair who is turning towards the saint with a frightened gesture is engagingly graceful and natural; she wears a long grayish-purple dress without a girdle. The horse is dappled grey." If we take Enlart's verbal descriptions as accurate, and there doesn't seem to be any reason not to, about 50 percent of the Carmelite church's frescoes have vanished and about 50 percent of the visual information of the ones still visible has faded away.

In the apse one can discern a series of Lusignan coats of arms in a checkerboard of squares with crosses and a rampant lion in pale yellow. To the right of the apse there is a figure in a splendid red robe that holds an orb in her left hand. Enlart argues that this is St Helena, an important saint indeed in Cyprus as it was she, legend has it, that brought a fragment of the True Cross to Cyprus. See if you can find the group of kneeling donor figures in the apse with their distinctive medieval head coverings. As you look at the center of the apse wall, they are up to your right, just above and to the left of the doorway. The one on the right is most legible, the center one less so, and the one on the left a mere ghost. In the north part of the apse one can still make out today a row of three saints. The one of the right hand side is the best preserved and this is St Nicholas with his bishop's mitre and wearing his white *omophorion* (bishop's vestments) with a light green under robe. Just to the left of his head you might be able to see (here's where those binoculars will come in handy) a small square scene that shows an event in St Nicholas's life. Here, the saint intervenes to save three knights who have been unfairly sentenced to death. They kneel on the ground, blindfolded, as St Nicholas grabs the sword from the executioner just as he is about to strike. To the right of St Nicholas's head is another of his miracles. George Jeffery identifies this as the legend of St Nicholas and the children in the salting tub, but I am pretty certain this is incorrect. Instead, what we see here is the story of the three virgin daughters whose father is too poor to afford their dowries. St Nicholas throws a bag of gold through the bedroom window one night so they can be properly married and not become adulterers. We can clearly see the three daughters lying in bed and the surprised father holding his hands up to the window, though the area just above is too damaged to see the actual bag of gold. The saint on the far right also had accompanying stories in little boxes around his body, but only one of these is partially legible and I have not been able to identify it.

On the south wall just west of the big open arch you might be able to see a trace of the painter working, even though his frescoes have long since disappeared. Some painters did a quick sketch of their figures with a stylus in the wet plaster before painting. On this wall you can see such an elegant drawing, done freehand and very curvaceous, of a human figure with dark drapery. He appears to be a monk saint, as we can still see his hood gathered behind his head. One can see this technique of sketching in the wet plaster on the St George fresco as well. Here the artist sketched out George's calf with graceful lines. On the north wall, near the west entrance, you can see the fine medieval graffiti signature of a man named Brucourt Alioueain. On the south wall you might be able to make out a figure with red drapery under an arch. Enlart suggests this might be St Catherine, whose cult was very prominent in the Famagusta area.

The west portal of St Mary of Carmel has some interesting sculptures such as the angel at the apex of the doorway, though it has lost its head (Fig. 99). He holds out a scroll and points with his finger to a passage which was likely written in black paint; probably a piece of scripture. At the side of the doorway, at the imposts, are weathered heads that look like monks with their cowls. The tympanum was plastered and frescoed and one can just make out the subject matter: the Virgin Mary with the infant Christ flanked by two pairs of angels. Just a bit of blue painting survives. The haloes are visible because they were done in relief in the plaster and so their outlines are quite clear and they give one a pretty clear idea of the composition. The fresco might date from a fairly late period when the church was turned over to Greek Orthodoxy. Indeed, several of the interior frescoes seem to be from a time after the Latin/Catholic control of the church.

The upper levels of the western façade are decorated with a set of three Lusignan coats of arms which seem to have been conceived of as part of the façade decoration (Fig. 100). But at some later date, again, perhaps when the church was converted to Greek Orthodoxy, a timber narthex or porch was added to the façade. A ledge for the roof's beams was carved into the façade, cutting through the coats of arms.

Sources for Carmelite Church: Enlart, 267-274; Jeffery, 137-140; Gunnis, 100-1; Michalis Olympios, "Networks of Contact in the Architecture of the Latin East: The Carmelite Church in Famagusta, Cyprus and the Cathedral of Rhodes," *Journal of the British Archaeological Association* 162 (2009): 29-66; P. Plagnieux and T. Soulard, 'Famagouste: L'église Sainte-Marie du Carmel', in *L'art gothique en Chypre*, ed. J.-B. de Vaivre and P. Plagnieux, Mémoires de l'Académie des Inscriptions et Belles-Lettres 34 (Paris 2006), 251–56.

Fig. 99: Sculpture of an angel over the main western portal of the Carmelite church, Famagusta.

Fig. 100: West façade of the Carmelite church in Famagusta.

Jacobite Church ('Tanner's Mosque' or 'Tabakhane'), Famagusta, 14th century

[35° 07' 36.10" N / 33° 56' 13.41" E]

Less than a hundred metres from the church of St Mary of Carmel is a medieval church often referred to as the 'Tanner's Mosque' because the small structure was used in the Ottoman period as a prayer hall for the men who worked as leather tanners in that quarter of the city (Fig. 101). But the building's original function was as a church, probably for the Jacobite community. The Jacobites were a sect from Syria that believed Christ had a single nature, that is, they rejected the notion that Christ had both a divine and human nature, and they were thus considered heretics by both the Greek Orthodox and the Roman Catholic Churches. They were referred to as 'Monophysites' and were established in significant numbers on Cyprus at least by the early 13th century. Despite their dubious status with the Roman Church, the Jacobites found refuge and some degree of prosperity in Famagusta by the 14th century. The northwest corner of the old city was the Syrian Quarter and was home to many Arabic speaking Christians — Jacobites, Nestorians, and Maronites among them — who had come to Famagusta in numbers during the 1290s and early years of the 1300s. Their presence there was noted by Jacobus de Verona, an Augustinian friar who visited Famagusta in 1335:

> Also in the same city [Famagusta] are several sects which have their own worship and their own churches. First, true Christians; secondly the Greeks, who consecrate not with unleavened wafers but with leavened bread; they do not elevate the Body of Christ, nor do they believe that the Spirit proceeds from the Son. There are also Jacobites, who are circumcised, and are baptized with the Greek rite. There are also Armenians, who perform their worship like true Christians, but say the service in the Greek tongue, also Georgians and Maronites...Also Nestorians, so called from the faithless Nestor, who say that Christ was only a mere man.
>
> *[Excerpta Cypria, 17]*

Records indicate a substantial Jacobite presence as early as the mid-13th century when, for example, in 1264 they are recorded as having a Bishop named Athanasius. It is likely that the other Syrian communities were also present at this time. These Syriac communities, with their own religious traditions, were often at odds with their Roman Catholic overlords and the papacy. Nevertheless, they seem to have flourished in Famagusta and kept their own churches.

The interior of the church consists of two groin-vaulted bays, separated by a transverse rib, with a semi-circular apse and semi-dome. The west portal of the church is quite wide and has slender colonnettes in its jambs with undecorated capitals. The voussoirs consist of a distinctive zigzagging moulding followed by a register of squared flower motifs and a row of what look like sprays of slender leaves (Fig. 102). Framing all of this is the Gothic hood mould typical of the Lusignan period. A large stone lintel has a square, raised section which may have been carved in relief — possibly a patron's coat of arms or a cross — but was chipped away when the building was converted to a mosque. All of this lends a sense of geometric purity and simple beauty. The tympanum is rough masonry today but it was originally plastered and frescoed as were the tympana of other churches in the vicinity.

Above the west façade doorway is a square window with heavy framing. Flanking this are small, slit-like rectangular windows which have trefoil *muquarnas* (scallop design), likely added as an Islamic decorative element to indicate the building's new identity as a mosque after 1571. At the very top of the façade is a little arch for the church's bell with flagstaff holders on either side.

The north side of the structure has two rectangular windows (they have mates in the south wall) with hood moulds. Each of these has three flower blossoms carved in relief. Below is another doorway with simple mouldings and small floral accents. Above the keystone of the door's arch are the remnants of a sculpture, probably originally an angel like the one above the west portal of St Mary of Carmel. Two lovely rainspouts also survive on this north side: dog-like faces with their ears sticking out and their spout-mouths open.

At the close of the 19th century Camille Enlart saw fragmentary frescoes of St Michael, St George and scenes from the life of Christ inside the church. One can barely make out some frescoes on the south wall of the interior.

Sources for Jacobite Church: Enlart, 299-302; [Enlart labeled this church "Unidentified Church 11"]; Jeffery, 155; Allan Langdale and Michael J. K. Walsh, "A Report on Three Newly Accessible Churches in the Syrian Quarter of Famagusta" *Journal of Cyprus Studies* 13, n. 33 (2007): 105-123.

Opposite: Fig. 101: The Jacobite church, also known as the 'Tanner's Mosque' or the 'Tabakhane', Famagusta.

Fig. 102: Arch of the main west portal of the Jacobite church, also known as the 'Tanner's Mosque'

Maronite Church (Church of St Anne), Famagusta, early 14th century

[35° 07' 32.90" N / 33° 56' 15.05" E]

The church of St Anne is well preserved with its nave and apse vaulting completely intact (Fig. 103). The church may have been built by Maronites in the 14th century. The Maronites shared the Syrian quarter of the city with the Nestorians, Armenians, and Jacobites, whose churches also survive in this quadrant of the old town. The Maronites were the most numerous Christian group after the Orthodox Greeks and many still live in Cyprus today, some even in the north, though there are only about 140 of them left. They were established in significant numbers by the early 12th century. George Hill estimates their population at that time as seven or eight thousand, with "some thirty villages", but Guita Hourani estimates a population as high as 20,000 and 60 villages in the 13th century, thus there could have been many Maronites coming to Cyprus at this time. But this trend was not to last, because by the Ottoman period the population of Maronites seems to have lessened significantly, perhaps because they were persecuted by both the Latins (Catholics) and the Orthodox Church on Cyprus, and at times had their churches and monasteries confiscated. Indeed, this church in Famagusta may well have been one of these Latin, Lusignan or Venetian-era confiscations. At some point and for some reason, the church did fall into Latin hands and was dedicated to St Anne. The Franciscans energetically tried to convert Maronites to Catholicism, and they seem to have had some success. By the late 12th century most Maronites in Palestine has accepted the jurisdiction of the Roman Catholic Church, and the Cypriot Maronites for the most part followed suit, while still keeping their distinctive liturgical language and rites. Because of this, they enjoyed a cozier relationship with the Roman Catholics than the Orthodox Christians on Cyprus did. The Maronites fought alongside the Latins when the Ottomans attacked Cyprus, and the Ottomans, after taking over the island, remembered this alliance and made life difficult for them. There were around 33 Maronite villages when the Ottomans conquered Cyprus, and twenty-five years later there were only 19. Many went to Lebanon and others to Malta. Many of those who stayed, under the pressures of persecution from the Ottomans, became Linobambaci ('linen and cotton'), that is, Christians who outwardly converted to Islam but in their hearts and minds remained Christian.

The interior of the church consists of a single hall with two groin vaulted bays and a polygonal apse with a ribbed vault over it (Fig. 104). Two transverse arches springing from corbels at the clerestory level demarcate the bays of the vaulting. In its general plan it has similarities to both St George of the Latins and St Mary of Carmel. The interior had

Fig. 103: Façade of the Maronite church, also known as the church of St Anne, Famagusta.

an interesting contraption, where a pulley was stored in a box-like room on the roof and it raised and lowered either a reliquary or lamp through a hole in the ceiling. Whatever it was, it must have added a dramatic theatrical element to the liturgies. George Jeffery suggested that it may have lowered a model of the dove of the Holy Spirit on to the altar.

Several frescoes and inscriptions decorate the interior, although some of them we only know from old photos taken in the 1930s. After 1974, this building was used as a storage depot by the military and the church was closed to the public until 2006. During this time the walls were covered by a protective concrete wall, which at the time of writing is still intact and blocking some of the frescoes. Still, one can see, barely, the remains of *The Assumption* over the founder's tomb on the north wall. Opposite this, in the western portion of the southern wall, images of Saints Catherine and Ursula are framed within a pair of arches with an ornate and colourful vine decoration. Their faces have gone, as has the orb that Catherine held in her left hand and the palm leaf in Ursula's hand, symbolic of her martyrdom. Yet we can be certain of their identification, despite the loss of their attributes, as their names are painted beside their heads. On the west wall two male saints, with halos in relief, are visible. Gone are the heraldic shields of Italy, the cross of Malta and the useful inscription which told Enlart not only the name of the church but also (mistakenly) the patron of the artistic work within.

The façade has a simple doorway which seems to have been made smaller with some additional masonry at some point. Perhaps there were structural concerns about the integrity of the lintel. Today the door is completely filled with concrete. In the tympanum, however, some pigments from a fresco survive and the subject matter was similar to the frescoed tympanum of St Mary of Carmel nearby: the Virgin and Child flanked by angels. Mary's large halo and her purple robe (*maphorion*) are visible. Above the portal are a row of corbels and post holes for a porch although here, unlike in the Carmelite church, the porch seems to have been part of the original plan. Above this level is a single lancet window and, above that, three corbels which carried a small, shallow wooden porch in front of the double bells which hung in the two arches of the belfry. At the top of the belfry is a flagstaff holder. Remnants of similar flagstaff holders can be found on the north and south sides of the belfry at the same level, just around the corner from the façade. More of these can be found at the top of the roof line of the north and south sides as well. The church must have presented a very impressive spectacle with its many richly coloured flags and banners flying in the persistent winds of Famagusta.

Sources for Church of St Anne: Enlart, 274-280; Jeffery, 140-3; Gunnis, 100; Allan Langdale and Michael J. K. Walsh, "A Report on Three Newly Accessible Churches in the Syrian Quarter of Famagusta" *Journal of Cyprus Studies* 13, n. 33 (2007): 105-123; Guita G. Hourani, *A Reading in the History of the Maronites of Cyprus From the Eighth Century to the Beginning of British Rule*, no date, on-line article.

Fig. 104: Interior vaulting of the Maronite church, also known as the church of St Anne, Famagusta.

Mary of Bethlehem or Church of the Nativity, Famagusta, 13th or 14th century

[35° 07' 33.42" N / 33° 56' 17.09" E]

This fascinating church is labeled "Ste. Marie de Bethlehem" on an old Genoese map of Famagusta while another map, produced during the last years of British rule on Cyprus, labels it "Church of the Nativity". The low façade originally looked like a triangular pediment, high in the center then sloping lower to the sides. The central portion of the façade, around the doorway, seems to have been repaired in modern times. Small drop corbels, typical of Lusignan times, flank the doorway on the façade. A flight of steps can be found immediately inside the dark interior, though removal of the soil that has washed into the church over the years may reveal one or two more. When I first went into this church the locals had been using it as a garbage dump, so hopefully it will have been cleaned up more recently. The first part of the interior consists of a single broad and pointed barrel vault (Fig. 105). A strainer arch curves around the middle of the vault from wall corbels, the north one being carved with a cross that strongly resembles the Lusignan cross of Jerusalem. This, as well as the dedication of the church, strongly suggests that it was originally a Latin church founded in the Middle Ages, even though there is evidence that, like so many other Latin Cypriot churches, it was later converted to Greek Orthodoxy. Post holes for an iconostasis seem to indicate this conversion. A niche in the south wall was likely a founder's tomb. Two more corbel shelves flank the large rectangular opening to the sizable rock-cut grotto portion of the church.

The grotto is not quite apsidal in shape but not quite rectangular either. In the northeast sector two niches have been carved, one with a masonry semi-dome constructed over top of it. Perhaps it was an aumbrey or piscina. There are very faint traces of plaster and fresco but these have long decayed. This church, like some other underground churches in Famagusta, reminds us that there were a considerable number of subterranean ecclesiastical monuments in the city, many of which may lie as yet undiscovered under modern homes. Some of these were entirely excavated from the living rock, while others, like the present church, were constructed over top of an ancient quarry.

Sources for St Mary of Bethlehem: Jeffery, 143. The Genoese map that labels the church 'Ste. Marie de Bethleem' (?) appears in Catherine Otten-Froux, "Notes sur quelques monuments de Famagouste a la fin du Moyen Age," in *Mosaic: Festschrift for A.H.S. Megaw*, edited by J. Herrin, M. Mullett, C. Otten-Froux (London: British School at Athens Studies, 2001), 145-154.

Unidentified Byzantine Church with grotto, Famagusta, 14th century

[35° 07' 36.73" N / 33° 56' 16.21" E]

This church, one of Famagusta's most fascinating ruins, was excavated by Theodore Mogabgab in 1936. It lies in the northwest corner of the city very near St Anne and the Jacobite church. A bust of Kemal Ataturk has been erected directly on top of the central part of the ruins. Still, one can clearly see the triple apses of the east end which survive up to about 70 cm in height. The church was more or less rectangular and about 50 feet in length and 35 feet wide. A couple of courses of stone still mark the general outline. Four column bases, likely pillaged from ancient Salamis, held columns that supported a small dome over the center of the church. These are hidden under the modern pavements of the monument. Substantial sections of the original pavements survived in 1936, though these had been shattered by the collapse of the dome, an event which Mogabgab dates from around the time of the siege of Famagusta in 1571. Mogabgab discovered the voussoirs of arches, indicating the existence of arcades in the interior, three arches in both length and breadth. Mogabgab also found several burials around the church, including a huge layer of various human bones which he thought indicated "a mass interment of remains removed from elsewhere." This could be significant because when the Ottomans conquered Famagusta they tore up the floor tombs in the Cathedral of St Nicholas, since they couldn't remain there if the building was to become a mosque. Those medieval bones could have been dumped here amongst the ruins of this church. But the most remarkable discovery made during Mogabgab's excavations was the entrance to a vast cave underneath the church. Just beside the south entrance (it had three, as is typical in Cypriot churches) was a small trapdoor which led 16 steps and 21 feet down into a subterranean cavern which may have been an early quarry. The stone staircase is covered by a pointed vaulting. The cave is almost as large as the church itself, 45 feet long and 17 feet wide with an 8 foot ceiling. A shaft which allowed light and air into the underground chamber contained, according to Mogabgab, "mass burials with a heap of detached skulls" along with "broken glass vessels, Byzantine and medieval shards, a small ring, two mother of pearl pendant crosses, remnants of a delicate chain, a few iron nails and spikes...". The "detached skulls" are particularly gruesome and one can easily imagine the decapitated heads of Famagusta's vanquished defenders dumped into the convenient pit of the shaft in 1571. Turkish military officials say that the cave was used as a command bunker in 1974 during the Turkish intervention, which is why a monument bust of Kemal Ataturk rests in the midst of it. Even though the cave's original access has been blocked up one can still visit it. One must simply walk down the little decline in the ground to the south of the church and one can gain access to rock-cut doorways. Perhaps this doorway was a way that local worshippers could have access to the underground shrine without having to pass through the church itself. Bring a flashlight and you can go to the back of the cave, in the direction of the church, and see the original stone staircase that led down from the church.

Sources for Unidentified Byzantine Church: T. Mogabgab, "An Unidentified Church in Famagusta," *Report of the Department of Antiquities, Cyprus* (Nicosia, 1939), pp. 89-96; Allan Langdale and Michael J. K. Walsh, "A Report on Three Newly Accessible Churches in the Syrian Quarter of Famagusta" *Journal of Cyprus Studies* 13, n. 33 (2007): 105-123.

Nestorian Church, Famagusta, 14th century

[35° 07' 30.76" N / 33° 56' 19.41" E]

The Nestorian church is one of Famagusta's most unique ecclesiastical monuments (Fig. 106-107). The Nestorians (also called Chaldeans) were an ancient sect that flourished from early Christian times in Syria. They, along with the Jacobites and Maronites, were also considered heretics. When the Latin Christians were methodically expelled from the shores of the Holy Land through the 13th century as Muslim armies advanced, many Nestorian traders, their fortunes linked with Latin merchants, also relocated to Famagusta. One Nestorian family, the Lachas, had legendary wealth and it was their largesse that built this church some time around 1360. The Cypriot chronicler Leontios Makhairas, writing in the mid-14th century, tells of the wealth of the Lachas family:

And there was great wealth there [in Famagusta]: all rich lords, such as were Sir Frances Lachas the Nestorian.... And the riches which they had are beyond my power to describe... For the merchant ships of the Christians which came from the West did not venture to do their business anywhere else but in Cyprus....and therefore the people of Famagusta were rich (and so was the whole island), and the land began to be an object of envy.
[Makhairas, 81]

But Makhairas also tells the story of how the family lost its wealth in the Genoese sacking of Famagusta, and the sons of Lachas the Nestorian, Tsoles and Tsetsious (also called, respectively, Joseph and George), lived meager lives indeed. George killed a man, according to Makhairas, and entered the Order of the Hospitaller Knights, but was very poor and Makhairas claims to have seen him begging for his meals. His brother Joseph went around selling sweetmeats in the villages. "He was a poor little fellow," writes Makhairas, "and him too have I seen" [Makhairas, 87]. In a single generation the Lachas went from celebrated affluence to being vagabonds and peddlers.

Like so many of Famagusta's structures this church also underwent substantial modification. It began as a much smaller, single nave church, but fairly soon the north and south side aisles were added, along with their accompanying semi-circular apses, thus increasing the building's space three-fold. After centuries of dereliction during the Ottoman period, when it was used as a camel stable, it was converted to Greek Orthodoxy in the late 19th century and even more remodeling altered the original medieval scheme. The Greeks dedicated the church to Agios

320

Fig. 107: The three apses of the Nestorian church, Famagusta.

Georgios Xorinos or "St George the Exiler", who had a rather uncharitable function. According to local legend, if you gathered dirt from the floor of this church and left it in the house of an enemy, it would cause either their death or exile within a year.

Several frescoes still exist on the walls, though they are much faded and in need of professional conservation. Some of the saints have their names written in Syriac script, indicating their medieval date and middle-eastern inspiration. In one case an image of a ship was scratched in the arms of St Meno, presumably so that the saint would protect the sailor's ship from harm on the high seas. It is one of many examples of ship graffiti in Famagusta's churches, the most extensive collection existing in the north apse of St George of the Greeks. Today the building is used as a theater and lecture hall by the local university, and public access is limited.

Sources for Nestorian Church: Enlart, 280-6; Jeffery, 144-7; Gunnis, 99-100; Michele Bacci, "Syrian, Palaiologan, and Gothic Murals in the Nestorian Church of Famagusta", *Deltion tes christianikes and arhaiologikes etaireias*, ser. IV, 27 (2006): 207-220; Michael J. K. Walsh, "'On the princypalle Havenes of the See', The Port of Famagusta and the Ship Graffiti of the Church of St George of the Greeks, Cyprus," *International Journal of Nautical Archaeology* (2007): 1-15.

The Latin and Other Quarters
(including outside the walls)

Agia Fotou (Photou), Saint Clare (Santa Chiara), Clarian Nunnery, Famagusta, (aka 'Underground Church'), mid 14th century

[35° 07' 41.32" N / 33° 56' 25.74" E]

In the northeast part of the old city, across from the soccer pitch and near the city's modern north roadway gate in the city walls, a stairway leads down to a small, man-made rectangular cavern. This is labeled 'Underground Church' on some signs and on some maps, which isn't very helpful as there are several other underground churches in Famagusta. In more modern times this underground cellar-like room was used by the Greek Orthodox Church as a shrine to St Fotou, a female saint who was thought to protect believers from the plague. She is a Greek version of St Clare, and so just beside St Fotou one finds the scant remains of the Gothic chapel of Saint Clare, and the outlines of the Poor Clares nunnery of Famagusta from the Lusignan period. Currently, the area has been recently excavated, revealing more clearly the plan of the nunnery and the chapel and some ancillary structures. The plan of another church was also uncovered, and some think that the church and monastery of Saint Dominic may also have been in this immediate area. The underground portion was probably part of the Latin medieval complex, serving as a storeroom or cellar, only being converted to a chapel after the late 16th century. It is not deep enough to have been a cistern although many masonry and rock-cut cisterns can still be found in Famagusta, some still open to the air and others buried or their mouths blocked up. At the time of writing excavations were going on in this area, trying to determine whether a church of San Domenico (Saint Dominic) and a monastery were also here. On Stephano Gibellino's 1571 print of the siege of Famagusta he labels a church in this location "S Dominico".

Sources for Agia Fotou and St Clare: Enlart, 293-4; Jeffery, 142-3.

Underground Church of Our Lady of the Golden Cave, (Outside the Walls) Famagusta, 13th or 14th century

[35° 07' 42.93" N / 33° 56' 00.64" E]

This impressive underground church is just outside the city walls of Famagusta's old city, about 110 metres northwest of the corner of the Martinengo Bastion (Fig. 108). To get to it you'll have to exit the walled city and go to the street intersection just outside the bastion. The site is surrounded by a modern 2 metre high stone wall and for safety reasons the gate is most often locked by the Department of Antiquities, though scholars and researchers can obtain the key from the Department. Or, if one is athletically inclined, the wall is by no means insurmountable. But be careful. A wide rock-cut stairway of about 20 steps leads down to a doorway that consists of masonry piers holding up a huge, solid stone lintel. Above the lintel the rock face seems to have been worked into a semi-circular lunette, which may at one point have been plastered and frescoed with an image of the Virgin Mary and Christ. Exposed to the elements, any paintings have long since vanished though the lunette's outlines are still quite visible. To the left just outside the entryway is a rock-cut cubicle of uncertain function. Some scholars believe that this is a tomb from the Bronze Age, and it is true that it resembles them, but it is more likely that it was excavated in more recent Lusignan times owing to the general popularity of underground churches in medieval Famagusta. It is very dark inside and this is another one of those instances where travelling with a good flashlight comes in handy. Be cautious when entering, as your eyes may not be used to the dark, and there are more steps leading down to the church's floor. Be cautious also because there is an opening to an *ayasma* or sacred well in the floor as well, although this was covered, barely, by a large chunk of concrete when I last visited. The chamber was lit by two shafts or light wells in the 'ceiling' on either side of the eastern part of the church, but these have been blocked up for safety reasons. High on the wall to the right of the apse-like niche in the east end are the vague remains of a series of coats of arms in the yellow and red colours associated with the Lusignans. Just a couple of the heraldic devices are legible, but one can see that a large section of the wall was at one time adorned with them. These decorations suggest that the church was originally Latin/Catholic and existed during the Middle Ages before it was converted to Orthodoxy, probably after 1571. The post holes on either side of the walls of the apse, which is simply a rectangular excavation in the east wall, indicate the presence of an iconostasis or altar screen at some point in the building's history. The candles and oil lamps that were used to illuminate the interior of this cavernous church must have been very striking in former centuries with its golden icons glowing in the dim light. One assumes that the name of the church was derived from a sacred icon of the Virgin with golden embellishments.

Fig. 108: The rock-cut staircase to the underground church of 'Our Lady of the Golden Cave' outside the walls near the Martinegno Bastion, Famagusta.

St George of the Latins, Famagusta, late 13th or 14th century

[35° 07' 36.27" N / 33° 56' 34.77" E]

St George of the Latins, not to be confused with Saint George of the Greeks or St George of the Latins in Lefkoşa/Nicosia, is one of Famagusta's earliest Latin medieval churches (Figs. 109-110). Built very close to the walls of the Lusignan castle, it is thought that construction might have begun on this church before the wider circuit walls of the city had been completed. Some evidence for this is found in subtle defensive and security elements of the architecture. The roof of the building had a low parapet of arrow loops or crenellations in the uppermost edge of the structure, still partly visible as a series of notches along the top of the north wall and visible with field glasses or a telephoto lens. The roof was accessible from a tower on the southwest corner of the façade. Though destroyed, one can still see some remaining steps of the spiral staircase that gave access to a timber walkway at the building's middle level (post holes are visible on the interior), which led in turn to an elevated guard's lookout, still visible on the west façade just to the left of the main entrance. A sentry's garret with a conical roof can be seen on the roof in the northwest corner. The view from there would have allowed someone to see ships coming towards the entrance to the port, which could only be entered from the north as a reef offshore protects all other approaches. This is still true today. One can see the reef by climbing atop the Sea Gate bastion. The doorway to the little guard's shack it still visible from the south.

The stone for the construction of the church might have come from various sources and this is evident in the different degrees of erosion and weathering, though these differences may also be explained by repair work on the structure in the 1940s. George Jeffery thought that some of the stones for the building were pillaged from the ruins of a Greco-Roman temple in Salamis, including columns that he claims supplied the raw material for the trilobed piers inset into the walls from which the ribs of the vaulting sprung. Yet the quarrying that was likely going on in Famagusta in these years for the castle moat could also have supplied much of the ready stone. In turn, the stones of the building's south wall were themselves quarried by British-era stone merchants who were very active in Famagusta in the late 19th century when the British were paying good money for cut stone to be shipped to Egypt to support the construction of the Suez Canal and the town of Port Said. Many of the stones of Famagusta's churches found their way there, much to the city's loss and the loss to future architectural restorers as well.

There are two theories explaining the destruction of the south side of the church while the north side remains in quite good condition. One

Fig. 109: The ruined church of St George of the Latins from the south, Famagusta.

hypothesis is that, like St George of the Greeks, this Latin counterpart received artillery barrages from the southeastern section of the city walls where the cannon fire was most concentrated during the 1570 siege of Famagusta. But Saint George of the Latins is quite distant from this part of the walls, beyond the range of most of the artillery positions. It is possible that barrages also came from the port, but this would have also led to the destruction of the apse which is in fact quite complete in its elevation. Another theory claims that the church was used as a gunpowder storage depot and that it was ignited and exploded outwards in a southern direction, thus destroying that side of the structure. One might recall that the Parthenon in Athens suffered a similar fate.

The tops of the external buttress piers were once adorned by magnificent white marble gargoyles, a few of which endure today though these are severely worn and weather-beaten. One depicts a monk pulling open his mouth as a water spout (Fig. 111), while another shows a bishop with his hands in prayer. Yet another depicts a strange dragon-like creature with a snaky, spiral tail and talons like an eagle. If you look closely at the tops of the other piers you can see the footings for the ones that have disappeared. A few other sculptures survive in better condition around the north portal. This portal must have been the most beautiful in Famagusta in its time. The north portal of the church of Saints Peter and Paul may have been inspired by St George of the Latins' splendid entryway. A high, sloping gable, prickling with leafy crockets, creates a triangular tympanum which is filled with blind tracery in a trefoil design. Flanking the lower part of the door are elaborate imposts with canopies which, like many such canopies in Cypriot Gothic architecture, may have held sculptures, though no record of these exists. Above the portal and to the right are three sculptures. One, a corbel figure of a bearded man with robes holds up a bracket with his hands (Fig. 112). Here, too, a sculpted figure may have stood atop. In another part, nearby, one can just make out the relief of a small dragon-like beast. The best preserved and most impressive of the north portal sculptures, however, is the corbel depicting a ferocious lion devouring a long-eared antelope (Fig. 113).

In the church's interior the capitals of the slender bundles of columns inset into the walls, from which the vaults' ribs sprang, are also beautifully carved and many of the foliate decorations, though weathered, are still lovely. One group is particularly compelling. Though at first appearing to be like the other capitals, it actually represents a flock of winged gargoyles whose double-bodies share common heads (Fig. 114).

Off the northeast corner of the interior of the church is a small chapel or vestry. It looks plain from the exterior but the interior has a beautiful ribbed vault, darkened by the fires of squatters. (During the inter-ethnic troubles in the 60s and 70s Turkish Cypriot refugees camped in the old,

Fig. 111: Marble gargoyle from St George of the Latins, Famagusta.

Fig. 112: Sculpted corbel from near the north portal of St George of the Latins, Famagusta.

Fig. 113: Sculpted corbel from near the north portal of St George of the Latins, Famagusta.

Fig. 114: Capitals with 'bat' designs from St George of the Latins, Famagusta.

abandoned churches). A trip to Lefkoşa and to the Church of St Catherine, about one hundred metres northeast of the cathedral of Santa Sophia, gives an idea of what Saint George of the Latins would have looked like, since St Catherine's is quite similar in size, plan and elevation. St Catherine's owes its survival to the fact that it was converted to a mosque (the Haydar Paşa Camii) and was thus repaired and maintained through the years.

Sources for St George of the Latins: Enlart, 258-262; Jeffery, 128-131.

Opposite: Fig. 115: Print by Stephano Gibellino of the Siege of Famagusta, 1571.

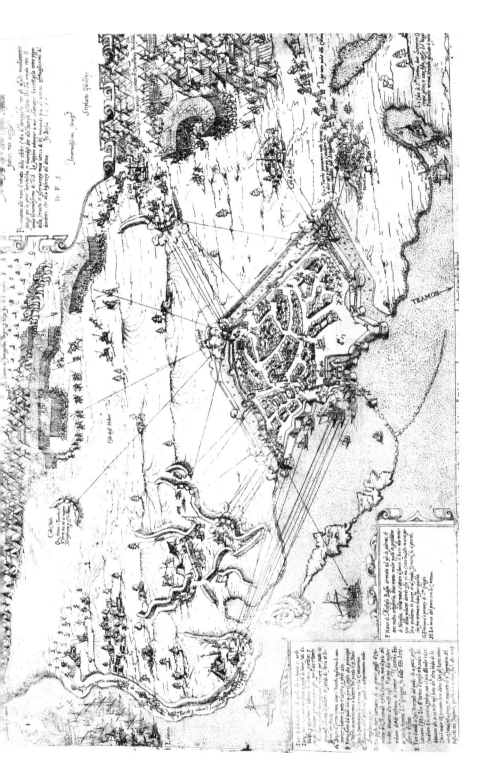

337

Church of St Anthony, Famagusta, late 14th century

[35° 07' 30.94" N / 33° 56' 40.82" E]

The designation of this church as the church of St Anthony is by no means certain, but there is a famous print from 1571 by the Venetian artist Stephano Gibellino that depicts the siege of Famagusta of that same year (Fig. 115). In that print, Gibellino numbers many of the buildings in the city and gives a legend along the bottom of the print. S. Antonio is number 3 and corresponds exactly to the place where the ruins of the church are today, along the inside of the port city walls just south of the Sea Gate. Enlart cites many Italian documents that mention a hospital and church of St Anthony in Famagusta, so it is certain that there was indeed such a church. If we can trust Gibellino, then these ruins may well be the ruins of the church of St Anthony of the Hospitallers. Part of the confusion might stem from the fact that the Templar church was also dedicated to St Anthony, and this was ceded to the Hospitallers in the early 14th century (see 'Twin Churches' entry below). As Enlart also notes, wedged between the wall and a main street running to the Arsenale in the southeast corner of the city, the buildings associated with the church developed in a north-south direction, thus explaining the long wall that runs parallel to the city walls at that point. The church itself was Byzantine in plan, with a single dome in the center, but with many Latin Gothic elements. The structure was thus one of those interesting hybrids typical of Cypriot medieval architecture. It had a narthex in its south side, where the main entrance was. Remnants suggest three bays of ribbed vaults in the narthex porch. The dome of the church was supported by four gray granite columns from the Granite Forum at the ancient Greco-Roman city of Salamis just north of Famagusta. Today they lie broken on the ground in the church's ruins. You can see six more of these columns, used by the Venetians, in the cathedral square of the city.

Sources for St Anthony: Enlart, 288-290.

Fig. 116: Franciscan church, with apse and former chapter house in foreground, Famagusta.

339

Franciscan Church, Famagusta, early 14th to 15th century

[35° 07' 29.65" N / 33° 56' 27.98" E]

Enough remains of the Franciscan church to get a good sense of its plan and elevation (Fig. 116). Similar in design to the Church of St Mary of Carmel but slightly smaller, the Franciscan church also had a single rib-vaulted nave with no side aisles. It resembles the Carmelite church in other ways too, including later renovations and additions of large funerary side chapels in the north and south walls. In both cases, these additions may have degraded the buildings' overall stability.

This church occupied a place of honour in the city, right beside the Lusignan royal palace, to which it was once directly connected. It was also the church closest to the cathedral, on the eastern side of the cathedral square, a location indicative of the respect enjoyed by the Franciscan Order in the Middle Ages. It is said that the Lusignan King Henry II, who may have been the principal patron of the building, often spent time in religious devotions in the church, using it as a private royal chapel. However, historical records also tell us that Henry's successor, Hugh IV, had little respect for the Franciscans and closed up the passageway that linked the palace with the church, using it instead as a cross-bow shooting gallery. Little remains of the north chapel, while the south chapel is the best preserved part of the entire structure. Tombstones and their inscriptions recorded by earlier explorers point to significant patronage by Genoese families. By 1395 Famagusta's economy was already in decline and a visitor, Nicholas Martoni, records a conversation with a Franciscan monk who complains that his alms were meager.

A chapter house was attached directly to the apse. This also still survives as it was reused to form the entrance to the Çafer Paşa hamam or bathhouse in the Ottoman period. Today, this bathhouse is a café-bar and the chapter house still serves as a foyer for the modern business. There are no remains of the monastic structures, their location now occupied by an elementary school's grounds.

Sources for Franciscan Church: Enlart, 262-267; Jeffery, 132-136.

The Church of Saints Peter and Paul (Sinan Paşa Camii), Famagusta, 14th century

[35° 07' 26.47" N / 33° 56' 25.55" E]

The church of Saints Peter and Paul is one of Famagusta's most impressive monuments (Figs. 117-118). After the cathedral of St Nicholas it is the largest structure that still maintains its architectural integrity after so many centuries. Since it is also similar in size and design to the ruined church of St George of the Greeks, Saints Peter and Paul gives us some sense of what that nearby church might have originally looked like. Saints Peter and Paul was constructed, chroniclers tell us, from a one-third portion of the profits from a single lucrative trading venture made by one of Famagusta's wealthiest citizens, Simon Nostrano. Built some time during the reign of the Lusignan King Peter I, who reigned from 1358 to 1369, Saints Peter and Paul represents the architectural expression of Famagusta's most prosperous and creative historical moment.

Like the cathedral, Saints Peter and Paul owes its survival at least in part to the fact that it was also converted to a mosque after the Ottoman conquest of 1571, when it was renamed the Sinan Paşa Cami. However, it has not been used as a mosque for over a century. Evidence of the conversion can be discerned in the minaret that was added atop the belfry tower on the southwest corner of the structure. The top section of the minaret fell down long ago, possibly in a large earthquake that happened in the 18th century, explaining its currently truncated form.

The minaret has a spiral staircase inside which gave access to the roof of the south side aisle and to a door which in turn led to a timber framed gallery on its interior. This gallery gave an uninterrupted view of the church's nave below. Its function was likely a segregated area for women since in the Middle Ages it was common to separate the genders during sermons and ceremonies. Indeed, it may have continued to serve that function when the building became a mosque since in Islam, too, women are segregated from the male 'congregation'. Another door on the opposite side gave access to the other end of the gallery from the north, and this connected up with a timber bridge, high off the street, which connected to the upper stories of the Venetian palace complex to the north (Palazzo del Proveditore). Thus the court ladies from the palace could move easily from their private parlours, across the elevated bridge, and directly into the gallery in the church for services.

One of the most impressive features of the structure is the view of its south flank with its two levels of flying buttresses cascading down from the heights of the building's roofline (Fig. 119). However, the lower set of buttresses were not part of the original structure (note there is only an upper set on the north side), but were added in subsequent centuries to

Fig. 118: Apses of the church of Saints Peter and Paul, Famagusta.

Fig. 120: North portal of the church of Saints Peter and Paul, Famagusta.

Fig. 121: Detail from the north portal of the church of Saints Peter and Paul, Famagusta.

Fig. 122: Detail from the north portal of the church of Saints Peter and Paul, Famagusta.

Fig. 123: Detail from the north portal of the church of Saints Peter and
Paul, Famagusta.

Opposite:
Fig. 124: Gothic rib vaults of the nave of the church of Saints Peter and
Paul, Famagusta.

348

help stabilize the south wall. Enlart suggests that the earthquakes of 1546 and 1568 may have necessitated the additional buttressing elements. On the roof of the structure, not normally accessible to the public, one can clearly see how the south wall had begun to bow outwards, perhaps because of differential settling of the building on that side. A large cistern was discovered in the southwest corner of the church, near the base of the belfry tower/minaret, thus perhaps making the foundations in that quadrant less secure than the builders may have wished. The pitched roof one sees today, as well as the cap on the minaret, is a recent construction of 2010.

On the south wall one finds additional evidence of the church's conversion to a mosque. Like most Cypriot churches, there were also entrances on the sides of the church. But here the original south portal was blocked up because it was too close to where the *mihrab* (the niche in the wall which indicated the direction to Mecca) was constructed on the interior wall. This was also done at Santa Sophia in Nicosia and in St Nicholas. The church's most impressive entrance is not, as might be expected, on the façade of the building. Rather, the north entrance — facing the royal palace — was given the most monumental and decorative expression (Fig. 120-121). This north portal, with its intricate gable, tracery, crockets, jamb columns, and dogtooth moldings also has sculptural reliefs of an angel swinging a censer on the left and the Archangel Michael with a basket of souls in his lap on the right (Figs. 122-123). These reliefs are among the best preserved examples of medieval figural sculpture on Cyprus. Even the decorations of foliage are beautiful and show leaf and vine motifs. Look closely at these vines and you'll see a couple of strange animals biting the tendrils.

The view of the east end of the church's exterior is splendid, with its high *trichonos* or triple-apse configuration. A large rectangular structure was at some point added to the lower level of the apses. These rooms may have functioned as a vestry for the church but also may have been added to assist in structurally supporting the apses.

The interior of Saints Peter and Paul is inspiring (Fig. 124). Flanking the wide nave are imposing sets of columnar piers with simple, squat capitals from which spring triple engaged colonnettes which themselves support the springing of the ribs of the five quadripartite (four-part) vaults. At the intersections of the ribs are bosses decorated with Lusignan coats of arms and symbols, including the multiple cross motif indicating the Lusignan claim to their lost kingdom of Jerusalem.

The interior houses a significant work of art high on the south wall just above the walled up south portal. There, in fragmentary form and much damaged, is a rare *sinopia*, an under drawing in red that was done in preparation for a fresco painting. The art historian Michael Walsh has identified the subject matter as the Forty Martyrs of Sebaste, a story of forty Roman soldiers who had become converts to Christianity and who were made to stand virtually naked beside a freezing lake by their pagan cohorts. The iconography is well known and the figures correlate with the conventional depictions: men shivering and leaning together, a man fainting while a friend supports him, and the others, scantily clad, huddled in the background. The *sinopia* may have been executed during the Genoese occupation of Famagusta or during the Venetian period. It is one of Famagusta's most important historical paintings and is in dire need of conservation.

In the more recent historical past the building has been put to several uses as a theater, and, for a time it was even the public library of Famagusta. For a long time it was used as the grain storage depot for the city, which is why even today some older people in its neighborhood still refer to it as the 'Buğday Camii' or 'Wheat Mosque.' It the springtime new wheat still sprouts up today in the small field to the south of the church, ancestors of seeds that fell from peoples' sacks ages ago. It had been unused and closed to the public for 35 years, but has been recently cleaned up and is now used as a community activities center.

Sources for Saints Peter and Paul: Enlart, 246-253; Jeffery, 151-154 ; Gunnis, 96; Michael J. K. Walsh, "Saint Peter and Paul Church (Sinan Paşa Camii) Famagusta: A Forgotten Gothic Moment in Northern Cyprus," *Inferno* 9 (2004): 1-9; Michael J. K. Walsh, "The Re-emergence of 'The Forty Martyrs of Sebaste' in the Church of St Peter and Paul, Famagusta, North Cyprus," *Journal of Cultural Heritage* 8 (2007): 81-86.

The 'Twin Churches' Famagusta: The Churches of the Templars, (13th century) and Hospitallers (14th century)

[35° 07' 31.73" N / 33° 56' 26.36" E]

Located 50 metres north of the Franciscan church are a pair of small churches commonly known as the 'Twin Churches' (Fig. 125). The north church is the larger and also the earliest, dating to some time in the 13th century. This church is believed to have belonged to the Knights Templar, functioning as their site of personal devotion and exemplifying their expression of patronage to the city's sacred sites. The Knights Templar was a military order of knights charged with protecting pilgrims and the pilgrimage routes to the Holy Land. Thus their mandate was closely linked to the crusades.

For a brief historical moment, the Templars were destined to become the masters of Cyprus when the island was sold to them in 1191 by King Richard the Lion Heart of England, who had conquered Cyprus by vanquishing its Byzantine despotic ruler Isaac Comnenus. The Templars, who were either short of funds or the will to govern a population resistant to their rule, soon chose not to pursue their ambitions on the island. Instead, Cyprus was sold the following year to Guy de Lusignan, the erstwhile King of Jerusalem who had lost his kingdom to Saladin and his Muslim armies. It is indicative of the Templars' power that they almost gained control of the entire island realm. Even when the Lusignans took over, the Knights retained much land and were a powerful presence on Cyprus and in Famagusta in particular. Documents demonstrate that in 1300 Famagusta's Templar Knights were very wealthy indeed. The Templars' position of power and influence was not, of course, limited to Cyprus. Their supremacy extended throughout the range of medieval Christendom. In fact, they became too dominant and were violently repressed by the papacy in the early 14th century. Their properties in Famagusta were confiscated and given to the other important knightly order of the Middle Ages, the Knights Hospitallers.

The Templar church is simple in design. It consists of three bays of ribbed vaults with a semi-circular apse with a single lancet window in its center. The sides of the building's exterior are supported by a series of simple masonry buttresses attached to the walls, a typical configuration in the churches of Famagusta. The west portal is a plain rectangular opening which had a shallow canopy extending over it, the supports for which can be seen flanking the doorway. There is a five-spoke circular window with trefoil tracery on the façade, and above that, one of three flagstaff holders. Almost all the churches of Famagusta had these flagstaff holders, and when we imagine what these structures must have looked like centuries ago, we can envision brightly coloured flags on tall

Fig. 125: The so-called 'Twin Churches'; the Templar church on the left and the Hospitaller church on the right, Famagusta.

wooden poles, adding height and dynamic movement to the elevations. It is probable that a banner with the red cross of the Templars once flew from this central holder. Archival photographs show that when Queen Elizabeth II was coronated in 1953, they put flags in the flagstaffs of the churches of Famagusta for the celebration.

As is true for many churches in Famagusta, the northern entrance was given pride of place. Here the north portal is wider than the façade entrance and has been given a framing in the form of an elaborate hood molding. It is thought that this entrance may have led to monastic buildings associated with the church, the ruins of which may lie below the parking lot that occupies this site today. Foundations of other structures lie to the east of the twin churches just beyond the apses.

The southernmost of the two churches has been identified as the Hospitallers' church. The Hospitallers, like the Templars, were a crusading knightly order but, as their name suggests, they provided hospitals for the sick along the pilgrimage routes to the Holy Land. A relief of a coat of arms of the Knights of St John of Jerusalem (a single equal-armed cross) on the lintel of the south portal supports this identification. This smaller church is only about two-thirds the size of the larger Templar church and consists of a single unribbed vault with an apse with one lancet window. The façade portal resembles the north portal of the Templar church, giving the façade more dignity. However, instead of a circular window, the Hospitaller's church has merely a single lancet on its façade. A truncated bell tower extends from the top of the façade at the middle, with flagstaff holders on the corners. It is altogether more humble and simple in comparison with the Templar church.

After the fall of the Templars the Hospitallers may have gained control of both of the churches. At least it seems that there was some attempt to unite the two buildings. A corridor creating a communication between the two was constructed, probably in the mid-14th century, and an exterior staircase was made between them, giving access to the roofs.

Camille Enlart saw frescoes in the Hospitallers church in the 1890s. Sadly, these have succumbed to the ravages of time.

Old timers in the neighborhood say that the Hospitallers church used to be the central meeting hall for the Cypriot chapter of the Masons. In the middle part of the 20th century some of Cyprus's wealthiest citizens were Masons and, in decades when automobiles were rare on Cyprus, everyone always knew when they were meeting because the road in front of the Hospitallers church was filled with the rare sight of dozens of motor cars.

Sources for Twin Churches: Enlart, 290-3; Jeffery, 131-2; Gunnis, 102. For a brief historical account of the Templars in Cyprus see Peter Edbury, "The Templars in Cyprus," in *The Military Orders: Fighting for the Faith and Caring for the Sick,* ed. Malcolm Barber (Aldershot: Ashgate, 1994), 189-195.

St Nicholas Cathedral (Lala Mustafa Paşa Camii), Famagusta, 14th century

[35°07' 29.34" N / 33° 56' 33.17" E]

There are few sites in Cyprus more impressive than the façade of the cathedral of St Nicholas in Famagusta, known as the Aysofya Camii from 1571, but called the Lala Mustafa Paşa Camii since 1954. As the sun moves around to the west during the late afternoon, you can sit at one of the cafes and be quite convinced that you're in Paris as the sun illuminates the quintessentially Gothic façade (Figs. 126-127). It is without question the largest and most complex of the churches of Famagusta and the jewel of Cypriot medieval architecture. Its plan consists of a nave and two side-aisles with each terminating at their east ends with polygonal apses (Fig. 128). The nave vaults are significantly taller than those of the side-aisles, providing wall elevation for a substantial clerestory, which is pierced by wide windows on the north and south. Corresponding windows are found below in each bay of the side-aisles. These are the essential elements of the plan and elevation of the great church, but a more detailed examination of its architectural features will help us understand the structure more thoroughly.

The Exterior of the Cathedral

The façade of St Nicholas cathedral has three horizontal and three vertical elements. Horizontally, there is the lower level which is dominated by the three entrances and the surrounding decoration. These portals are an impressive trio, recessed and surrounded by multiple arches and crowned with high, pitched gables. The second level is dominated by a large central rose window with beautiful tracery, but which also has a section (on the left) of the balustrade with quatrefoil tracery that originally spanned the width of the central façade. The central window is flanked by surfaces marked by lancets of blind tracery. From a distance one can see rectangular doors low down on these lancets. These doors led to timber staircases — no longer there — that allowed one to climb to the roof of the cathedral, but also gave access to walkways on top of the aisles. The uppermost level of the façade consists of the tops of the two towers at either side. Should this have been a cathedral built in northern climes, the central space at this upper level would have been filled with the triangular end of a pitched roof. However, such roofs were never constructed on Latin Cypriot churches as there was no threat of snow and rainfall was sparse (Fig. 129). Instead, the tops of the vaults were covered in a layer of mortar to protect the vaulting. This is one of the main characteristics that differentiate the Cypriot churches from their

Fig. 126: Façade of the cathedral of St Nicholas (Lala Mustafa Paşa Camii), Famagusta.

Opposite: Fig. 127: North side of the cathedral of St Nicholas (Lala Mustafa Paşa Camii), Famagusta.

356

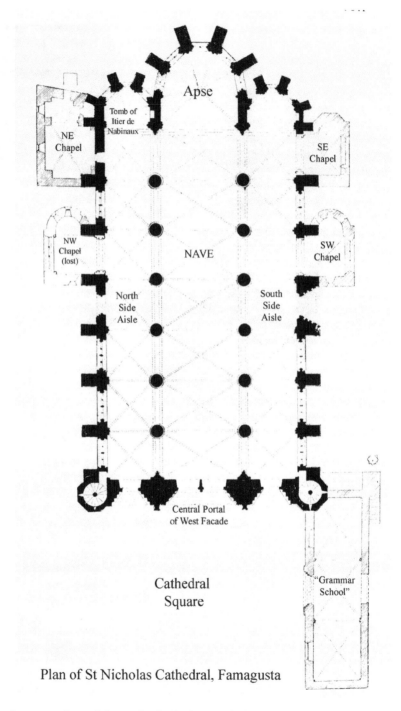

Apse

Tomb of
Itier de
Nabinaux

NE
Chapel

SE
Chapel

NW
Chapel
(lost)

NAVE

SW
Chapel

North
Side
Aisle

South
Side
Aisle

Central Portal
of West Facade

Cathedral
Square

"Grammar
School"

Plan of St Nicholas Cathedral, Famagusta

Fig. 128: Plan of the cathedral of St Nicholas, Famagusta [from
Camille Enlart, Gothic Art and the Renaissance in Cyprus].

358

Fig. 129: Vaulting of the roof of the cathedral of St Nicholas, Famagusta, from the north tower.

European counterparts. Certainly, the lack of a high and steeply pitched roof makes the structures look quite different, proportionally, from those in Europe.

Vertically, the façade is divided into the three sections corresponding to the central nave and the two side aisles of the church's interior. The church has the conventional three entrances: the central one opening to the nave and the smaller flanking ones opening to the side aisles (Fig. 130). Each of the portals is splayed, that is, inset into the façade to provide a shallow shelter immediately before each door. The central portal is divided by a slim trumeau with an engaged colonnette whose capital supports a small base, over which a Gothic canopy hovers a few feet above. These canopies are also found flanking in the jambs of the doorway. Though statues may have occupied these areas, there is no record of them. The masons, nevertheless, were accustomed to putting in such elements into the jambs and did so here as well, even though no sculpture may ever have been meant to occupy them. Look into the tops of the little canopies and you'll see little Gothic 'rib vaults' with central bosses with relief designs such as the *Agnus Dei* ('Lamb of God') and the Lusignan Rose. However, there are substantial remnants of other figural sculptures around the portals and, in fact, in many places on St Nicholas' façade. Look closely at the bottom ends of some of the decorated arches and you'll see animal figures, and sometimes even human figures, that have had their heads removed because of the building's conversion into a mosque. Here and there, above the canopies of the central portal for example, you'll see the claws of lion-like animals with manes and snake-like tails whose faces have long been lost. There's one small dragon that the iconoclasts missed, however. See if you can find him. He's to the right of the central doorway. His head and face survive to this day. Other decapitated animals can be seen here and there, but there are also some higher up on the façade that survive in fairly good condition. Also, look at the apexes of the decorated arches with leafy motifs and you will often see the Green Man with foliage growing out of his mouth and nose. On the towers are some impressive survivors. On the south tower there is a dragon-like creature that holds some unfortunate smaller beast in his claws below. Also on the south tower is a nude man (you can see his testicles and penis) who holds his head in his hands. Likely he symbolizes sins of the flesh, and he repents of his sins or, perhaps, he realizes that his sins will land him in hell. One the north tower is a strange figure who seems to be dressed in armor or perhaps a suit of mail. Is he holding a bouquet of flowers or some kind of knobby club? Beside him, to the north, is a much damaged figure that seems to have had a long tail with scales on it, like a mermaid. Nobody knows what these fantastic creatures mean but they are typical features of Gothic architecture. It's one of those times

Fig. 130: Main portals of the cathedral of St Nicholas, Famagusta.

361

where having a pair of field glasses will help you appreciate the building. There are also some small animal figures decorating the apse as well, very high up. They usually can be found at the bottom ends of the leafy decorative arches and mouldings.

While looking carefully at the façade's decorations and architectural elements, you will also see, especially in the south tower midway up, the radial fracturing of an impact crater caused by one of the cannon balls shot by the Ottoman army in 1571. In other parts of St Nicholas, you can see rounded holes where the cannon balls went right though the walls.

The tympana of the three western portals are glazed with traceried windows, a fairly uncommon way to fill this space, though it also appears at Reims in France, which is often spoken of as being the inspiration for Saint Nicholas. Endearingly, St Nicholas cathedral is often referred to as the 'daughter' of the great cathedral at Reims. Camille Enlart thought there were many similarities between the two and remained convinced that St Nicholas was constructed by architects and masons from the Champagne region, of which Reims is the principal city. More recent scholars, however, have demonstrated that some elements of St Nicholas can be traced to German Gothic structures of the Rhineland, such as Cologne. Since masons and model books travelled widely in the Middle Ages it is perhaps not so surprising to see several similarities from myriad regional sources.

There were reasons why the Lusignan kings may have made reference to Reims cathedral since that was where the kings of France were crowned. Similarly, St Nicholas in Famagusta was where the Lusignan kings had their coronation ceremonies as kings of Jerusalem after they had been crowned kings of Cyprus in the cathedral of Santa Sophia in Lefkoşa/Nicosia. The appearance of St Nicholas thus recreated and made reference to the lineage of French royalty, therefore implying Lusignan correlation with them.

The south side of the cathedral offers the best view of the flying buttresses, piers, and side chapels of the structure (Fig. 131). The view from this side also makes clear the significant reconstruction of the vaults and buttresses which took place sometime after 1571. The nave vaults all through the central section of the church were either destroyed or structurally compromised from the barrages of the 1571 Ottoman siege, but even earlier damage could have occurred during the earthquakes of 1546 and 1568. There was also a severe earthquake in 1735. Alexander Drummond makes mention of it when he visits Famagusta in 1745: "In the year 1735, the town was greatly damaged by an earthquake: the Cathedral church of Sancta Sophia (St Nicholas was sometimes called this), which has been converted into a mosque, fell in and buried in its ruins above two hundred Turks who were at worship when the shock

Fig. 131: South side of the cathedral of St Nicholas, Famagusta.

Fig. 132: *The remaining medieval (Lusignan-era) flying buttresses of the south side of the cathedral of St Nicholas, Famagusta.*

happened" [*Excerpta Cypria*, 274]. It is no wonder that the later architects, commissioned to make repairs, constructed inelegant but sturdy buttresses to replace the more refined and delicate ones that failed. The first two bays of the nave from the west still have the original, more decorative flyers with their tracery quatrefoils (Fig. 132). The tops of these bands have channels carved in the top to direct rainwater into drain pipes in the piers. This is also why the windows of those middle sections do not have any of their original Gothic tracery.

It is on the south side that one finds a rare historical document that has helped architectural historians date the structure (Fig. 133). On one of the piers is a deeply cut inscription in abbreviated medieval French. It records a moment in the history of the church's construction:

In the year of Christ 1311 of the 4th of August the money provided for the building of the church of Famagusta was paid down and Bishop Baldwin began the work in the same year on the 1st day of September, of which work six vaults of the two aisles had been completed and ten vaults of the aisles and eight vaults of the nave remained to be built.

A similar 'construction update' inscription can be found at the cathedral of Reims. Although the inscription doesn't tell us exactly when the cathedral was begun or when it was finished, it nonetheless lets us know of its partial progress by 1311.

The apse of St Nicholas is particularly striking (Fig. 134). One can enjoy a good view of it from the top of the Sea Gate bastion, particularly in the morning sun. Since there are no flying buttresses here to counteract the thrust of the vaulting of the interior (since there is no ambulatory), the wall is articulated by piers which give strong vertical accents to the five facets of the polygonal apse. There are two levels to the apse, both with a series of tall lancet windows, which have been filled in with geometric stucco designs to make the windows appear more like a mosque's. The demarcation between the lower and upper levels is made clear by the strong horizontal elements of a series of projecting corbels. These corbels supported a wooden gangplank which enabled one to walk — along with the gallery on the façade and on the roofs of the side aisles — the entire distance around the cathedral at that level.

The lancet windows of the upper level are crowned with gables with large rosette designs (Fig. 135). The gables were originally bristling with crockets, though many of these have fallen off over the centuries. Despite the damages, these decorative elements still magnificently convey the literal sense of the corona or crown which is particularly rich in this context, since it is not only the crown over the altar — that is, the crown

Fig. 133: Medieval French inscription on a pier on the south side of the cathedral of St Nicholas, Famagusta.

Opposite:
Fig. 134: Upper part of the central apse, the corona, of the cathedral of St Nicholas, Famagusta.

367

of Christ as King of Heaven — but the crowns of the Lusignan kings of the Holy City of Jerusalem who were coronated there. In medieval symbolism the crowns of earthly kings were synonymous with the crown of Christ's rule in heaven, and thus also their reigns were blessed by God. At Famagusta, as at Reims, earthly kings were not only coronated, but anointed by God to rule.

The finials on top of the piers and towers are also significant aspects of the exterior decoration of the cathedral. Much damaged by the trials and tribulations that this building has suffered through the centuries, not the least of which are lightning strikes during winter storms, few of these elements endure. One, on the southeast corner of the apse, still survives in its entirety.

There were four chapels attached to the cathedral: two on the south side and two on the north. The one on the north that still survives could well have been the sacristy of the cathedral rather than a chapel proper. One of the other chapels on the north side has been completely destroyed, though the outlines of its foundations are still visible. The westernmost pair, on both the north and south sides (which includes the ruined northern one), were very likely built at the same time and have a similar plan. They were open to the church through wide arches but these, along with the accesses to the other chapels, were walled up when the church was converted to a mosque. All of these chapels have been left completely derelict and the public is not given access. However, a generous donation at the mosque ticket desk might get you access to the northeastern chapel/sacristy, which is today used as a storage shed. There was a small medieval tomb slab cracked in two on the floor in 2007, presumably of a youth who was interred in the cathedral, but this has vanished. If you gain access to the chapel, look up into a window on the north wall and you'll see an Ottoman repair of the window with a Venetian inscription block, clearly an insult to the Venetians and their rule on Cyprus. In gaining access to the north flank of the cathedral one also can see the remaining ground plan of the second, now ruined chapel. On the wall beside it one can see the large Gothic arch that used to give access to the main part of the church, now walled up.

The Interior of the Cathedral:

The interior of the cathedral consists of a high central nave with lower flanking side aisles (Fig. 136). While not nearly as large as some counterparts in Western Europe, it is still an impressive sight. The nave vaults are 21.85 metres high, about half the height of the nave of Amiens cathedral in France. The interior length of St Nicholas is 52.5 metres, about half the length of a football pitch. Here, too, it is more modest in dimensions compared with its European counterparts, as Amiens is 133

Fig. 135: Gables of the upper part of the central apse, the corona, of the cathedral of St Nicholas, Famagusta.

metres in length. Yet even while it may lack the monumental dimensions of Europe's great cathedrals, St Nicholas is still a stunning building. In a strange way, stripped of all its Catholic ecclesiastical furniture, including its altar, pews, altarpieces, and other common accretions that typify the interiors of currently functioning cathedrals (the conversion of St Nicholas into a mosque long ago cleared out these elements), it is a more pleasing space because of it. If one likes to appreciate the architecture alone, the bare bones interior of St Nicholas might come as an agreeable surprise. Only the *dikka*, the raised wooden platform in the nave (used by the imam to recite *surahs* from the Koran), and the *mimbar* against the south wall interrupt the clarity of the architectural forms. The apse of the nave is very clearly visible, even in its lower level, since there is no longer an altar or an altar screen, as there would have been centuries ago when the building still functioned as a church. The nave arcade is supported by large, rounded stone columns 5.10 metres in circumference, six on each side, from which spring the elegant Gothic arches. Look at the bases of these and you'll see a version of those ubiquitous Lusignan symbols, these ones, as in Famagusta's castle, resembling medals on a general's military jacket.

The large windows of the side aisles and clerestory allow ample light to enter the interior space and illuminate the nave, and this makes it much lighter inside than many northern cathedrals that have darker stained glass in the windows. The tall lancets of the apse light up the apse vaulting, which is a lovely sexpartite (six part) vault with an impressive spray of ribs extending from the central boss (Fig. 137). The columns, ribs, and voussoirs of the nave arcade are all left today in the natural limestone, while the other mural surfaces are covered in white plaster. It is an attractive ensemble, but we must remember that many of the wall surfaces might have been decorated with colourful frescoes centuries ago. Nobody knows if underneath the plaster some medieval or Renaissance period paintings survive.

Only some of the clerestory windows still maintain their original stone tracery designs, while the plaster patterns of the remaining windows date from renovations in the British period. Note that original tracery survives in some of the clerestory windows closest to the western façade of the building, but that in most of the other windows it is lost. Recall that there was a tremendous earthquake in Famagusta in the 18th century, as mentioned above, and it is reported that many of St Nicholas' vaults fell in. While in the central apse note the *piscina* (a niche in the wall for the storage of liturgical instruments and holy water), which still has its open tracery work.

The south aisle, which is where the *mihrab* is today (the niche in the wall that indicated the direction to Mecca and thus the direction to pray

Fig. 138: Detail of tomb effigy of Bishop Itier de Nabinaux, cathedral of St Nicholas (Lala Mustafa Paşa Camii), Famagusta.

towards), has some interesting elements in it. Note that the *mihrab* itself actually is a filled in open arch. This arch once led to a funerary chapel that actually still survives attached to the southern exterior to the church. There are two of these and one can see them while walking around the south side. The more easterly of the chapels was also a funerary chapel, and it, too, was opened to the south side aisle and has since been walled up. Both are closed to the public, which is a shame since they are quite marvelous.

Chroniclers tell of dozens of carved tomb slabs in the flooring of St Nicholas' cathedral, virtually all of which were destroyed in 1571. Only one seems to survive in the church itself, having been moved to the north apse. It is in the part of the mosque sectioned off for women, but there is rarely anyone there so it is usually possible to visit, except during prayer time. The effigy is under a wooden lid and is much worn, but the figure and inscription are still legible (Fig. 138). It is the tomb of Bishop Itier de Nabinaux, a Franciscan monk who was ordained bishop of Famagusta around 1360. He died from a chill he received from swimming in the sea in 1365.

The Environs of the Cathedral:

As in most European cities, the cathedral was the center of civic life and several subsidiary buildings surrounded the main church structure. The Bishop's palace seems to have taken up much of the area to the north and the east of St Nicholas. Though much has been lost of this compound, a significant amount remains. Along the north side, for example, there is still an arcade which opens on to the street which leads to the Sea Gate. These vaulted spaces are used today as retail stores and it is quite likely that this was their function in medieval times as well. The rents from the spaces would have generated income for the bishop and the cathedral building. Another level may have existed on top of this arcade but this vanished long ago. Scant remains still exist to the east of this row of shops, including a barrel vaulted rectangular structure of uncertain function. A well, now covered up, was located just off the northeast corner of the cathedral and this may have provided water not only for sacred rituals but also for the bishop's domestic use. The small church immediately to the east of the cathedral apse could well have been the bishop's private chapel. It is currently under restoration (2011) and while it was certainly a Latin Catholic chapel or church originally it shows signs of having been converted to Orthodoxy at a later date, after 1571 one presumes. Post holes high in the wall in front of the apse indicate alterations made to support the ends of an iconostasis. It is a simple construction, simply a slightly pointed barrel vault with two strainer arches resting on four V-shaped corbels on the walls. On the exterior walls, on the west, north, and south sides it seems several posts were inserted to support the roofing of porches.

Otherwise there is little that remains of the Bishops' residence, though excavations might reveal more of the foundations of whatever was once there. A monastery is also thought to have existed just east of the apse along the modern short street where some stone buildings have been restored. One of them is a pub appropriately called 'Monk's Inn'; the 100 metre long street is named after William Dreghorn, who lived in the old town and wrote guidebooks for Salamis and Famagusta. He was a much loved character in Famagusta and I was sad not to have been able to meet him. He passed away a year before I came to Famagusta.

The parvis or cathedral square still provides an open space in front of the west façade of the cathedral/mosque today. Extending from the cathedral's southwestern corner is a structure which may have been a grammar school, a common ancillary institution appended to cathedrals. It seems to have been built rather late in the history of the complex. Certainly it was much renovated by the Venetians as Venetian coats of arms in white marble decorate its façade. There was a second storey above it and access is still found from a stone staircase on the southern, external wall of the building. It is worth climbing up there to get closer views of the cathedral façade. The interior of this structure is rib vaulted but in a heavy, utilitarian style. Its most distinctive feature is the ornate arched doorway that faces the cathedral square. There are many decorative mouldings, perhaps recycled from earlier medieval churches, and one can make out some sculptures, a pair of which seems to illustrate a man fighting with a lion-like creature. On the left there is a dragon with web-like wings. The slender white columns, while at first looking like marble, are in fact modern reproductions just painted white. Their capitals, too, are modern restorations, though they may well be accurate reconstructions. One of the most distinctive features of the building is the two large circular windows, about a metre and a half in diametre, with their banded frames that look like a ribbon wrapping a hoop. Look below these and you'll see large pieces of classical Greco-Roman period marbles with sculpted decorations. At one time they were set up to make a stone bench all along the length of the structure at that side of the square. The section closest to the cathedral is the most impressive. It's a long relief with running animals in the circles of a vine motif. There's a lion, an ox, and a deer with antlers. All of these fragments very likely came from Salamis. We are reminded that the cathedral square was also a place for ritual and ceremony, including executions, and that city and church officials may have used this long bench as a place from which to view the proceedings.

As one looks at the façade of the cathedral, to the far left is a domed Ottoman *medresse* or Koranic school, one of the few Ottoman structures on Cyprus (see later entry). Ottoman tombs are also found here, such as the small tomb shrine of Mehmet Omar Effendi. In front of the *medresse* is a pair of granite columns on pedestals, probably taken from Salamis by the Venetians who erected them here to imitate the two columns at the Bacino waterfront beside the Doge's Palace (Palazzo Ducale) in Venice. Like the columns in Venice, one was probably surmounted by a statue of St Theodore, an old patron saint of Venice, while the other was topped by a statue of the Lion of St Mark, Venice's later patron saint.

To the far right, as one looks at the façade, are two large slabs of marble under a modern canopy, right in front of the animal frieze just mentioned. On one of them there is a coat of arms and the barely legible remnants of a medieval inscription. It is the tomb slab — taken from the cathedral's floor — of a 'Dame Remodin', who is otherwise unknown to history. Today, these slabs are used to lay out the bodies during Muslim funerals at the mosque.

Sources for St Nicholas Cathedral: Enlart, 222-245; Jeffery, 116-127; Gunnis, 90-5; Michael J. K. Walsh, "A Gothic Masterpiece in the Levant. Saint Nicholas Cathedral, Famagusta, North Cyprus," *Journal of Cultural Heritage* 6 (2005) 1–6; Allan Langdale, "The Marginal Sculpture of St Nicholas Cathedral," in *Medieval and Renaissance Famagusta: Studies in Art, Architecture and History*, eds. Nicholas Coureas, Peter Edbury, Michael Walsh (London: Ashgate, 2012).

The Greek Quarter

The Greek quarter is the southeast quarter of the city, which is today the least developed part of the city. There are four Greek Orthodox/ Byzantine churches in the area: St George of the Greeks, St Symeon/Agios Epiphanios, St Nicholas, and Agia Zoni. It is also where one can access the Çanbulat bastion in the southeast corner, which is also a good place to exit the city walls and begin a walking tour of the moat, while a staircase on the inside of the walls brings you to the terraplein so that you can walk along to the bastions atop the south walls. In this corner of the walls was also the Arsenale of the Venetian era city, where armaments were stored.

St Symeon (Agios Epiphanios), Famagusta, 12th – 13th century

[35° 07' 25.69" N / 33° 56' 37.18" E]

The church of St Symeon (Agios Epiphanios), which today is attached and contiguous with the church of St George of the Greeks (next entry), was the earlier 'metropolitan' or cathedral of the Greek Orthodox community in Famagusta before the larger St George of the Greeks supplanted it in the mid-14th century (Fig. 139). There was also record of a St Symeon monastery, presumably attached to this church, which was associated with St Catherine's in Sinai, and thus had prestigious connections. The remnants of that monastery may lie to the east of the surviving structure. The original church was a smaller, single-domed structure, but in the 13th and later centuries the church was enlarged with other domes and an aisle along the south flank, greatly enlarging its size. Eventually it had 3 domes, one of which survived to the early 20th century. If one looks carefully, one can see the curving pendentives in the upper architecture, indicating where the domes were. Some of the earlier church was destroyed, and other parts added, to create the entrances from St Symeon into the new and cavernous interior of St George of the Greeks. The fact that the old church was incorporated into the newer church indicates the veneration that it had in the Middle Ages, and it is likely that St Symeon still functioned as an important shrine even as an appendage to the larger metropolitan. St Symeon was also famous for purportedly being the resting place, for a time, of one of Cyprus's most important early Christian saints, St Epiphanios, the famous early bishop who had formerly been interred in the south apse of the basilica at Salamis (Constantia) that bears his name. This is why some scholars believe that the church should more properly be referred to as Agios Epiphanios.

Sources for Agios Symeon/Agios Epiphanios: Thomas Kaffenberger, *Hagios Georgios in Famagusta: Ein Beispiel des Kulturtransfers. Baugeschichtliche Untersuchungen*, unpublished MA thesis, Johannes Gutenberg University, Mainz, 2010.

Fig. 139: Church of St Symeon, Famagusta

379

St George of the Greeks, Famagusta, 14th century

[35° 07' 26.32" N / 33° 56' 37.01" E]

Saint George of the Greeks is the second largest church in Famagusta and served as the cathedral or 'metropolitan' for the Byzantine Orthodox community through the late Middle Ages and Renaissance period (Fig. 140). As Thomas Kaffenberger notes, it was probably begun around 1349 just after a terrible outbreak of the plague inspired liberal donations to the Church in the hope of winning God's mercy. It is also possible that the church was constructed as a commemoration of the return of an Orthodox bishop to Famagusta, as the Papal document called the *Bulla Cypria* of 1260, which curtailed the powers of the Orthodox Church on Cyprus and made it subservient to Latin Catholicism, had exiled the Orthodox bishopric to the remote town of Karpasia. However, in the mid-14th century the bishop was allowed to return to Famagusta and this grand metropolitan seems to have been, at least partly, a monumental expression of that important ecclesiastical victory for Cypriot Orthodoxy. Indeed its scale seems almost celebratory and intended to be equivalent to the impressive scale of the Latin Catholic cathedral of St Nicholas merely 100 metres away. Found in the southeast corner of the city, which was the Greek quarter, its southern flank was exposed to the heavy bombardment of the Ottoman gunners during the siege of 1570-71, yet it was the north side that collapsed. Though nothing of the nave or aisle vaults survives, the semi-domes of the three apses still maintain their integrity. These apses and semi-domes, from both the interior and exterior views, comprise the most striking elements of the building (Fig. 141).

Saint George of the Greeks was built alongside a much older and smaller Byzantine church called St Symeon/Agios Epiphanios (previous entry). This ancient and venerable edifice eventually had the two-aisle and two-apse configuration very common to modified Orthodox structures through the Middle Ages. The southern wall of St George of the Greeks incorporated the northern transept wall of the earlier church (probably one of the oldest sections) and, further west, the architects opened up a broad arched access from the larger church to the smaller. Today one can still pass from one to the other. St Symeon thus became a veritable chapel to the larger, later building, its stones having been imbued with the sanctity of the ancient bones of St Epiphanios, Cyprus's most important Christian saint.

St George of the Greeks is an Orthodox church but adopts the configuration of a Latin Catholic structure, with a large central nave and two flanking side aisles with arcades. As in the nearby St Nicholas cathedral, large columnar piers provided the support for the arches of the side aisles and the church's vaulting. There are four of these on

Fig. 140: Ruins of the church of St George of the Greeks, Famagusta.

Fig. 141: St George of the Greeks (St Symeon at left) from the southeast, Famagusta.

each side. In these columns can be read one element in the story of the building's structural misfortunes. Originally the columns were slender, and these thinner columns can be seen today, revealed by the breaking away of the outer stones that once sheathed them. These first columns were not strong enough, so an extra collaring of stones was gathered around them to reinforce them. However, even these thicker columns suffered compression fractures because of the weight of the vaulting. Everywhere on what remains of them is the vertical cracking caused by the tremendous pressures of the weighty superstructure. In the column in the building's northwest corner, look low into a hole of broken stone and you'll be able see a part of the iron clamps that used to hold the collaring blocks in place.

If you look up to the now exposed rubble fill of the eastern vaulting you see how the internal fabric of the structure was constructed. There are large earthenware pots ensconced in this mass of stones and concrete. These vases were placed there to lighten the weight of the vaults themselves, supposedly to relieve the supports. However, clearly this was not a good construction method and may even have contributed to the building's demise. It may reflect a lack of confidence of the builders in the technology of the rib vaults, a lack of assuredness that was, it seems, well-founded.

In other elements, too, Byzantine architectural conventions seem to have given way to the Latin Gothic style in St George of the Greeks, such as the three west entrances and the circular rose window on the façade, once filled with tracery. It is assumed that French masons, perhaps after working on St Nicholas, were given work on the Greek structure (or were they Greek masons who had worked alongside masons trained in European methods and styles?). The ambitious size of the new Orthodox metropolitan, 42.2 metres in length, 21 metres wide, with nave vaults 19.8 metres high (only about a metre less than St Nicholas cathedral's), may have convinced the architects to allow the masons to stick with a form they were experienced with. Even the side aisles' vaults were a towering 12.5 metres in height. Yet St George of the Greeks, like so many churches on Cyprus, may have had a another hybrid element to it. An engraving of the skyline of Famagusta from the southeast, made by the Dutchman Cornelis van Bruyn in 1683, shows a high drum and dome on what can only be St George of the Greeks. It is possible that the artist was exercising artistic license. Since stone merchants long ago carried away the blocks of any collapsed dome, they also took away the evidence that might have given us more unambiguous information about the building's superstructure. While many architectural fragments lie scattered on the ground inside the church, none of these definitively indicate a domical structure. The clearest evidence that there was indeed a dome on

St George of the Greeks lies in the building's plan. The key lies in the intercolumnations, the distances between the columns in both the north and south rows. Counting from the façade towards the apse number in your mind the columns from 1 to 4 on your left and 5 to 8 on your right. The distance between 2 and 3 and 6 and 7 is about 7 metres. However, the distance between columns 3 and 4 and 7 and 8 is only about 5 metres, and the other columns in the east and west are also about 5 metres apart. So we have this large open section in the middle of the church that is 7 by 7 metres. When constructing a dome one creates first a square in the ground plan with supports at the corners of the square. This square will be transformed into an octagonal drum for the dome, and then the circular base of the dome rests upon this. So in elevation one gets this geometric progression of shapes: square, octagon, circle. For the first this is exactly the configuration we have here with the 7.0 metre wide nave and the columns 7.0 metres apart. It suggests a dome about 6 metres in diametre. So the ground plan of the building implies a dome, supporting the accuracy of van Bruyn's drawing. One thing is sure, the vaults and hypothetical dome disappeared long ago. Indeed, the traveler Richard Pococke may have recorded in his writings the exact date of the moment of destruction. Noting a huge earthquake in Famagusta in 1735, he wrote that, "St George's, one of the most magnificent [churches in Famagusta], was thrown down by the earthquake" [Excerpta Cypria, 255]. Alas, he doesn't tell us if it had a dome.

The story of the dome and its collapse can also be analyzed by considering the columns more closely. Bear with me as this is all a bit 'architectural'. The circumference of St George's original slender columns was 4.42 metres, significantly thinner than the columns of St Nicholas cathedral, where the columns had a circumference of 5.10 metres. Yet the vaults of Saint George were almost as high as St Nicholas', and if there was a dome then the highest point of St George was about 5 metres higher than St Nicholas. Moreover, the intercolumnations at St Nicholas were about 4.57 metres, and we have already noted an intercolumnation of 7.0 metres for St George. So St George's columns were spaced more widely at least on two sides, were thinner, and had more total weight to bear. By the time the problems were evident and the earlier columns bolstered with their additional collaring of stone, bringing them up to a circumference of 7.13 metres, the damage had already been done. It would appear that the critical weakness showed itself mostly in the northwest corner of our four main supporting piers, as it is here where one can see, even in the outer collaring of stone, the dramatic tendrils of pressure fractures that look like forked lightening cracking down the shaft. Thus what little remains of the building can still tell us tales of its construction and destruction.

Along the interior walls one can see many shallow, arched insets. There are seven along the north wall and only two on the south. These niches are very common features in the churches of Famagusta. They are funerary niches where patrons or ecclesiasts were interred, and their sale helped churches and monastic communities raise money. The honour of having such a tomb in an important church could usually be gained only by a large initial gift and some property or sum of money that could maintain the tomb and prayers for the deceased in perpetuity. Note the sloping brackets on each side, which held a slab of stone that might have had either an effigy of the deceased or a dedicatory inscription, or both, carved in it. Alas, none of these survive in place. Some remnants of frescos survive, however, in the intrados (interior faces) of some of these arches, especially on the one in the south wall near the west entrance. Another, the one on the north wall second from the north apse, has a figure of St George, the church's patron saint, still visible. On the wall above this niche are barely visible the legs of two standing men with red stockings and robes with green lining. Their heads are almost invisible. They seem similar to the depictions of military saints. Favorite military saints included Saints Theodore, Procopios, or George, the latter who, we have already noted, appears in the niche below and was the church's patron saint. In Byzantine/Orthodox art military saints often appear in pairs and frequently wear courtly dress such as these figures. One must imagine, then, these niches and their surrounding walls brilliantly painted, and the sumptuous tomb slabs covered with beautiful textiles and family coats of arms. The two tomb recesses in the north and south that are inside the border of the bema step must have been the most prestigious as they were in the most sacred location closest to the altar. Ironically, many architectural historians, Camille Enlart among them, thought that the constructing of these niches in the north side undermined the strength of that wall, which fell and took the vaulting with it.

There are small rooms, like cubicles, off of the north sides of the side aisles' apses. Each may have been the equivalent of either a vestry or sacristy, or had a combination of functions. Although they are usually dirty inside, it is worthwhile to stick one's head into these little cubicles and see the little semi-domes with carved elements made to look like gothic rib vaults. Perhaps the most simple and likely explanation is that they were storage niches for liturgical vessels and other ceremonial items, since the north and south apses would have functioned as the *prosthesis* and *diaconicon* respectively. The southernmost cubicle has two niches inside, and each of the two is graced with an elegant lancet-shaped window. The northern one also has metal hinges and a clasp in the wall outside the opening, suggesting a wooden door with a locking mechanism. Similarly, in the south cubicle, the interior with the little 'rib vault' seems to have had a wooden door on it. Each small room may thus have been used to store valuable liturgical vessels such as a chalice or candlesticks or other ritual objects of precious materials that needed to be locked away in a safe place.

Notice that the area just in front of the apse is marked by a bema or a step that elevates that portion of the church's floor. This is a typical feature of Byzantine or Orthodox churches. The edge of the bema also marked the position of the iconostasis that would have restricted visibility into the apses. If you look high on the walls on either side of the church you'll see post holes that mark the end points of the timber-framed iconostasis. All of this is, of course, long gone. Note, too, that the bema bisects the two easternmost columns. Take a close look at the southernmost and you'll see some surviving part of the barrier above the bema. Low down you'll also see a row of those distinctive Lusignan symbols of a tapering element with a small ball at the bottom; in this instance resembling the hanging military medals of a decorated general (this motif has many variations).

The flooring of St George of the Greeks is interesting in another way, however. There is an elevated platform extending into the nave from the bema step and continuing right up to the second set of columns from the west facade. Unlike the bema's elevation, this is not a common feature in Byzantine churches. Since this church was the most important in the region it may have provided a special zone set off for meetings of high ecclesiasts, or perhaps this platform played a role in certain ceremonies appropriate for Famagusta's metropolitan. An *ambo* or elevated pulpit may have been located at the center of this platform or tribune, giving the bishop a place from which to read scripture or give sermons. It could have been demarked further by a low fencing, a common feature in Byzantine churches, thus segregating it off for special ceremonial events, though no tangible evidence of this remains. Indeed, one might think of this as an uncommonly wide *solea* (see entry on Agia Trias), its broad dimensions indicative of the ceremonial requirements of the metropolitan of a prosperous city.

In the great central apse of the interior one can see the *synthronon*, the semi-circular steps upon which the bishop would have been enthroned during special religious occasions. Chilling testament to Famagusta's violent past is found behind the *synthronon*, where the wall is peppered with bullet holes. One finds this in the side apses as well. This is likely evidence of iconoclasm after the Ottomans' sacking of the town in 1571. Ottoman soldiers had a kind of matchlock musket (*tüfek*) that could have done this kind of damage. Look high above and you'll also see a cluster of such holes in the center of the semi-dome. It is likely that from there once gazed down an image of Christ Pantocrator (one might recall the post-1974 shotgun holes in the Pantocrator of the dome of the Antiphonitis church). One can imagine elated Ottoman soldiers taking pot shots at the image of the conquered Christian god after they triumphantly entered the city in 1571.

There are frescoes in both side apses as well. In the north apse one can see fragmentary and faded remains of a row of saints, some of whom, on the right, have an inscription that refers to a Synod, a famous Fifth Ecumenical Council that took place in Constantinople in 553 CE. The depictions of saints associated with that Synod might have had a particular political charge, as the Synod was held without the permission of the Roman Pope. In other words, that Synod represented the first time that the Eastern Orthodox/Byzantine Church asserted its divine authority without the consent of the Western, Latin Catholic Church. Given what was mentioned earlier about St George of the Greeks signifying Orthodoxy's reassertion of its authority in Famagusta, these frescoes might well have had a particular resonance with the idea of resistance against Catholic oppression by associating the earlier historical subservience to Rome to the present Cypriot situation. The church itself, like the Fifth Ecumenical Synod, becomes associated with a reassertion of Eastern Orthodox autonomy from Roman ecclesiastical hegemony. Visible are, from left to right, St Makedonios of Tamassos and St Athanasios, both Cypriot saints and, further to the right St Basil and St Spyridon (also Cypriot), and at the far right St Hippolytus and St Hadrian.

One might also discern in the north apse some ship graffiti, most of it dating from the 19th century. Mariners carved these images of their ships not as acts of vandalism, but because they believed that the saints would protect their ships from harm. Votive graffiti, one might call it. If you look closely, you'll find a lot of such ship graffiti in Famagusta. While in the north apse, look up to your right near the edge of the wall and you'll see two 19th century graffiti dates: 1878 and 1881. In that same area note some squared sections where the frescoes look like they've been cleaned. They're a lighter colour. Italian art restorers came in 2007 and did some test patches to find out what kind of residues were on the frescoes. In most lights you can discern a pale brown cloudiness over all these paintings. This is caused by the build-up of olive oil deposits. In former times priests used to spruce up their faded frescoes by rubbing olive oil into them. This made the colour more vivid for a short time. However, over the years, the coatings made them more and more faded as the oil dried and absorbed dust and soot. The patches that the Italian restorers put on the frescoes were soaked in a solution that dissolved this cloudy organic residue.

The best time of day to look for graffiti and to view these frescoes is near sunrise or sunset, when there isn't direct light and cast shadow. The same is true for the paintings in the south apse. Here, one can make out scenes from the life of Christ, such as the *Betrayal* (upper left), *Descent from the Cross* (middle left), and *Entombment* or '*Epitaphios*' or anointing of Christ's body (lower left). If you have a telephoto lens or some binoculars, zoom in on Christ's face in the *Betrayal*. It's one of the only faces that survives in all of Famagusta's frescoes and one can make out Christ's stern look as Judas steps in to give the betraying kiss. The figure of Judas is remarkably dynamic, swooping in with his red garments flying. Note the dark brownish colour of Judas' clothing. It may be painted in a pigment that Cyprus was, and still is, famous for: Cyprus Umber. Once you notice it, you'll see that it's used a lot in the frescoes of the church.

It is likely that above the single window of the south apse was a scene of the Crucifixion, now lost. You might be able to see the bottom of the wood of the cross set into a little mound a few feet above the central window. On the right side one can see a continuation of the story with the first scene of the *Resurrection* as angels open Christ's tomb, and above this the *Anastasis*, also associated with the *Resurrection*, but this time the Second Coming of Christ. The opened lids of sarcophagi lie crossed at his feet, symbolizing Christ's triumph over death.

In the central apse one can make out the robes of a row of saints low down, though these are difficult to see as the paintings have been severely weathered. Higher up in the central apse, but below the moulding of the semi-dome, on the left side one can see a series of halos of saints whose faces have been chipped out. Look also above the windows of the central apse to the left and right and you'll be able to see the crossed wings of cherubim. If you have binoculars or a good telephoto lens look carefully at the upper moulding running around the curve of the central apse. On the left half you'll see a stone dog's tooth moulding that is very typical in Lusignan-era Cypriot architecture. One assumes that this was the original decoration. In the right half, however, note that it was later covered in fresco with an extensive Greek inscription running along both its upper and lower profiles.

As you are standing in the central apse and looking towards it, glance to your right and you'll see an arch in the south wall that has incorporated one of the ends of the church of St Symeon/Agios Ephimianos. In a band running along the under part of the moulding of that arch you'll see a well-preserved strip of ornamental fresco with diamond shapes and leaves that look like Christmas trees. It gives you some idea of the decorations that once covered many of the walls and niches of the church centuries ago.

Another *Crucifixion* scene, very much faded, can be seen high on the interior wall of the southwest corner of the church. The shadowy image of Christ on the cross is quite visible in silhouette. Weeping angels fly in from either side of the cross, while Mary (left) and St John (right; see his hand gesturing towards Christ) and others mourn below, their halos discernable against the light background. Many flecks of the blue of Mary's robe are visible on the left, and if you look closely at the two halos close together you can imagine the fainting Virgin being supported by another figure, maybe Mary Magdalene, also in blue. The rectangular panel nailed to the cross above Christ's head read 'INRI', the initials meaning 'Jesus of Nazarth, King of the Jews', which the Romans had mockingly placed there. In the sky above, flanking the top of the cross, the circular orbs of the moon and sun sadly witness the cosmic event.

While looking at that wall, notice some post holes nearby on the south wall and note a slender Gothic window. In fact this 'window' was a doorway that gave access to what might have been the *gyneconitis* or women's gallery, which was mostly a wooden structure. You can get a better view of the door from the south exterior, where there are also some projecting corbels to support a walkway. This upper gallery was accessed by climbing the spiral staircase in the southwest tower, which you can see by entering the door in that corner of the church's interior. The steps only go up a few stairs but you can see the dramatic spiral of the broken steps going up the hollow shaft of the tower. From the exterior you can see the door in the tower that led to a balcony and to the door to the timber-framed gallery inside.

Tucked into that corner in that south wall (southwest corner, about 15 feet up) there is a indistinct image of John the Baptist, whose head inclines to the left and who holds out his hands in worship. That it is John is indicated by the vertical strip of wool hair shirt that can be seen in the opening of his robes. This was almost certainly part of the triad known as the Deisis. If you have been to Hagia Sophia in Istanbul you have seen a mosaic of that subject in the upper gallery. John the Baptist, in the Deisis configuration, faces Christ from the right, while Mary is found on the far left, also facing Christ and in a pose similar to John's. Both the Christ and Mary figures of the group have vanished long ago, but one can make out the edge of the throne upon which Christ sat.

There are very mute remnants of other frescoes in the church. Inside the main west portal on the wall on either side were a row of saints in the upper register and larger images of saints, or angels such as the Archangel Michael, lower down. Rows of saints also flanked the upper level around the large arch that leads into St Symeon/Agios Epiphanios. In the northwest corner, up high on the north wall, once can also make out the halo of some sacred figure. It is more visible than the others because the round halo was embossed with many little circles.

Scattered on the ground one can also see large blocks of stones with four little arms extending from them. These are found in other ruined Gothic churches in Famagusta. They are the capstones of the ribbed vaults where the ribs converged at the apex of the vaults, a kind of keystone of the vault. Often, they had coats of arms or crosses decorating them. When you visit the church of Saints Peter and Paul or Saint Nicholas cathedral, you can still see these uniquely shaped stones playing their structural role. There are other architectural fragments as well, such as parts of the vaults or wall sections with the triple-lobed compound piers that led up to the ribs of the vaults. Lying on the ground in the central apse is a single piece of white marble with a capital carved on it. This noble piece gives us a good sense of some of the more valuable stone revetments that used to grace this edifice.

The exterior view of the apses in the morning sun is one of the great sights in Famagusta, especially in the spring when the grasses are green and the sky a brilliant blue. One can easily see the orange streaks of rust below some of the holes which still hold the iron cannon balls shot into them over 436 years ago. Three such projectiles still inhabit the upper portions of the façade of the church, surrounded by other radial fractures indicative of high velocity projectiles. St Nicholas cathedral is also full of such impact craters. On the upper portion of the façade there is a row of large corbels projecting outwards, suggesting that they may have supported a porch. This balcony may have been where the Orthodox Bishop of Famagusta blessed crowds assembled in the square before the church, now a dirt parking lot. On the northwest corner of the church is a relief of the Green Man with foliage coming out of his moustache and beard. He appears in many places in Famagusta's churches. The beautiful portals of St George of the Greeks still have some of their elegant mouldings and capitals, mute evidence of its once glorious decorations.

Photographs from the Mogabgab Archive show that there was a special mass and celebration in the hollow shell of Saint George of the Greeks to commemorate the coronation of Queen Elizabeth II in 1953. This, and recalling the bullet holes in the apses of Saint George, reminds me of a story once told to me by a Greek Cypriot friend. At the time of the coronation the British festooned Famagusta with red, white, and blue lights, like Christmas lights the colours of the Union Jack. At the time there was already enmity against the British, and some enmity between Greek and Turkish Cypriots. Greek schoolmasters were reported to have paid a piaster to boys with slingshots who would shoot out the red lights, leaving only the white and blue of the Greek flag. Turkish schoolmasters responded by paying the same to other boys to knock out the blue lights, leaving only red and white, the colours of the Turkish flag. If only they had stuck to that.

Sources for St George of the Greeks: Enlart, 253-258; Jeffery, 147-151; Michael J. K. Walsh, "'On the princypalle Havenes of the See', The Port of Famagusta and the Ship Graffiti of the Church of St George of the Greeks, Cyprus," *International Journal of Nautical Archaeology* (2007): 1-15; Thomas Kaffenberger, *Hagios Georgios in Famagusta: Ein Beispiel des Kulturtransfers. Baugeschichtliche Untersuchungen*, unpublished MA thesis Johannes Gutenberg University, Mainz, 2010.

Agios Nicolaos (Nicholas), Famagusta, 14th century

[35° 07' 23.50" N / 33° 56' 40.21" E]

Agios Nicolaos, not to be confused with the cathedral of St Nicholas, is a half-ruined Byzantine church of the two-aisled type located about 100 metres south of St George of the Greeks in the Greek quarter of Famagusta (Fig. 142). Both aisles terminate in semi-circular apses. Four substantial rectangular piers hold up an octagonal drum, which is surmounted by a dome. When trying to imagine the dome of St George of the Greeks (previous entry), take this drum and dome and triple its size and you'll get an idea of what that earlier dome looked like. The church's pendentives (the four triangular sections which support the drum of the dome) are pierced by three holes in each section. These holes lead to hollows in the masonry called acoustic cavities, which were fairly common in Byzantine churches in Cyprus. The cavities consist of pottery vases inset behind the wall surface, which is why they are sometimes called 'acoustic vases'. The concept was an ancient one, discussed by the ancient Roman architect Vitruvius, who recommended using sets of vases (*echeia*) in theaters to help amplify and resonate the sound. A vase could actually be attuned to a certain tone to amplify specific notes, though, from a scientific perspective, it is unlikely that amplification actually took place, even if resonance was intensified. In Byzantine worship, singing was a central part of the liturgies of monks and priests and these resonating vases made the sound reverberate in the acoustic cavities, thus making the chants more impressive sounding. The vases thus played a crucial role in defining the acoustical environment of the church, making it seem as if interior wasn't governed by the same physical rules as the 'real' world outside. The manipulation of sonic characteristics of the interior was thus aimed at making the church seem more heavenly and augmenting the sanctity of the space. Today swallows use them as convenient nests.

In the drum of the dome, a section below one of the windows seems to have been eroded by the persistent raising and lowering of something on a rope. It could have been a rope to ring the bells of the church or to raise and lower a chandelier used to light the interior. A fresco of Christ in Limbo on what remains of the south wall, visible to George Jeffery around 1915, has now vanished.

Sources for Agios Nicolaos: Jeffery, 155.

Agia Zoni, Famagusta, 15th century

[35° 07' 21.89" N / 33° 56' 39.17" E]

Agia Zoni, about 50 metres southwest of Agios Nicolaos, is a small Byzantine church with a Greek cross plan and a dome which dominates the structure. It is dedicated to the Zoni, or the sacred girdle of the Virgin. According to some accounts of the Assumption of the Virgin Mary, St Thomas was the only witness to the event. Mary gave St Thomas the belt-like band of cloth, the Zoni, from her garments as a tangible souvenir of the miracle. At some point this church must have had a piece of cloth that was part of the sacred relic of the Zoni. There is a fragmentary fresco of the archangel Michael on the interior, which is usually closed to the public.

Other Famagusta Churches, Including Unidentified Church Ruins in Famagusta

Church of the Stavros (Mustafa Paşa Tamisi; Enlart's No. 19), Famagusta, late 14th or early 15th century

[35° 07' 23.59" N / 33° 56' 31.55" E]

This small rectangular church, almost chapel-like, is in very good condition. Very likely there were many such small religious buildings in Famagusta, giving rise to the myth that there were 365 churches in Famagusta, one for every day of the year. These smaller edifices were often damaged by earthquakes then pillaged for stone in later centuries. Since this building seems to have been converted into a small neighborhood mosque or *mescit* some indefinite time after 1571, it has been maintained. Additionally, it serves as a holy shrine and some Muslim burials are still revered there in the small graveyard along the north side of the building. It has a simple but very elegant portal on the west side, with dog-tooth mouldings in the voussoirs of the arch and a marble lintel block which had a Lusignan era coat of arms on it, now erased. There are fan-shaped corbels in the top corners of the doorway, and the impost blocks feature pretty flower designs. Above the portal is a lovely Gothic double window. The north doorway, the one most often used as the entrance today, is simpler but still has a marble lintel and fan-shaped corbels. The interior consists of a single barrel vault with transverse strainer arches springing from wall corbels. However, a cluster of three engaged colonnettes in the north wall near the apse suggests that at one time a ribbed vaulting may have been present or intended. The apse is semi-circular on the interior, but pentagonal on the exterior, not an uncommon formation in Cypriot churches. Today, there is a *minbar* (stepped pulpit) and *mihrab* (niche in south wall indicating direction to Mecca) in the mosque, and the chap who attends the building might strenuously attempt to convert you to Islam. A donation may expedite your escape.

Ruins of Unidentified Church (Enlart's No. 14), 80 m east of St George of the Greeks, Famagusta, 14th century

[35° 07' 26.81" N / 33° 56' 38.72" E]

It is a real pity that this small church did not survive, because it may well have been one of Famagusta's most beautiful Gothic edifices (Fig. 143). It was a diminutive church, perhaps even a chapel, and seems to have been similar in design to St George of the Latins, though half its size. All that is left is part of the lower sections of two bays of the north wall. One can see the two inset arches of founder's tombs down low, with the triple bundles of the colonnettes that would rise up the wall to spring into the ribs of the vaults above. The lower sections of two Gothic mullioned windows can be seen above. Look carefully at the very bottom of the windows and you can see the stub of the mullion or the band of stone that bisected the tall window. Both on the interior and exterior of the church, the window frames were beautifully moulded. A single colonnette survives in the corner, which was the northwest corner of the structure, with its sculpted capital. Originally the church consisted of three rectangular ribbed vault bays with a three-facet apse in the east. The small part of the west façade that survives shows that there was a tower in the corner.

Sources: Enlart, 294-6.

Opposite:
Fig. 143: Ruin of unknown church (Enlart's No. 14), Famagusta.

399

Ruins of Unidentified Church (Enlart's No. 15), Famagusta, late 14th or early 15th century

[35° 07' 23.99" N / 33° 56' 33.49" E]

Enlart claims that this fragmentary ruin of a small chapel-like church, about 12m long, occupies a spot on Stephano Gibellino's 1571 print of the siege of Famagusta (Fig. 115) marked S.BAR. This may mean 'Santa Barbara' or, more likely, 'St Barnabas', a popular local saint whose main Orthodox church and monastery is about 8 kilometres north of Famagusta. However, the number 9, which marks the spot of the church on the print, isn't exactly where these ruins are, though they're not far away, so this is very conjectural. Enough of the church remains to be able to envision its full size and the structure of its vaulting. Even more survived in Enlart's time (1880s) because a drawing he made includes three windows along the church's north side, whereas we see only one today. It seems to have been an open rectangular space of three Gothic rib vaulted bays with no apse but just a flat east end. Small niches survive in the east wall and at least one of the corbels for the springing of the rib vaults survives with its leaf designs. The ruins of the appended buildings have not been identified. Could this have been the private chapel of a palatial residence?

Sources: Enlart, 296-7.

Ruins of Unidentified Church (Enlart's No. 17), 50 m southwest of Saints Peter and Paul, Famagusta, 14th century

[35° 07' 24.39" N / 33° 56' 24.99" E]

This fascinating church, just a stone's throw south of Saints Peter and Paul, has a rather magnificent portal that, while very much eroded, still gives a strong impression of how ornate it was with its leafy crockets along the south side of the gable. The most interesting aspect of this church is found on its interior. Although all of the vaults are gone, one should look closely at the sculpted corbels which have the faces of 'the Green Man' a common motif in medieval Cypriot architecture. The Green Man is a fantastic figure, a pagan motif, which has leaves or greenery sprouting from his mouth or nostrils, or, as is the case here, he seems to have an enormous leafy moustache. Several of these naively carved brackets survive, and their almost cartoon-like realization is part of their vernacular charm. In the apse, which is a three-facet configuration, one can see the step of the bema that raised the floor level of the apse area. There is also a niche in the wall and, in the walls near the entrance, some arched alcoves for founders' tombs with the slanting brackets that used to hold the tomb slab. On this slab perhaps a candle burned for the deceased's soul, or flowers could be left in memory of the dead. Outside the church, on the north and south walls, you can see crudely hewn rows of post holes for timber framing. These are evidence of buildings that used the convenient stone walls for constructing houses, probably in Ottoman times. Many of Famagusta's churches have such post-holes.

Sources: Enlart, 297-8.

Ruins of Unidentified Church (Enlart's No. 18), 80 m southwest of Saints Peter and Paul, Famagusta, 14th century

[35° 07' 23.57" N / 33° 56' 25.65" E]

This church, much ruined, lies directly south of the church just discussed above. It was a domed Byzantine church but one can see the very scant remains of its Gothic style portal. Just the top part survives, but one can still see a nice small round window with its 4-lobed Gothic tracery in it. Essentially, most of the west end and the east end survive, but nothing of the north and south walls. The doorway is walled up now, but the apse of the church in the east end is visible, with part of the semi-dome intact. The apse of the north aisle also survives on the left. One can also see that the west end had three portals. Just above the finial at the apex of the central west portal, beneath the circular window, is a small niche. Today, there is just a block of stone there, but Enlart in the 1880s saw a crumbling statue which he could not identify. Had this statue survived it may have told us the dedication of the church. Above the circular window is the bottom portion of a flagstaff holder. Enlart notes that he saw a photograph, taken by Monsieur L. de Clercq in 1860, that shows an arched belfry above the flagstaff holder. These notations remind us that every century sees significant disappearances of fragments of these magnificent churches.

Sources: Enlart, 298-9.

Fortifications and Venetian Period

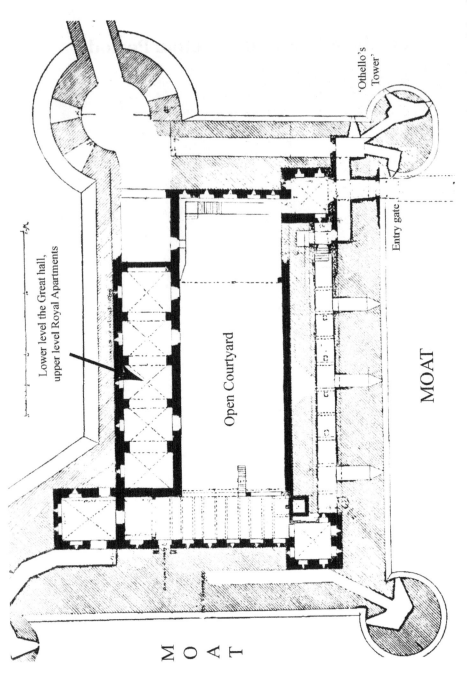

The plan shows, continued, are the original medieval Lusignan castle, and the shaded

'Othello's Tower'

Entry gate

MOAT

Lower level the Great hall, upper level Royal Apartments

Open Courtyard

M
O
A
T

The Medieval and Venetian period Castle, Famagusta, 13th to 16th century

[35° 07' 38.78" N / 33° 56' 37.07" E]

When the Lusignans gained control of Cyprus they seem to have immediately begun fortifying Famagusta, the island's principal port. One of the main components of the fortifications had been a castle in the northeast corner of the city that protected the entrance to the harbour (Fig. 144). Famagusta's anchorage is naturally protected by a reef about half a kilometre from the eastern city walls. This reef is visible from atop the Sea Gate bastion. Thus the mouth of the harbour was in the north, and the castle, in part, was meant to protect this entrance. Still, there were other defensive measures put in place, including a jetty that stuck out from the castle towards the opening to the port, as well as a tower built on the reef that allowed for a chain to be pulled across the harbour entrance. A similar tower was erected in Girne/Kyrenia and this chain tower is still visible in the old port there.

The Lusignan era castle is an impressive complex. It had a moat around the two sides that did not face the sea, much of which is still intact. Reports from early travellers indicate that the moat was at least partially filled with sea water. This has led to some misunderstandings about whether the moat of Famagusta's city walls were also filled with water, but that is impossible since much of the bedrock of this much longer moat lies several feet above sea level. But certainly the castle moat seems to have had water in it. Nicholas Martoni, an Italian notary, visited Famagusta in 1394. Of the harbour and castle he wrote:

> The castle of the city is fine, and is nearly all in the sea, except perhaps a fourth part on the city side, and there are fine ditches there constructed on either side which are filled with the sea water, and remain always full of the said water, making the said castle impregnable. The city of Famagosta has a pretty fine harbour, protected from every wind. And in this harbour in front of the city gate is a wooden jetty, a stone's throw in length, and vessels come up to this jetty, and therefrom merchandise is carried to the vessels.
>
> *[Excerpta Cypria, 22]*

Felix Faber, a monk who went on a pilgrimage to the Holy Land in 1483, was also impressed with the harbour, and recorded in his diary that Famagusta was "...set on the seashore, and has a port most convenient from fleets" [*Excerpta Cypria*, 45]. Today, we see Venetian period circular bastions at the castle's corners, two of which are still plainly

Fig. 145: 'Othello's Tower' and the entrance to the Lusignan era castle, Famagusta.

Fig. 146: View of the upper level Royal Apartments looking south in the medieval castle, Famagusta.

407

408

visible, including the one at the castle's main gate (SE corner) which was christened 'Othello's Tower' by the British in an attempt to bolster tourism to the city in the early 20th century. In Shakespeare's play *Othello* it does not specify that Othello lived in Famagusta, but merely in a port of Cyprus (Fig. 145). But the name stuck and most guidebooks still refer to it as 'Othello's Tower'. Originally, the medieval, Lusignan-era bastions were square in plan, and the circular Venetian ones incorporated or replaced these earlier towers, and remnants of these earlier ones can be made out in the southeast and southwest parts of the structure.

Above the entrance gate to the castle, which has a fine old wooden door with iron sheathing (perhaps dating from the Ottoman period), is a partially restored relief of the lion of St Mark, the emblem of the Venetians. The lion stands beside a tower, which may represent the castle itself or even the chain tower in the harbour. The inscription records that the Venetian renovations on the castle were instigated by Nicolo Foscareno, Prefect of Cyprus, in 1491. These renovations included the demolishing of the Lusignan royal apartments in the north upper level, the modernizing of the four bastions, and the thickening of the walls wherever possible to withstand the barrage of iron cannon balls.

The aforementioned royal apartments are worth looking at closely (Fig. 146). They are on the high terrace in the north, above the huge vaulted hall. There were many large windows facing south and west in this upper section, and one can still see the recessed niches for the windows where stone benches were set up so one could enjoy the view. I imagine court ladies in fine medieval dress sitting here watching festivities or competitions in the large court below. The castle is essentially a rectangle enclosing this large courtyard in the center. The royal apartment rooms were clearly rib-vaulted, as the lower parts of the tri-lobed compound piers still exist along the walls. One of the rooms, the easternmost, has an apse in it, which suggests it may have been a chapel.

At the ground level of that same northern section is an imposing room, a Great Hall, with its soaring vaults still intact (Fig. 147). It's an impressive sight and one can imagine magnificent royal banquets there with colourful banners, flags, and coats of arms with the sound of music and the smell of roasted meats from the hunt. One can visualize long wooden tables with members of the Lusignan court seated for a medieval feast.

However, while the castle may have been a fortified royal residence, its primary function was military, and this function became even more pronounced under Venetian management. The sturdy bastions with their crenellations are clear evidence of this essential purpose. There are also many tunnels in the castle — one should bring a good flashlight if wanting to explore them — where one can find significant aspects of Venetian modifications. The northwestern and northeastern parts were the sectors most adapted by the Venetians after they gained control of Famagusta. Going down the dark tunnels in the area facing the port you can come across cramped and utilitarian double and triple cannon placements angled to the directions most efficacious for defending the long walls of the port which were thin compared to the thick, earthen-backed land ramparts. If Ottoman ships could be kept out of the harbour and thus far enough away, their ship mounted cannons would be less effective against these leaner defenses.

Even while the Venetians seem to have done some updating on the castle, reports from the 16th century seem to indicate that they also used it for other purposes. Christopher Fürer, who visited Famagusta in 1566, noted that the castle was used as a prison. Perhaps, for the Venetians, the city walls were the main focus of their defensive strategy and the castle was in this respect more of a liability than an aid, since they had a limited number of defenders to disperse around the considerable circuit of city walls. The problem was noted by the silk merchant Jacques le Saige of Douai, who visited Famagusta in 1518 and observed:

> The walls of Famagosse are all freshly repaired [by the Venetians], and there is a very grand boulevard. In brief it is an impregnable city if it had a sufficient garrison. But there are only 800 soldiers in the pay of the Venetians, for they have the whole land of Cyprus under them.
>
> *[Excerpta Cypria, 57]*

Moreover, at least in 1553 when the Englishman John Locke visited, this garrison was very poorly paid. Of the soldiers' poor horses he wondered, "...but truly I marvell how they live being so hardly fed, for all the sommer they feede onely upon chopt straw and barley for hey they have none..." [*Excerpta Cypria*, 70]. Nicholas le Huen, a Carmelite monk who visited Cyprus in the last quarter of the fifteenth-century, also noted the grim circumstances of the soldiery. In a prophetic passage, he wrote of Cyprus: "It is today under the Venetians, and they are in danger of losing it in no time, for the soldiers or gendarmes they have there are not paid, and have not wherewithal to live, except meanly and very ill at their ease" [*Excerpta Cypria*, 50-1]. Indeed, in the defense of Famagusta in 1570-71 when the Ottomans besieged the city, a shortage of manpower was a decisive factor in the Venetian defeat.

It is uncertain how much the Lusignans actually used the castle. Soon after its construction, building began on a palace in the center of Famagusta across the square from St Nicholas cathedral. Very little of this palace complex survives, and it was much enlarged to the west by the Venetians to create the Palazzo del Proveditore, but we do know that the Lusignan royals most often resided in the palace in the town while in Famagusta, so the castle may not have been used very much as a residence.

The same Christopher Fürer mentioned above tells a story of a man who had been imprisoned in the castle by the Venetians for many years. Apparently the Venetians became lenient jailers because the man, Pietro Paolo, of the Scaligeri family of Verona, who had been exiled to Cyprus, was free to leave his cell and wander around the city as long as he didn't leave the walled part. Pietro was forbidden to get married, but that didn't stop him from having a mistress and siring a son and two daughters. The daughters married well to Belgian men – one of them became a schoolteacher – and his son became a doctor of medicine. They were good hosts, too, for Fürer notes that, "...both of these throughout our stay in Famagusta did us many kind offices" [*Excerpta Cypria*, 78].

The courtyard of the castle is filled with interesting architectural fragments and inscription blocks. There is a lovely white marble capital with a relief of the Virgin and Child on it. Anywhere else it would be in a museum in a place of honour. Another capital has a knight on horseback wielding a sword against an enemy. There's a well-preserved panel with the ubiquitous lion of St Mark holding the book with the Latin inscription: "Peace to you, Mark my Evangelist".

Sources for the Castle of Famagusta: Enlart, 444-454; Jeffery, 101-105; see also Christian Corvisier, in *L'Art Gothique en Chypre*, eds. Jean-Bernard de Vaivre and Philippe Plagnieux (Paris: 2006), pp. 351-366.

The City Walls of Famagusta, including the Ravelin, Land and Sea Gates, and the Martinengo Bastion, 13th to 16th century

GPS Co-ordinates for the bastions of Famagusta's city walls (listed clockwise from the Ravelin/Land gate in the SW corner of the city), are below. Turkish names of some bastions are given in italics:

The Ravelin [*Ak Kule*]: 35° 07' 17.00" N / 33° 56' 22.71" E
Diocare Bastion: 35° 07' 22.51" N / 33° 56' 18.52" E
Moratto Bastion: 35° 07' 34.83" N / 33° 56' 10.86" E
Pulacazara Bastion: 35° 07' 34.83" N / 33° 56' 10.86" E
San Luca Bastion: 35° 07' 38.79" N / 33° 56' 09.66" E
Martinengo Bastion (NW corner): 35° 07' 41.20" N / 33° 56' 07.49" E
Del Mezzo Bastion: 35° 07' 44.77" N / 33° 56' 15.49" E
Diamante Bastion (NE corner): 35° 07' 46.59" N / 33° 56' 25.60" E
Signoria Bastion: 35° 07' 44.24" N / 33° 56' 28.90" E
The Sea Gate/Porta del Mare: 35° 07' 33.58" N / 33° 56' 40.34" E
Arsenale Bastion [*Çanbulat*] (SE corner;): 35° 07' 22.83" N / 33° 56' 51.60" E
Camposanto Bastion: 35° 07' 18.98" N / 33° 56' 45.12" E
Andruzzi Bastion: 35° 07' 16.63" N / 33° 56' 37.70" E
Santa Napa Bastion: 35° 07' 16.46" N / 33°56' 32.24" E
Land Gate (Limissol Gate; SW corner): 35° 07' 17.29" N / 33° 56' 22.81" E

Famagusta had been a small harbour with some light fortifications as early as 1211 but we know very little of these early defenses. Significant fortification work seems to have begun around 1300, firstly on the castle and the seaward or eastern wall. This is not surprising, since the Lusignans would have made it a priority to provide safe haven for themselves and for their interests in the city, which revolved mainly around the security of the docks and anchorage. A mole extending from the castle into the sea was built, thereby constricting the harbour entrance towards a natural shoal that still protects the port. Enlart notes that peasant labour was conscripted for work on the new defenses, and that by 1368, citing the fourteenth-century chronicler Leontios Makhairas, the chain tower at the entrance to the harbour was completed.

By 1372 the Lusignan king, Peter II, expanded the defenses of the arsenal, as Enlart notes, in anticipation of an attack by the Genoese. But by this time, certainly, the city had a circuit of walls and very likely a dry moat of some kind. Famagusta was blessed with outcroppings of rock that invited as much quarrying out ditches as building up walls, and this is a feature of significant portions of the landward walls where upwards of one half of the mural elevation is of natural rock, making the defenses difficult to undermine. The Genoese attack came in 1373, and Famagusta was lost to the Lusignans for almost a century, even while they continued to control the rest of Cyprus. Only in 1464 did the Lusignans finally retake Famagusta, but at great expense and to regain a once thriving city that the Genoese had exploited into virtual dereliction. Travellers such as Nicholas Martoni, who landed in Famagusta in November of 1394, made note of the city's decline: "But now the Genoese hold the said town… but a great part, almost a third, is uninhabited, and the houses are destroyed, and this has been done since the date of the Genoese lordship" [*Excerpta Cypria*, 22]. It is likely that the Genoese did some work on the fortifications — Makhairas says that they added height to the walls [Makhairas, 435] — but, generally, they seem to have been loath to invest heavily in their new conquest and so might be expected to have added minimally to the defenses. Still, Martoni could add that "The said city has finer walls than any I've seen in any town, high with broad alleys [moats] round them, and many and high towers all around" [*Excerpta Cypria*, 22].

There are few civic fortifications as impressive and historically important as the walls of Famagusta, and yet they remain woefully understudied, even though they are incomparable compendia of medieval and early modern military architecture. They are also relatively unscathed by the sometimes distorting ministrations of modern restoration. As in other Venetian ports beyond Venice, Famagusta's walls integrate both terrestrial and marine defensive components, thus adding to their complexity and sophistication.

The walls of medieval Carcassonne in France, often championed as being the most complete European city walls in existence, were almost entirely reconstructions of the nineteenth-century. In contrast, the walls of Famagusta are very largely just as they were five centuries ago. Almost three and a half kilometres in circuit, they are marvelously complete, with each of their two major landward, corner bastions and eleven more subsidiary bastions intact. Enhancing the appeal of these extraordinary fortifications, the integrity of the horseshoe-shaped moat and the mural works and counterscarp are also virtually complete. Even the *glacis* of the western defenses still retains its sloping topography. Many of the *cavalieri* platforms are in excellent condition. The tunnels in the walls are in a respectable state, especially in the west and south walls, though many of these were modified and walled up for use as jail cells in the Ottoman period. More recently, since 1974, the Turkish army has altered some bastions on the north flank of the city (principally the Martinengo). These have recently been reopened for the first time in decades. Hopefully, conservation and restoration projects will continue on these incomparable fortifications. I have a vision of the moat being transformed into a lovely park with walkways and children's playgrounds and green gardens; a place to go for a stroll with the family in the mornings or evenings, with places to buy a coffee or tea and sit for refreshments under the shade of a tree. So, too, could the seaside at the port be transformed into a yacht marina and a tourist esplanade with shops and outdoor cafes. Currently, the public has no right of entry to the portside, and even year-round citizens of Famagusta have no access to the sea in their city that lies on the sea, unless, of course, they work at the docks. Whenever I visit Dubrovnik, Croatia, with its restored walls and walkways, I think of what modern Famagusta could become.

As Famagusta's strategic importance and wealth increased there was significant expansion of the walls, moat and counterscarp. When the Venetians assumed suzerainty in the late fifteenth century, they were obliged to enhance and refurbish these walls in preparation for the inevitable Ottoman assault that would utilize modern artillery and siege tactics, both naval and terrestrial, which the Lusignan walls and bastions were ill-equipped to repel. Walls were thickened by the backing of substantial terrepleins (which also facilitated transport of munitions atop the walls and provided ancillary gun platforms), the bastions were totally rebuilt, and, in the case of the northwest corner of the city, an entirely new complex dominated by the daunting Martinengo Bastion was constructed. Yet even these 'modern' walls were built at a time when such military architecture was quickly becoming outmoded. The accelerated rate of obsolescence might be illustrated by observations made by a number of sixteenth-century travellers. One visitor, Jacques le Saige, who arrived in Famagusta in 1518 (about thirty years after the Venetians had taken over), not only admired the walls but noted that they were recently refurbished:

> We were greatly astonished to see so great a city. For vessels cannot come nigh but for reason of the rocks, and the walls too are terribly thick, and there are fosses lined with masonry along the town. Hence you might gather that one might attack it from without and yet be unable to injure that city... The walls of Famagosse are freshly repaired, and there is a very grand boulevard. In brief it is an impregnable city.
>
> *[Excerpta Cypria, 57]*

In 1552 Daniel Ecklein, from the German city of Arrau, thought that Famagusta's walls had the best land and sea defenses of all the towns he had seen in his travels as a pilgrim. In 1553 the English pilgrim John Locke found the fortifications stalwart and impressive and it is likely that in the thirty-five year interim between le Saige's and Locke's visits modernizing work continued. Similarly, a decade later, in 1563, Elias of Pesaro wrote admiringly to his brother that "Famagusta...is a fortified town, girt with a double wall, commanded by a fine large and solid castle." In 1566, the pilgrim Christopher Fürer could unhesitatingly evaluate the city as "well fortified." Yet Giacomo Diedo, a Venetian Senator, described Famagusta in 1570, merely four years later, as "small and weak [needing] men of valor, whose strength and high spirit should make up for the defects of its fortifications." Perhaps none of these earlier travellers, mere tourists after all, had Diedo's insight into what kinds of tribulations those defenses might have to endure. Famagusta's walls thus stood at the cusp of anachronism: in one year magnificent and in the next deficient, they were testaments to the rapid progress in the weapons and strategies of siege warfare. The Famagusta renovations represent the necessity of having to adapt to the realities of gunpowder, high explosives, and devastating cannon barrage. It was an actuality that these walls eventually had to confront in a heroic defense legendary in the annals of war, the Ottoman siege of 1570-71, documented visually in the famous print by Stephano Gibellino (Fig. 115) and in numerous dramatic literary accounts such as Paolo Paruta's *Storia della Guerra Cipro* of 1571.

Nevertheless, though the walls of Famagusta may have prefigured the waning days of the relevance of the walled city, the ramparts, in their ultimate test, did not fail. Rather, disease and starvation among the dwindling surviving Venetian defenders led to eventual surrender. The besieged seem to have been the "men of valor" Diedo indicated as requisite, for a small but resolute group of defenders held off an imposing Ottoman war machine for almost a year.

The Venetian campaign of refurbishing the walls, beginning around 1491 and continuing over the next eighty years, proceeded on many fronts and involved several aspects of the defenses. The Commune of Famagusta sent the following petition to the Venetian Senate, an indication of the difficulties of securing professional builders to guide such ambitious projects so far from home:

[Please send] two master builders to work the kiln and a vessel to transport the lime to Famagusta. These, together with eight or ten master builders to arrange the broken stones in the trench and to work on the inclined wall, and in order to manage all of them, would you please send an engineer to supervise the construction, and with a mandate such that no local officer may put a stop to anything that we build, because many orders had been given by Your Highness's local officers, but none of them is competent, which is inconvenient, and therefore if Your Sublimity were not to order this mandate, the constructions will not be completed promptly

[Enlart, 447; trans. Beatrice Basso]

The bastions were thickened considerably with sheathings of additional stone and their interiors dramatically reconfigured to facilitate the quick delivery of heavy munitions. Crenellations (assuming that they existed in the earlier Lusignan bastions) were usually replaced by sloping aprons with cannon positions. In some cases, however, such as in the Andruzzi bastion, a crenellation system was retained but modified for small artillery, arquebuses or muskets. The walls were made thicker by tons of earth backing, which also created substantial level areas at the tops of the ramparts (*terrepleins*) for the erection of several huge *cavaliere*, raised platforms of earth faced with squared masonry. These platforms gave defenders a significantly better view of enemy movements, encampments, and artillery positions, as well as greater range for Venetian cannon and additional protective height. All along the curtain walls one sees today the evidence of arrow loops, anachronisms for the Venetians, which were hastily filled with stones. Elsewhere, old medieval gateways were blocked up and mural elevations extended.

The two most dramatic modifications were at the two landward corners of the city. The southwest corner was also where the principal land gate was situated. Below the lofty Lusignan-era polygonal bastion that had the older land gate at its base, the Venetians built a new ravelin complex in a roughly arrow-shaped formation in 1544, incorporating an earlier medieval tower or ravelin that stood separate from the walls (Fig. 148-149). The situation at the former ravelin and old medieval gate is complex. The tall polygonal tower that is in the city walls was once the main gate to the city (Fig. 150). This gate was protected not only by being a large tower itself, but by a smaller tower that stood on its own just across from the gate, completely free from the city walls. This was the old ravelin, which was absorbed by the new complex built around it by the Venetians. This is what one sees today, and why what guidebooks call 'The Ravelin' isn't really a ravelin any more at all. The Venetians expanded the moat outwards to accommodate the larger configuration, and two new gates with long drawbridges extended from either side (Fig. 151). This substantial addition bolstered the southwest corner of the city walls with an immense bulwark integrated into the city's main defensive array, thus dramatically improving the level of protection for the newly positioned main gates and their approaches (Later, a new gate would be opened up beside this ravelin, the current land gate for the city). The upper part of the new ramparts bristled with cannons, while the top of the old Lusignan polygonal bastion now served essentially as a *cavaliere* or lookout and secondary gun platform. It's well worth going up there as the view into the ravelin complex is impressive (Fig. 152). Wide ramps were constructed to efficiently supply it with munitions. This gave the southwest corner a double level of firepower over the distant and mid-range of the battlefield, but also substantially greater enfilading fire into the moat in both northerly and easterly directions. The free-standing ravelin was eventually fully integrated into the main wall circuit with two

Fig. 148: View of the Ravelin complex from the west, Famagusta.

417

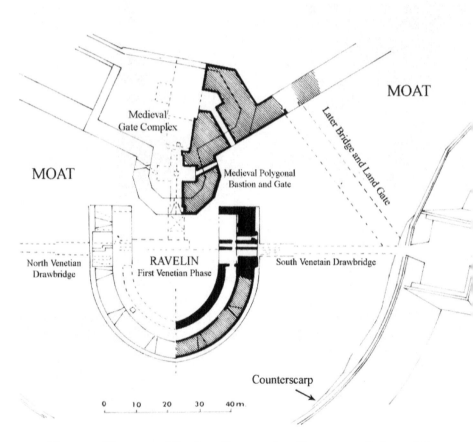

MOAT

MOAT

Medieval
Gate Complex

Medieval Polygonal
Bastion and Gate

Later Bridge and Land Gate

North Venetian
Drawbridge

RAVELIN
First Venetian Phase

South Venetain Drawbridge

Counterscarp

0   10   20   30   40 m

Fig. 149: Diagram of the Ravelin complex, Famagusta [adapted from George Jeffery, Description of the Historical Monuments of Cyprus, 1918].

418

Fig. 150: The Ravelin interior, looking towards the old polygonal tower and medieval gate of Famagusta.

Fig. 151: South flank of the Ravelin complex, Famagusta, with south drawbridge gate (left) and modern bridge and gate into the city (far right). Including the 'wings' attaching the Ravelin to the main city walls. Moat in foreground and medieval polygonal bastion background.

Fig. 152: Looking into the Ravelin from the top of the medieval polygonal bastion, Famagusta.

'wings' as the defensive qualities of the ravelin were in later years seen to be of dubious advantage. A section from Lorini's *Delle fortificatione* of 1597 addresses the ravelin's defects:

> But this defense has been found in our time to be not only imperfect but highly dangerous to the garrison. The ditch around the ravelin is difficult to enfilade and becomes a cover for the enemy, and after mining operations the enemy easily occupies the ravelin and captures the entrance to the city.
>
> *[Jeffery, 108]*

There are some interesting things to see while walking around the 'Ravelin'. First of all, the old medieval entrance gate itself, modified by the Venetians, is really wonderful. A long tunnel connects the inside of the city with the exterior gate, which would have had some kind of bridge. Now, one walks across a small modern walkway into the compound. One can see to the north and the south two gates that used to have independent drawbridges. The slots for the chains can still be seen in both. Note how well protected they are on their flanks. One can walk on the different levels of the complex, but the upper levels really afford a great 'defender's view' of the moat. Look west to the stone wall of the counterscarp and you'll see the wall pocked with musket fire, mute evidence of the pitched battles fought on these ramparts between the Ottomans and the Venetians in 1570-71. Paolo Paruta gives a description of the last moments of defence of the ravelin by the Venetian defenders:

> The attack was truly terrible. The Turks fought stoutly, inflamed by the certain hope of that day gaining the city. Our men kept well together, and held their ground with desperate courage. The enemy might enter their defences, but could not drive out the defenders, as fast as the Turks approached they were scattered, killed, hurled back: and blows which fell on so dense a crowd never fell in vain. This third attack continued for five hours, and was most bravely met. But the soldiers who were set to defend the ravelin at the Limisso gate were thrown into disorder by the enemy's fireworks, and were unable to manoeuvre in the small space they could command, so that when at the other points assailed by the enemy the battle was well nigh done, they were still engaged, and suffering very severe losses.
>
> *[Excerpta Cypria, 114]*

When at the lowest level of the ravelin complex, one can see a ditch carved partly out of the living rock. The rock is shattered with huge cracks visible. This may be from a massive explosion that took place there

Fig. 153: The Venetian Sea Gate bastion from the port side, with marble framing and the Lion of St Mark, Famagusta.

423

Fig. 154: The upper part of the Venetian Sea Gate bastion with the Lion of St Mark, Famagusta.

during the siege. Look around on the ground inside the ravelin, and you may well see iron cannon balls that have lain there for over 400 years. Also, if you go down into the moat just outside the ravelin, you will find the mouth of a tunnel in the counterscarp, dug by Ottoman soldiers to try to gain access to the moat for nocturnal mining expeditions. Indeed, if one has an eye to see it there are many such traces of that siege still visible in the walls of Famagusta. In one section of the southern walls, not far from the Çanbulat bastion, a stone catapult ball the size of a beach ball is still embedded in the wall. While exploring the Ravelin keep your eyes open for the fine Lusignan coat of arms carved in relief on slabs of white marble, evidently retained by the Venetians when they renovated the ravelin complex.

Another significant addition to the walls was the construction of a broad new circular bastion at the port. This bastion greatly increased firepower into the harbour and provided much needed auxiliary fire towards the sea entrance that was only partially protected by the castle's towers. But the Sea Gate (*Porta del Mare*) was also, as its name indicates, the principal entrance to the city from the harbour (Fig. 153). As such, and since it was the gate through which most Venetian visitors would arrive, the gate was articulated in a manner that many who traveled to Venetian ports of call would have found familiar and reassuring. The portal, which, unhappily, can today only be seen from the Othello tower in the castle, is framed with late fifteenth century style revetments with a standard architectural vocabulary and iconography: a pediment with the lion of St Mark, a Latin inscription in classicizing lettering, and coats of arms, in this case those of Nicolo Priuli (Fig. 154). The inscription reads NICOLAO PRIOLI CYPRI PRAEFECTO MCCCCLXXXXVI [Nicolo Priuli, Prefect of Cyprus, 1496]. The lion of St Mark, the empire's primary signifier, was not merely a symbol of Venice. It assured the travellers the protection of the saint even at the furthest fringes beyond the Venetian lagoon, thus legitimizing the expansion of Venice's economic and military reach under the saint's emblem. The portrayal of the lion is in many ways standard, but there was a particular variation on the theme, which is represented here; the forepaws are on the land and the rear paws are in the sea, indicating the dual terrestrial and maritime aspects of Venice's empire.

Like other such portals and monuments in the distant ranges of the Venetian Empire, Famagusta's Sea Gate makes use of spolia. The white marble panels and discs of red marble (now bleached) came from the ruins of the ancient Greco-Roman city of Salamis just five miles north of Famagusta. Upon entering the monumental gate visitors found themselves in an unexpected and imposing interior: a single, broad dome. This expansive space and the novelty of such an architectural feature (unlike the usual interior spaces of military architecture, although the

Famagusta Gate in Nicosia is also domed) may have powerfully reiterated the prowess of Venetian engineering skill by utilizing a complex form associated with ancient Rome. It must have been inspiring and reassuring for Venetian travellers and traders to find such a remarkable and impressive architectural element in the hinterland of the realm. There was a gate here in medieval times as well, but that older bastion and gate was destroyed by the Venetians in their rebuilding. It was through that earlier gate that Queen Caterina Cornaro passed as she left her island kingdom for the last time.

The most impressive Venetian addition to the walls of Famagusta, the Martinengo Bastion, is found at the northwest angle of the trapezoidal perimetre of the defenses and was the most ambitious single element of the Venetians' architectural projects in Famagusta (Fig. 155-156). The Venetians had inherited fortifications with many weaknesses, but the most vulnerable corner had been the northwestern. It is this most urgent concern that motivated the Senate to dispatch the young military architect Giangirolamo Sanmichele — the nephew of the principal Venetian military engineer and architect, Michele Sanmichele — to Cyprus. The Martinengo Bastion, if not designed by Giangirolamo, is Sanmichelean in design. The Martinengo would be Famagusta's most modern configuration in keeping with recent innovations in military design, which took modern cannons and artillery into account and increased both the defensive and offensive capabilities of the bastion. The story of the young architect Giangirolamo is a sad one. Poised to inherit his famous uncle's mantle as Venice's premiere military architect, he was married in Venice and immediately sent to Cyprus. Giorgio Vasari, the famous biographer of artists and architects, wrote of the young man's diligence and hard work on the island, and of his coming down with a fever and dying in Famagusta, where he was buried in the cathedral. Unhappily, we do not have his tomb marker.

The Martinengo is an angled bastion of a type invented in the fifteenth-century. The designs of these types of bastions were dramatically distinct from the rounded demi-lunes ('half-moons') that had characterized medieval fortifications. Particularly in the sixteenth century, European cities undertook ambitious building and renovation campaigns — Famagusta was not alone in this — to update their fortifications in order to adapt to innovations in cannon technology and siege warfare. The angled bastion was the most striking manifestation of this process of modernization. The Martinengo thrust out from the curtain wall and functioned as a huge gun platform, which, along with the *cavaliere*, multiplied offensive firepower, thus helping to keep the besiegers at a distance and diminishing the efficacy of their cannon. At the same time, the curled *orrechiae* ('ears') provided enfilading fire to sweep the moat in

Fig. 155: The Venetian period Martinengo Bastion, Famagusta.

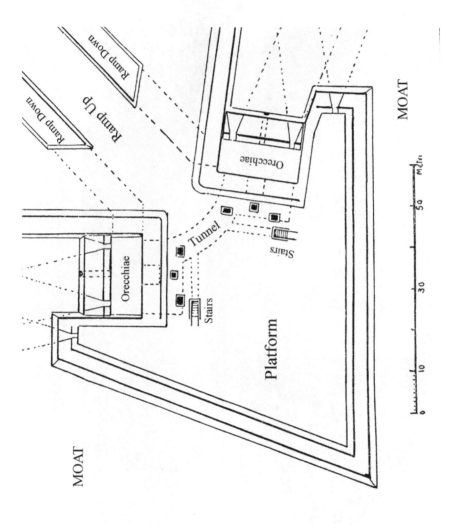

Fig. 156: Plan of the Martinengo Bastion, Famagusta [adapted from George Jeffery, *Description of the Historical Monuments of Cyprus*, 1918].

428

two directions, defending the ditch from a protected position (Fig. 157). The Venetian era walls of Lefkoşa/Nicosia, the capital of Cyprus, were expressions of the most contemporary and ideal configuration: circular in plan with broad, obtuse bastions at regular intervals. It was one of the few instances where the ideal of the architects and theorists was actually constructed. But Famagusta's walls were, of course, not built from scratch by the Venetians, and thus each bastion was modified in specific ways for existing conditions.

An indication of how the Venetians wanted the Martinengo to function is conveyed by its severely acute angle. Since the Martinengo had to work somewhat alone in its quadrant it had to, along with its *cavaliere*, cover a great range both bilaterally and in the enemy's distant field. It thus thrust out to a sharp point, in contrast to the broad angled bastions of the Lefkoşa/Nicosia fortifications, which were planned to work collectively in series along the consistent curve of the curtain walls. The sharper angle of the Martinengo was also dictated by the lay of the original walls and the moat, which necessitated that the *orrechiae* be swept back so as to enfilade the sections (and, in turn, so that the responding bastions could enfilade around the Martinengo with no dead ground beneath it). Additionally, the high, level ground to the northwest of the bastion was an ideal staging ground for enemy attacks, and the sagittal profile of the Martinengo presented its sloping and dramatically raking faces to that area, thus helping deflect and deflate enemy fire from that direction. A marble relief of the lion of St Mark (the likely subject, though only the frame for it remains) defiantly stared down the besiegers from the crest of the bastion.

The Martinengo's construction, however, consisted of more than the dramatic promontory of its apex and its cusped *orrechiae*. Wide ramps descending to the *orrechiae* and ascending to the upper ramparts and flanking *cavaliere*, provided an efficient infrastructure for the movement of munitions and the rapid deployment of men and supplies from one position to another. In addition, a broad, curving barrel-vaulted tunnel united the two *orrechiae*, thus enabling defenders to respond quickly to shifts in enemy strategies, feints, or diversions. The considerable smoke generated by cannon was efficiently carried away by numerous chimneys, thus keeping the tunnel's air clear.

The designs that facilitated lateral repositioning were complemented by the potentials for effective vertical troop relocations. The lowest defensive element of the complex was a postern gate that allowed, for example, nocturnal excursions into the moat to thwart enemy mining operations. The next level up included the quartet of large guns of the *orrechiae*, while another tier along the crest of the bastion also incorporated artillery placements. Yet another elevation was supplied by

Fig. 157: One of the orrechiae or 'ears' of the Martinengo Bastion, Famagusta.

the towering platforms of the nearby *cavaliere*. One could move among these vertical levels almost as quickly as one could change positions laterally, through stone staircases set within protective, sloping archways. A well-organised group of defenders could thus attain, in alteration, defensive or offensive postures with expeditious adaptability.

One of the most interesting of the ensemble is the secret tunnel beneath the postern gate. One can access the postern gate by descending the staircase from the western *orrechiae*. Just on the inside of the heavy door of the gate was a trap door that opened on to a tunnel that went into the moat. Was this tunnel dug by besiegers or defenders? I think that this tunnel was dug by the defenders. Should enemies get to the postern gate and try to ram it in, opening the trap door inside actually bolstered the door of the postern. Defenders could then enter the tunnel, creep underneath the enemies in the moat, and pop up unexpectedly from another hidden trap door in the ground, thus being able to attack from behind the soldiers occupied with the postern gate.

Despite the representation of pitched battles at the Martinengo in Stephano Gibellino's print of 1571 (Fig. 115), the written accounts of the Ottoman siege focus on the attacks along the southern flank of the city, which included the Ravelin in the west and the Arsenal at the east end. Today the Martinengo seems relatively unscathed while many parts of the southern walls still bear the wounds of 1570-71. In addition, the number of cannon balls found in the southern half of the city is far greater than in the northern. It could very well be that the Martinengo's considerable capacities were never pressed into service.

Sources for City Walls, Ravelin, and the Martinengo Bastion: Enlart, 444-454; Jeffery, 101-116; There is a fairly detailed discussion of Famagusta in Leone Andrea Maggiorotti, *Gli Architetti Militari*, vol. I (Rome: 1932 or 33), pp. 433-453 [N.B. "Anno XI E. F."/ Year 11, 'Era Fascista']; Michel Balard, "Famagouste au Debut du XIV Siecle, in *Fortifications, Portes de Villes, Places Publiques dans le Monde Mediterranean*, ed. Jacques Heers (Paris: Presses de l'Université de Paris-Sorbonne, 1985), pp. 279-299; Gianni Perbellini, "I castelli di Cipro e le crociate" in: *La fabbrica dei castelli crociati in Terra Santa*, ed. L. Marino (Florence, 1997), 110-117; Gianni Perbellini, "Outline of Fortified Networks in Cyprus" *IBI Bulletin* 48 (1992): 3-16; Gianni Perbellini, "The Venetian Defences of Cyprus" *Fort* 16 (1988): 7-44; Gianni Perbellini, Le Fortificazioni di Cipro dal X al XVI Secolo," *Castellum* 17 (1973): 7-58; Nicolas Faucherre, "L'Enceinte Urbaine de Famagouste," in *L'Art Gothique en Chypre*, eds. Jean-Bernard de Vaivre and Philippe Plagnieux (Paris: 2006), pp. 307-350. Allan Langdale, "At the Edge of Empire: Venetian Architecture in Famagusta, Cyprus," *Viator, Medieval and Renaissance Studies* 41, n. 1 (2010), 155-198.

The Lusignan Palace, the Venetian Palace of the Proveditore, and Triple arch Gateway, Famagusta, late 15th to 16th century

[35° 07' 29.09" N / 33° 56' 30.07" E]

The Venetian palace, or Palazzo Proveditore (the Proveditore was the Venetian military administrator of Cyprus) was built partly in the same location and partly west of the medieval Lusignan Royal palace that preceded it, though little of the earlier structure remains (Fig. 158). The original construction of the Lusignan palace directly across from the cathedral made clear the institutional symbolism of kingship's close relationship with the Church: while the cathedral was the house of Christ, the King of Heaven, the palace was the house of the kings of men. Sacred and secular thus mirrored one another, giving clear indication of the medieval notion of the divine right of rule. St Thomas Aquinas, it might be noted, dedicated his treatise *On Kingship* to a king of Cyprus. But the correlation may have been even more important for royalty that resided in Famagusta, for the Famagusta Cathedral was also the site of the second coronation of the Lusignan kings. Santa Sophia in Lefkoşa/Nicosia was the first site of coronation where the Lusignan kings were crowned as kings of Cyprus, while a second coronation at Famagusta conferred the crown of Jerusalem. Jerusalem was, of course, the Holy City and the city that was the reflection of God's heaven on earth. To relate the palace of the Lusignan kings to the Famagusta Cathedral, then, was also to reconfirm their title to Jerusalem and their hope to regain it.

It is in this same square, after the coronation of the Lusignan king Peter II in 1369, that an argument arose between the consuls of Genoa and Venice. A custom had been established whereby each consul would lead the king's horse across the square after coronation, but the two began to dispute over who should be on the left and who on the right, the latter being the place of honour. Tempers flared and a street battle broke out between Venetians and Genoese and several lives were lost. Peter sided with the Venetians in the conflict and paid dearly for his alliance. A few years later, in 1373, Genoa responded with force, attacking Cyprus at several ports and avenging themselves against the Lusignans. Famagusta was taken and remained in Genoese hands for almost a century until 1464.

From the center of the cathedral square, looking west, one sees the three magnificent arches of the Venetian entrance to the palace complex (Fig. 159-160). Four monolithic, unfluted granite columns segregate the three rounded arches. These are four of the six grey granite columns in the piazza (the others are free-standing, in front of the *medrese*) from the so-called 'Granite Forum' in Salamis, where one can still see fragmentary

Fig. 158: Remains of the walls of the cortile of the Venetian Palazzo del Proveditore (Governor's Palace), Famagusta.

Fig. 159: View west from the top of the minaret of the Lala Mustafa Paşa Camii (St Nicholas cathedral), Famagusta, with the Venetian Triple Arch gateway in foreground, the Venetian Palazzo del Provveditore in the background, with the church of Saints Peter and Paul in the far

434

Fig. 160: The Venetian Triple Arch gateway, Famagusta.

Fig. 161. The west side of the Ottoman madrasa, with the two Venetian spolia columns, spolia from

Fig. 162: The 'Tomb of Venus', in the Triple Arch gateway, Famagusta. It used to sit between the two columns in front of the cathedral in Venetian times. Compare the sarcophagus at Bellapais in Fig. 75.

pillars lying on the ground. The columns project from the wall, and in the entablature above are Doric style triglyphs and metopes (Note: except for the northernmost metope, the rest of the upper level above the capitals is a 20th century reconstruction). The use of the austere Doric style, along with the scored and rusticated masonry of the arches and piers, communicates a stern, monumental dignity. The classical references, not surprising in a Venetian Renaissance work of architecture, are also found in the triple arch motif itself, which refers to the triple arches of the Roman imperial triumphal arch. This façade was no doubt seen as an expression of Venetian imperial authority here in Venice's most eastern outpost. The Venetian coat of arms of Giovanni Renier, who was the Captain of Cyprus in 1552, decorates the hanging keystone of the central arch. A second story existed above this triple archway, and at least one source mentions balconies above. The design and some of the decorative elements of the triple archway are reminiscent of the triple archway at the Venetian fortress of San Andrea in Venice, designed in 1535 by Michele Sanmichele. We do not know the name of the architect of the Venetian arches at Famagusta, but it is tempting to credit the design to Michele Sanmichele or his nephew Giangirolamo Sanmichele, who arrived in Famagusta in the late 1550s to modernize the city's defenses and who may have also designed the spectacular Martinengo bastion.

The Renaissance style of the triple archway was also echoed in the two columns, also *spolia* from Salamis, which had been erected by the Venetians in front of the cathedral entrance (Fig. 161). At some unknown date they were moved either by the Ottomans or, later, by the British, to their present location along the west side of the *medrese*. These two columns also played a role in classicizing the architectural vocabulary of the heart of the city. The Renaissance style architecture superseded the medieval, Gothic style, thus mirroring Venice's ascendance over its French predecessors and modernizing the look of the city's core.

An important artifact just inside the arches of the palace entrance also played a role in this process of classicization. The so-called 'Tomb of Venus' (Fig. 162) is a Greco-Roman sarcophagus which formerly rested, some sources say, between the two aforementioned pillars in the city square (Stephano Gibellino puts it there in his famous print image of the siege of Famagusta; Fig. 115). Now, it is found just inside the Venetian triple arches. This was a tangible reference, like the actual Roman pillars themselves, to the greatness of the Roman imperial past. With these many references, the Venetians equated themselves and their empire with that of the ancient Romans who also once controlled the Eastern Mediterranean. Further, the Venetians associated themselves with Venus, partly owing to the similarity in the sounds of the names — Venus and Venezia — and the legendary tomb became a complex classical allusion to Venice's rule over Greek lands and islands. But there is another element to these pillars that speaks to the nature of Venetian control on Cyprus. It was between these columns that criminals were punished or even put to death. The same things occurred between the two monumental columns in Venice itself. So the tomb of Venus may have been more than a pretty antiquity decorating Venice's newly won town square. It may well have played a role in corporal punishment of the citizenry who resisted Venetian rule.

Behind the Renaissance style rounded arches of the Venetian arcade are the older, pointed arches of the earlier Lusignan palace. A few more of these can be seen in the south as one walks through the now open courtyards, but any remnants of the Lusignan palace have either been destroyed or were integrated into the Ottoman period structures along the south flank of the plaza. A bit further west one comes to the remaining high walls of the Venetian palace. These walls give muted but still impressive indication of the palatial rooms which must have served the Venetian court of the Proveditore. Note how the windows and door are emphasized with a style of masonry called *alle diamante*, where the stones are faceted (Fig. 163). Generally, the lower, ground level rooms would have been given over to business, storage, and administration, while the second level would have included kitchens and banqueting halls. The uppermost levels of the palace would have been the domestic quarters, including bedrooms. As mentioned earlier in the section dealing with the Church of Saints Peter and Paul, a bridge extended from the upper stories of the southwestern corner of the palace complex, crossing the street and allowing direct access to the upper gallery of the church's interior. Whatever the function, this bridge would have made a veritable court chapel out of Saints Peter and Paul for the inhabitants of the palace. One can also find a medieval church of unknown dedication appended to the northwest corner of the palace complex.

During Ottoman times part of the structure was used as a prison, and its most famous prisoner now gives his name to the cathedral square, the 19th century Ottoman poet Namik Kemal, whose bust in bronze can be seen near the Venetian columns. Today, the plaza formed out of the cortile of the Palazzo del Proveditore is filled with some of the cannons and cannon balls which led to the end of Venetian rule on Cyprus.

Sources for the Palazzo del Proveditore and Triple Gateway: Enlart, 463-468; Jeffery, 158-9; Allan Langdale, "At the Edge of Empire: Venetian Architecture in Famagusta, Cyprus," *Viator, Medieval and Renaissance Studies* 41, n. 1 (2010), 155-198.

'Biddulph's Gate' or 'Bulwer's Arch' (Entranceway to a Venetian Palazzo), Venetian, Famagusta, 16th century

[35° 07' 33.28" N / 33° 56' 29.58" E]

This portal was once the noble and ornate entrance to one of Famagusta's Venetian period houses or *palazzi* (Fig. 164). Sadly, only the entrance survives, free-standing like a sculpture at the roadside. The portal only narrowly escaped destruction as it was once scheduled for demolition in the late nineteenth-century. In an effort to save it, Her Majesty's High Commissioner in Cyprus, Sir Robert Biddulph, bought the property so as to avert the portal's demise and ever since it has been known as 'Biddulph's Gate.' A drawing by Enlart from around 1896 shows the gate in an era when the sculpture was in better condition — the lion holding a shield is quite discernible — and one of the door's flanking columns was still in place.

Sources for Biddulph's Gate: Enlart, 454; Jeffery, 158; Allan Langdale, "At the Edge of Empire: Venetian Architecture in Famagusta, Cyprus," *Viator, Medieval and Renaissance Studies* 41, n. 1 (2010), 155-198.

Opposite:
Fig. 163: Details of the alla diamante faceted masonry around the doorways of the Venetian Palazzo del Proveditore, Famagusta.

442

'The Queen's Palace' (A Venetian Noble's Palazzo), Venetian, Famagusta, late 15th or early 16th century

[35° 07' 32.05" N / 33° 56' 29.64" E]

Just to the northeast of the *Palazzo del Proveditore* are the remnants of another *palazzo* that may have been a renovation of a large medieval house. It reveals much about what some of the finer *palazzi* in Famagusta may have looked like in the Venetian period. It is sometimes called the 'Bedestan Palazzo' or the 'Queen's Palace' because it corresponds to a *palazzo* of that name in Stephano Gibellino's famous print of the siege of Famagusta (Fig. 115) and its location agrees with the historical record indicating that Caterina Cornaro vacated the larger palace and moved to a smaller palace nearby and just to the north. It consists of a two-storied L-shaped block (although it could have been U-shaped, as the western end has been lost) around a rectangular cortile with a simple loggia. The main entrance of the Bedestan Palazzo is articulated with elegant faceted stones, just like the windows and portals of the *Palazzo del Proveditore*. It is currently a private home so it is unlikely that you will be able to see the interior courtyard.

Sources for the 'Queen's Palace': Enlart, 456; Jeffery, 158; Allan Langdale, "At the Edge of Empire: Venetian Architecture in Famagusta, Cyprus," *Viator, Medieval and Renaissance Studies* 41, n. 1 (2010), 155-198.

Opposite:
Fig. 164: The so-called 'Biddulph's Gate (or 'Bulwer's Arch'); a portal of a former Venetian palace in Famagusta.

Ottoman Architecture in Famagusta

Çafer Paşa Fountain, Famagusta, Ottoman, 1601
[35° 07' 29.41" N / 33° 56' 29.87" E]

Following their conquest of Cyprus in 1571 the Ottomans initiated several projects aimed at improving the capturing, storage, and availability of fresh water in both the cities and the countryside. The Venetians had made significant progress in the city's water supply, but by 1571 these earlier efforts had proven insufficient. New aqueducts played a crucial role in water transport and distribution and, in Famagusta, several public fountains were constructed to give citizens access to clean water. The Çafer Paşa fountain is just one of the many fountains that can still be seen while walking about the old city, though none have water flowing in them today (Fig. 165). The fountain consists of a single pointed arch attached to the north end of the Venetian triple archway palace entrance, though 19th century photographs show that it was originally several feet south of its current location. The stones used to construct the arch, and the moulding along the top, were no doubt taken from one of the medieval churches. Indeed, the height, width, and depth of the arch is highly reminiscent of the sort of funerary niches found in many of the medieval churches of Famagusta. It may even have come from the Franciscan church just a few metres away. The theme of recycled funerary elements continues in the marble tub into which the water poured. Could it have been a sarcophagus from an ancient tomb? The fountain included a low drain hole, still visible, perhaps for watering animals. The back wall of the fountain is dominated by a large slab of marble with a series of cartouches of Ottoman calligraphy; verses that sing the praises of Çafer Paşa and make note of his commissioning of many public works to improve the town. Parts of the inscriptions claim that: "The fountain has brought good health to the citizens of the old city of Famagusta and has cured many illnesses with its healthy waters... Çafer Paşa is like these healing waters, bringing freshness and life to the city... God has bestowed power and a good nature to Çafer Paşa who is the ruler of the land and seas". The inscription is full of such hyperbole and is written with many rhymes in an elegant, poetic style. Of course, it is entirely possible that this fountain was built by the Venetians but merely repaired by Çafer

Paşa, who then put his celebratory inscription on it to claim full credit. It wouldn't have been the first time conquerors did this kind of thing.

It is interesting to go behind the fountain because one can still see the water holding tank and, extending to the north and west, the line of the pipes which brought water to the fountain.

Fig. 165: The Ottoman period Çafer Paşa fountain, Famagusta.

Çafer Paşa Hamam, Famagusta, Ottoman, 1605

[35° 07' 29.67" N / 33° 56' 28.76" E]

Just beside the fountain, the Çafer Paşa Hamam extended the aquatic theme of Çafer Paşa's civic patronage in the form of a public bath house for the enjoyment and hygiene of the citizens (Fig. 166). As in the instances of the churches in Ottoman Cyprus, other secular Gothic structures were reassigned for other uses. In this case, the chapter house of the Franciscan church was converted into part of the new bath house, with additional rooms and domes constructed northwards.

The medieval chapter house of the church of St Francis, a box-like structure which consists of a single groin vault, must have been added to the Franciscan complex at a somewhat later date after the construction of the church because as one goes into the structure today one can see how the building cuts off the lower part of the central lancet window of the apse. In a way it is quite fortuitous because the blocking off of the window preserved its splays, moulding, and part of the mullion, making it perhaps the best preserved section of medieval fenestration in the city. It is uncertain what the function of the chapter house section of the baths may have had in terms of the bathing sequence, perhaps it was just the changing room or the cool plunge bath, but certainly the hot rooms and steam rooms were in the added domed sections northwards. These hot parts of the Çafer Paşa hamam consist of a large central dome, raised on an octagonal drum, with four smaller domes and corresponding rooms radiating off of it. The smaller rooms would have been the hottest. Beyond this are a couple of hallways, where the furnace of the bath house might have been.

Yet another part of the Franciscan Church may have been integrated into the function of the bath. A rectangular vaulted room to the west of the back of the domed section (to see it you must walk around and into the Franciscan church) might have been a kind of reservoir for the bath's water supply.

Fig. 166: The Ottoman period Çafer Paşa hamam or bath, incorporating the former chapter house of the Franciscan church, with the Franciscan church ruins in the background, Famagusta.

The Medrese, Famagusta, Ottoman, late 16th early 17th century

[35° 07' 30.26" N / 33° 56' 32.24" E]

A *medrese* was a school for young men, attached to a mosque, where they were taught lessons from the Koran. The Ottomans seem to have used some surviving architectural elements left over from the Lusignan period in creating what I think is the most pleasing Ottoman structure in Cyprus (Fig. 167). The reused section is a set of Gothic vaults in the south part of the current structure. This may have been part of the Bishop's palace in the Middle Ages. The Ottomans took this and built a large dome beside the arcade, then added another arcade at a right angle to the first, creating almost a porch on the west face. An entrance with elegant *muquarnas* designs in the semi-dome was constructed in the north. It is yet another example of cultures using the remnants of earlier buildings to create something new. Today the building is used as a restaurant, and it is worthwhile to dine there or have a drink just to see the interior of the structure. As you enter the monumental north portal, look up high above and to the left and you'll see a large lintel block of dark stone with a wonderfully preserved Syriac inscription (Fig. 168). The block must have been imported from a church in the Middle East as it reads:

Line 1: To the honour of the holy Trinity, this church of Mar Behnam was established in the days of the Patriarch Mar Ignatius, son of Ephrem, from Qal'at [Antta (near Mardin)....]

Line 2: Jacob and Barsaumo at the expense of the faithful through the concern of Salam son of QBL. Let everyone who reads (this) please pray for him and for his parents and for everyone who has participated either in world or in action; it was completed the year [....]

The 'Ignatius' of the inscription is probably the patriarch Ignatius Abdallah, who lived in the middle of the 16th century. It was he who sent Moses of Mardin to Europe in 1555 to print the first New Testament in Syriac, which was published in Vienna in 1555.

Look along the bottoms of the windows in the structure's interior, under the central dome, and you will see channels that used to carry streams of water. It was thought that the sound of running water calmed the students while they were studying their Koranic verses, but also alluded to the Rivers of Paradise that awaited devout Muslims.

Sources for Medresse: Thanks to Sebastian Brock for the translation of the Syriac inscription.

Fig. 167: The Ottoman medrese just to the north of St Nicholas cathedral (Lala Mustafa Paşa Camii), with the Venetian granite columns on the west face, Famagusta. To the right is the small former, domed tomb kiosk of Omar Effendi.

Fig. 168: Large stone block imported from Syria with Syriac inscription in the medrese, Famagusta.

The Kertikli Hamam, Famagusta, Ottoman, mid-17th century

[35° 07' 38.25" N / 33° 56' 22.71" E]

In a peaceful residential neighborhood in the northern section of Famagusta, a ten minute walk from the cathedral square, lies the impressive ruin of a mid-seventeenth century Ottoman period hamam or bathhouse (Figs. 169-170). This structure is fascinating because the bathhouse was created by re-adapting a medieval bathhouse or factory to a new use as an Ottoman-style hamam. This tendency to reuse earlier medieval structures, as we have seen, was a common practice during Ottoman rule on Cyprus. The Kertikli Hamam is not unique in Famagusta in this regard, for another Ottoman bathhouse, the Çafer Paşa Haman of 1605 (see earlier entry), had integrated the chapter house of the Church of St Francis into its fabric.

The Kertikli hamam consists of three main sections. One was a long arched structure, now completely lost except for its foundations, running east to west along the south side. There is some evidence that this barrel vaulted section may have been bisected by a cross vault creating an axial entrance hall from which the wings extended both east and west. It is likely that the changing rooms and cool bath (*soğukluk*) were in this section of the complex. It is also in the southwest part of this section where the main water supply arrived. Today, one can see a small archway which may have been the terminus of the underground channel which directed water here from the main aqueduct of Famagusta further to the center of town about 360 metres south of the hamam. The construction of a road has obscured whatever remains of the southern wall, which probably also was the entrance to the bath owing to the usual axiality of this building type elsewhere in the Ottoman world.

Another section of the complex includes the impressive domed rooms of the hot (*sıçaklık*) and warm (*hararet*) baths and the steam room. There are six of these rooms, all roughly rectangular and each of a different size. Each room also has a different sized dome over it, with differing perforations that allowed natural light into the rooms. They were once glazed. An elderly woman in the neighborhood claims that when she was a child boys knocked out the last of the glass with rocks. In some of these rooms are niches which may have held lamps or implements used in bathing or massage, such as sponges or brushes. If you look at the lights of these domes and focus your eyes in a certain way, patterns emerge.

The Ottoman bath finds its inspiration in the Roman baths of the ancient world. The Roman division of rooms into hot, warm, and cool rooms (*caldarium, tepidarium, frigidarium*), often along with a kind of sauna or steam room (*sudatorium*; see entry on the baths at Salamis),

Fig. 169: The Ottoman Kertikli Hamam, Famagusta.

Fig. 170: Perforated domes of the Ottoman Kertikli Hamam, Famagusta.

453

found its parallels in the Ottoman hamam. Roman baths were also known to provide sensual services from massage to prostitution, and these activities, too, defined the social function of the Ottoman bath, even though early Ottoman baths were often built as appendages to mosques where the intended function was to provide the opportunity for thorough bodily cleansing before prayer. But this more ritual function was quickly secularized in Ottoman society and the hamam emerged as a place where men could enjoy both women and young boys, receive massages, and drink wine. The Kertikli Hamam is found at the north edge of the old town of Famagusta, and its location outside of the town's center may have defined it as a seedier counterpart to the aforementioned Çafer Paşa bathhouse, a more elegant hamam which was located across the town square from the city's main mosque.

At the rear of the building (north), in a low depression in the ground, one can see something that looks like a doorway, but this was the furnace of the bath structure which was used to heat the air and water for the complex. If it was consistent with the function of other Ottoman baths, a huge metal cauldron for water sat over a fire while the fire's hot air was blown into the spaces beneath the floors created by the brick hypocausts. Remnants of these hypocausts, made of circular bricks stacked like coins, can be seen in some of the rooms.

The north hall of the complex (and the west, though this section has been destroyed), which includes the furnace, may have been a bathhouse or may originally have been some kind of medieval factory in the Lusignan period. It is tempting to think that it was a sugar factory, as sugar refining was a major industry in Cyprus during the Middle Ages. The processing of sugar required the same elements that the later hamam would also require: heat and water. But in other sugar refining sites in Cyprus one usually finds remnants of a very specific type of conical pottery used in the process. No such distinctive pottery has been found here, so this idea is not well supported. On the north wall on the far left is a filled in arched opening that may have been the furnace of the earlier, medieval structure. In this fill may be the archaeological evidence needed to more certainly define the function of the original building.

Few remains give us any sense of the decoration of the complex, though in the southeast corner room one can barely make out a couple of fresco line drawings of fish, a suitably aquatic design for a bath house.

Other Ottoman Structures in Famagusta

Visitors to Famagusta can also see several other smaller monuments testament to the rich Ottoman heritage on Cyprus. The Akkule Camii was built just inside the land gate of the city fortifications, right at the entrance to the old medieval tower and gate that one now goes through to get to the ravelin complex. It is called the Akkule or 'White Tower' because this was the Ottoman name for the Ravelin, as it was from here that the white flag of Venetian surrender was unfurled in 1571. It was built in 1618, ostensibly as a convenient place of prayer for the guards who protected the city gate. Technically it's not a mosque but a *mescid*, a small prayer hall. It's currently the tourist information office so you can go there and get maps and other information on the city. There is a marble plaque above the main doorway with elegant calligraphy of a surah from the Koran. The mihrab or prayer niche inside is also very attractively carved though covered over with white paint. Just by the inside of the land gate tunnel, you can see how the little mosque literally melds with the walls of the former Venetian defenses.

Just a few metres away, but outside the land gate, you will see a large, domed Ottoman tomb with a marble decorated relief facing the road as you walk out of the old city. The relief is probably ancient, from Salamis, and is one of the many examples of spolia or reused architectural elements in Cyprus. It's a lovely fragment, with an egg and dart moulding along the top and a wide band of a vine motif with fleshy leaves below. There are three domed tombs here and several smaller rectangular graves all around. They date mostly from the 17th century and are not well cared for at this time. In some cases trees grow out of the tombs, so neglected they have become. Perhaps the small field can be turned into a civic park and better maintained by the municipality. There are a few other Ottoman tombs scattered in the old town. Along the south flank of the church of Saints Peter and Paul, under the arches of the flying buttresses, is the tomb of Mehmet Çelebi, who was once an Ottoman ambassador in Paris. His tombstone has lovely Ottoman script adorning it. There are also Ottoman graves at the Stavros church, now the Mustafa Paşa Tamisi, where the cenotaphs are covered in cloths of green, which is the colour associated with the Prophet Muhammad. If the Çafer Paşa and Kertikli Hamams weren't quite enough for you, there's also the ruin of the Kizil Hamam near the west walls about 200 metres north from the land gate entrance. There were probably several domes to the bath, but today there remain only the vestiges of two of them. They are still impressive, however, and, like the Kertikli Hamam, you can see the clay tubes in the broken walls that once sluiced hot air to keep the walls warm. In one part of the bath the foundation for an octagonal fountain survives, and you can easily imagine an elegant dome over it with sunlight coming in the perforations of the dome and making shafts of light through the steamy atmosphere of the bath house. The benches for the sweating patrons still exist around this fountain. Whenever I see it I can hear the tinkling of the water from its spouts.

Other Ottoman Structures in Northern Cyprus

Arif Paşa Aqueduct, Gaziköy/Afenteia, Ottoman, 17th century

[35° 09' 22.76" N / 33° 33' 49.97" E]

Especially in the 1600s, after the conquest of Cyprus in 1571, the Ottomans began ambitious engineering projects to improve all aspects

of water storage and distribution on the island of Cyprus in an attempt to boost its agricultural productivity and the hygiene of the cities. One of the most impressive remnants of these hydrological projects is a 300 metre long section of the Arif Paşa Aqueduct just 1 km west along the main road out of Gaziköy/Afanteia (Fig. 171). It is a widely held belief that aqueducts are elevated above ground but, in fact, even those more monumental and famous aqueducts built by the ancient Romans, were 85 percent underground. Arched, elevated channels were used only to bridge hollows and valleys to keep the water running at a consistent downward slope. This section of the Arif Paşa Aqueduct bridges just such a depression in the landscape before disappearing again below ground on its way south. The source of the water was, ultimately, the Kyrenia Mountains in the north, which on most days are visible from the aqueduct itself. An additional feature of this specific section of the aqueduct is that it makes a sharp turn in direction, thus following the contours of the landscape to maintain its consistent level of declension. The channel which carried the water, about 2 metres off the ground at the highest point, is visible along most of the section, carried by dozens of surviving supporting arches. At a few points one can discern sluices that could be opened to drain water out of the main channel to irrigate fields in the vicinity. Although not as impressive and monumental as the Abu Bekir aqueduct near Larnaca, this smaller feat of Ottoman engineering is still worth a visit. Drive there on the smaller country roads rather than taking the main roads and you'll see the beautiful landscape of rural Cyprus, especially lovely in the springtime. The aqueduct looks especially impressive rising out of a sea of freshly sprouted wheat.

Sources for Arif Paşa Aqueduct: N. Yıldız, "Aqueducts in Cyprus," *Journal for Cypriot Studies* 2.2 (Spring, 1996): 89-112.

Fig. 171: The Ottoman Arif Paşa Aqueduct near Gaziköy/Afenteia.

459

The Gambili (Kambyli) Hamam, Hisarköy, 17th -18th century

[35° 18' 03.89" N / 33° 06' 10.78" E]

Hidden in some trees in the western outskirts of Hisarköy is a delightful but very small ruined Ottoman bath house (Fig. 172). Originally, it might have served a single house, perhaps the household of an important citizen of the village. One story is that it belonged to the local *sheik* or *agha*. At most, it seems to have been able to comfortably seat no more than 6-8 bathers. It could be that the village was so small that this was sufficient for everyone's use.

The bath has its single dome surviving almost completely, and one can go down into the bath itself though caution is advised because of its advanced state of ruin. One can see the elegant niches in the walls with their ogee arches. Also visible near the floor line is the arched conduit through which the hot air originally flowed beneath the now lost pavements. One really feels like an archaeologist exploring this old ruin, and it's a good exercise to try to imagine what the building was like when new. Hopefully the locals will clear away the area and stabilize the architecture to help preserve it for the future.

Fig. 172: The Ottoman period Gambili (Kambyli) Hamam, Hisarköy.

461

Appendix I: Lusignan and Venetian Era Class Structure and Ethnic Groups on Cyprus

I have decided to provide a brief and admittedly cursory overview of aspects of the social classes and ethnic groups of the island during the centuries from 1100 to 1571 when the Ottomans conquered the island. Such a perfunctory introduction as I provide here can hardly do justice to five centuries of life on Cyprus let alone the other historical eras. I include it nevertheless to provide at least a general sense of some elements of social classes and some aspects of ethnic diversity during the medieval period as most tourists will most likely be interested in the rich remains of the middle ages. My hope is that these notes that follow will encourage readers to expand their research to include modern historical writings on medieval and Venetian Cyprus and, indeed, the history of all of Cyprus's eras. As in the rest of the volume, I use primary texts from travellers of the period. However, these observers cannot always be trusted to be accurate and one should always take their often observations with a grain of salt.

There were several ethnic groups in Cyprus. Some of these were briefly dealt with in the book when discussing buildings associated with specific populations such as Nestorians, Armenians, Jacobites, and Maronites. However, other peoples marked by either religious, ethnic, or class distinctions such as serfs, Jews and slaves are dealt with below. This sketch of the social contexts of the medieval buildings discussed in this volume suggests a rural community mostly made up of labourers who were slaves, serfs or *parici* and the vast percentage of these people were Greek speaking and Orthodox Christian. In the sections on Jews and slaves I have drawn much from essays by Benjamin Arbel.

It is probable that the majority of the Cypriot population in the Middle Ages and during the Venetian period were peasants who worked in agriculture or shepherding, though this was by no means a fixed or stable percentage during the centuries of Latin rule. For many, there were few chances for social mobility and visitors to the island often note that the population was heavily taxed. There were many merchants and traders in Cyprus, reflected in the active commercial enterprises in the main ports. The working class were divided into three principal groups: the *parici*, the *perpiriarii*, and the *lefteri*.

Parici (Gk. *Paroikoi*, "neighbours"; serfs): The *parici* (sing. *parico*) were the lowest class on Cyprus and were virtually slaves of the property owners in a feudal system of social organisation. They were probably all Greek speaking. They had to pay their masters 50 besants a year, no small sum, and give the lord one-third plus one-tenth of all the agricultural produce that was the fruit of their labour, about 40% of the total. These people could be sold or traded like chattel, even for a horse or dog. Lords were allowed to punish any member of the *parici* in the most violent way, as long as he did not draw blood or kill him, because in Lusignan Cyprus feudal nobles could not exercise high justice unlike parts of Western Europe. Many seemed to have beaten their serfs or put them in stocks. Stephen de Lusignan, writing around 1572, noted the situation of the *parici* and how the Venetians had at least put an end to one of the humiliating practices:

> When the kings gave the villages to this or that lord, they gave them, along with the villages, the jurisdiction over the...*Parici*. They had the power to put them in jail, to put them in chains, banish them, submit them to rope torture, and to whip them; but they could not take blood from them, nor kill them, because this right belonged to the king. However, the noblemen could sell, buy, or exchange them, so that they were like slaves.... Some of these masters of the villages were nearly tyrants, and they traded the *Parici* with dogs, or horses, or falcons. The Venetians therefore made it a law that the *Parici* could be exchanged only with other human males and females. But some of these masters did terrible things to them, and in excess; and those poor wretches, in order to free themselves from such treatment, are forced to give their master as much money as he requests.
>
> *[Sources History Cyprus X, 39]*

Any serf from the age of 15 to 60 had to work 2-3 days a week for their masters. The luckier *parici* did receive a wage for this work but it was a pittance. For an entire day's labour a serf would earn about 6 *quattrini*, an amount as diminutive as it sounds: one *quattrini* was 1/7680th of a single ducat. It will come as no surprise that there were many lords who reneged on paying their *parici* at all, as indicated by a proscription passed in 1489 (the first year of official Venetian rule) outlawing the practice and imposing fines on parsimonious lords. *Parici* could purchase their freedom but the cost was high, between 60-100 ducats, an amount any *parico* was unlikely to ever amass at a salary of 6 *quattrini* a day. Even if the amount had been saved the master was under no obligation to accept it. However, a lord could free a *parico* without a charge if he so wished. In 1563 the Archbishop Livio Podocataro of Nicosia freed a *parico* who had worked for him because he had been such a devoted servant.

The Lusignan kings were, as might be expected, the largest 'owners' of *parici*. Sometimes, cash-strapped kings raised money by selling freedom. The price could be as low as 50 ducats if the king wanted many takers. At other times, during the reign of James II, for example, the price went up to 100-200 ducats, but came with extra benefits such as the right to become a priest upon gaining liberty. At one point there seems to have been some creative accounting with regard to the manumission of *parici*. In 1494 Venice's Council of Ten demanded that they be able to review any sale of *parici* manumission. They had discovered that some owners were supposedly selling freedom at a discounted rate as low as 25 ducats. This was fine, on the face of it, but it was also believed that this was the amount reported to the Treasury when, in fact, the owners had received much more than that amount. In an attempt to rein in this fraudulent practice many of the *parici* who had been sold at the supposedly discounted rate were rounded up and returned to servitude. Many *parici* left their babies at the doors of the cathedral of Santa Sophia in Lefkoşa/Nicosia because any infant left there was a foundling (Gk. *vreta*) and became the responsibility of the Church and free.

There were instances of peasant rebellion. Taking advantage of the Mamluk invasion of 1426, which caused total chaos in Cyprus, the peasants themselves rose up, some killing their masters, and they began looting and pillaging, eventually setting up captains in Lefka, Limissol, Oreini, Peristerona, and Morphou, and even proclaiming a new king, Alexis. However, the rebellion was soon quelled and the briefly reigning monarch of the dispossessed was presently dangling unregally from the gallows.

Parici were not allowed to travel freely, being obliged to stay on the property of their owner. They could journey further afield only if they received a license. Should a *parico* try to escape Cyprus there were, in the Venetian period, severe penalties for ship captains who conveyed such human cargo, but rewards for returning the fleeing serf back to the owner. If someone restored a runaway *parico* the lord was obliged to pay a reward of 10 ducats plus the cost of transporting him back. A ship captain who knowingly transported a *parico* would be fined the huge sum. Escaping *parici*, as might be deduced from the number and severity of the laws and the fines governing them, were a problem for the Venetians. In 1490, just after the Venetians had taken control of the island, they calculated that escaping *parici* were a significant drain on the island's resources. Since population depletion was a general problem for the Cypriot economy at this time the Venetians tried to curb the exodus, promulgating draconian laws to staunch the flow while at the same time inducing emigration from the Morea in Greece to repopulate the island. The most likely place for *parici* to flee was the island of Rhodes, and anyone harbouring a serf there could be fined a ducat a day for sheltering them. Still, in 1518, the Venetian chronicler Marino Sanudo estimated that there were 500 serfs, escapees from Cyprus, living on Rhodes.

When an Ottoman invasion seemed imminent, the Venetians conscripted 5000 *parici* and *francomati* for the defense of Cyprus. Later, in a grossly transparent act of social 'charity' the Venetian Senate freed all *parici* when the Ottomans declared war, hoping that the masses of freed Greek Cypriots would then come to Venice's aid when the Turks attacked Cyprus. But the Venetian Rectors of the island refused to enact the proclamation of comprehensive manumission.

Perpiriarii: This group was only slightly better off than the *parici*, paying less per year to their feudal lords — 15 besants per annum rather than 50. They paid this fee in coins called 'hyperpers' (also called gold besants or 'nomisma'), from which the name of their class was adapted. They were officially, though often not in practicality, 'free', as their group had been granted a block privilege in centuries past. Many of these had been civil servants or wealthy burghers of Nicosia.

***Lefteri* (Gk. *eleutheroi*, It. *francomati*):** *Lefteri* were *parici* who had gained partial liberties either by purchasing it or having it granted by their feudal lord. Still, they needed to donate a portion of their labour. Children of *lefteri* parents were themselves free only if born after the conferring of freedom, while those born earlier remained *parici*. So, too, the offspring of a *lefteri* who married a *parici* woman; their children would revert to *parici* status. Such interclass unions were discouraged for, as Stephan de Lusignan noted around 1572, they muddied the waters of the social hierarchy:

> Further, if a *Leftero* or a *Leftera* marries a *Parica* or a *Parico*, their children will all be *Parici*; and in some places they divide the children between them. Therefore a law was enacted that a priest cannot marry a *Parica* with a *Leftero*, or a *Leftera* with a *Parico*, because of their future children.
>
> *[Sources History Cyprus X, 40]*

Priests were thus forbidden to solemnize these marriages, and it should also be noted that a similar law was passed forbidding priests to marry Orthodox and Catholic Christians ('Greeks' and 'Franks').

One historical event demonstrates how such classes could be treated. In an attempt to discern whether there were some *parici* posing or claiming to be *lefteri*, the Lusignan King James II, in 1468, had a mandate read out by the town criers in all the villages and towns of Cyprus. The proclamation exhorted all *civitains* (low ranking civil servants) and *paracivitains* (local village police) to round up all the people — men, women, and children — who were not natives of the town and who were not certain to be *lefteri*, arrest and bind them, and take them to the local Bailie where their claims to *lefteri* status would be scrutinized. If found to in fact be *parici* they would be punished and sent back to their masters or confiscated as property by the king. Any citizen or *lefteri* that protected or harboured them, or who failed to report a *faux-lefteri*, would be fined the substantial sum of 25 ducats. As one might expect, there was trade in false certificates of manumission. However, anyone caught supplying a false document for a *parici* was harshly penalized with a 100 ducat fine.

White Venetians: These were people of Greek or Syrian descent who had been made Venetian subjects and thus enjoyed some benefits from the Venetians. Most of them lived near the southwestern Cypriot port city of Paphos where they paid 300 ducats per year to the Venetian captain for the privilege of their status. In Lusignan times they also paid a special fee to the king on St Mark's feast day (April 25th). There were also a few who had in a similar fashion became Genoese subjects, called 'White Genoese'.

Stratiotai: This group was originally a division of mercenary soldiers who were brought to Cyprus in Byzantine times to garrison the island's towns, but also to patrol the coast, which was particularly prone to pirate raiding. The establishment of an auxiliary coastguard was necessitated by Islamic expansion in the eastern Mediterranean and the subsequent pillaging that came with it. The name of this group comes from the hearth tax (i.e. a tax per household — different from the taxes levied on agricultural produce, which was called *paroikoi*) or *stratia* that was imposed to pay for the *stratiotai's* protection services. The Lusignans eventually abolished the *stratiotai*, but kept taxing the people with the *stratia*. Later, during the Venetian period, Albanians and Macedonians were still brought in to act as coastguards for the island. However, Stephan de Lusignan, writing in the years just after the Ottomans conquered Cyprus, notes that *Francomati* (*Lefteri*) were also obliged to keep watch on the coasts, apparently assigned and disciplined by the Albanian *stratiotai*. He describes their state of readiness:

> All the *Francomati*, that is, the free farmers, go and perform this task of watching the coast as their turn comes, and they have to watch from one evening to the next. Each guard consists of two farmers, each of which is obliged to watch for a certain number of hours. They keep a fire hidden and have combustible materials prepared, and they are obliged to make as many fires as is the

number of ships they see. The other guard stations respond as soon as they see the fires. They blow their trumpets, and immediately ride off to the places where the fires are lighted. To keep the farmers that are on watch from falling asleep, some Albanians have the task of riding around and punishing those who have left their post.

[Sources History Cyprus X, 110]

But if ships were spotted, it was the Albanian *stratiotai's* responsibility to track them. Lusignan, again, describes how they worked.

Over the whole island they usually keep a thousand horses from Albania.... The task of the officers is this: when they see suspicious ships and privateering vessels they are obliged to keep pace with them by horse all along the coast till they reach the next guard station. The next guard keeps pace with them until they leave the island. This is done to prevent them from coming ashore and doing damage.

[Sources History Cyprus X, 109-110]

These descriptions are fascinating indicators of the methods used to secure the island from coastal incursions from late Byzantine through Venetian times. In the later Venetian period, *parici* were also used to keep watch on the coast by day, while the *francomati* served the coastal night watch.

Jews in Cyprus

When Ptolemy Soter conquered Jerusalem in 320 BCE he is said to have transferred Jews to Cyprus, so their presence dates from at least Hellenistic times. Still others sought work in the Cypriot copper mines during the time of Christ. We know that in the first century CE there were already many Jews living in Cyprus. St Paul is said to have preached to Jews in Cyprus, almost certainly at Salamis, where in 45 CE St Barnabas also preached Christianity to Jews in the synagogue and was later killed by them for his heresies. In Paphos there must have been many Jews at this time as Paul converts several when he visits the city in these early years. But the Book of Acts records that others even before Barnabas and Paul prostylized to the Jews of Cyprus:

Now they which were scattered abroad upon the persecution that arose about Stephen traveled far as Phenice and Cyprus and Antioch preaching the word to none but unto the Jews only. And some of them were men of Cyprus.

[Acts 11: 19-20]

Today, people in Paphos will point to a marble column where they say St Paul was tied as he received 39 lashes. Some Jewish converts became leaders in the early Christian community on Cyprus, such as St Heracleidios and St Auxibius of Soli.

In the years 115-116 CE, during the reign of the Roman Emperor Trajan, Cypriot Jews took part in the huge Jewish rebellion of that year, which was brutally repressed by the Romans. So significant was the rebellion on Cyprus it is estimated that between 120,000 and 240,000 people were killed, both by the Jewish rebels, led by Artemion, and by Trajan's general Lusius Quietus who was sent to suppress the resistance. In a corrupted form Quietus' name gave us the historical name of the war, the 'Kitos War', though it is also known to scholars as 'The Second Jewish-Roman War'. The insurgence apparently destroyed Salamis and non-Jews were slaughtered by the thousands by the rebels. After the Romans had defeated these rebels, Jews were forbidden to live on Cyprus on pain of death. But there is evidence that Jews returned to Cyprus in the ensuing centuries and their population in the 7th century must have once again been significant as Jews from the mainland city of Tyre exhorted their Cypriot counterparts to join them in a conspiracy against Greeks in 610 CE.

After the 7th century we hear little about the Jews of Cyprus until the 12th century when Benjamin of Tudela visits between 1160 and 1173. He notes that there are Orthodox Jews on Cyprus, but also a heretical Jewish sect variously called 'Cyprians', 'Kaphroseins', or 'Epikursin' — this last denoting 'Epicurians', a blanket denomination for heretic Jews — who take Sunday as their Sabbath and who have been excommunicated by Orthodox Jews. Another Jewish scholar, Abraham Ibn Ezra, wrote a text refuting their ideas in the middle of the 12th century. Thus their numbers must have been large enough to warrant this response.

Certainly, by the 14th century Jews were again fairly numerous in Cyprus. Famagusta and Nicosia, the island's two largest cities, both had Jewish quarters, though by the Venetian period it seems as if the only significant population of Jews was in Famagusta. One source suggests that the Nicosian Jews had been attacked during an Easter celebration and had fled to Famagusta where, one supposes, the ethnic climate was less antagonistic. Yet they may not have been all that numerous. By 1568, at any rate, when a survey of Jews in Famagusta was done, the population was around 175 people, including children, although this probably represents a decline from the 14th century numbers. In 1563 Elias of Pesaro had estimated just 25 families, so it seems that the Jewish population might have been on the rise again, almost doubling in the five years between Elias' arrival and 1568. But in that same year, fearing that Jews were working as spies for the Turks, 'foreign' Jews — that is, Jews not born in Cyprus — were expelled from the city. Jews were also found in the countryside, and 14th century documents refer to Jewish tanners in the village of Psimolophou.

The location of Famagusta's Jewish quarter was very likely just inside the Land Gate, in the southwest corner of the city. In Stephano Gibellino's 1571 print of the siege of Famagusta the word *zeucha* is printed in that location. Enlart thought this a version of the Venetian *zecca* (mint) and thus concluded that Gibellino was indicating the position of Famagusta's mint. Benjamin Arbel sees *zeucha* instead as Venetian dialect for *giudecca*, or Jewish Quarter. This location, just inside the town from the Santa Napa bastion, is also echoed in the nickname of the bastion, the Giudecca Tower. In Gibellino's print he also notes a topographical point he labels *Colle degli Hebrei*, a low hill southwest of the city, which likely marks the cemetery of the Jews, which we know was outside the city.

Famagusta was known as having a very diverse population in the 14th and 15th centuries, and even the Jewish population, as Arbel notes, was itself diverse, with Jews coming from all points of the Mediterranean and Black Seas. But Jews were not always welcome. Arbel cites an instance in 1497 when Jewish families who may have been expelled from Portugal in that year were subsequently turned away by the Venetians when they appeared on Cypriot shores.

As in many places in Europe Jews were obliged to wear some distinguishing badge, a rule that had been established throughout Catholic lands by the Lateran Council of 1215. On Cyprus it was implemented in the early fourteenth century by John del Conti, the Latin archbishop of Nicosia. Elias of Pesaro, who visited Cyprus in 1563, made note of Jewish doctors in Famagusta who wore black hats with small, round yellow badges on them. Elias sees this as a kind of honour for them, because other Jews had to wear very prominent yellow head coverings.

> A man is lucky if he knows medicine, for the Greeks respect the Jews as good doctors, and trust them...there are two Jewish doctors, a Portuguese and a Roman, who earn more and make a fine income by their profession. They are all held in great respect, and wear a black hat with a yellow badge no bigger than the small coin called *issarion*, a privilege allowed to no other Jews, who are all obliged to wear, as at Venice, a head-covering entirely of yellow.
>
> *[Excerpta Cypria, 76]*

Elias, himself a Jew, has left us a fascinating snapshot of Famagusta in 1563, near the end of the Venetian era on Cyprus. He had left Italy for the Holy Land, considering moving there with his family. It is likely that he left from Venice, because he notes that ships leave every month to go to Famagusta. But when he arrived he heard that the plague was raging in

Syria and thought better of continuing his journey. Stuck in Famagusta, he wrote a letter that has survived the centuries. Lingering in the town allowed Elias to make some detailed observations about Jewish life. He describes the synagogue as "large and fine...supported by a community of about twenty-five families, Levantines, Sicilians, and Portuguese." But he also observes that, "Hatred, discord and jealousy reign among them." So all was not peaceful, it seems, in the Jewish quarter. The Jews in Famagusta make their living lending money, at rates of twenty or twenty-five percent. There seems, indeed, to be a credit crunch in Famagusta, as Elias observes that:

> As soon as the Christians see a fresh Jew arrive to stay here they ask him if he wants to lend money. If he says yes, they are kindly toward him, and he need not fear that the other Jews will look askance at him as though he were poaching on their preserves. The country is big enough to feed them all.
>
> *[Excerpta Cypria, 74]*

It is customary, according to Elias, to treat the lender well and bring him a gift after the loan has been agreed upon, of a value of three or four percent of the total loan amount. For small loans, it might be just a chicken or some oil or cheese, but for large loans it might be a substantial present. Elias notes that, as in Crete and Corfu, the majority of Cyprus's inhabitants are Greek speaking and Orthodox Christians, and he claims that they had anti-Semitic attitudes:

> For all the gold in the world they would not eat anything that a Jew has touched, and would never use his cooking utensils. Suppose a Jew wishes to buy anything from them he must not touch it but must describe what he wants: anything he touches he must keep.
>
> *[Excerpta Cypria, 74]*

This was consistent with other places in Christian lands. But Elias has some prejudices of his own, and describes the Greeks in unflattering terms. He claims that, "Their intelligence is less developed, their manners are peculiar." But he goes on in an even nastier tone:

> They do not allow their women to show themselves in the town by day; only at night can they visit their friends and go to church. They say this is by way of modesty, but it is really to avoid the frequent adulteries, for their rule of life is thoroughly perverse. They are all liars, cheats, thieves. Honesty has vanished from their midst.
>
> *[Excerpta Cypria, 74]*

He was not the only visitor to point out the lax morals of the Cypriots and the amorousness of their women.

There were also Jewish scholars in Famagusta. Arbel notes the presence of Moshe Rova, who translated works from Arabic into Italian (one thinks that he might have been able to make a good living helping traders negotiate), as well as Yom-Tov ben Faraji, a biblical scholar. Rabbi Eliezer Ashkanazi was a scriptural scholar, and lived in Famagusta in the 1560s.

Jews were not allowed to own property outside of their designated quarter in Famagusta, and this accords with treatment in other Mediterranean lands. In one instance, Jews who did not pay sufficient reverence for a Christian religious procession passing by were punished by the Venetian governor with a fine upon the whole Jewish community. In 1553 a papal order was given to outlaw the Talmud, and in Famagusta Hebrew books were burned by the Venetian authorities, echoing similar events throughout Roman Catholic dominions.

Anti-Semitism in Cyprus, as in Europe, also led to their special exploitation in times of economic stress. As George Hill notes: "In 1310 the Lord of Tyre extorted 100,000 white besants from the Jews of Nicosia, Famagusta, and other places". It is also recorded that the Genoese, when in control of Famagusta, also exploited the Jews. Makhairas, however, notes that the Genoese also robbed Christians.

When the Genoese saw the immeasurable wealth which they had gotten from the prince, they again robbed the wretched town [Famagusta], knights, burgesses, and wealthy people, and also the two Jewish quarters of Famagusta and Lefkosia

[Makhairas, 437].

...and they pillaged Lefkosia twice or thrice, and did much damage. They pillaged Famagusta twice or thrice and did many things to vex people, and they put men to torture so that they confessed their riches, and then they robbed them. And whatever men had either in secret or openly they carried off, both from Jews and from Christians

[Makhairas, 403].

The Greek Cypriot chronicler Kyprianos instructs his countrymen to recall the ancient proscription against the Jews on Cyprus and says that, while the law is no longer in effect, there were other ways to prevent members of 'the detested race' from settling among them. But he was upbraided for his prejudices by another Orthodox Cypriot, Sakellarios.

By the late 19th century, a census revealed that there were only 127 Jews in the whole of Cyprus, and only 4 in Famagusta where they had occupied an entire quarter in the Middle Ages and Venetian period. George Jeffery notes a village called Margo (on the road midway between Larnaca and Nicosia) where there was a Jewish community of small size in the late 19th and early 20th centuries.

There is a coda to that last statistic and, in a way, to Elias of Pesaro's desire to move his family to Palestine four centuries ago. Famagusta was the site of detention camps when Jews tried to establish a Jewish state in the Holy Land after World War II. These early Zionists took boats that were diverted to Famagusta because the British, who then controlled both Cyprus and Palestine, were keen to stop them from getting to their destination. Similarly, some Jews who did manage to get to the Holy Land were then deported and detained in Cyprus, many at camps at or near Famagusta. It is estimated that 55,000 Jews were held there.

Slaves and Slavery in Cyprus

Slavery was an integral part of the Mediterranean economy and social structure for thousands of years and this continued in the medieval and Venetian periods in Cyprus, and included both Christian and Muslim owners and slave dealers. Our principal document informing us about slavery in Cyprus, and specifically in Famagusta, the island's busiest port, comes from the richly informative records of the Italian notary Lamberto di Sambuceto, who was in Famagusta from 1296 to 1307, but substantial information also comes from the records of a later visitor, the Venetian notary Nicola de Boateriis, who worked in Famagusta between 1360 and 1362. Benjamin Arbel has written of these records and examined their information and implications. Although, as he warns, it is difficult to come to firm conclusions about the general circumstances of slavery on Cyprus from just two sets of documents, there is nonetheless much that is conveyed either directly or through inference. The commercial transactions having to do with slavery, either purchasing or freeing (manumission), often record the gender, age, and colour or ethnic origin of the slave. At times the price is also mentioned, either the price paid by the new owners or the price paid by the slaves to purchase their freedom.

Piracy and raiding were the principal ways that slaves were acquired, and it seems that around 1300 the Genoese were the most ambitious slave traders in the Mediterranean. But they were not the only brokers from European lands. Traders from Piacenza, Pisa, Ancona, Barcelona, Messina, and Palermo are also indicated. Venetians do not appear in Sambuceto's records, but we know that they were also active, concentrating their efforts, however, on the island of Crete, which they controlled. It might surprise people to know that in this period most slaves were Greek (*Rhomaioi*; i.e. Byzantines), taken from islands or coastal towns in the Aegean Sea frequented by Genoese ships, or the south or west coasts of what is today Turkey. Records indicate, however, a wide ethnic diversity, including Jewish and Armenian slaves. Black slaves from Africa were also present, supplied by North African Muslim slave merchants, but they were the minority on Cyprus.

The average age of purchased slaves was quite young, at 18.5 years. Male slaves were slightly more often mentioned in Sambuceto's records than female: 49 compared to 37 in his records where gender is noted. Prices varied widely. A 22 year old Saracen woman fetched 200 besants, while a 12 year old girl from Samos and a 20 year old young woman were purchased for only 30 besants apiece. Between Sambuceto's time in Famagusta and Boateriis', separated by 50 years, there was an almost 60% increase in the average price of slaves, which Arbel attributes to the general rise in the demand for manpower in the Mediterranean at this time. The Black Death of 1348 had killed so many people that there was a shortage of workers.

Slaves could be freed by their owners without charge or for a fee set by the owner. In one sad case, a woman named Lucia de la Cava freed her slave Nicola de Negroponte for 300 white besants, a grossly inflated sum that, as Arbel writes, reflected "a blatant exploitation of the slave's desperate wish to return to freedom," as the owner could have easily purchased two or more healthy slaves with the money she received from Nicola. Sometimes it seems that people were enslaved essentially to be held for ransom before relatives or others could pay for their freedom and safe return. Arbel notes a case of six Jews who were enslaved, but who were redeemed by another Jew from Palermo for 700 white besants. Other cases are happier. Some slave owners freed their slaves willingly and with no charge. Often, this freedom was only gained upon the master's death, such as the case of the two shipbuilding assistants who were freed upon the passing of their master, the ship carpenter Giulianus de Sur. Testaments and wills indicate many Christians had slaves, even though they believed slavery was wrong. In some cases Boateriis' notes that owners freed slaves for the sake of their salvation or for the remission of their sins. The Cypriot chronicler Leontios Makhairas also thought slavery was immoral. Indeed, he claims that Famagusta was lost to the Genoese in 1373 because God wanted to punish the Cypriots who practiced it:

And if you wish me to tell you how it was that Famagusta was taken, I say that this was allowed by God because of our sins. And not Famagusta only: it would have been just that they should have taken all Cyprus as well, because of our many sins. And to tell you about it openly: first of all was the sin of the slaves. The land of the Greeks was being ravaged, and the men were being brought over

to the islands as slaves and captives, and our people treated them
so hard-heartedly, that they used to throw themselves down from
the roofs and kill themselves, and some of them cast themselves
into pits, and others hanged themselves, for the heavy torments
which they made them endure, and because they were famished.

[Makhairas, 465]

Since the Genoese were the principal slave traders it's hard to see
the logic, but it does give us insight into the grim lives of the slaves on
Cyprus; suicide and starvation were apparently common among them. In
one exceptional case in 1373 the Constable Sir James de Lusignan found
himself unprepared in terms of manpower for a Genoese attack on Cyprus,
and in an attempt to quickly bolster his number of defenders promised
freedom to any murderers, criminals and slaves who joined his ranks.

Although slave holding on Cyprus seems to have declined during the
Venetian era there were still slaves being used at that time on the large
agricultural estates and in the sugar factories of Episcopi, which were
owned by the Cornaro family. Makhairas' sobering observations quoted
above are echoed in the much later diary of the English traveller Richard
Wrag, who visited Cyprus in 1575 and who reported retrospectively on
the Venetians' treatment of their slaves or *parici*:

> Before it came in subjection to the Turks, while it was under the
> Venetians, there were many barons and noble men of the Cipriots,
> who partly by usurping more superiority over the common people
> then they ought, and partly through their great revenues which
> yearly came in by their cotton wooll and wines, grew so insolent
> and proud, and withall so impiously wicked, as that they would
> at their pleasure command both the wives and children of their
> poore tenants to serve their unclean lusts, and holding them in
> such slavery as though they had beene no better then dogges,
> would wage them against a grayhound or spaniell, and he who
> woon the wager should ever after holde them as his proper goods
> and chattels, to do with them as he listed...

[Sources History Cyprus V, 13]

Scholars disagree on the relative merits and demerits of Venetian rule
on Cyprus, and the accounts of travelers similarly record both positive
and negative evaluations of the Venetians' brief tenure on the island.

The Linobambaci

The Linobambaci, which means 'linen and cotton', is a sect in Cyprus
that has an interesting story. They are Christians who, when the Ottomans

conquered Cyprus, purported to convert to Islam, but in their hearts remained Christian. They took up Turkish dress and names, learned to speak Turkish, and went to the mosque and conveyed their outward life entirely like Turkish Muslims, all the while in their minds thinking 'Jesus' when they spoke the name of 'Allah'. Amongst themselves, however, they used Christian names and followed all of the Orthodox religious festivals and rites, including baptism. By doing so they managed not to pay the heavy taxes that were levied on Christians of the realm. Many Maronites, especially a group living just north of Nicosia, seemed to have responded to increasing persecution from the Ottomans by faking their conversion to Islam and becoming Linobambaci.

Sources for Medieval Class Structure and Ethnic Groups: George Hill, *History of Cyprus*; J. Hackett, *History of Orthodox Church in Cyprus*; Makhairas, *Recital Concerning the Sweet Land of Cyprus*; Benjamin Arbel, "The Jews in Cyprus: New Evidence from the Venetian Period," *Jewish Social Studies* 41, n. 1 (1979): 23-40; Benjamin Arbel, "Slave Trade and Slave Labor in Frankish Cyprus 1191-1571," *Studies in Medieval and Renaissance History* 14, ser. 2 (1993): 151-190; Costas Kyrris, *History of Cyprus*, Nicosia, 1985; Dalia Ofer, "Holocaust Survivors as Immigrants: the Case of Israel and the Cyprus Detainees," *Modern Judaism* 16 n. 1 (Feb., 1996): 1-23; Danny Goldman and Michael J. K. Walsh, "Stranded in Boğaz, Cyprus: the Affair of the Pan Ships, January, 1948," *Journal of Cyprus Studies* 15 (2009): 41-64; on the Linobambaci see section in Charles Frazee, *Catholics and Sultans: The Church and the Ottoman Empire 1453-1923* (Cambridge University Press, 1983).

Appendix II: Inaccessible Churches and Monasteries in Northern Cyprus

One of the unfortunate circumstances for lovers of historical architecture is that some sites are (at the time of this book's preparation) inaccessible to the public because they are in military zones. Visitors doing research on the sites and using earlier guidebooks and maps might thus make long trips to places they are unable to see. These sites include the church and monastery of St Spyridon at Erdimli/Tremethousa, the church and monastery of St John Chrysostom at Kousoventis below Buffavento, and the Akhiropietos church and monastery near Lapithos. The latter is still worth a visit to see the nearby church of St Evlalios and the nearby Lambousa fish traps. One hopes that these will someday be open to the public to visit. There is reason for hope. As recently as 2006 a sector in the Syrian quarter in Famagusta, where there was a small military detachment, was opened, thus allowing visitors to explore three previously inaccessible churches. The rock-cut and frescoed chapel of Agia Mavra (aka Agia Mavri or *Chrysokava*; see Jeffery, 322), just south of the castle of Kyrenia, seems also inaccessible today.

Appendix III: A Note on Carob Houses

Travellers along Cyprus's beautiful north coast may come across large, rectangular stone structures located in isolated coves. Carob was a major export from the 18th through to the early 20th century, and these buildings are carob bean warehouses, where the fruits of the Cypriot carob crop would be brought and stored for export. Small ships would take the carob from these storage structures to new markets. My favorite one is not far from Kayalar/Orga on the north coast. It can be viewed from the main road as it sits in a lovely little bay where the carob ships could have taken shelter (Fig. 173). It can be found at 35° 22' 04.43" N / 32° 59' 53.63" E.

Cyprus was well known for its carob for centuries. When the Russian Orthodox monk Bars'kyj visited Cyprus in 1730 he saw some large carob houses: "They harvest such an abundance of carob tree fruit (Saint John's Bread), that there are many large buildings filled with it. They move it with shovels, like manure, and great merchants arrive who fill many ships with it and transport it to different kingdoms" [*Sources History Cyprus* III, 12]. Carob was called not only 'Saint John's Bread' but also 'Locust Bean' or 'Turkish Horns', though the word 'carob' derives from the Greek word *keras*, meaning 'horn', referring to the curving shape of the pod of the carob. Carob was used as a sweetener and it could be made into syrup, which was also once produced on Cyprus. As Seigneur de Villamont observed as he passed near Limissol in 1588, "Beyond Limisso we crossed a beautiful plain full of olives, fig trees and notably carob trees. This is an evergreen tree, with a long fruit of delicious taste" [*Excerpta Cypria*, 172]. But the crop seems to have been an important one even a bit earlier, as Christopher Fürer makes note of their abundance in 1566. Richard Pococke, too, in 1738, around the same time that Bar'kyj visited, made observations on the uses of Cyprus's many types of trees:

> They also have common juniper on the mountains and pine trees in great numbers, with which they make tar. They have likewise the carob, called in Greek, *Keraka*, which is supposed to be the locust tree, the fruit of which in this island exceeds that of any other country, growing like a flat bean, and is exported both to Syria and Egypt.
>
> [*Excerpta Cypria, 266*]

Constantius, the Archbishop of Sinai, travelled through Cyprus in 1766 and also recognized the commercial importance of carob to the island:

A tree not held in so much account, but still reckoned among the products of the island, spreads its shade over many parts, and its fruit makes by itself quite a commerce. This is the Carob. The sea coast between Scala and Lemesos is thick with these trees, and Lemesos is the chief depot and place of sale.

[Excerpta Cypria, 310]

The carob storehouses one can see on the north coast mostly date from the 19th century when the British tried to encourage its export in an attempt to make Cyprus more commercially profitable.

Fig. 173: A British period carob storage house on the north coast near Kayalar.

Appendix IV: The Inçırlı Cave near Çinarlı/Platani

While this book deals with archaeological sites and examples of architecture and art, one of the most interesting things to be seen in the northern part of Cyprus is the Inçirli Cave near Çinarlı (Fig. 174). At the time of writing, the cave was locked up and one must get the key from the *muhktar* of the village of Çinarlı before driving a couple of kilometres east and south to the cave opening [35° 19' 29.48" N / 33° 46' 10.19" E]. The opening of the cave is marked by a fig tree that locals think has special powers. The cave gets its name from this fig tree as the word *incir* in Turkish means 'fig'. The cave is a real wonder, winding about for about 100 metres with many eerie stone formations, stalactites and stalagmites. A set of lights is strung throughout, but one must be cautious while exploring.

Fig. 174: Inside the Inçrlı Cave near Çınarlı/Platani.

Appendix V: Sites Organised by Region

It is difficult to know how to organise the material in a guidebook such as this. Generally, I have organised the entries chronologically, dealing with the Neolithic Age first, then the Bronze Age, then the ancient Greco-Roman, Early Christian and Byzantine, and so on up through the Lusignan and Venetian and Ottoman periods. But, of course, this isn't how people travel, so I've made a list below of the sites organised by region. With the cities of Famagusta and Nicosia, this is not a problem, as all the buildings are within walking distance of one another in the walled towns and a simple map from the tourist office will be a sufficient guide. But for the others the following may help you make most efficient use of your travels as you visit the different districts. You are encouraged to study your maps to check locations as well. Since various maps have either Greek town names or just Turkish names, it is sometimes difficult to navigate through northern Cyprus, so I have also included below a bilingual listing of the towns and villages of the region. Map 1 gives only a general listing of some towns and sites.

Karpas Peninsula: Refer to Map 2. Panagia Kanakaria, Sykha church, churches at Afendrika, Agios Philon, Agia Trias, Apostolos Andreas, Bronze Age fort site at Nitovikla, Kral Tepesi, tombs near Avtepe/Elisi, tombs near Kaleburnu/Galinoporni, ancient Neta village site, Panagia Elousa, Agios Thrysos, Phoenician statues in quarry.

Area just north of Famagusta: Refer to Map 3. Ancient Greco-Roman city of Salamis, the Cenotaph of Nicocreon, St Barnabas, the Royal and Cellarka Tombs, the Bronze Age city of Enkomi, Avgasida Monastery, church of Agios Sergios, Trapeza church (west of Famagusta).

Area in and around Iskele/Trikomo: Church of St James, Panagia Theotokos, Panagia Tochniou monastery, Panagia Kyra, Lusignan chapel in Sınırüstü/Syngrasi, Kantara castle.

Area between Famagusta and Nicosia: Agios Ephimianos near Akdoğan/Lysi, the Arif Paşa aqueduct, the Absinthiotissa Monastery (north slope of Kyrenia Mountains), the İnçirli cave.

Northwest Region: Church of the Panagia and Gambili Hamam at Hisarköy/Gambili, the Pigadhes Altar, Agia Irini/Paleokastro.

Girne/Kyrenia Mountains: [see also Kyrenia entries below] On north slopes: Panagia Kriniotissa, St Hilarion Castle, Antiphonitis, Armenian Monastery (Sourp Magar). On south slopes: Buffavento Castle, Panagia Absinthiotissa.

Girne/Kyrenia City: Kyrenia Castle and bastions, Kyrenia shipwreck.

West of Girne/Kyrenia near the Coast: Karaman/Karmi (Edremit) tombs, Lambousa Fish Traps, Agios Evlalios, Sina Monastery, Başpinar/Lapta mills and aqueducts.

East of Girne/Kyrenia near the Coast: Bellapais, Vounous, Vrysi, Tatlısu/Akanthou, Panagia Pergaminiotissa, Melandryna monastery, Hellenistic tomb between Mersinlik/Phlamoudi and Kaplıça/Davlos.

Morphou/Güzelyurt Region (see Map 2): St Mamas, Toumba tou Skourou, Soli, Vouni.

Karamanian Sea

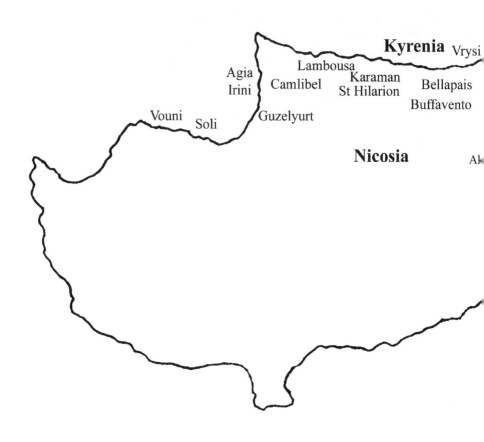

Kyrenia Vrysi

Lambousa
Agia   Karaman   Bellapais
Irini   Camlibel   St Hilarion
                                              Buffavento

Vouni   Guzelyurt
        Soli

Nicosia   Ak

Map 1: Principal Sites and Towns

Principal Sites & Towns in
the Northern Region of Cyprus

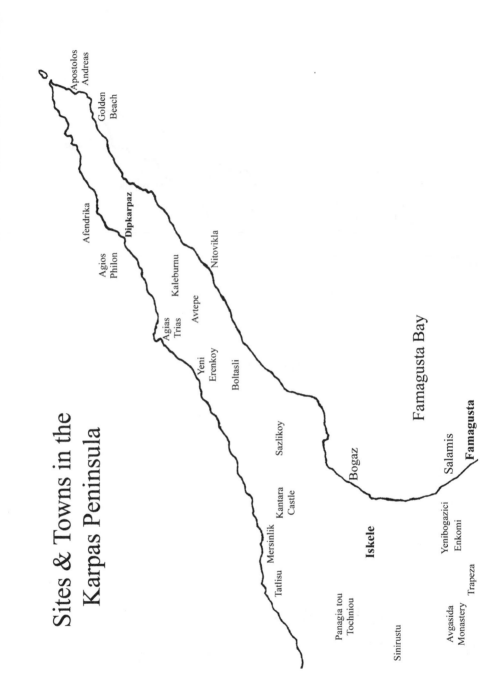

Sites & Towns in the Karpas Peninsula

Apostolos Andreas

Golden Beach

Afendrika

Dipkarpaz

Agios Philon

Nitovikla

Kaleburnu

Avtepe

Agias Trias

Yeni Erenkoy

Boltasli

Sazlikoy

Famagusta Bay

Kantara Castle

Bogaz

Mersinlik

Salamis

Tatlisu

Famagusta

Iskele

Yenibogazici

Enkomi

Panagia tou Tochniou

Sinirustu

Avgasida Monastery

Trapeza

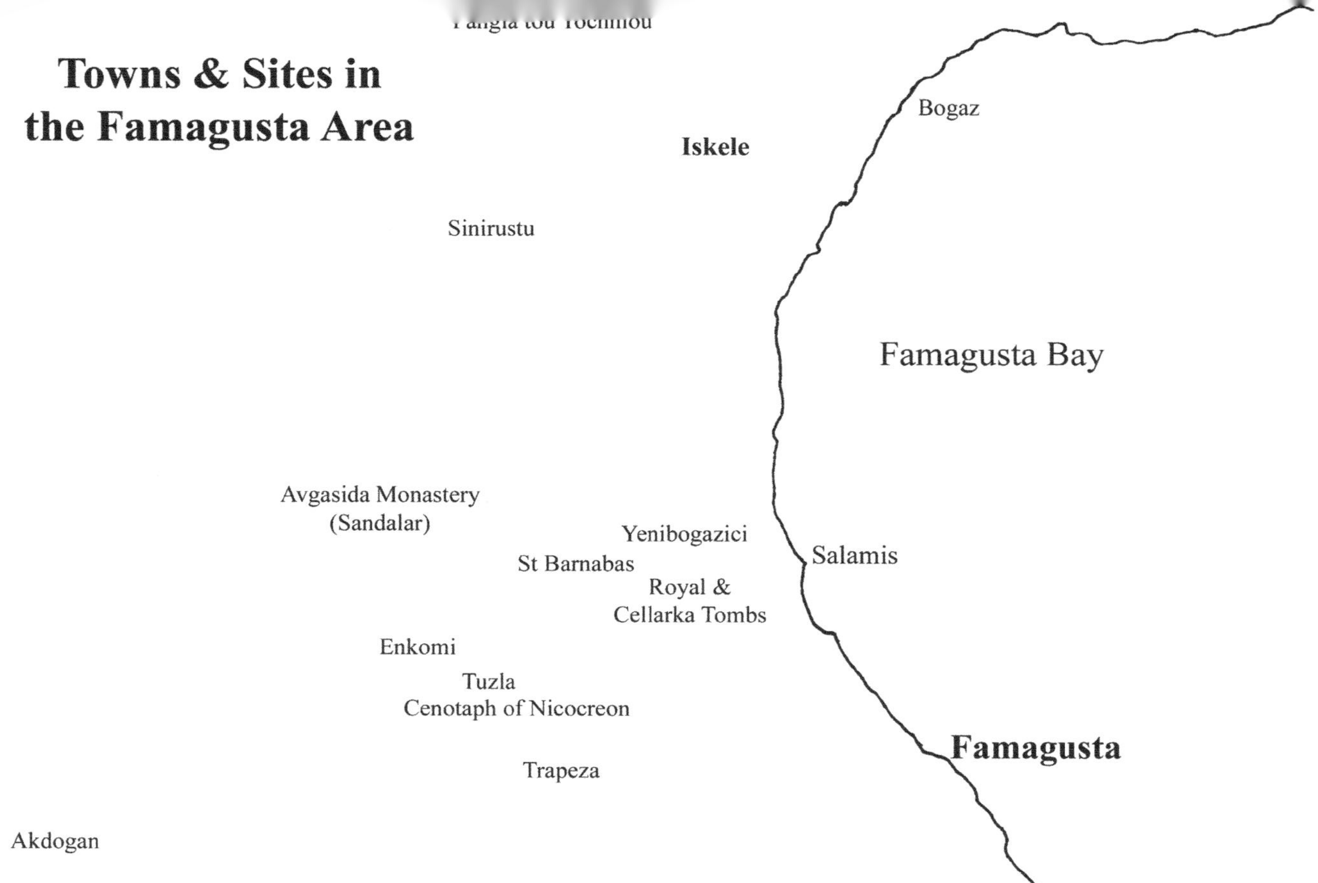

Towns & Sites in
the Famagusta Area

Bogaz

Famagusta Bay

Iskele

Salamis

Yenibogazici

St Barnabas

Royal &
Cellarka Tombs

Sinirustu

Famagusta

Tuzla

Enkomi

Cenotaph of Nicocreon

Trapeza

Avgasida Monastery
(Sandalar)

Akdogan

Map 3: Towns and Sites in the Famagusta Area

Towns and Villages of Northern Cyprus: Turkish / Greek / Turkish

Note: Only towns relevant to the sites in this book are listed. It should be noted that in both Greek and Turkish place names there is considerable variation in the transliterations in different books and maps.

Turkish Name	Greek Name
Akdoğan	Lysi
Aslançak	Karavas
Avtepe	Agios Symeon (Symeon) or Elisi
Bahçeli	Kalogrea
Baspinar	Lapta
Boltaşli	Lythrangomi
Çamlibel	Myrtou
Çatalkoy	Agios Epiktitos
Gazimağusa (Mağusa)	Famagusta
Girne	Kyrenia
Güzelyurt	Morphou
Hisarköy	Kambili
Iskele	Trikomo
Kaleburnu	Galinoporni
Kapliça	Davlos
Karaman	Karmi
Lapta	Lapithos
Lefkoşa	Nicosia
Mersinlik	Phlamoudhi
Sazliköy	Livadia
Sınırüstü	Singrasi
Sipahi	Agia Trias
Tatlısu	Akanthou
Taşlıca	Neta
Tuzla	Enkomi
Yeniboğaziçi	Agios Sergios

Greek Name	Turkish Name
Agia Trias	Sipahi
Agios Symeon (Symeon) or Elisi	Avtepe
Agios Epiktitos	Çatalkoy
Agios Sergios	Yeniboğaziçi
Akanthou	Tatlısu
Davlos	Kapliça
Enkomi	Tuzla
Famagusta	Gazimağusa (Mağusa)
Galinoporni	Kaleburnu
Kalogrea	Bahçeli
Kambili	Hisarköy
Karavas	Aslançak
Karmi	Karaman
Kyrenia	Girne
Lapithos	Lapta
Lapta	Baspinar
Livadia	Sazliköy
Lysi	Akdoğan
Lythrangomi	Boltaşli
Morphou	Güzelyurt
Myrtou	Çamlibel
Neta	Taşlıca
Nicosia	Lefkoşa
Phlamoudhi	Mersinlik
Singrasi	Sınırüstü
Trikomo	Iskele

Glossary of Terms

Acheiropoietos: (Gk. αχειροποίητα) "Not made by human hands," i.e., made by God's hands. Refers to the miraculous production of holy icons or buildings. It is the name of a famous monastery on the north coast of Cyprus, just west of Kyrenia. It is currently inaccessible to the public.

Acoustic Vases: Clay vases placed in the webbing of vaults or the pendentives of a domed church. In theory, they improved the resonance of sound in the church and thus the sonorousness of the chants of monks and priests. Vases were also placed in the vaulting of churches to lighten the weight load of the vaults, thus making them easier to support [see *pendentives*].

Alla Diamante: Italian, meaning 'diamond style'. It describes a of type masonry where the faces of the blocks are faceted at angles. Usually these decorate the frames of doorways or windows [compare *ashlar masonry, rusticated masonry*].

Ambo (or Ambon): An elevated pulpit for preaching in Byzantine churches. Usually having a small staircase leading to the pulpit platform [see *solea*].

Ambulatory: A semi-circular path in the apse of a church formed by a series of columns or piers running around the inside curve of the apse. Common in medieval pilgrimage churches, where pilgrims would visit a series of altars set up in the ambulatory. Often the side aisles of the church flow directly into the apse ambulatory, while in churches without ambulatories, the side aisles terminate in the east end in chapels or separate apses.

Angled Bastion: A type of pointed bastion invented in Italy in the 15th century in response to the rise of the use of cannons in besieging cities [see *bastion, demi-lune, orillon, curtain wall*].

Apodyterium/-ion: Changing room in a Roman bath or in a Baptistery.

Apron: A sloping upper part of a battlement or fortification, at the crest of the walls, for helping deflect enemy artillery fire. Aprons are present, for example, at the tops of the battlements of the Martinengo bastion in Famagusta.

Apse: Usually at the east end of a church, the apse is most often semi-circular in plan, though polygonal (i.e. three or five-sided) apses are found in Cyprus. Also common in Cypriot churches are triple-apse designs where a central, larger apse — corresponding to the width of the nave inside — is flanked by smaller apses corresponding to the church's side aisles. Single and double-aisled churches also often had apses. In the church's interior, the main or central apse marks the place where the altar is located. In double aisled Cypriot churches from the Middle Ages, sometimes there was a Latin or Catholic altar in one apse and an Orthodox altar in the other [see *trichonos*].

Arcade: A general term to indicate a series of arches [see *arch*, *voussoirs*].

Arch: A building technique using trapezoidal stones set into a semi-circular or arcing formation. The stones used in the arch are called 'voussoirs'. The stone at the apex of the arch is called the keystone [see *keystone*, *voussoirs*].

Arrow Loop: A slender, beveled opening in a fortification wall used by archers for shooting arrows at the enemy.

Ashlar Masonry: Squared, cut, and finished stone used in a wall. The wall is smooth and the blocks tightly fit [see *rusticated masonry*].

Atrium (pl. atria): An open courtyard in front of an early Christian church. The atrium was often surrounded by a covered portico or arcade.

Aumbrey: A niche in the wall, near the altar, where sacred vessels such as the chalice for mass were kept [see *diaconicon, prosthesis, piscina*].

Ayasma: A holy well or spring in or near a Byzantine church. It supplied pure water for ablutions, baptisms and other rites. Often, the water from sacred springs was thought to be miraculous or curative.

Baptismal Font/Pool: A baptismal font is usually a stone bowl or other container of holy water used in baptism. A baptismal pool refers to a larger pool, usually set in ground, in which the person baptized is fully emerged in the water. On Cyprus there are many instances of cross shaped 'processional type' baptismal pools, where the celebrant walks down steps into the pool for full emersion. See discussion of church of Agia Trias [compare *phiale*].

Baptistery: A room or rooms, including a baptismal pool or font for baptizing new Christians [see *apodyterium, chrismarion*].

Basilica: A term used to describe an early Christian church with a nave and flanking side aisles, often with a semi-circular apse.

Bastion: A tower-like projection from the fortification walls of a city. Medieval bastions tended to be of a semi-circular type called demi-lunes or "half-moons." The Martinengo bastion in Famagusta is an angled or pointed bastion [see *angled bastion, demi-lune, orillon*].

Battering: A sloping segment of walls of a castle, bastion, or city wall fortification. It helped make a high wall more stable and wider at the base. Some bastions were battered for their full height.

Bay: A single vault section in a series of vaults. Vaulted churches are usually constructed as a succession of such bays, which are often visible because of the delineation of the ribs of the vault. However, not all vaults are rib vaults. Still, it is usually possible to discern the X-shaped cross structure of a bay even when ribs are not present [see *rib vault, vault*].

Bema: The sanctuary of a Byzantine or Orthodox church in the apse and in the area immediately in front of the apse. Separated from the nave of the church by an iconostasis or templon. Slightly elevated above the level of the nave [see *iconostasis, templon, pastophoria*].

Boss: A decorative stone usually found at the center crossing of the diagonal ribs of a rib vault. In Cypriot Gothic churches the bosses are usually carved with coats of arms, crosses, or floral designs. Sometimes called a roof boss. [see *keystone, vault, rib vault*]

Buttress: Any masonry element which helps support a wall, vault, or arch. Sometimes a pier buttress lends weight and strength to a wall to counteract and equalize the thrust of the interior vaults. The flying buttress is often used in larger medieval churches and cathedrals. The 'flyer' is an arch which is directed precisely at the convergence of the thrust of the vaults in the interior; then this force is carried by the flyer to an external pier buttress. This system relieves the walls of the load of the vaults, allowing for larger windows. This is the technology that allowed for a greater amount of light in Gothic churches [see *flying buttress, pier buttress*].

Caldarium: Hot bath area of a Roman bath complex [see *tepidarium, sudatorium, frigidarium, apodyterium*].

Capital: The crowning, transitional element on top of a column or pier. In classical architecture the three most common orders are the Doric, Ionic, and Corinthian. Each had distinctive capitals. Gothic architecture too had capitals at the tops of the slender colonnettes of portals or the large columns which comprised the arcades of the church interiors. Often they were decorated with simple leaf designs [see *column, pier*].

Catechumen: Those receiving training and education to become Christians, as yet unbaptized. 'Catechumena' refers to a part of the church where the unbaptized could observe liturgical ceremonies.

Cavaliere: A raised platform on top of city wall fortifications that allowed a better view of the attackers' positions and to allow greater range for artillery fired from the city. Horses were used to pull carts carrying cannons and cannon balls to the high gun platforms, thus the word 'cavaliere' is derived from the Italian for horse, 'cavallo' (related to the English word 'cavalry'). Wide ramps led up to the cavaliere to facilitate the rapid delivery of munitions and guns. Such ramps can be found at the Martinengo Bastion in Famagusta [see *bastion, demi-lune, terreplein*].

Chapel: A small room or appendage to a larger church or a tiny building on its own. Chapels had their own altars and usually served either private devotion or a funerary function. At times chapels were dedicated to specific saints.

Chrism: The blessed or consecrated oil or unguent used for anointing. Used in Orthodox ceremony of the 'chrismation', where oil is placed on the celebrant's head after baptism. Only the patriarch can consecrate chrism, and this is distributed to bishops for baptismal rites. Often made of olive oil with some other aromatic oils or scents.

Chrismarion: Room, often attached to a baptistery, where people were anointed with chrism, or consecrated oil [see *chrism*].

Clerestory: An upper level in a church which has windows to admit light into the church's interior. In Gothic architecture the clerestory is the row of window high in the walls of the nave above the arcade of the side aisles.

Cloister: An open courtyard in a monastery, usually with vaulted arcades surrounding it.

Column: A cylindrical shaft set vertically to support a horizontal member such as a lintel or arch.

Colonnette: A small, usually slender column.

Colonnade: A series of columns.

Corbels: A masonry projection built out from the mural surface. Sometimes these supported porches or timber constructions but often in Cypriot Gothic architecture they supported the springing of the ribs of vaults in the interiors of the churches. Sometimes, as at Bellapais Abbey, these corbels are carved into figural sculptures.

Counterscarp: The cliff-like part of the moat that lays opposite the city walls. Sometimes, as at Famagusta, the counterscarp was faced with stone masonry so as to make escape difficult for anyone who found themselves trapped in the moat. Also at Famagusta, in the lower levels of the stone cliffs of the counterscarp, shelf-like indentations were carved so defenders could lie in wait at night for the enemy to enter the moat.

Crockets: A Gothic decorative device that most often looks like a leafy projection. They can be found prickling along the gables of Gothic doorways [see *gable*].

Curtain Wall: The long stretches of open wall in the fortifications of a walled city extending between bastions [see *bastion, enfilade*].

Demi-lune: Literally "half-moon". A French term describing the half-circular plans of medieval style bastions on city walls. The majority of Famagusta's bastions are of this type.

Diaconicon: Part of a Byzantine or Greek Orthodox church where the liturgical vessels are stored. Similar to a vestry or sacristy. In some Latin churches this is called an aumbry. Sometimes they are merely niches in the wall, sometimes they are larger rooms, which are usually then referred to as pastophoria [see *aumbrey, piscina, prosthesis, sacristy, vestry*].

Dome: A circular or oval-shaped hemispherical vault of curved masonry. Essentially an arch rotated in construction 360 degrees [see *drum, pendentive*].

Dormitory: A structure in a monastery where the monks' cells and sleeping rooms are found. Also called a 'dorter'.

Drip Course: A horizontal, slightly projecting moulding along a wall that directs rain from the walls' surface so that it can drip to the ground rather than run down the walls. Also called a drip stone or drip moulding [see *hood mould*].

Dromos: (pl. dromoi) A downward sloping, open, alley-like area in front of a Bronze Age tomb.

Drum: This term has two meanings in architecture. The first meaning refers to the drum of a column. A column drum is a cylindrical element that is stacked with other segments to make up a column [Note: Not all columns are made this way; some are 'monolithic', carved from a single piece of stone]. The second meaning refers to the circular or octagonal vertical element upon which a dome sits. It is common to see domes carried on drums in Byzantine and Greek Orthodox churches in Cyprus. Usually the drums are pierced with a few small windows to allow light into the dome interior. Sometimes also called a 'tambour'.

Enfilade: Crossfire from bastions to protect the moat and curtain walls of a city from enemy attack. The term 'enfilading fire' is also used to refer to this type of crossfire [see *angled bastion, bastion, curtain wall, moat, orillon*].

Engaged Column: A column imbedded into or attached to a wall or pier.

Etimasia (Ητοιμασία): See *Hetoimasia*.

Finial: The crowning element of a pier or other vertical element in Gothic architecture. Generally cone-like in shape it usually has many little crockets or leaf-like projections on it. Also called a pinnacle.

Flying Buttress: An arching element extending from the wall of a Gothic church at the point of convergence of the thrust of the interior vaults. The flyers convey the force of the weight of the vaulting to the sides and ultimately on to pier buttresses that stand apart from the wall surface. This technique allowed Gothic builders to free the walls of the weight of the vaulting, thus allowing large windows to occupy the clerestory levels of the church [see *clerestory, vault, buttress*].

Fresco: A painting done on wet plaster so that the colours bind with the plaster as it dries [see *sinopia*].

Frigidarium: Cold pool of a Roman bath complex [see *caldarium, sudatorium, tepidarium*].

Frons Scenae: High backdrop wall of a Roman theater. Often had niches with statues of the Muses or Roman emperors [see *orchestra, parodoi, proscenium*].

Gable: A triangular frame over a Gothic doorway. Sometimes they have crockets on their slanting sides and a finial on the apex of the gable.

Glykophilousa: Name of the Virgin meaning "Virgin of Tenderness". Refers to icons where the Virgin and Christ child are gently caressing or embracing one another.

Gymnasium: Greco-Roman structure for athletic training and sometimes functioning as a kind of hostel for athletes [see *palaestra*].

Gynaeconitis: Gallery for women and children in a Byzantine or Greek Orthodox church.

Hamam: A Turkish bath.

Hegumen: Greek word indicating the abbot of an Orthodox monastery.

Hetoimasia: The preparation of the throne of heaven for the second coming of Christ. It is a common motif in the rim of dome frescoes as part of the Christ Pantocrator image. It shows an empty throne with instruments of the passion (lance, crown of thorns), with Mary and St John the Baptist leading a procession of angels or saints [see *Pantocrator*].

Hodegetria: Literally meaning 'the one who shows the way', the name given to the Virgin Mary but, more specifically, of icons of the Virgin and the Christ child where Mary gestures towards the infant on her lap.

Hood Mould: A moulding which projects over a window or door to frame its upper portion. Although an attractive aesthetic element its function is not entirely decorative, since it also functions as a drip course, preventing erosion on the arched window or doorway below [see *drip course*].

Hypocaust: Short brick or stone pillars underneath the floor of a Roman bath that created empty spaces for the hot air to circulate and heat the water and rooms [see *caldarium, praefurnia*].

Icon: A religious painting for devotion in Byzantine and Greek Orthodox Christianity. Icons were thought to have significant religious power, especially those depicting the Virgin Mary and the infant Christ [see *iconostasis, iconoclasts, iconodules*].

Iconoclasts: Literally, 'breakers of images'. Those who believe that images should be banned in religion because the images themselves are worshipped instead of God, thus promoting idolatry. In Byzantine history iconoclasts destroyed many religious images, especially in the 8-9th centuries.

Iconodules: Literally 'image lovers'. Those who support the use of images and icons in religious devotion.

Iconostasis: In Byzantine or Orthodox churches the tall screen, decorated with many icons, that separates the bema platform and apse from the nave of the church. Earlier demarcating screens were sometimes called 'templons' or 'templon screens', though these did not have icons on them. Earlier templons or chancel screens were low parapets, like low fences with small columns. They did not hinder the congregation's view of the liturgical ceremonies. After the victory of the iconodules over the iconoclasts in the 9th century, the veneration of icons steadily increased in orthodoxy and the iconostasis became the main element of church furniture to display a church's collection of important icons. Thus the iconostasis grew and grew in size to the point of virtually blocking the congregation's view of the altar and the apses [see *iconodules, iconoclasts, templon, bema*].

Intercolumnation: The distance between two columns.

Jambs: The inset lower parts flanking a Gothic doorway. Sometimes, sculptures of saints are found there (called 'jamb statues') though if they ever existed in Cypriot portals none have survived. Often slender colonnettes with small capitals are placed in the jambs.

Keystone: The stone at the apex of an arch which distributes the weight above to the voussoirs of the arch [see *voussoirs*].

Koimeterion: The English word 'cemetery' is ultimately derived from this Greek word that means 'resting place', implying cemetery or burial grounds. It can refer to a place in a church that had burials and/or funerary functions.

Lancet: The typical slender Gothic window with a pointed top. Sometimes filled with tracery [see *tracery*]

Lavabo: A container or fountain for water used in ritual washing.

Lintel: A horizontal element, usually a slab of stone, spanning an opening between two supporting vertical elements. Most commonly used to create doorways or windows.

Machicolations: Projections at the top of a fortification wall, often above gates, which have holes in them to allow hot oil or other things to be dropped or poured on top of besiegers.

Mandorla: An almond shaped, halo-like capsule surrounding the figure of Christ. Often seen in images showing Christ enthroned in heaven or ascending to heaven.

Maphorion: The purple mantle worn by the Virgin Mary. The purple is symbolic of Mary's imperial role as Queen of Heaven.

Medrese (or madrasa, medresse): A school for teaching the Koran and Muslim religious philosophy. Usually associated with a mosque.

Metropolitan: Essentially an Orthodox cathedral. The principal urban church of the Orthodox faith in a city.

Mihrab: The niche in the wall of a mosque which indicates the direction to Mecca, towards which Muslims pray.

Minaret: The tower of a mosque from which the muezzin would make his call to prayer. In Ottoman architecture it is a tall, slender, pencil-like tower with a high pointed roof [see *muezzin, serife*].

Moat: The deep ditch surrounding city wall fortifications. Sometimes dry or sometimes filled with water [see *counterscarp, curtain wall*]

Mosaic: A technique in which small bits of glass or fired, glazed clay squares or stone, are organized into a pictorial or decorative design in floors, walls, or ceilings [see *tesserae, opus sectile*].

Moulding: Any narrow projecting stonework courses that runs along an arch, roofline, or any other part of a wall surface. There are many designs or profiles of mouldings with several specific names. They can have complex combinations of concave and convex profiles. A common type of decorative moulding in medieval Cypriot architecture is called 'dog tooth' moulding, but it looks like a row of flowers with four sharp petals radiating out from a central bead.

Muezzin: The man who sings out the call to prayer to Muslims five times a day. In former times, the muezzin would climb the minaret and make his call. Today, loudspeakers are used [see *minaret, serife*).

Mullion: A vertical element like a slender column that divided a Gothic lancet window into vertical bands [see *lancet, tracery*].

Muquarnas: A type of Islamic decoration where the inside of an arch, vault, window, or door is articulated by a web of prismatic geometric shapes.

Narthex: An enclosed hall at the front of a church that acts as a transitional zone from the exterior to the interior of the church. Usually it is a long, rectangular room running the full width of the church's façade.

Nave: The nave is the main, central aisle of a church. Often, the nave is higher and wider than the flanking side aisles. It leads directly to the main apse and altar.

Necropolis: Literally 'city of the dead'. A term for an ancient cemetery.

Opus Sectile: A form of decoration in which different types and colours of stone are cut into shapes and set into a design in a floor or wall. Usually they are used to make geometric patterns in pavements [see *mosaic*].

Orchestra: Semi-circular area surrounded by seating in a Roman theater. In Greek theaters is round. Found below the stage in Roman examples. Often had an altar in the center [see *frons scenae, parodoi, proscenium*].

Orillon (Ital. Orecchiae): Cusped portion of a type of angled or pointed bastion that became popular in the Renaissance period. It created hidden alcoves from which enfilading fire could protect the curtain walls of a city fortification and yet be protected from enemy artillery, as in the Martinengo Bastion in Famagusta or the bastions of Nicosia. Because they curled around and were on either side of the main head of the bastion they were given the name 'ears' in French (*orillon*) and Italian (*orecchiae*) [see *angled bastion, enfilade*].

Palaestra: Greco-Roman open courtyard for wrestling practice and athletic training [see *gymnasium*].

Panagia: Means "all holy" in Greek and is a general term used to refer to the Virgin Mary. It is usually followed by a term further describing an attribute of the Virgin, such as 'Panagia Theotokos', which means 'All Holy Bearer of God'.

Panspermia: Funerary rituals involving placement of fruits and seeds in tombs or in funerary pyres to spread the seeds of life. In contemporary Greek funerary rituals it is known as 'pankarpia'.

Pantocrator: Image of Christ as ruler of the universe. Usually found in domes or in the semi-domes of apses of Byzantine churches.

Parekklesion: In Byzantine architecture a chapel, sometimes used for burial.

Parodoi: Entranceways to a Roman theater [see *frons scenae, orchestra, proscenium*].

Pastophoria: Side chapels on either side of a bema of a Byzantine church [see *bema*].

Pendentives: The curved, triangular shapes that are created when building a dome from a square base [see *dome, drum*].

Peristyle: Means columns all around. A peristyle court is an open court with columns around it, supporting either horizontal lintels or the springing of arches. The atria of early churches were peristyle courts [see *atrium*].

Phiale: In Byzantine churches a font, sometimes small and bowl like, for holy water. Some of the fonts in larger churches, such as the one in the atrium of the basilica of Campanopetra at Salamis, was a large construction with columns holding up an elegant roof over an octagonal pool.

Pier: A vertical masonry element usually square or rectangular in plan that supports a horizontal element or springing of an arch.

Pier Buttress: A solid masonry pier built into a wall to stabilize the wall. Greater stabilization is needed in vaulted buildings so many medieval churches have pier buttresses. In Gothic buildings that utilize flying buttresses, the pier buttresses stand away from the upper walls of the building, attached to the vaulting by the flyers [see *flying buttress, vault*].

Piscina: A niche in the wall in the interior of a Latin church in the apse near the altar. Used as a shelf to store holy water for the washing of liturgical instruments for church services.

Polycandelon (-lion): A metal chandelier-like holder that held small glass oil lamps for lighting. Associated with Byzantine churches.

Portal: A doorway, but one usually more elaborate and monumental than a simple door.

Portcullis: A heavy grating, usually of an iron webbing or grid, which could be raised and lowered in a gateway. An iron portcullis survives in the sea gate at Famagusta.

Postern Gate: A small door providing clandestine exits or escapes from a fortified city. Used for surprise forays against an enemy or to obtain supplies and smuggle them back into the city when it was under siege.

Praefurnia: The furnace of a Roman bath complex used to heat the air [see *caldarium, frigidarium, sudatorium, tepidarium*].

Proscenium: The stage of a Roman theater [see *frons scenae, orchestra*].

Prothesis: Place in a Byzantine or Greek Orthodox church where the priest prepares the bread and wine for the liturgy.

Quadripartite Vault: A vault with ribs that divide the bay into four triangular sections [see also *rib, webbing*].

Quatrefoil: A type of Gothic tracery design in which the design creates four cusped sections [see *tracery, trefoil*].

Ravelin: A large bastion built beside the main gate of a walled city but detached from the walls. The purpose of the Ravelin was to give the gate extra protection from attackers [see *bastion*].

Refectory: A structure in a monastery where the monks ate their meals [see *cloister, dormitory, trapeza*].

Relic: A body part of a saint or an object that was connected to a saint or member of the Holy Family. These sacred relics sanctified altars and pilgrims would travel great distances in the Middle Ages to visit the shrines associated with the relics of Christ, Mary, the Apostles, and the saints.

Rib: Part of a rib vault. A projection or moulding that delineates the structure of a vault and directs the weight and forces of the vault. The ribs that run directly across a vault are called transverse ribs, while the ones forming an X in the vault bay are called diagonal ribs. Most Gothic vaults in Cyprus are quadripartite, which means that each bay or vaulting section is divided into four by the ribs — essentially, a rectangular shape with an X through it [see *quadripartite vault, vault, webbing*].

Rusticated Masonry: Squared stones where the facing is left rough or only partially finished. Often gives a wall or building a strong, military feel such as in a castle [see *ashlar masonry, alla diamante*].

Sacristy: Place where the priests and other attendants to a liturgy are clothed and where preparations for the mass are made. [see *vestry, diaconicon, prosthesis*]

Şerife: A porch on an Ottoman minaret which looks like a projecting collar around the minaret. Originally it provided an elevated porch for the muezzin to make the call to prayer. In later Ottoman architecture it simply became a decorative element of the minaret [see *minaret, muezzin*].

Side Aisles: Side aisles are the flanking aisles on either side of the nave [see *nave*].

Sinopia: A rough sketch under-drawing done in preparation for a fresco painting, usually done in a rust or red coloured paint [see *fresco*].

Solea: A passageway up the center of the nave of a Byzantine church, demarked by a waist high, fence-like set of stone panels often supported by short columns. The solea demarked a ritual path for the priest and sometimes terminated in (or incorporated) an ambo or pulpit [see *ambo*].

Spolia: Literally, 'spoils'. Spolia are any remnants taken from an older civilization and reused by contemporary conquerors. Often, these spolia are works of art or fragments of architecture. For example, the Venetians took columns from ancient Salamis and reused them in the monumental entrance to their palace in Famagusta. Frequently, such spolia are also used symbolically, to represent the new civilization having conquering the territories of the earlier one.

Stomion: [Gk. "Mouth"] The mouth or entrance to a Bronze Age tomb.

Sudatorium: Steam or sweat bath area of a Roman bath complex [see *caldarium, frigidarium, tepidarium*].

Synthronon: A semi-circular set of steps along the inner wall of the central apse of an Early Christian or Byzantine church. It provided a place for the bishop and other officials to sit during ceremonial occasions and masses.

Templon: A fencing or screen, usually with a series of piers or columns and a low balustrade of stone, which segregated the bema of a Byzantine church from the main body of the church. Found in earlier Byzantine churches, it allowed more visibility into the apse than the later iconostasis which eventually replaced it. Often, today, one finds fragments of these early templons incorporated into the fabrics of the later churches [see *bema, iconostasis*].

Tepidarium: Warm bath area of a Roman bath complex [see *caldarium, frigidarium, sudatorium*].

Terreplein: [from Ital. *terrapieno*, i.e. 'filled with earth'] A French term indicating wide area at the top of a thick, usually earthen fortification wall.

Tesserae: The small bits of glass or bits of glazed clays which are used to make mosaics [see *mosaic*].

Theotokos: Name for the Virgin Mary meaning 'bearer of God'. In images of the Theotokos Mary holds a circular frame in front of her womb, with the infant Christ depicted inside.

Thymiaterion: Stand for burning incense. Used in cult worship both in the pagan Greco-Roman world but also for devotions in Byzantine churches or chapels.

Tracery: The lace-like decorative stonework which is typical of Gothic art. When these intricate designs simply decorate a wall they are referred to as 'closed' or 'blind tracery'. When they appear as open work or in widows they are called 'open tracery' [see *lancet, mullion, trefoil, quatrefoil*].

Trapeza: (Gk. 'table') Name of a refectory in a Greek Orthodox monastery, where the monks and abbot ate their meals.

Trefoil: A type of Gothic tracery design in which the design creates three cusped sections [see *tracery, quatrefoil*].

Trichonos: A word to describe the three-apse formation of the east end of many Cypriot churches [see *apse*].

Trisagion: Greek for 'thrice holy'; sung by the priest as part of the Orthodox divine liturgy.

Trumeau: A vertical element in the middle of a Gothic portal which divides the portal into two doors and helps support the lintel which spans the top of the portal [see *lintel*].

Tumulus: A man-made mound or hill, usually marking a tomb (pl. tumuli).

Tympanum: The space above the lintel of a doorway enclosed by the shape of the relieving arch above it. In Cypriot churches a fresco was sometimes painted on plaster in the tympanum over a doorway. In Famagusta's cathedral, a window was placed in the tympanum (pl. tympana).

Vault: A building technique using the concept of the arch but extending and sometimes rotating the arch to encompass larger interior spaces. There are many types of vaults. For example, a simple arch extended in space creates a tunnel or barrel vault. The intersecting of two simple vaults at right angles created a more complex groin vault. A rib vault is a sophisticated type of groin vault where ribs are constructed to direct the thrusts of the vaults to very specific areas. The masonry in the interstices between the ribs is called the webbing [see *arch, bay, rib, quadripartite vault*]

Vestry: A room near the altar in a church where the priest's vestments and other sacred instruments are stored. [see *sacristy, prosthesis, dianconicon*]

Voussoirs: The wedge-shaped stones in the curving part of an arch [see *arch, keystone*].

Webbing: Part of a vault. The webbing is the masonry in the curving faces of a vault between the ribs [see *rib, quadripartite, vault*].

Index